Logic, Language and Philosophy

A SYSTEMATIC EXPOSITION of classical propositional and predicate logic, supplemented with concise introductions to many-valued logics, intensional logic (briefly covering a variety of modal logics), and pragmatics. Special features include many interesting and thought-provoking excursuses on related topics and important texts on philosophical aspects of logic, as well as study and discussion questions and suggestions for further readings.

–Valentin Goranko, Stockholm University

A NEW INTRODUCTION to logic with a fresh format combining a systematic exposition of the technical material with excursus on a number of philosophical themes from the nature of logical constants and the normativity of logic to proof theoretic semantics, conditionals, descriptions, truth, reference and Gricean pragmatics. The book covers besides classical logic (with natural deduction and some metalogic) also many-valued logic and intensional logic, and includes many useful exercises on the technical material and summaries (with study and discussion questions) of a well thought selection of classical and more recent philosophical texts. An excellent first encounter with logic for a philosophically oriented audience.

–Maria Aloni, University of Amsterdam

Logic, Language and Philosophy is a terrific new addition to the crowded field of logic textbooks. What sets it apart from the rest is Liu and Stokhof's inclusions of expert discussions of issues connected to logic from various parts of philosophy and linguistics, as well as discussions of the main authors and texts that made advances in these areas. I highly recommend this book. It is not just another introduction to logic, but something bigger and better than that.

–Thomas Hofweber, University of North Carolina at Chapel Hill

Logic, Language and Philosophy

An Introduction to Standard Logic

Fenrong Liu
Martin Stokhof

CSLI
PUBLICATIONS
Center for the Study of
Language and Information
Stanford, California

Center for the Study of Language and Information
Leland Stanford Junior University
Printed in the United States
28 27 26 25 24   1 2 3 4 5

Names: Names: Liu, Fenrong, author. | Stokhof, M. J. B. (Martin J. B.), author.

Title: Title: Logic, language and philosophy: a short introduction to standard logic / Liu Fenrong and Martin Stokhof

Description: Stanford, California : Joint Research Center in Logic, Tsinghua University & University of Amsterdam, [2024] | Includes bibliographical references and index. | Summary: "This book provides a first introduction to two key systems that play a role in any variety or application of logic: classical propositional logic and classical predicate logic. It also contains pointers to variations and alternatives, to logics that deal with a wider range of concepts. This book provides examples of the application of logic to philosophical problems, and illustrates some of the philosophical problems that are raised by logic itself. This book aims to give the reader a first glimpse of the wide variety of tastes, smells, and textures that await them once they have trained their palate to appreciate the standard dishes of the logic cuisine. " — Provided by publisher.

Identifiers: LCCN 2024006537 (print) | LCCN 2024006538 (ebook) |
ISBN 9781684000821 (paperback) |
ISBN 9781684000838 (ebook)

Subjects: LCSH: Logic

Classification: LCC BC71 .L58 2024 (print) | LCC BC71 (ebook) | DDC 160–dc23/eng/20240418

LC record available at https://lccn.loc.gov/2024006537 LC ebook record available at https://lccn.loc.gov/2024006538

CIP

∞ The acid-free paper used in this book meets the minimum requirements of the American National Standard for Information Sciences—Permanence of Paper for Printed Library Materials, ANSI Z39.48-1984.

CSLI Publications is located on the campus of Stanford University.

Visit our web site at
`http://cslipublications.stanford.edu/`
for comments on this and other titles, as well as for changes and corrections by the author and publisher.

Contents

Preface

Another introduction to logic? Do we really need one? There are many introductions available that cover the logical materials that form the core of this book. Proposition logic, predicate logic, including their natural deduction proof systems, can be learned and taught using a variety of sources. So why add another one?

The main reason is provided by the nature of the course from which this book originates, more in particular the diverse backgrounds of the students that take it. For a number of years we have been teaching introduction to logic to undergraduate students at Tsinghua University come a wide variety of disciplines: science and engineering, philosophy, the humanities and social sciences, computer science, mathematics and artificial intelligence.

Teaching logic to such a diverse group of students is a challenge, one that we try to meet by combining the teaching of the core concepts and techniques of logic with philosophical discussions. The topics of these discussions concern not just classical applications of logic in the analysis of philosophical problems, they also address philosophical questions that are raised by logic itself. Thus, the book aims to give the students also an overview of various ways in which logic and philosophy interact. Our approach here is thoroughly ecumenical: we do not push one particular philosophical point of view. On the contrary, we hope that by exposing students to different philosophical perspectives, the book will also foster critical and independent thinking.

Another characteristic of this book is that logical materials are introduced with an emphasis on the connection between logic and language. The contrast between formal and natural languages is made explicit, the uses of the formal languages of logic in the representation of the meaning of natural languages is highlighted, as are their limitations. The connection between meaning and use, and that between semantics and pragmatics as the systematic study thereof, is an integral part of this.

So, the course and the students for which this book is written form its main inspiration. We hope the book will inspire similar courses, since teaching logic to students with different disciplinary backgrounds has tremendous advantages. The discussion sessions that intersperse those that are devoted to the logical materials provide unique opportunities to address fundamental questions from a variety of viewpoints. Each student will have their own take on the questions discussed depending on their disciplinary background, and it is this variety that forces everyone (including the teachers :-)), to reflect on the assumptions inherent in their specific disciplines.

The book originated over a number of years in which we taught the course and refined the materials. The feedback that we have gotten from students has been very valuable. We should single out the comments and suggestions we have received from our TAs during those years: Haibin Gui, Yang Sun, Yiyan Wang, Jialiang Yan, Qian Chen, Penghao Du, Qingyu He, Rui Fan. We thank them all.

The book appears simultaneously in English and Chinese. The contributions of Yiyan Wang and Lei Li have been pivotal in preparing the final versions of both editions, and we are very grateful to them. Finally, we thank Johan van Benthem for his insightful comments on an earlier version, as well as Dikran Karagueuzian and Kenneth Perry at CSLI Publications for their valuable feedback.

Fenrong Liu & Martin Stokhof

1

Introduction

1.1 Reasoning and logic

Logic, thus is the common understanding, is 'the science of reasoning'. But what exactly is reasoning? And in what sense is logic its science?

The term 'reasoning' covers a wide range of phenomena, from formal proofs in mathematics to the loose kind of connections we make in everyday conversations between observations, judgements, assumptions, and the like. A strictly ordered sequence of steps that derives, say, the Pythagorean theorem from the Euclidean axioms according to fixed rules counts as reasoning. But so does looking out the window, observing heavy rain clouds and deciding to take an umbrella when going out. Reasoning is done in language, but also 'in the mind', or with pictures, or in any other medium that allows us to represent and process information.

Reasoning often takes the form of argumentation where the goal is to convince an audience or readership to accept a particular conclusion by providing arguments for it. Argumentation is the core of science, of course, where we argue for a particular theory or hypothesis on the basis of experimental data or conceptual considerations. But argumentation also plays a prominent role outside science: in law and politics, in theology and speculative philosophy, in business and in the arts, in everyday conversations: argumentation is everywhere.

Not all reasoning and argumentation is of the same nature. There is what is called 'deductive' reasoning, where given the truth of some sentences, called the 'premises', the truth of another, called the 'conclusion', necessarily follows. Mathematical reasoning is of this kind. But we also have what is called 'inductive' reasoning, where from a finite number of observations that function as premises, we draw a general conclusion. This is often what we find in experimental and observational sciences. And another differentiator is that we can consider the truth of premises and conclusion, or rather their probability.

Given this variety of forms and functions of reasoning and argumentation, one might wonder in what sense logic is 'the science' of all that?

There is an everyday use of the term 'logic', more common perhaps now than in the past, where it serves to indicate a pattern of more or less necessary connections. Thus, one may find such expressions as 'the logic behind the measures taken by the government', or 'the logic behind his madness', or 'the strange logic of supply and demand in on-line trading'. These terms refer to connections between certain actions, rules, and statements that follow a certain pattern. They serve to explain why things are as they are, to predict future events, and so on. This use of the term refers directly to the patterns themselves: it is the patterns that constitute the logic.

But the term 'logic' is also used in another sense, not to refer to such patterns, but to the discipline that studies them. Thus we speak of 'Aristotelian logic' to refer to the works of the Greek philosopher Aristotle,[1] of 'Mohist logic' to refer to works by the Chinese thinker Mozi and his school,[2] of the 'mathematical logic' of Frege and Russell, and so on.[3] All these uses of 'logic' refer to systematic studies of certain reasoning patterns.

These two uses of the term are related: particular logical systems focus on particular patterns of reasoning. That is why they are often used more or less interchangeably. Thus 'Aristotelian logic' can refer to a particular set of reasoning patterns, as well as to Aristotle's systematic treatment of them.

1.2 Arguments and argument schemes

Not all aspects of argumentation fall within the scope of logic. Traditionally, a distinction is made between logic and rhetoric. Whereas logic focusses on the validity of arguments, rhetoric is concerned with their persuasive force. One could say that logic deals with arguments that are used to convince, and rhetoric with arguments that are meant to persuade. Thus rhetoric focusses more on psychological processes induced by arguments, whereas logic studies their systematic properties.

The central concept of any logic is that of validity. We distinguish between arguments that are valid and those that are not. Consider the argument in (1):

(1) a. Some employees are from abroad
 b. All people from abroad need working permits
 c. So, some employees need working permits

Here we have two premises, (1a) and (1b), and a conclusion, (1c). Intuitively this a valid argument: in any situation in which (1a) and (1b) are both true, (1c) must be true as well.

Contrast this with (2):

(2) a. All employees are from abroad
 b. All company owners are from abroad
 c. So, some employees are company owners

This is not a valid argument, since we can imagine a situation in which (2a) and (2b) are both true, but (2c) is false. Note that also if all three, i.e., (2a), (2b) and (2c), are true, the argument as such is still flawed.

Now what distinguishes the valid argument (1) from the invalid (2)? One way to find out is to change elements in the sentences making up these arguments and see whether that changes their status. For example, suppose we change 'employees' to 'bus drivers', as in (1′):

(1′) a. Some bus drivers are from abroad
b. All people from abroad need working permits
c. So, some bus drivers need working permits

That is still a valid argument: apparently, that the first premise and the conclusion are about employees is not relevant. With similar substitutions, we can figure out that 'be from abroad' and 'need a working permit' are also not relevant: we can substitute these expressions by any other, and as long as we do so uniformly, we get another valid argument.

However, what we cannot change are the expressions 'some' and 'all'. For example, if we replace 'all' in (1b) by 'some' we get:

(3) a. Some employees are from abroad
b. Some people from abroad need working permits
c. So, some employees need working permits

And this is no longer a valid argument.

By changing elements we can thus identify those on which the validity of an argument depends. These are called 'logical constants', and non-essential elements 'logical variables'. The distinction is captured in the notion of an 'argument scheme'. An argument scheme is a skeleton that is obtained from a concrete argument, by replacing anything that does not contribute to the validity by variables. Here we use A, B, C as variables that range over nouns and verbs. The argument scheme underlying (1), (1′) and other variants is (4):

(4) a. Some A are B
b. All B are C
c. Some A are C

This is a valid argument scheme: any uniform substitution of concrete expressions for the variables A, B, and C will result in a concrete valid argument.

What holds for valid arguments and valid argument schemes, also applies to invalid ones. By the same method, we can then conclude that the invalid argument (2) is an instantiation of the invalid argument scheme (5):

(5) a. All A are B
b. All C are B
c. Some A are C

The extraction of argument schemes from concrete arguments is a process of *formalisation.* Argument schemes such as (4) and (5) are formulated using a mixture of natural language and formal language expressions. As we shall see in modern logic natural language is altogether done away with and completely formal languages are used to formulate argument schemes and to study their logical properties.

1.3 The anatomy of a logical system

A logical system, or 'logic' for short, is characterised by three key ingredients.

First of all, there is the formal language it employs. The main elements here are specifications of the set of logical constants and that of the logical variables. The set of logical constants defines what the logic is about, its descriptive scope, i.e., the range of argument schemes that it is intended to cover. The specification of the logical constants and logical variables is often called the 'vocabulary' of the formal language. Then there is a set of rules that specify how starting from the vocabulary one can build the set of all the expressions of the formal language. Vocabulary and rules together form the first ingredient: the syntax of the logic.

But expressions as such are not enough, they need to be interpreted. This is the second ingredient of the logic. The logical constants are assigned fixed meanings, ones that account for the contributions they make to the validity of argument schemes. The meanings of logical variables are characterised in terms of the type of meaning they have. This gives us the meanings of the expressions that make up the vocabulary. But we also need to specify the meanings of all the complex expressions that together make up the formal language. To this end another set of rules is formulated. Corresponding to each syntactic rule that defines a way to combine expressions into more complex ones, there is a corresponding semantic rule that defines the meaning of the complex expressions in terms of the meaning of its component parts. Interpretations of the vocabulary and semantic rules together form the second ingredient: the semantics of the logic.

The third and last ingredient of the definition of a logic is a specification of the intuitive concept of validity. As we shall see, there are a number of ways to define the validity of argument schemes. The main opposition here is that between a semantic approach and a syntactic one. As the name suggests, a semantic definition of validity proceeds in terms of meaning. Such a definition corresponds to the intuitive concept that we used before: an argument scheme is valid if whenever the premises are true, the conclusion is also true. But one can also approach validity in terms of the concept of a proof: an argument scheme is valid if we can obtain the expression that is its conclusion from those that are its premises using a set of derivation rules.

A final word about the way in which syntax and semantics of the formal language of a logical system are related. Given a vocabulary, the syntactic rules define what the expressions of the language are by specifying a finite number of ways of combining given expressions into new, more complex ones. The semantics follows this pattern exactly: starting from the meanings assigned to the expressions that make up the vocabulary, there is a semantic counterpart for each syntactic rule that specifies the meaning of the complex expression in terms of the meanings of its component parts. This syntax – semantics parallelism is characteristic for the large majority of formal languages employed not just in logic, but also in mathematics, computer science, and other fields. This core conception of how syntax and semantics relate is often called the 'principle of compositionality': the meaning of a complex expression is a function of the meaning of its parts and the way in which they are syntactically related.

1.4 Logic as a many-splendored thing

'Logic' is in a sense a misleading term because, as we have seen, it is highly ambiguous. It refers to an academic discipline, i.e., to what one studies or takes courses in. But it can also be used to refer to general, normative principles that characterise a certain institution or form of behaviour, to particular ways of thinking, reasoning and argumentation. And 'logic' is the term that refers to formal systems that can be used to study all this.

The plural of 'formal systems' has to be acknowledged. Different formal systems study different types of reasoning and argumentation. Thus there are systems that focus on reasoning with temporal expressions, or with modal ones, or with quantificational ones. That is one source of multiplicity. But there is another one, which is that there is no one, 'correct' or 'true' formal system that characterises 'the' correct or true form of reasoning about a certain domain. So, even with the same coverage in terms of what aspects of reasoning are being investigated, there is often a range of alternatives that give different accounts of what the logic of that particular aspect is supposed to be. Thus we have different logics for propositional reasoning, and different ones for quantificational expressions, for modal and temporal expressions, and so on.

This book focusses on a couple of core formal systems. If we can use a gastronomical metaphor, in order to appreciate the variety that a certain cuisine has to offer, it is best to start with learning how to prepare and appreciate a number of standard dishes. This is what any introductory book must offer. But a good cookbook will also provide some pointers to variations on those standards, and thus provide an entrance to the endless variety and depths that characterise a good cuisine.

Logic is such a cuisine: it contains a dazzling variety of formal systems, concepts, techniques, all with their associated meta-logical results. Some of these systems are there just for their own sake, like many parts of pure mathematics. Others are closely tied to very specific and particular applications. And these applications as such can come from a wide variety of fields: from philosophy, linguistics, economics, psychology and cognitive science, from mathematics, computer science, ...

This book will provide a first introduction to two key systems that play a role in any variety or application: classical propositional logic and classical predicate logic. But it will also contain pointers to variations and alternatives, and to logics that deal with a wider range of concepts. As for applications, the focus will be on language and philosophy. These two are intimately related, for obvious reasons: philosophical analysis is concerned with fundamental concepts and these concepts are expressed in language. Of course, although, or perhaps because, the connection between philosophy and language is intimate, it is not therefore obvious and unproblematic. Philosophical concerns require careful linguistic analysis, and in turn, the analysis of language raises fundamental philosophical questions.

The details are intricate, numerous and fascinating. What follows will not be able to do justice to that, but it does aspire to give the reader a first taste of the role that logic can play here. That will be done in two ways. First of all, we will provide some examples of the application of logic to philosophical problems. And secondly, we will give pointers to philosophical problems that are raised by logic itself. In that way we hope to give the reader a first glimpse of the wide variety of tastes, smells and textures, that await them once they have trained their palate to appreciate the standard dishes of the logic cuisine.

2

Excursus: logic in philosophy

2.1 The topic

In the western tradition logic has always been an integral part of philosophy. Aristotle established logic as a systematic philosophical discipline along with, and connected with, other philosophical disciplines, such as metaphysics, epistemology, ethics. The basic structure remained in place for many centuries, although the contents and also the relative importance of the various elements varied. Logic was central in the scholasticism of the European Middle Ages, but lost some of its prominence with the advent of modern philosophy, in which epistemological questions came to occupy center stage.

By the eighteenth century logic was still a recognised part of the philosophical curriculum, but its importance for other philosophical disciplines was declining. The term 'logic' came to have a much wider use, but as the systematic study of formal aspects of reasoning, logic had become of lesser importance.

That changed with the advent of modern formal logic in the late nineteenth and early twentieth century. The limitations of the classical Aristotelian logic had long been acknowledged, but never adequately overcome. By making a radical break with natural language as the primary vehicle for philosophical and logical analysis, modern logic provided a much more powerful set of systematic, formal tools that could be applied in a wide range of areas, including philosophy.

Thus a new age of intensive interaction between logic and other philosophical disciplines emerged. Modern analytic philosophy was shaped by the application of modern logic, and continues to thrive in virtue of the application of ever more sophisticated logical tools. The foundations of this tradition were laid by a number of authors, such as De Morgan, Boole, Bolzano, Peirce, and, if not the most important definitely the most influential: Frege and Russell.

2.2 The authors

Gottlob Frege

Gottlob Frege (1848 – 1925) was in the first place a mathematician, who found himself forced to become a logician, and who counts as a philosopher of language only retrospectively. For Frege himself this variety of professional identities was not quite relevant: he always approached the problems that confronted him during his intellectual development from the same broad, philosophical perspective. That nowadays Frege is considered to be a logician and a philosopher of language is largely due to the fact that we now view these as separate disciplines, to both of which Frege happens to have made decisive contributions.

Frege the logician is the author of *Begriffsschrift* (Frege, 1879), which counts as the first systematic exposition of modern logic. But Frege turned logician because he had to: he was driven to his logical investigations by a mathematical motive. The background of that is the foundational crisis in mathematics. Where mathematics had served as the paradigm of certain knowledge for centuries,[1] the development of non-Euclidean geometries and the paradoxes in Cantor's set theory had instigated doubts about the very foundations of mathematical knowledge. Frege, who was particularly interested in the arithmetical foundations of analysis, tried to base arithmetic on logic: the programme of logicism. In order to carry out this programme a logic was needed that was adequate for reasoning about relations. Specifically, what was required was a logic that could deal adequately with relational judgments with more than one quantified argument, such as 'Every natural number is equal to the sum of two natural numbers'. Within the broadly Aristotelian logical framework, still prevalent at the time, the basic form of judgments was that of subject – predicate, and that was inadequate to deal with relational judgments. The system that Frege presented in *Begriffsschrift* is the first fully developed system that overcomes this limitation.[2]

Frege's main motivation for the construction of a formal system of logic was that he felt that a proper foundation of mathematics could only be achieved on the basis of a logic in which mathematical reasoning could be formalised in a completely explicit way. That he considered arithmetic as the most fundamental part of mathematics is, of course, not by accident. Especially after the development of analytic geometry by Descartes, number theory was, and perhaps still is, considered the most fundamental mathematical discipline. Showing that arithmetic can be based on pure logic would then restore the certainty of fundamental mathematics that has been put into question by the foundational crisis.

At some point in his logical investigations Frege looked at more general issues regarding meaning, which brought him to look at language more generally, going beyond the formal languages of logic and mathematics. In this context he developed his platonic perspective on meaning, and it is this body of work that has earned him the title of 'founding father of analytic philosophy'. On this view, which has been developed and defended by authors such as Dummett, Geach, Austin and Anscombe, Frege is a direct ancestor of early Wittgenstein, and, together with Russell and G.E. Moore, one of the creators of what is called the 'linguistic turn' in philosophy.[3] From this point of view the importance of Frege's work is mainly located in his semantic investigations, and the corresponding ontological views.

There is no denying that the influence of Frege on Russell and early Wittgenstein, and through them on the entire tradition of analytical philosophy, is real and profound. Nevertheless it is primarily a systematic appraisal, one that can be made only in hindsight: we can now see that Frege in fact played that role. But if we want to assess Frege in his historical context, then looking at him and his work in hindsight might very well distort the picture. That nowadays we value Frege's work mainly from an analytic perspective, or, even more narrowly, from the perspective of the philosophy of language, does not mean that he himself saw what he did in that way.[4] In the literature on Frege there are also authors who try to interpret him in his contemporary context, and who come to a different appraisal of the nature of the intellectual setting in which Frege himself situated his work. On this view, defended among others by Hans Sluga[5] the main motivation of Frege's work is epistemological, rather than language-oriented. The dominant paradigm in German philosophy in the mid-nineteenth century was naturalism, not some form of Kantian idealism. This naturalism came with a radical form of empiricism,[6] which, according to Sluga, is the background against which we should interpret Frege's philosophy. Frege's aim was to re-instate Kant's form of anti-empiricism. Empirical laws, Frege argued, depend on induction. And induction presupposes arithmetic. If it can be shown that arithmetic is *a priori*, then this would vindicate Kant's claim that not all knowledge is empirical. Frege does differ from Kant in considering arithmetic to be analytic, whereas Kant was of the opinion that it is synthetic.[7] Thus the reduction of arithmetic to logic, in addition to providing a way out of the foundational crisis in mathematics, makes a key contribution to the Kantian epistemological project.

As was mentioned, such a reduction presupposes a logic with adequate expressive power, and that is what Frege developed in his *Begriffsschrift* from 1879. After completing that work he set himself the task of providing a satisfactory philosophical analysis of the concept of number, which he laid down in his *Grundlagen der Arithmetik*, which appeared in 1884 (Frege, 1884). A formal analysis of arithmetic in logical terms is the topic of the *Grundgesetze der Arithmetik*, of which the first volume appeared in 1895 (Frege, 1895). Then something unexpected happened: Russell discovered that the axioms that Frege used in the first volume allow the derivation of a paradox. Frege made an attempt to repair this. His revision appeared in an appendix to the second volume of *Grundgesetze*, which was already in print when Frege was confronted with Russell's discovery. However, it soon became clear that his revision failed to solve the problem, and Frege abandoned the programme of logicism.[8]

Bertrand Russell

The influence of Bertrand Russell (1872 – 1970) on the development of western analytic philosophy can hardly be overestimated. Together with G.E. Moore he shaped philosophy in the UK and beyond through his many writings on a wide range of topics and through his influence on a number of famous students, including Ludwig Wittgenstein. Some of his works addressed highly technical issues in the philosophy of mathematics, formal logic, epistemology and ontology, and were intended for a readership of specialists. But he also wrote for a more general audience on topics in philosophy, politics, educational reform, marriage, and so on.

Russell was born in an aristocratic family, and received the education that was common at the time in those social circles. He studied mathematics in Cambridge, but also developed broad interests in philosophy, politics and social issues. (His first publication was on German social democracy.)

His early years were devoted to what has become known as the 'revolt against idealism', and to philosophy of mathematics and logic. Philosophy in England in the second half of the 19th century was heavily under the influence of British Idealism, a form of idealism that was promoted by, among others, Bosanquet and Bradley, and that had strong roots in the German idealism of Kant and Hegel. Russell initially was trained in this tradition of speculative metaphysics, but in the late nineties of the 19th century, together with G.E. Moore, rebelled against it. Initially, his main reason for rejecting idealism was its insistence that all relations are 'internal', i.e., can be understood in terms of properties of the things related. Through his training in mathematics, Russell saw that this could not work for asymmetrical relations in mathematics. For example, the relation 'being smaller than' between natural numbers cannot be explained in terms of properties of the numbers themselves.

For Russell this led to a rejection of the basic tenets of idealism, including its insistence on a form of holism, and its view that thought and fact cannot be distinguished. In contrast, Russell came to promote a kind of philosophy that was more practically oriented and that needed to be conducted in close connection with the empirical sciences. An early statement of these ideas can be found in *The Problems of Philosophy*, from 1912 (Russell, 1912). Logic, according to Russell, was the most useful tool that philosophy could use.

Russell did his most productive work in philosophy of mathematics around the turn of the century. His early work in this area led to the 1903 *The Principles of Mathematics* (Russell, 1903). He became acquainted with Frege's ideas and his work in logic and the foundations of arithmetic. As was mentioned above, he discovered a paradox in Frege's *Grundgesetze*, but he adopted the programme of logicism that was set out by Frege, and, together with his one-time mentor Alfred North Whitehead, produced the monumental *Principia Mathematica*, the three volumes of which appeared between 1910 and 1913 (Russell & Whitehead, 1910, 1912, 1913).

After the publication of *Principia* Russell turned to more general philosophical problems in ontology and epistemology, and to politics and social issues. In his philosophical work, he adopted various views, from a rather physicalistic ontology in his early philosophy of logical atomism to the later view of neutral monism, according to which the physical and the mental are on a par, being two different organisations of the same ontological base. His views on how we can acquire knowledge of reality likewise shifted. And they continued to do so over the many years that Russell was philosophically active. An attribution of particular views to Russell therefore always has to be temporally qualified. But a constant element in Russell's philosophical work is his conviction that logic and of logical analysis are central to all philosophy.

Russell did not just write about political and social issues, he was also actively engaged in these matters. He was a conscious objector in World War 1, stood for parliament but wasn't elected, visited Russia, China and Japan, opened an experimental school, and after World War 2 actively opposed the nuclear policies of both western and eastern nations during the cold war period. He received the Nobel prize for literature in 1950, and over all the years also managed to have a very productive academic career. He published a large number of books and articles, lectured extensively in various countries, notably the US, and held academic positions in Cambridge and in Chicago. His *A History of Western Philosophy* (Russell, 1945), which was published in 1945, became one of the most widely read books on the topic.

The selections that are treated below stem from Russell's early period, and highlight his rejection of speculative philosophy and his insistence of logic as 'the essence of philosophy'. Another important contribution of Russell's, viz., his analysis of definite descriptions and the distinction between knowledge by acquaintance and knowledge by description will be treated in chapter 17.

2.3 The texts

Frege, Preface from Begriffsschrift

The text comes from the preface of Frege's seminal work, the *Begriffsschrift*. In a few pages Frege provides an insight into his motives for developing the formal system that is presented in the book. These concern mainly the nature of natural language and its role in science and in philosophy, and the contrast with the kind of formal language that Frege develops.

Frege's exposition seems straightforward, but on closer inspection we can distinguish in the text three slightly different perspectives on the relationship between natural language and formal languages, each motivated by different considerations.[9] The three perspectives can be labelled 'extension', 'improvement' and 'reform'.

From the perspective of 'extension' one views a formal language as a means to extend the expressive power of a natural language. This happens, e.g., when we add elements of symbolic systems, such as calculus or the periodic system, and of scientific vocabulary to our everyday natural language. Think of using 'H_2O' to refer to water, or of using 'delta' as a term for a quantitative difference.

The perspective of 'improvement' is slightly different. Here one considers the way in which a natural language expresses certain things to be defective in some sense, and provides a formal language to do better. Precision and explicitness are main considerations. Think of notation for basic arithmetic: it can be done in natural language, but using the formal notation makes things more precise and more easy and survey-able.

The third perspective is that of 'reform'. This is where one considers certain aspects of natural language not just to be lacking in expressive power or cumbersome, but actually misleading and as such an obstacle in the way of proper philosophical and/or scientific investigation. This perspective is closely related to the conception of an ideal language.

In the preface of *Begriffsschrift* Frege writes about his motivations to move from the use of natural language to the definition and application of a fully formal language at several points. And each of the three perspectives just mentioned seems to be represented at some point in his exposition.

Thus when Frege writes:

> ... I found the inadequacy of language to be an obstacle; no matter how unwieldy the expressions I was ready to accept, I was less and less able, as the relations became more complex, to attain the precision that my purpose required. This deficiency led me to the idea of the present ideography.

he seems to be taking the first perspective: natural language lacks the means to express things with the precision that is needed.

Then there is the comparison of a natural language to the eye and a formal language to the microscope. Here the second perspective, that of 'improvement', seems to be taken. The eye is versatile but lacks sharpness, the microscope provides sharpness but is 'a one-trick pony'.

The third perspective, that of reform, appears to be the one that inspires the passage where Frege refers to philosophy and its task 'to break the domination of the word over the human spirit'. That domination is due to 'the misconceptions that through the use of language almost unavoidably arise', and it can be exposed by using a formal language. Frege was certainly not the first to lament the inadequacy of natural language for proper philosophical analysis and scientific thought. But unlike his predecessors, he had something to back it up: his 'conceptual notation', the first fully explicit example of a formal logical system with sufficient expressive power.

Russell, selections from Our Knowledge of the External World

The selections come from *Our Knowledge of the External World* (Russell, 1914), which is a compilation of the lectures Russell gave during a visit to the Lowell Institute in Boston. John Slater's introduction gives a detailed overview of the context in which the lectures were written.[10]

In the first chapter we find Russell's criticisms of philosophy as it has been done in the past. Note Russell's use of the term 'philosophy' indicates the western tradition only. Also it is remarkable that he gives a very broad characterisation: there is the classical tradition; evolutionism; and the new kind of philosophy that he himself espouses: the philosophy that uses the logical-analytic method.

Russell's main criticism of the classical tradition is connected to what he deems to be the goal of any form of intellectual engagement with the world, i.e., to produce knowledge. That is where the classical tradition fails:

> [. . .] the great systems of the past serve a very useful purpose, and are abundantly worthy of study. But something different is required if philosophy is to become a science [. . .]"

Interestingly, Russell does acknowledge that rational reasoning, and thus logic, plays an important role in the classical tradition. So it is not a lack of logic, but a wrong use of it, that is the problem. The difference between the traditional, wrong use, and the new, right use resides in how logic interacts with experience, i.e., with empirical knowledge.

'Evolutionism' is the term Russell uses for what he considers the trend of his time: a philosophy based on views that are borrowed from biology, in particular Darwin's theory of evolution. It favours an organic, holistic and continuous, dynamic view of the world, in contrast to the mechanistic, static view that can be associated with classical mechanics.

Russell's criticism is two-fold. He rejects the claim of evolutionism that its worldview is supported by biology. And he objects to what he views is an exclusive focus on moral issues. So, evolutionism is not sufficiently in accordance with experience, i.e., what science tells us about the world, and it does not deal with the kind of questions that Russell thinks philosophy should address, i.e., it does not produce the kind of knowledge that it is the task of philosophy to supply. This is connected with his rejection of Bergson's claim that, next to the intellect, intuition is also a reliable source of knowledge.

The second chapter is devoted to an exposition and defence of the claim that logic is the essence of philosophy, i.e., that:

> [...] every philosophical problem, when it is subjected to the necessary analysis and purification, is found either to be not really philosophical at all, or else to be, in the sense in which we are using the word, logical.

Russell is quick to note that the exact meaning of this claim depends on what is understood by 'logic'. He dismisses classical, Aristotelian logic and the scholastic variants out of hand, and Bacon's inductive method is not regarded as necessary for 'a perfected science'. Russell investigates in some detail the views on induction of John Stuart Mill, who ties induction to the law of causality. The upshot of Russell's discussion is that logical principles as such can *not* be derived from experience.

Hegel's conception of logic, according to Russell, is a kind of speculative metaphysics that aims to uncover fundamental properties of the world by purely *a priori* reasoning. Although it claims to be a departure from classical, Aristotelian logic, it is not, Russell claims.

Russel then sets out to show that the first real departure from the traditional logic of the western tradition came about with the advent of formal, mathematical logic, as developed by Peano and Frege. Their crucial insight was that not all judgements are of the Aristotelian subject – predicate form, ascribing a property to an entity. Relational judgments and quantified judgments have a different logical structure, and thus warrant different ontological conclusions.

Thus, the key element in Russell's analysis of the philosophical importance of mathematical logic is the notion of logical form. The logical form of a proposition is not a constituent of it, it is the way in which its constituents are put together. Logical form in this sense is what philosophical logic is all about. Knowledge of logical forms is the basis of all understanding and of all inference. The task of philosophical logic is 'to extract this knowledge from its concrete integuments, and to render it explicit and pure.'

Russell illustrates this with an analysis of relational judgments and of various logical properties of relations, emphasising the crucial role they play in scientific and everyday reasoning. He then goes on to discuss how various logical forms determine facts, assertions and propositions. He distinguishes between atomic, molecular, and general logical forms, at each level. Our knowledge of these forms is a form of self-evident, general knowledge that is essential for reasoning, and that cannot be explained as a result of sensory experience, but must rather be considered as a precondition for it.

Thus for Russell logic, the new logic that is, 'has the effect of enlarging our abstract imagination'. The value of its application in philosophy is that 'it [makes] possible at last to see what kinds of problems may be capable of solution, and what kinds must be abandoned as beyond human powers.'

2.4 Study and discussion questions

Study questions

Frege

- Which division does Frege make in 'truths that require justification'? And where in that division are the truths of arithmetic?
- What requirements should a language that is suited for expressing logical inference meet according to Frege?
- Wherein does Frege locate the innovation of his formal language?
- In which two directions does Frege see possible extensions of the application of his formal language? And what additions would be needed for those?

Russell

- How does Russell evaluate the 'logical-analytic' method in comparison with traditional methods?
- What does Russell mean with the opposition between 'construction' and 'inference' ?
- Which two main sources does Russell regard as the roots of the classical tradition in philosophy?
- What is the gist of Bradley's argumentation against the reality of relations? (see the passage quoted on p. 4–5.)
- What difference does Russell claim there is between the way logic is used in the classical tradition and the role it plays in a scientific philosophy?

- What distinction does Russell make between fact, assertion, and proposition?

Discussion questions

- Can you think of examples of philosophical problems that involve misunderstandings that are related to natural language?
- And how would a formal language (of logic, of mathematics, or a programming language, ...) be able to help?
- Are all philosophical problems amenable to rational treatment? What are the characteristics of problems that are not?

2.5 Further reading

Michael Dummett's books on Frege, Dummett (1973a, 1985, 1992), though contested in various ways, remain excellent introductions to the various elements of Frege's thought. For an early alternative approach, see Sluga (1980);. In addition to the old translations of Frege's work by Geach, Black and others, there is the collection edited and translated by Michael Beaney, Beaney (1997). A good collection of recent work on Frege is Ricketts & Potter (2010).

An early but still relevant introduction to Russell is Pears (1967); see also the more recent Griffin (2003).

On the origins of the analytic tradition and the role of Frege and Russell, see Soames (2014). On the 'pre-'history of modern logic in relation to philosophy, see Lapointe (2018).

Recent work on the relevance of logic to philosophy includes that of Timothy Williamson, Williamson (2013).

Part I

Proposition Logic

3
Proposition Logic: Syntax

3.1 Introduction

The first stage of our journey through logic land deals with proposition logic, a simple logical system that nevertheless can be used to examine the validity of a substantial range of arguments and that can serve to illustrate a number of key features of logical systems. One of them is the use of formal languages, which is the main topic of this chapter.

But before we dive into that, a quick indication of the range of proposition logic is in order. The term itself may serve as an indication. A proposition is what is expressed by a sentence in natural language (hence, one also finds the name 'sentential logic' being used). Proposition logic is thus concerned with logical relations between sentences. That means that the internal components of sentences, i.e., nouns, verbs, adjectives and other types of sub-sentential expressions, are left out of consideration. They will be treated later, when we study predicate logic. Proposition logic is concerned with the logic of expressions that connect sentences.

A simple example will illustrate what is, and what is not, at stake. Consider the following argument:

> A: Shopping malls will be open, provided the reproduction rate of the virus stays below 1
> B: But that will only be the case if travel from outside remains restricted and social distancing rules are obeyed
> C: Travel restrictions are lifted
> (*All*): So shopping malls will remain closed

This simple example uses various tools for reasoning: a conditional premise: 'If the reproduction rate of the virus stays below 1, then shopping malls will be open'; another conditional premise: 'If travel restrictions are lifted or social distancing rules are not obeyed, then the reproduction rate will not stay below 1; a given: 'Travel restrictions are lifted'; and a conclusion: 'Shopping malls will remain closed'.

The argument is valid, as some reflection shows. As was already noted in the introduction, we can isolate the parts of an argument that matter for its validity by checking which parts can be changed without affecting that validity. For example, we can replace 'Shopping malls will be open' by 'Schools will be open' and we get another valid argument. What we cannot do, for example, is change one of the conditional premises into a disjunctive one, e.g., 'Travel restrictions are lifted or the reproduction rate does not stay below 1'.

That kind of tinkering shows that the logical structure of the argument is something like this:

If p, then q; if r or s, then not q; r, so not p

Any concrete argument that has this logical structure will be valid, and the structure itself we call an 'argument scheme'. Proposition logic is all about the study of the validity of argument schemes that rests on the use of expressions such as 'if . . . , then . . . ', 'not', 'or', and the like.

In order to be able to study the validity of argument schemes involving these expressions we first of all need a good way of representing them. For that we use a formal language.

3.2 Formal languages

A formal language that we can use to study proposition logical argument schemes needs to meet three conditions. First of all, it needs to provide the means to represent basic sentences, i.e., sentences that do not have any logical structure that proposition logic can make use of. Secondly, it needs to contain representations of the logical elements that determine the validity of proposition logical arguments. And finally, it needs to show how these elements operate, i.e., how they form new sentences.

The first condition is met by specification of a vocabulary of proposition letters. These will represent basic sentences.[1] For that we use lower case letters: $p, q, r, \ldots$, and whenever this is convenient, we use them also with subscripts: $p_1, p_2, \ldots, p_n, \ldots, q_i, \ldots$

Next we need representations of the logical elements. These are called 'connectives'. We use $\neg, \wedge, \vee, \rightarrow, \leftrightarrow$. They are meant to represent sentence negation, conjunction, disjunction, conditionals, and equivalence, respectively. How they do that, will be a matter of the meaning that we assign to these expressions. That will be a topic for chapter 5. But for now, think of $\neg$ as 'not', or 'it is not the case that'; of $\wedge$ as 'and'; $\vee$ as 'or'; $\rightarrow$ as 'if . . . , (then) . . . '; and $\leftrightarrow$ as 'if and only if'.

Finally, the third requirement, viz., shows how the connectives can be used to form new sentences from given ones. That is the task of specifying the syntax of proposition languages. It requires a definition of how proposition letters and connectives can be used to define the set of all the formulas of such a language.

In order to be able to state the syntax in an efficient way, we need to be able to refer to arbitrary formulas. For this we use so-called 'meta-variables': Greek letters $\phi, \psi, \ldots$, with subscripts $\phi_1, \phi_2, \ldots, \phi_n, \ldots$ where necessary. They stand for arbitrary formulas.

With that we have all the ingredients to define what are the formulas of a language of proposition logic L, based on a vocabulary of proposition letters VOC_L.

Definition 1 (Syntax)
Let VOC_L be a set of proposition letters. The formulas of L, given VOC_L, is the set of expressions:

1. All proposition letters in VOC_L are formulas of L
2. If ϕ is a formula of L, then so is $\neg\phi$
3. If ϕ and ψ are formulas of L, then so are $(\phi \wedge \psi)$, $(\phi \vee \psi)$, $(\phi \rightarrow \psi)$, and $(\phi \leftrightarrow \psi)$
4. Only that which can be generated by the clauses (1)-(3) in a finite number of steps is a formula of L

The first three clauses give a recipe for getting formulas; (4) adds that only that which has been achieved according to this recipe is a formula.[2] A reminder: proposition letters and the formulas that can be constructed from them are the actual formulas of the language. So $p \wedge q$, $(p \vee q) \wedge (p \vee r)$, and so on, are formulas of the language. Per contrast, ϕ, ψ are variables that range over concrete formulas, and that means that their values can be the same. That is why 'If ϕ, ψ are formulas, then so is $(\phi \wedge \psi)$, also covers $(p \wedge p)$, $((q \rightarrow r) \wedge (q \rightarrow r))$, and so on.

One of the remarkable features of a formal language such as this one is the lack of ambiguity. In fact, this is what you might call a 'design characteristic'. Whereas natural languages allow for expressions that are ambiguous, counting on context to make clear what the intended meaning is, no such liberties are allowed when constructing formal languages.[3]

Hence the use of brackets. Without them a string such as $p \wedge q \vee r$ would be ambiguous between $((p \wedge q) \vee r)$ and $(p \wedge (q \vee r))$. Using brackets to indicate what formulas are combined avoids the problem. Thus each step in the construction of a complex formula introduces a pair of brackets. The exception is the construction of a negation: no brackets are needed because negation applies to a single formula. Note that when the construction process has ended, the outermost pair of brackets is superfluous; thus we write $(p \wedge q) \vee r$ instead of $((p \wedge q) \vee r)$. Likewise when we use metavariables: we write $(\phi \rightarrow \psi) \rightarrow \chi$ instead of $((\phi \rightarrow \psi) \rightarrow \chi)$

In table 3.1 we list the connectives and their intended meanings, which will be fully specified in chapter 5.

Connective	*Composite formula*	*Meaning*
$\neg$: negation	$\neg p$: negation of p	it is not the case that p
$\wedge$: conjunction	$p \wedge q$: conjunction of p and q	p and q
$\vee$: disjunction	$p \vee q$: disjunction of p and q	p or q
$\rightarrow$: implication	$p \rightarrow q$: (material) implication of p and q	if p, then q
$\leftrightarrow$: equivalence	$p \leftrightarrow q$: (material) equivalence of p and q	p if and only if q

Table 3.1: Connectives and their meanings

A couple of remarks on terminology: $\wedge, \vee, \rightarrow$ and $\leftrightarrow$ are called 'binary' connectives, and $\neg$ is called a 'unary' connective; in a conjunction $\phi \wedge \psi$, ϕ and ψ are called 'conjuncts', and in a disjunction $\phi \vee \psi$ as the 'disjuncts'; in an implication $\phi \rightarrow \psi$, ϕ is usually referred to as the 'antecedent' and ψ as the 'consequent'.[4]

Exercise 1 For each of the following expressions determine whether it is a formula of proposition logic:

a. $\neg(\neg p \vee q)$
b. $p \vee (q)$
c. $p2 \rightarrow (p2 \rightarrow (p2 \rightarrow p2))$
d. $p \rightarrow ((p \rightarrow q))$
e. $(p \rightarrow p) \rightarrow (q \rightarrow q)$
f. $\neg(q)$
g. $p \vee \neg p$
h. $p \vee q \vee r$
i. $\neg p \vee \neg\neg p$
j. $(p \vee p) \leftrightarrow p$

3.3 Construction trees and induction

A characteristic feature of formal languages is their step-by-step syntactic construction. This enables the implementation of the principle of compositionality, via step-by-step semantic interpretation. The details of that follow in chapter 5, we now take a closer look at the syntactic aspect.

The way in which a formula is constructed using clauses defined in definition 1 can be visualised by means of so-called 'construction trees'. In figure 3.1 is an example, viz., the construction tree of $(\neg(p \vee q) \rightarrow \neg\neg\neg q) \leftrightarrow r$.

The nodes in the tree are adorned with a formula and the number of the clause in definition 1 that was used to produce it. All construction trees start with nodes labelled (1), as all formulas are built from proposition letters. The clause number gives the main connective, i.e., the connective that was the last to be introduced and thus characterises a formula as a negation, conjunc-

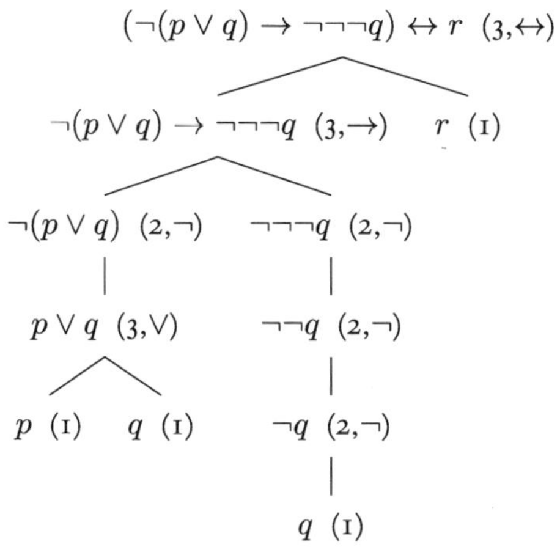

Figure 3.1: Construction tree $(\neg(p \vee q) \to \neg\neg\neg q) \leftrightarrow r$

tion, and so on. Each formula has one and only construction tree: there is no ambiguity thanks to the use of brackets.

A useful notion that can be defined in terms of construction trees is that of a formula ϕ being a sub-formula of some formula ψ: ϕ is a sub-formula of ψ if and only if ϕ is a node in the construction tree of ψ. Note that this means that every formula is a sub-formula of itself.

Exercise 2

a. Draw the construction tree of $((p \vee q) \vee \neg r) \leftrightarrow (p \vee (q \vee \neg r))$. Give the subformulas of the formula.
b. Give all formulas that can be made out of the following sequence of symbols by supplying brackets: $p \wedge q \to r$. Also supply their construction trees.
c. Classify each of the following sentences as an atomic formula, a negation, a conjunction, a disjunction, an implication, or an equivalence:

i.	$p \to q$	v.	$\neg(p \to q)$
ii.	$\neg p$	vi.	$(p \to q) \vee (q \to \neg\neg p)$
iii.	p	vii.	$\neg(p_1 \wedge p_2) \wedge \neg p_2$
iv.	$(p \wedge q) \wedge (q \wedge p)$	viii.	$(p \wedge (q \wedge r)) \vee p$

Construction trees do not only provide a nice way to visualise the syntactic structure of a formula, they are also useful for proving things. For that we take another look at the last clause of Definition 1, which reads:

> Only that which can be generated by the clauses (1)–(3) in a finite number of steps is a formula in L.

This is also referred to as the 'inductive clause' of the definition.

At first sight definition 1, in particular clauses (2) and (3) might look circular: aren't we defining here what a formula is in terms of formulas? It is the base clause (1) and the induction clause (4) that save the day. The base clause (1) defines a certain subset of formulas in terms of another notion, viz., the proposition letters in the vocabulary. And that is specified completely independently from definition 1. So we have at least some formulas that are not defined in terms of formulas. Clauses (2) and (3) do that, but note that the formulas on which they draw are of lesser complexity than what they define. Then comes clause (4). This states that only what can be constructed using (1), (2) and (3) can count as a formula. And that means that clauses (2) and (3) are not circular, it only requires that ultimately any formula is constructed starting with proposition letters.

Definitions such as definition 1 in which objects are said to have some property P only if they can be construed from other, simpler objects that are P, and ultimately from some group of objects which are simply said to be P, are called 'inductive' definitions.[5] The corresponding sets of objects are often called 'inductive sets'. Inductive definitions generate a method for proving things about such sets, called 'inductive proofs'. Quite generally, for every inductive definition there is a corresponding kind of proof by induction.

Let us return to formulas to illustrate this. Because the set of formulas is defined inductively, there is a simple method by which we can prove that all formulas have some particular property. In order to prove that all formulas have a property A it is sufficient to show that:

1. proposition letters have property A
2. if a formula ϕ has A, then $\neg\phi$ does too
3. if ϕ and ψ have property A, then $(\phi \wedge \psi), (\phi \vee \psi), (\phi \rightarrow \psi)$ and $(\phi \leftrightarrow \psi)$ do too

That this is sufficient is because of the induction clause (4), which assures us that every composite formula must be composed of some simpler formula(s) from which it, then, inherits the property A. A proof of this sort is called *a proof by induction on the complexity of the formula*, or also: a proof by induction on the length of the formula.

As an example of a proof by induction, consider the following simple, but rigorous proof of the fact that all formulas of proposition logic have an equal number of right brackets and left brackets.

Fact 1
All formulas ϕ of a language of proposition logic have an equal number of right and left brackets.

Proof. By induction on the complexity of formulas:

1. proposition letters have no brackets
2. suppose ϕ, ψ have an equal number of brackets
3. then $\neg\phi$ has an equal number of brackets, since no brackets are added or deleted
4. and $(\phi \wedge \psi), (\phi \vee \psi), (\phi \rightarrow \psi)$ and $(\phi \leftrightarrow \psi)$ have equal number of brackets since exactly one left bracket and exactly one right bracket is added

□

Step 1 is often called the 'base step'. Here it refers to the first clause in definition 1 of formulas. Step 2 the 'induction step' (or the 'induction hypothesis'). Steps 3 and 4 mirror the clauses in definition 1. The induction step is justified by the fact that definition 1 is an inductive definition.

Informally, one can look at a proof like this as follows. We can prove the fact for the basic case of proposition letters by inspection; this is step 1. Then steps 3 and 4 show that the property in question is preserved by the construction of complex formulas if the less complex formulas have the property. This is the hypothesis in Step 2. Since nothing else but what is constructed as in steps 3 and 4 is a formula, the proof is conclusive.

Another useful consequence of inductive definitions is that they allow for other inductive definitions. Thus since the notion of a formula is inductively defined we can define a function $(\ )^\sharp$ from formulas to natural numbers as follows:

$$
\begin{aligned}
(p)^\sharp &= 1 \\
(\neg\phi)^\sharp &= (\phi)^\sharp \\
(\phi * \psi)^\sharp &= (\phi)^\sharp + (\psi)^\sharp, \text{for each two-place connective} *
\end{aligned}
$$

What $(\ )^\sharp$ does is give the number of proposition letters in the formula ϕ.

Exercise 3 The *operator depth* of a formula of proposition logic is the maximal length of a nest of operators occurring in it. Example: $((\neg p \wedge q) \wedge \neg r)$ has operator depth 3.
Give a precise definition of this notion, using the inductive definition of formulas.

Exercise 4 What notions are defined by the following definitions by induction on formulas?

a.

$$p^* = 0$$
$$(\neg\phi)^* = \phi^*$$
$$(\phi \circ \psi)^* = \phi^* + \psi^* + 1$$

b.

$$p^\flat = 0$$
$$(\neg\phi)^\flat = \phi^\flat$$
$$(\phi \circ \psi)^\flat = \phi^\flat + \psi^\flat + 2$$

c. Prove by induction that for all formulas ϕ: $\phi^\flat = 2\phi^*$.

3.4 Applying a formal language

Proposition logic is about the validity of arguments that is based on connectives. As we shall see in chapter 7 that is done in a way that abstracts from actual arguments. However, that does not mean that there is no connection. We can translate statements and arguments that are made in natural language into the language of proposition logic and then see whether a certain argument is valid or not, or what a particular statement means from the logical perspective.

Note that doing so usually involves a certain amount of ingenuity and tinkering. An example of that appeared already in the introductory section, where the sentence 'Travel restrictions are lifted' was considered the negation of the sentence 'Travel restrictions remain in place'. One sentence is treated as the negation of the other although there is no explicit negation in either. This means that representation of natural language in a logical language is a matter of representation of content, not of form. That requires insight in how natural languages express content, which may differ from one language to the other.

Here are a few more examples of such divergences between form and content that one needs to be aware of when applying the language of proposition logic.

Negation can function at sentence-level, but also occurs as a modification of sub-sentential expressions, such as verb phrases, adverbs, and adjectives, as the examples in (1) illustrate:

(1) a. It is not the case that the Yankees won the 2004 World Series
b. Prisoners do not have full constitutional rights
c. I go to the museum not that frequently
d. He is very unfriendly

Conjunction is not necessarily expressed using 'and'. In English there is a whole range of expressions that indicate conjunction, e.g., 'but', 'while', 'even though', 'though', 'also', as the following examples show:

(2) a. Food colouring appears to change the color of water, but no chemical change occurs
b. Even though chemicals we are exposed to every day can be toxic, you can protect yourself from chemical exposures

c. Although they are very dangerous, extreme sports are getting more and more popular
d. Elements have many physical properties. They also have chemical properties

These expressions do differ in their usage, of course. For instance, 'but' is used to indicate a contrast, while 'even though' indicates that a particular fact does not make the rest of the statement untrue. These kinds of differences are matters of communicative use, and fall outside the application of the formal language of proposition logic.

Expressions of implication in natural language often leave out 'then', sometimes 'if . . . , then . . . ' is omitted altogether. Here are some examples of ways to express implication:

(3) a. You go, I will go too
b. You will get your payment only if you complete the work
c. In order for us to complete the project on time, it is necessary that we speed up the process
d. In order for people to resume their normal activities, it is sufficient that a vaccine is available
e. As soon as the energy supply stops, the endothermic reaction stops as well

What can be captured in a formal language and what not, depends on a number of factors. As was already indicated some aspects of meaning in natural language are intimately tied to communicative use, which formal languages lack. More on that in chapter 26. In other cases, it is a matter of how the formal language is designed, i.e., what is intended to do that determines which aspects of meaning are captured and which are left out of consideration. We will come back to this in chapter 5.

The next exercise is about representing sentences of English using the language of proposition logic. The idea is to make explicit the connectives that are present in the sentence, either explicitly or implicitly.

Here is a simple example:

- If I have lost if I cannot make a move, then I have lost
- Key: p: I can make a move; q: I have lost.
- Representation: $(\neg p \to q) \to q$

We see that we always need two things:

1. a formula that is the proposed translation; and
2. a key that specifies what the proposition letters used stand for

Exercise 5 Represent the following sentences by proposition logical formulas. Preserve as much of the structure as possible and in each case give the key.

a. If Ann and Bill are murderers, then Carol is innocent

b. If Carol is guilty, then Donald's testimony is correct
c. If Donald's testimony is correct, then Bill is the murderer
d. Every crime of theft is a crime of property infringement, and every crime of theft is an intentional crime
e. If Ann attends the party, then Bill, Carol, and Donald all attend the party
f. If Ann did not attend the party, then at least one of Bill, Carol and Donald did not attend the party
g. If Ann did not attend the party, then Bill, Carol and Donald did not attend the party
h. If at least one of Bill, Carol and Donald did not attend the party, then Ann did not attend the party
i. My shield is very strong. No matter how sharp a spear is, it cannot pierce my shield
j. My spear is very sharp. No matter how strong a shield is, my spear can pierce it
k. You are not the fish, you do not know the happiness of the fish
l. You are not me, you do not know that I do not know the happiness of the fish

The representation of arguments is an extension of this form of application of a logical language. Arguments basically consist of a number of sentences, which as the premisses and conclusion of the argument. The representation of sentences has been illustrated. Arguments are a central topic in chapter 7.

4
Excursus: logical constants

4.1 The topic

The idea that the meaning of a logical constant is exhausted by a specification of the rules for its use, raises a question if things are turned around: does every specification of a set of rules for use define a *bona fide* logical constant? Or is more at stake?

The question as such is of paramount importance, since it touches directly on the question what logic is. In chapter 1 we stated that logic is about the validity of arguments that depends on logical constants. That is a working definition of what logic is that is satisfactory if we have some independent means of establishing what logical constants are.

But that issue turns out to be hard to decide, and it is one that logicians and philosophers continue to wrestle with. It will not be solved here, but the aim is to show how in the context of a deductive view of validity the question has taken on a particular form. It was shaped that way by Arthur Prior as early as 1960. Prior's paper gave rise to lots of reactions and Belnap's paper is a good representative.

4.2 The authors

Arthur Prior

Arthur N. Prior (1914 – 1969) was a logician and philosopher who is best known for his pioneering work on tense logic. Born and educated in New Zealand, Prior worked there and in Australia before moving to the United Kingdom in the mid-1950s. He worked with contemporaries such as J.C. Smart, Peter Geach, and William Kneale, and the young Saul Kripke. Among his students were Max Cresswell and Kit Fine.

Prior was one of the first to develop a logic of temporalities, a.k.a. as 'tense logic' (Prior, 1957, 1967). His approach is based on the philosophical view that events, and with them the things that occur in them, move through time, from being future to being present to becoming past. Descriptions of events are essentially temporal, and their truth or falsity therefore depends on the time at which they are evaluated. This view of time is often called the '*A*-series', and it stands in contrast to the view that holds that events are essentially a-temporal, and hence their descriptions tense-less, the so-called '*B*-series'.[1] The *A*-series perspective seems to derive some support from languages such as English in which verbal tense is an important structural component of grammar. However, in formal semantics other approaches are explored as well, such as event-based semantics.[2]

Prior's interest in logic, although focussed on tense logic and modal logic, also included the history of logic and the philosophy of logic. His paper 'The Runabout Inference Ticket' (Prior, 1960) is an instance of his interest in the latter. Although it does not discuss the matter explicitly, it addresses one of the central questions in the philosophy of logic, viz., what is a logical constant? Logical theories are generally identified by the expressions that function as logical constants in them. Thus, propositional logic is concerned with certain propositional connectives, predicate logic with both the propositional connectives and the quantifiers, propositional tense logic with propositional connectives and tense operators, and so on. This raises the question what determines whether a type of expression counts as a logical constant. Any answer to that question is a determination what logic is, and is not, about, and thus embodies a conception of what logic is.

It may seem straightforward to come up with an answer, but it is actually surprisingly complex to do so in a way that satisfies everyone. Different answers have been given, and although here are certainly a number of properties that everyone agrees a logical constant should have, there is no universal agreement on the matter.

Prior's paper is an early contribution to this debate, and it is formulated in terms of inference. This has two aspects: it concerns the conclusions that can be drawn from a statement in which a logical constant occurs, and the premises from which such statement can be concluded. Later, in chapter 10, we will study this conception more thoroughly.

Nuel Belnap

Prior's short paper 'The Runabout Inference Ticket' led to a couple of immediate responses, and eventually continued to play a key role in later discussions about inference, meaning and the scope of logical theories. Later on we will see some examples of more recent responses, Belnap's paper is an example of an early one: his paper 'Tonk, Plonk and Plink' (Belnap, 1962) appeared a year and a half after Prior's.

Nuel D. Belnap (b. 1930) is an American logician and philosopher, who works in structural proof theory and in philosophical logic. He is well-known for his work on theories of truth (in particular the so-called 'prosentential theory of truth, see Grover et al. (1975)), on the logic of questions (see Belnap

& Steel (1976), and on tense logic and logics of agency (the so-called 'STIT'-logic, see Belnap et al. (2001)). His most recent work is in tense logic and is concerned with the investigation of the logic of branching space-time, and the consequences for issues involving (in)determinism and free will.

4.3 THE TEXTS

Prior, 'The Runabout Inference Ticket'

The paper is very short, and very influential. It starts with the introduction of the concept of an 'analytically valid inference'. That is an inference that is, first of all, valid, and, secondly, depends on nothing but the meanings of the expressions involved. The distinction between analytic and synthetic truth harkens back to Kant. It can be understood in slightly different ways, but a commonly accepted characterisation is that a statement is analytically true if and only if it is true solely in virtue of what the expressions in the statement mean; standard example: 'Bachelors are unmarried.' Prior extends the notion of analyticity to inference, an analytically valid inference being one that is valid solely in terms of the meanings of the expressions involved.

Prior illustrates the concept with the familiar example of conjunction, noting that given the meaning of 'and', the inference of *p* and *q* respectively from '*p* and *q*' is valid because of what 'and' means. And for the same reason the inference of '*p* and *q*' from *p* and *q* is valid as well. A key observation that Prior makes is that any inference pattern can be accounted for by defining a connective with the required properties.

This gives Prior what he needs to make the next, and surprising step: the introduction of the 'runabout inference ticket'. It is provided by the introduction of a new propositional connective 'tonk'. The meaning of 'tonk' is specified in terms of the inferences it allows:

- Infer '*p* tonk *q*' from *p*
- Infer *q* from '*p* tonk *q*'

Note that there is nothing unusual about the inference patterns as such: the first pattern is displayed by disjunction 'or', the second by conjunction 'and', and both are perfectly healthy ways of drawing inferences. The combination in one connective 'tonk', however, is toxic: anything can be inferred from anything. Obviously, 'tonk' is not a proper logical constant. But the question is why?

One obvious reaction might be that one should not introduce such a connective in the first place. But that leaves the question what, from a logical point of view, are proper connectives and what are not, unanswered. If we accept the account in terms of analytical validity of inferences involving 'and', then we seem forced to accept the same account for inferences involving 'tonk'.

Prior's text ends with a tongue-in-cheek reference to the 'usefulness' of his result, clearly indicating that he regards the argument he has given as a *reductio ad absurdum* of the view on inference that forms its starting point.

Belnap, 'Tonk, Plonk and Plink'

Belnap's paper is one of the first reactions to Prior's provocative contribution, and it has been very influential in the debate of it over the years. Like Prior's paper, Belnap's reaction is short but contains a forceful argument.

Belnap first considers the suggestion that it is misguided to analyse connectives in terms of derivability, without a prior semantics. Obviously, this would invalidate Prior's introduction of 'tonk'.

However, Belnap does not think this is a valid objection. In logic, as in many other branches of philosophy, he claims, there are two main lines of thinking. The analytic way defines wholes in terms of their parts. And the synthetic way defines parts in terms of the wholes they occur in. The analytic line of thinking is exemplified in the semantic approach to validity, which starts with defining the meanings of connectives with truth tables and then proceeds to analyse the validity of inference in terms of them. The synthetic mode, which is the line taken by, for example, natural deduction, works in the reverse order: it characterises connectives in terms of the role they play in valid inferences. Belnap considers both approaches useful, and hence does not accept the objection.

Belnap's solution starts from the observation that we need certain general assumptions about the concept of inference ('deducibility' is the term that Belnap uses) in order to control what are, and what are not, legitimate definitions of connectives. Belnap then proceeds to define such a set of assumptions, using a Gentzen-style formulation. The addition of a new connective, indicated by Belnap as 'plonk', to a given system is legitimate if the new system is a conservative extension of the initial system. This means that all inferences that are valid in the new system involve the new connective 'plonk', i.e., the addition of 'plonk' does not lead to additional valid inferences not involving 'plonk'.

The justification for this demand is that the initial system, without the new connective, is complete for its connectives: all valid inferences are captured by it, hence any extension that produces new ones that do not involve the new connective is inconsistent.

Belnap goes on to discuss how one would incorporate another constraint, viz., that connectives that are introduced are unique. In the setting of a syntactic, synthetic approach this means that the definition of a connective should characterise a unique role in inference patterns.

4.4 Study and discussion questions

Study questions

Prior

- What does Prior understand by an 'analytically valid inference'?
- Formulate the rules Prior gives for the 'tonk'connective as introduction and elimination rules.
- What does transitivity of deduction mean, and what role does it play in Prior's argument?

Belnap

- How does the objection to Peano's definition of the arithmetical operation '?' that Belnap discusses work?
- Give an example that shows that the addition of 'tonk' to Belnap's system is inconsistent.
- Explain why having the axiom $A \vdash B$ would make the addition of 'tonk' conservative.

Discussion questions

- Prior's argument can be read as a *reductio ad absurdum* of the idea that what characterises logical constants is that they give rise to analytically valid inferences. Discuss what constitutes the intuitive attractiveness of that account. Do you see a way in which it can be modified so as to avoid Prior's *reductio*?
- Can you think of a connective that is not in the standard set of propositional logic that can be added in a conservative manner to the system of natural deduction? If so, provide the definition and show that the conservativity requirement is met.
- Try to find examples of phenomena outside logic and philosophy for which the analytic and the synthetic mode of investigation, respectively, would seem most suited. Are there general characteristics of these phenomena that determine which mode is more appropriate?

4.5 Further reading

Another early response to Prior's paper is that of Stevenson (Stevenson, 1961). The debate about the nature of logical constants has continued, see MacFarlane (2017), Cohnitz & Estrada-González (2019, chapter 4).

5

Proposition Logic: Semantics

5.1 Introduction

In the previous chapter we introduced the language of propositional logic, in this one we will be looking at its semantics. We have used the connectives with an informal stipulation of their meanings: $\neg$ to stand for negation, $\wedge$ for conjunction, and so on. But strictly speaking, these expressions are just meaningless signs, until we assign a meaning to them.

In doing so we face a number of choices. If we take our clue from the counterparts of connectives in natural languages then we see that these often quite complex meanings, that may even change with the context in which they are used. Do we need to take all of these on board in designing the semantics for a language of propositional logic? We already noticed that the communicative use of natural language is not something that has an obvious counterpart in a formal language. This suggests that we need to separate those aspects of meaning that relate intrinsically to the communicative use in context from more general ones.

That gives us a first selection. Another one comes from what we want to do in propositional logic, viz., study the validity of arguments based on connectives. The concept of validity that we use then dictates what kind of meanings we need to assign to the connectives. Informally, a valid argument is one in which the conclusion is true if all of the premises are. Thus validity is a matter of connections between the truth and falsity of sentences.

That provides us with the second selection criterion: connectives are assigned meanings that are truth-functional, i.e., that express certain relations between the truth values of the sentences that they connect.

What that means, and what aspects of the intuitive meanings of natural language connectives can and cannot be captured in this way is the topic of the following section.

5.2 Truth, truth conditions, truth tables

The focus on truth and truth-functionality implies that we are only looking at sentences that are true or false.[1] We denote truth values with the symbols

1 for 'true' and 0 for 'false'. Since we are interested in systematic relations between truth and falsity, all other aspects can and should be ignored. As far as propositional logic is concerned, meaning is a matter of truth conditions.

How is that implemented? Semantic interpretation follows the lead of syntax. This is the principle of compositionality, which was already introduced in chapter 1. The construction of a formula dictates how its interpretation proceeds. It starts with the proposition letters occurring in the formula, and then interprets each step in its construction, applying the semantic interpretation of the connective that is introduced in that step.

So the first step is to interpret proposition letters. Since proposition letters have no connections with each other, this means that we start with an assignment of truth values to the proposition letters. Different interpretations make different assignments, and all of them are relevant, so in the interpretation of complex formulas all combinations of interpretations of proposition letters are potentially relevant.

Then we need to interpret the connectives. Connectives combine one (negation) or two (the other connectives) formulas to form a new one. The interpretation of the result is determined by the component formulas in a specific way: that is the semantic interpretation of a connective. Concretely this means that a connective determines what the truth value of the whole formula is given the truth values of the component part(s).

This can be formally implemented in a number of ways. We will start with making use of so-called 'truth tables'. Later, in chapter 7 we will look at another way of specifying the semantic interpretation of the language of proposition logic.

A truth table is a table in which all the possible combinations of truth values a number of formulas are systematically related. They are an effective tool to study semantic relationships between formulas. That will be their use in chapter 7, where the validity of propositional arguments is studied. But we can also use them to define the interpretation of the connectives, and of complex formulas. We start with the connectives.

5.3 Semantics of connectives

5.3.1 Negation

Negation is a relatively simple matter. It turns a true formula into a false one, and a false one into a true one. That is exactly what is described in the truth table 5.1:

The left ('input') column lists all possibilities with regard to truth and falsity of an arbitrary formula, using 1 and 0 as standing for 'true' and 'false',

ϕ	$\neg\phi$
1	0
0	1

Table 5.1: Truth table for negation

respectively. And the right ('output') column displays the interpretation of the negation of a formula: if ϕ is true, $\neg\phi$ is false, and if ϕ is false, $\neg\phi$ is true.

There are more ways to express the negation of a sentence than by means of 'not' or 'it is not the case that'. See the examples in table 5.2, where each of the sentences in the left column is the negation of the corresponding sentence in the right column.

Porcupines are unfriendly	Porcupines are friendly
John is neither at home nor at school	John is either at home or at school
No one is at home	Someone is at home
John is never at home	John is sometimes at home
John is not home yet	John is home already
John has never yet been at home	John has on occasion been at home

Table 5.2: Forms of negations

5.3.2 *Conjunction*

The truth table for conjunction is given in table 5.3.

ϕ	ψ	$\phi \wedge \psi$
1	1	1
1	0	0
0	1	0
0	0	0

Table 5.3: Truth table for conjunction

This is more or less self-explanatory. A conjunction is true if and only both conjuncts are true, and false otherwise. Do note that this truth table, and hence the logical connective $\wedge$ accounts for only part of the meaning of corresponding expressions in natural language.

To give one simple example, a conjunction in natural language is often interpreted as involving temporal order; see the contrast between:

(1) a. He finished his studies and took a job
b. He took a job and finished his studies

The natural interpretation of such sentences is that the second event mentioned happened after the first. Then these sentences do not have the same truth conditions. However, as the truth table for conjunction makes clear, $\phi \wedge \psi$ is true if and only if $\psi \wedge \phi$ is. Arguably, the order effect is connected with the communicative use. Note that it is cancellable:

(2) He finished his studies and took a job, but I don't know what he did first

This is not a contradiction, which indicates that the order effect does not belong to the truth conditions of the sentence, but has to be explained in terms of communicative function. More on that in chapter 26

It is relevant to note that conjunction is sometimes just a part of what natural language expressions mean. Consider the following example:

(3) The capsule failed to reach its intended orbit because the navigation system malfunctioned

For sentence (3) to be true both component sentences have to be true as well. So (3) implies (4):

(4) The capsule failed to reach its intended orbit and the navigation system malfunctioned

But for (3) to be true more is needed, there also has to be a causal relation between the two. And that is not captured by the logical conjunction.

A similar story can be told about the other example. This indicates that we can use propositional logic in such cases to study part of what goes on in arguments in which such sentences occur, but that some aspects that are relevant for truth are not captured.

5.3.3 *Disjunction*

For the disjunction the truth table is as given in 5.4.

ϕ	ψ	$\phi \vee \psi$
1	1	1
1	0	1
0	1	1
0	0	0

Table 5.4: Truth table for disjunction

According to table 5.4, a disjunction is true if and only if at least one of its disjuncts is true. So this is the truth table for what is called 'inclusive' disjunction, i.e., disjunction that does not exclude that both disjuncts are true., as is the case in the following example:

(5) One can learn English by watching films or by interacting with others

But there is also an alternative use, which in English is expressed by the 'either ... or ...' construction, that does exclude this. It is, aptly, called 'exclusive' disjunction. Sometimes a separate connective ∞ is introduced for exclusive disjunction and its truth table given in 5.5.

ϕ	ψ	$\phi \infty \psi$
1	1	0
1	0	1
0	1	1
0	0	0

Table 5.5: Truth table for exclusive disjunction

Consider the following example:

(6) You can have either a cookie or an ice cream

Another construction which can be used to express an exclusive disjunction is with 'unless':

(7) We are going to see a film tonight, unless we are going to the beach this afternoon

In what follows, unless otherwise stated, 'or' is understood to be inclusive, as is also usual in mathematics.

5.3.4 *Implication*

The truth table for (material) implicationis given table 5.6.

ϕ	ψ	$\phi \to \psi$
1	1	1
1	0	0
0	1	1
0	0	1

Table 5.6: Truth table for material implication

This truth table may need some clarification, as it may not appear to be intuitive in all respects.

The second row does not present a problem: $\phi \to \psi$ is false if ϕ is true and ψ is false. This is intuitive: a claim that if ϕ is the case then so is ψ can be shown to be false by showing that ϕ is true but ψ is false.

But that also supplies us with a justification for the other rows. In fact, ϕ being true with ψ being false is the only situation in which we can claim that $\phi \to \psi$ is false. And since sentences are either true or false, that means that in all other situations $\phi \to \psi$ is true.

This certainly is reasonable in case ϕ and ψ are both true, and in case they are both false. This leaves the situation in which ϕ is false and ψ is true. Here, perhaps, one would say that the truth value of the implication as a whole cannot be decided. However, consider the following examples:

(8) If a number is larger than 10, then it is larger than 5.

This sentence is true. Suppose we pick arbitrary numbers to check whether what the sentence states is the case. The one situation in which an implication is false, viz., where the antecedent is true and the consequent is false, cannot arise: there is no number n such that $n > 10$ and $n \not> 5$. No matter what number n we pick, it holds that if $n > 10$, then $n > 5$. Note that this also covers the situation in which we happen to pick a number smaller than 5, i.e., in which the antecedent is false. And this also includes the situation in which we pick a number between 10 and 5, i.e., the situation in which the antecedent is false and the consequent is true.

So, if we accept that (8) is a true sentence, then we assign the implication the meaning that is specified in truth table 5.6.

This means that the implication of propositional logic is an adequate representation of the use of 'if . . . , (then) . . . ' in mathematics. But not only there. Cf.,:

(9) If you drive too fast, you get a ticket

Unlike in the case of (8) here all four situations, i.e., all four distributions of truth values over antecedent and consequent, are possible. It is clear that if you drive too fast but don't get cited, (9) would be false. But in all other situations we would accept it as true. Even if you keep to the speed limit but get a ticket for ignoring a red traffic light.

That is not to say that a propositional logical implication is always an adequate representation of a conditional sentence. We come back to that in chapter 6.

Note that in natural language, sentences that express implications do not necessarily contain 'if . . . , (then) . . . '; cf.:

(10) In order for the liquid to dissolve, it is necessary that it is heated to at least 60°C

This can be rewritten using *if . . . , (then) . . .* :

(11) If the liquid dissolves, it is heated to at least 60°C

And note that the same holds for:

(12) In order for the vapour to disappear, it is sufficient that the pressure is lowered to 990 Hpa

which can be represented as:

(13) If the pressure is lowered to 990 Hpa, the vapour will disappear

5.3.5 *Equivalence*

Finally, the truth table for material equivalence is given in table 5.7:

ϕ	ψ	$\phi \leftrightarrow \psi$
1	1	1
1	0	0
0	1	0
0	0	1

Table 5.7: Truth table for material equivalence

According to table 5.7, $\phi \leftrightarrow \psi$ is true if and only if ϕ and ψ have the same truth value.

Occurrences of 'If and only if' in natural language are rare, outside the context of mathematics and logic. But of course there are other ways to express equivalence. An example is the English 'provided':

(14) Travel restrictions are lifted, provided the reproduction rate stays below 1 and social distancing rules are obeyed

As predicted by the truth table for equivalence, this sentence says the same as the conjunction of two conditionals:

(15) If travel restrictions are lifted, then the reproduction rate stays below 1 and social distancing rules are obeyed

(16) If the reproduction rate stays below 1 and social distancing rules are obeyed, then travel restrictions are lifted

In mathematical and logical contexts, 'if and only if' is often expressed as 'iff' or $\Leftrightarrow$.

Exercise 1 Observe the following truth tables and figure out which connective each of them corresponds to:

a.

ϕ	ψ	?
1	1	0
1	0	1
0	1	1
0	0	1

b.

ϕ	ψ	?
1	1	1
1	0	0
0	1	0
0	0	0

c.

ϕ	ψ	?
1	1	0
1	0	0
0	1	0
0	0	0

d.

ϕ	ψ	?
1	1	1
1	0	1
0	1	1
0	0	1

5.4 Semantics of complex formulas

Truth tables are an effective and intuitive way to specify the semantic interpretation of the connectives of a propositional logical language. But they can also be used to represent the meaning of complex formulas. All the ingredients for that are in place: we have assignments of truth values to all the proposition letters and interpretations of the connectives, the expressions that form more complex expressions from simple ones. They can be represented in what is called a 'composite truth table' for a formula.

A simple example is given in table 5.8.

p	q	$p \wedge q$
1	1	1
1	0	0
0	1	0
0	0	0

Table 5.8: Composite truth table for $p \wedge q$

In accordance with the principle of compositionality, the semantic interpretation of $p \wedge q$ is determined by that of its component parts, viz., p and q, and by the way in which these are combined, viz., by means of $\wedge$. The composite truth table is then constructed by looking at all possible assignments of truth values to p and q, and then apply the interpretation of $\wedge$ to each of them.

The result looks like truth table 5.3 that gives the semantics of $\wedge$, of course. But note that this use of truth tables is different: they are not definitions, but calculations of the interpretation of complex formulas.

This is clear if we look at a more complex example, as given table 5.9.

Again, we start with the possible combinations of truth values of the proposition letters occurring in the formula. Then we apply the interpretation of the connectives that are used in each step of the construction of the formula. I.e., for each combination, we first calculate the truth values of $\neg p$ and $\neg q$ (using the truth table of negation); then we calculate the truth values of $\neg p \rightarrow \neg q$ (using the truth table of the implication); and finally we determine the truth values the formula as a whole (using the truth table of negation again).

Another example, involving three proposition letters, is given in table 5.10.

p	q	$\neg p$	$\neg q$	$\neg p \to \neg q$	$\neg(\neg p \to \neg q)$
1	1	0	0	1	0
1	0	0	1	1	0
0	1	1	0	0	1
0	0	1	1	1	0

Table 5.9: Composite truth table for $\neg(\neg p \to \neg q)$

p	q	r	$p \vee q$	$\neg r$	$(p \vee q) \wedge \neg r$
1	1	1	1	0	0
1	1	0	1	1	1
1	0	1	1	0	0
1	0	0	1	1	1
0	1	1	1	0	0
0	1	0	1	1	1
0	0	1	0	0	0
0	0	0	0	1	0

Table 5.10: Composite truth table for $(p \vee q) \wedge \neg r$

Here three proposition letters occur in the formula, giving rise to eight different assignments of truth values to each of them. For each of these eight combinations we then determine the truth value of each of the sub-formulas and finally that of the formula as a whole.

It will be clear that this is a perfectly general procedure with which we can determine the interpretation of any formula ϕ of a propositional language:

- Determine which proposition letters $p_1, \ldots, p_n$ occur in ϕ
- Draw a table with 2^n rows and fill each with a unique combination of truth values assigned to $p_1, \ldots, p_n$
- Follow the construction tree of ϕ and add a column of each sub-formulas of ϕ and calculate its truth values in each of the rows

Exercise 2 Make truth tables for a, b, c, e, f, g, h from exercise 5 in chapter 3.

5.5 Semantics revisited

We now have a language and a semantics. The next step is to use that to define propositional logic, i.e., an account of the validity of propositional arguments. That is the topic of chapter 7. However, before turning to that, we present the semantics of propositional language in a different format. The truth table method that has been introduced above is a perfectly adequate way of formulating the semantics of propositional logical language. And, as we will see later in chapter 7, truth tables are also a convenient tool for checking the validity of proposition logical arguments. However, if we want to formulate and prove general facts about propositional logical validity another way of stating the semantics will prove to be convenient. Also, this way of stating the semantics of a logical language will be the format that is used later on, when we turn to predicate logic and other logical systems.

This formulation of the semantics starts with the concept of a 'valuation.' Valuations are functions that assign a truth value to each of the formulas of a propositional language. Not any function will do, however, only those that are in accordance with the interpretations that we want to assign to the connectives will qualify.

The definition, which is called a 'truth definition' for the language L, runs as follows. Let FORM_L be the set of all formulas of a propositional logical language L, based on a vocabulary of proposition letters, VOC_L. Let $\{0, 1\}$ be a set of truth values.

Definition 2 (Semantics)
A valuation V is a function from FORM_L to $\{0, 1\}$ that meets the following requirements:

1. $V(p_i) \in \{0, 1\}$, for all $p_i \in \text{VOC}_L$
2. $V(\neg\phi) = 1$ iff $V(\phi) = 0$
3. $V(\phi \wedge \psi) = 1$ iff $V(\phi) = 1$ and $V(\psi) = 1$
4. $V(\phi \vee \psi) = 1$ iff $V(\phi) = 1$ or $V(\psi) = 1$
5. $V(\phi \rightarrow \psi) = 1$ iff $V(\phi) = 0$ or $V(\psi) = 1$
6. $V(\phi \leftrightarrow \psi) = 1$ iff $V(\phi) = V(\psi)$

If we check the clauses in this definition against the truth tables for the connectives, we see that they match. Note that we only need to specify when a formula of a given form is true, the rest follows from the fact that V is a function that assigns every formula either 1 or 0.

Exercise 3

a. Reformulate the truth definition as a specification of the conditions in which a formula is false.
b. Motivate that the two formulations are equivalent

That the truth definition and the truth tables define the same semantics for the language of proposition logic rests on the fact that for any given formula ϕ only a finite number of valuations really matter, viz., those that assign different truth values to one or more of the proposition letters that occur in ϕ. In effect each row in the composite truth table of ϕ corresponds to a distinct set of valuations, viz., those that agree on the proposition letters in ϕ.

Given this correspondence between valuations and truth tables, it is a matter of convenience which semantic method we use. But note that the finiteness of the factors that are relevant for the interpretation of a formula is crucial here. If the assignment of a truth value to a formula would depend on a parameter that could have an infinite number of values, finite representations such as composite truth tables would no longer be available. A case in point is time: in a logic where formulas are true relative to a point in time, finite truth tables are no longer an option, assuming that time is infinite.

6

Excursus: conditionals

6.1 The topic

The analysis of material implication in classical two-valued logic is the one that is standardly used, despite the fact that it has some odd properties that some have even called paradoxical: the so-called 'paradoxes of material implication'. One example is what is often called the 'paradox of entailment': given the semantics of the material implication a formula of the form $(p \wedge \neg p) \rightarrow q$ is always true, no matter what propositions p and q represent.

The analysis of material implication goes back to Frege and Russell and in the context of reasoning in mathematics, about mathematical objects and their properties and relations, it is perfectly adequate. And given that connectives in classical logic are truth-functional it is arguably the only analysis that is available. However, some of its logical properties are distinctly odd if one compares them with the meaning of conditionals in natural language. This fact has, of course, been noted already early on in the development of classical truth-functional logic.

Almost immediately after the publication of Russell & Whitehead's *Principia Mathematica*, in 1911 – 1913, C.I. Lewis objected to the concept of material implication as adequate for how conditionals in natural language function, and proposed what he called 'strict implication'. Strict implication is analysed in terms of a primitive concept of possibility, and informally reads as follows: A strictly implies B if and only if it is not possible that A is true and B is false.

Other early work that aimed at overcoming some of the difficulties worked with so-called 'many-valued logics', about which more in chapter 22. However, Lewis' idea of strict implication was the more influential one, and it has led to a plethora of different analyses over the years. It turns out that different ways of dealing with the paradoxes of material implication also have repercussions for the analysis of causal conditionals ('If the stone will hit the glass, it will cause it to break'), counterfactual conditionals ('If I hadn't stricken the match, it would not have lightened'), and so on.

6.2 The authors

Peter Suber

Peter Suber (b. 1951) is an American philosopher and logician who worked on a wide variety of topics in the area of epistemology, such as scepticism and Kantian analysis of arithmetic and geometry, and on issues in philosophy of law, such as civil disobedience.[1]

The text is part of notes that Suber made for a course on logic which he has taught for many years at Earlham College.

David Sanford

David Sanford (1937 – 2022) was an American logician and philosopher who worked primarily in the area of philosophical logic and analytical metaphysics, on such topics as disjunctive predicates, mereology, vagueness and the Sorites paradox, and the analysis of causality.

The text is the first chapter of his 1989 book (revised edition 2003) *If P, Then Q: Conditionals and the Foundations of Reasoning* (Sanford, 1989).

6.3 The texts

Suber's text is a short introduction to the paradoxes of material implication as they arise in classical truth-functional logic. He identifies two sources of them, and goes on to discuss these in terms of the tensed relationship between relevant connections between antecedent and consequent and truth-functional connections. As was also noted above, Suber, too, indicates that in certain contexts the material implication is adequate. He then goes on to discuss very briefly the effect of the paradoxes of material implication for the classical analysis of the validity of arguments.

The text by Sanford gives an extensive analysis of the way in which conditionals are expressed in natural languages such as English. He focusses on the question of what it is in reality that makes a conditional statement true, and illustrates what is at stake with reference to statements about causal relationships, and statements that ascribe dispositional properties.

6.4 Study and discussion questions

Study questions

Suber

- Which two sources of paradoxes of material implication does Suber distinguish? And in what sense are they 'paradoxical'?

- Is there a difference between the two examples that Suber gives of each?
- Which of the two gives rise to the paradox of entailment?
- Which intuitive requirement on ordinary implications is lost by truth-functionality? And why?
- How does Suber argue that an implication with a false antecedent is true? And how does that show that paradoxes of material implication 'are acceptable to some of our intuitions'?
- Why does Suber raise the question of whether paradoxes of material implication also apply to arguments?
- And how does he argue that they do not?

Sandford

- Why does Sanford hold that the study of conditionals is of general importance?
- What is the connection between deliberation, planning and conditional reasoning?
- Why are the terms 'antecedent' and 'consequent' potentially misleading? What alternative terminology does Sanford propose?
- What are non-declarative conditionals? And why are they usually not taken into account in theories of conditionals in logic and philosophy?
- What conception of truth does Sanford use? And what problem do conditionals present for that conception?
- What is the connection between conditionals and Hume's conception of causation?
- And how do conditionals play a role in Mill's dispositional account of physical existence?

Discussion questions

- Recall what Frege said about the relationship between natural language and the language of logic in the preface of his *Begriffsschrift*. Can that be used as a justification for the discrepancy between the meaning of material implication and the meaning of conditionals in natural language? And what can be said about that from the point of view that Russell defends in his *Our Knowledge of the External World* ?
- Explain why C.I. Lewis' strict implication is not truth-functional. Connect this with what Suber says about the relationship between relevancy and truth-functionality.
- Are there any elements of Sanford's analysis of conditionals in English that do not transfer to Chinese? If so, what are these? And then what are the consequences for the general conclusions that Sanford draws from his analysis?

- Explain why Suber claims that the paradoxes of material implication, even though they may be problematic for the analysis of natural language conditionals, do not pose a problem for the validity of arguments. Illustrate with an example. Can you see a connection with the concept of strict implication of C.I. Lewis?
- Discuss what problems one would encounter if one would try to analyse statements that ascribe dispositional properties in truth-functional terms.

6.5 Further reading

The paradoxes of material implication have given rise to different analyses of implication. One approach is to use many-valued logic, which will be treated in chapter 22.

The *locus classicus* for relevance logic is Anderson & Belnap (1975) For a recent overview, see Bimbó (2006) and Jago (2013). For a more general overview that includes also other non-classical logics, see Priest (2008)..

For an extensive overview of philosophical approaches to conditionals, see Arlo-Costa (2019). Conditional sentences in natural language are also a widely studied topic in formal semantics, see von Fintel (2011).

7
Proposition Logic: Validity

7.1 Introduction

Chapters 3 and 5 have given us a language and its interpretation. This allows us to represent sentences and arguments in such a way that their propositional structure is made explicit. What we do not yet have is a logic. Logic, recall, is concerned with the validity of arguments, i.e., with systematic connections between the truth and falsity of the sentences forming an argument. So we need to see how validity is to be defined. Then we have a proposition logic.

We will first look at an important relation between proposition logical formulas, viz., that of logical equivalence. Next, we introduce some general concepts, viz., that of tautology, contradiction and contingency, and have a closer look at how they relate. Finally. we will define the concept of validity and illustrate it by means of some applications. Together these concepts constitute the logic of propositions.

Logical systems are not only applied, they are also objects of study themselves. Thus if we inquire into properties of a logical system, we engage in what is often called 'meta-logic'. We end this chapter with an illustration of that type of endeavour. It concerns the expressive power of the system of proposition logic.

7.2 Equivalence

Consider the composite truth table 7.1. Here we have two different formulas $p \rightarrow q$ and $\neg p \vee q$. As the table shows, these two formulas are true and false

p	q	$\neg p$	$p \rightarrow q$	$\neg p \vee q$
1	1	0	1	1
1	0	0	0	0
0	1	1	1	1
0	0	1	1	1

Table 7.1: Composite truth table for $p \rightarrow q$ and $\neg p \vee q$

under exactly the same conditions, they are what is called 'logically equivalent'.

Note that the equivalence of $p \to q$ and $\neg p \lor q$ does not depend on p and q being the proposition letters occurring in them: $r \to s$ and $\neg r \lor s$ are equivalent as well. And neither is it relevant that the first is an implication with proposition letters as antecedent and consequent and the second a disjunction of a negation of a proposition letter and another proposition letter. What matters is logical form: any formula of the form $\phi \to \psi$ is equivalent with one of the form $\neg\phi \lor \psi$.

Again, we can use a truth table to show this:

ϕ	ψ	$\neg\phi$	$\phi \to \psi$	$\neg\phi \lor \psi$
1	1	0	1	1
1	0	0	0	0
0	1	1	1	1
0	0	1	1	1

Table 7.2: Composite truth table for $\phi \to \psi$ and $\neg\phi \lor \psi$

Logical equivalence is defined as follows:

Definition 3 (Logical equivalence)
ϕ and ψ are logically equivalent iff for all valuations V: $V(\phi) = V(\psi)$

Instead of a truth table we can also use the definition to show that two formulas of a given form are equivalent. Here is a simple example, an equivalence that is known as 'the law of double negation'.

Fact 2 (Double negation)
ϕ and $\neg\neg\phi$ are logically equivalent

Proof. Take an arbitrary valuation V. Suppose $V(\phi) = 1$. It follows that $V(\neg\phi) = 0$ (truth definition, clause 2), and $V(\neg\neg\phi) = 1$ (same).
Similarly for the case that $V(\phi) = 0$. □

This illustrates a proof strategy: if we need to prove that something holds for all of an infinite number of cases, it suffices to prove it for an arbitrary instance.

A truth table would also do the job:

ϕ	$\neg\phi$	$\neg\neg\phi$
1	0	1
0	1	0

Table 7.3: Composite truth table for $\neg\neg\phi$ and ϕ

The last example is a composite truth table which demonstrates that $(\phi \vee \psi) \vee \chi$ is equivalent to $\phi \vee (\psi \vee \chi)$, see table 7.4.

ϕ	ψ	χ	$\phi \vee \psi$	$(\phi \vee \psi) \vee \chi$	$\psi \vee \chi$	$\phi \vee (\psi \vee \chi)$
1	1	1	1	1	1	1
1	1	0	1	1	1	1
1	0	1	1	1	1	1
1	0	0	1	1	0	1
0	1	1	1	1	1	1
0	1	0	1	1	1	1
0	0	1	0	1	1	1
0	0	0	0	0	0	0

Table 7.4: Composite truth table for $(\phi \vee \psi) \vee \chi$ and $\phi \vee (\psi \vee \chi)$

This equivalence is known as the 'associativity' of $\vee$. A similar result holds for $\wedge$. The associativity of $\vee$ and $\wedge$ means that we can leave off brackets in formulas of this form: we can write $\phi \wedge \psi \wedge \chi$, $(\phi \to \psi) \vee (\psi \to \chi) \vee (\chi \to \phi)$ etc.

Exercise 1 presents a number of well-known equivalences.

Exercise 1 Prove the equivalence of the formulas listed in six of the following items. Use truth tables for three cases, and the definition of equivalence for the other three:

a. $\phi, \neg\neg\phi, \phi \wedge \phi, \phi \vee \phi, \phi \wedge (\phi \vee \psi), \phi \vee (\phi \wedge \psi)$
b. $\neg\phi, \phi \to (\psi \wedge \neg\psi)$
c. $\neg(\phi \vee \psi), \neg\phi \wedge \neg\psi$ (De Morgan's Law)
d. $\neg(\phi \wedge \psi), \neg\phi \vee \neg\psi$ (De Morgan's Law)
e. $\phi \vee \psi, \psi \vee \phi$ (commutativity of $\vee$)
f. $\phi \wedge \psi, \psi \wedge \phi$ (commutativity of $\wedge$)
g. $\phi \wedge (\psi \vee \chi), (\phi \wedge \psi) \vee (\phi \wedge \chi)$ (distributive law)
h. $\phi \vee (\psi \wedge \chi), (\phi \vee \psi) \wedge (\phi \vee \chi)$ (distributive law)
i. $\phi \to \psi, \neg\phi \vee \psi, \neg(\phi \wedge \neg\psi), \neg\psi \to \neg\phi$
j. $\phi \to \psi, \neg\psi \to \neg\phi$ (law of contraposition)
k. $\phi \leftrightarrow \psi, (\phi \to \psi) \wedge (\psi \to \phi), (\phi \wedge \psi) \vee (\neg\phi \wedge \neg\psi)$
l. $(\phi \vee \psi) \wedge \neg(\phi \wedge \psi), \neg(\phi \leftrightarrow \psi), \neg\phi \leftrightarrow \psi$
m. $(\phi \vee \psi) \to \chi, (\phi \to \chi) \wedge (\psi \to \chi)$
n. $\phi \to (\psi \wedge \chi), (\phi \to \psi) \wedge (\phi \to \chi)$
o. $\phi \to (\psi \to \chi), (\phi \wedge \psi) \to \chi$

Logically equivalent formulas always have the same truth values. This means that if ψ occurs in χ, it can be replaced by ϕ without any effect on the truth value of χ. We use the notation $[\alpha/\beta]\gamma$ to refer to the result of replacing occurrences of β in γ by α.

Theorem 1 (Substitution)
If ϕ and ψ are logically equivalent, then χ is logically equivalent with $[\phi/\psi]\chi$

Proof. By induction on the construction of χ. Observation: ϕ, ψ, χ are complex: proposition letters are by definition not equivalent and do not have subformulas.

- $\chi = \neg\psi$. Then $[\phi/\psi]\chi = \neg\phi$. Since for all $V: V(\phi) = V(\psi)$, we also have that for all $V: V(\neg\phi) = V(\neg\psi)$
- $\chi = \psi \wedge \xi$. Then $[\phi/\psi]\chi = \phi \wedge \xi$. Since for all $V: V(\phi) = V(\psi)$, we also have that for all $V: V(\psi \wedge \xi) = V(\phi \wedge \xi)$

The other cases are left to the reader. □

What the substitution theorem illustrates is the truth conditional nature of the meaning of formulas of a propositional language. Because only their truth conditions matter, equivalent formulas, which have identical truth conditions, can be substituted without changing the meaning.

Here is a simple example where theorem 1 is used to derive an equivalence using equivalences mentioned in exercise 1:

- $\phi \to (\psi \to \chi)$ iff $(\phi \wedge \psi) \to \chi$ (n.)
- $\phi \wedge \psi$ iff $\psi \wedge \phi$ (f.)
- $\phi \to (\psi \to \chi)$ iff $(\psi \wedge \phi) \to \chi$ (theorem 1)

Exercise 2 Show on the basis of equivalences of exercise 1 that the following formulas are equivalent:

a. $\phi \leftrightarrow \psi$ and $\psi \leftrightarrow \phi$ (commutativity of $\leftrightarrow$)
b. $\phi \to \neg\phi$ and $\neg\phi$
c. $\phi \wedge (\psi \wedge \chi)$ and $\chi \wedge (\psi \wedge \phi)$
d. $\phi \infty \psi$ and $\phi \leftrightarrow \neg\psi$
e. $\phi \infty \neg\psi$, $\neg\phi \infty \psi$, and $\phi \leftrightarrow \psi$

There is a connection between material equivalence and logical equivalence. A simple illustration is given in table 7.5.

ϕ	$\neg\phi$	$\neg\neg\phi$	$\phi \leftrightarrow \neg\neg\phi$
1	0	1	1
0	1	0	1

Table 7.5: Composite truth table for $\phi \leftrightarrow \neg\neg\phi$

Because for any valuation $V: V(\phi) = V(\neg\neg\phi)$, it follows that for any valuation $V: V(\phi \leftrightarrow \neg\neg\phi) = 1$.

Obviously, this holds for any two logically equivalent formulas and the corresponding material equivalence, as is expressed in fact 3.

Fact 3
ϕ and ψ are logically equivalent iff for every valuation $V: \ V(\phi \leftrightarrow \psi) = 1$

The proof of an equivalence such as this typically proceeds in two steps, one proving the logical implication from left to right ($\Rightarrow$), the other that from right to left ($\Leftarrow$):

Proof.

$\Rightarrow$: Suppose ϕ and ψ are logically equivalent. Then every valuation $V: V(\phi) = V(\psi)$. By condition 6 of the truth definition 2, it follows that $V(\phi \leftrightarrow \psi) = 1$, for every V

$\Leftarrow$: Suppose that $V(\phi \leftrightarrow \psi) = 1$ for every valuation V. Then there can be no V such that $V(\phi) \neq V(\psi)$, since otherwise $V(\phi \leftrightarrow \psi) = 0$ which contradicts the assumption. So for every $V: V(\phi) = V(\psi)$, and thus ϕ and ψ are logically equivalent.

□

7.3 Tautology, contradiction, contingency

7.3.1 *Tautology*

Formulas which are always true, such as $\phi \leftrightarrow \neg\neg\phi$, form a special category. They are called 'tautologies':

Definition 4 (Tautology) A formula ϕ is a tautology, notation: $\models \phi$, iff for all $V: V(\phi) = 1$.

Thus we get an alternative formulation for Fact 3:

Fact 3 (Alternative formulation)
ϕ and ψ are logically equivalent iff $\models \phi \leftrightarrow \psi$

As was the case with logical equivalence, that a formula is a tautology can be shown either by giving a composite truth table, or by reasoning about the truth definition.

For example, that $\models \phi \rightarrow (\psi \rightarrow \phi)$ is shown by the composite truth table 7.6. It is also shown by the following reasoning:

Proof. Suppose $\not\models \phi \rightarrow (\psi \rightarrow \phi)$. Then there must be a $V: V(\phi) = 1$ and $V(\psi \rightarrow \phi) = 0$. But if $V(\phi) = 1$, then also $V(\psi \rightarrow \phi) = 1$ and hence we have that $V(\phi \rightarrow (\psi \rightarrow \phi)) = 1$. This contradicts the assumption, which thus has to be rejected. □

ϕ	ψ	$\psi \to \phi$	$\phi \to (\psi \to \phi)$
1	1	1	1
1	0	1	1
0	1	0	1
0	0	1	1

Table 7.6: Composite truth table for $\phi \to (\psi \to \phi)$

This proof instantiates another very common proof strategy, so-called *reductio ad absurdum*. Using this strategy a fact is proven by showing that the assumption that it is not true leads to a contradiction.

Exercise 3 Show that the following formulas are tautologies (for each ϕ, ψ and χ):

a. $\neg\phi \to (\phi \to \psi)$ (*ex falso sequitur quodlibet*)
b. $\phi \vee \neg\phi$ (principle of excluded middle)
c. $(\phi \to (\psi \to \chi)) \to ((\phi \to \psi) \to (\phi \to \chi))$
d. $(\phi \to \psi) \vee (\psi \to \phi)$
e. $((\phi \to \psi) \to \phi) \to \phi$ (Peirce's law)

Obviously all tautologies are equivalent with each other: if $V(\phi) = V(\psi) = 1$ for all V, then $V(\phi) = V(\psi)$ for all V:

Fact 4 If $\models \phi$ and $\models \psi$, then $\phi \Leftrightarrow \psi$

If ϕ is not a tautology, i.e., $\not\models \phi$, then there is a valuation V such that $V(\phi) = 0$. Such a V is called a 'counterexample' to ϕ (being a tautology).

Consider truth table 7.7.

p	q	$\neg p$	$\neg q$	$p \to q$	$\neg p \to \neg q$	$(p \to q) \to (\neg p \to \neg q)$
1	1	0	0	1	1	1
1	0	0	1	0	1	1
0	1	1	0	1	0	0
0	0	1	1	1	1	1

Table 7.7: Composite truth table for $(p \to q) \to (\neg p \to \neg q)$

In case $V(p) = 0$ and $V(q) = 1$, we have $V((p \to q) \to (\neg p \to \neg q)) = 0$. Thus, a valuation $V\colon V(p) = 0, V(q) = 1$ is a counterexample that shows that $\not\models (p \to q) \to (\neg p \to \neg q)$.

It is important to note that we cannot say whether a formula of the form $(\phi \to \psi) \to (\neg\phi \to \neg\psi)$ is a tautology or not without information about

ϕ and ψ. If for example we choose p for both ϕ and ψ, then we get the tautology $(p \to p) \to (\neg p \to \neg p)$, and if we choose $p \vee \neg p$ and q for ϕ and ψ respectively, then we get the tautology $((p \vee \neg p) \to q) \to (\neg(p \vee \neg p) \to \neg q)$. But if we choose p and q for ϕ and ψ respectively, then we arrive at the sentence $(p \to q) \to (\neg p \to \neg q)$ which, as we have just seen, is not a tautology.

Exercise 4 Determine whether the following formulas are tautologies. If one is not, give a counterexample. (Why is this exercise formulated with p and q, and not with ϕ and ψ as is exercise 3?)

a. $(\neg p \vee \neg q) \to \neg(p \vee q)$
b. $((p \vee q) \wedge (\neg p \to \neg q)) \to q$
c. $((p \to q) \to p) \to ((p \to q) \to q)$
d. $((p \to q) \to r) \to (p \to (q \to r))$

7.3.2 *Contradiction*

Tautologies have counterparts, viz., formulas which are always false, i.e., ϕ such that for every V: $V(\phi) = 0$. Such formulas are called 'contradictions'. Stock examples are those of the form $\phi \wedge \neg\phi$, see table 7.8.

ϕ	$\neg\phi$	$\phi \wedge \neg\phi$
1	0	0
0	1	0

Table 7.8: Composite truth table for $\phi \wedge \neg\phi$

The relationship between tautologies and contradictions can be expressed in the following two facts.

Fact 5
If ϕ is a tautology, then $\neg\phi$ is a contradiction.

Proof. Suppose ϕ is a tautology. Then for every V: $V(\phi) = 1$. But then for every V it must hold that $V(\neg\phi) = 0$. So according to the definition, $\neg\phi$ is a contradiction. □

An analogous proof shows that:

Fact 6
If ϕ is a contradiction, then $\neg\phi$ is a tautology.

Just like tautologies, all contradictions are equivalent.

7.3.3 *Contingency*

And then there is a third kind of formulas called '(logical) contingencies'. These are neither tautologies nor contradictions, i.e., formulas ϕ such that there is a $V: V(\phi) = 1$ and a $V: V(\phi) = 0$. In the truth table for a contingent formula there is at least one row with 1 and at least one with 0. Unlike tautologies and contradictions, contingencies are not all equivalent. Simple examples are two proposition letters p and q.

We do have:

Fact 7
ϕ is a contingency iff $\neg\phi$ is a contingency.

Proof.

$\Rightarrow$: Suppose ϕ is contingent. Then there is a $V: V(\phi) = 1$ and a $V: V(\phi) = 0$. For the first we have $V(\neg\phi) = 0$ and for the second $V(\neg\phi) = 1$, which means that $\neg\phi$ is contingent.

$\Leftarrow$: analogously.

□

Exercise 5 Let ϕ be a tautology, ψ a contradiction and χ a contingency. Which of the following sentences are (i) tautological, (ii) contradictory, (iii) contingent, (iv) logically equivalent to χ:

a. $\phi \wedge \chi$
b. $\phi \vee \chi$
c. $\psi \wedge \chi$
d. $\psi \vee \chi$
e. $\phi \wedge \psi$
f. $\phi \vee \psi$
g. $\chi \rightarrow \psi$

Exercise 6 Prove the following general assertions:

a. If $\phi \rightarrow \psi$ is a contradiction, then ϕ is a tautology and ψ a contradiction
b. $\phi \wedge \psi$ is a tautology iff ϕ and ψ are both tautologies

Exercise 7 Refute the following general assertion by giving a formula to which it does not apply:

a. If $\phi \vee \psi$ is a tautology, then ϕ is a tautology or ψ is a tautology
b. If $\phi \wedge \psi$ is a contradiction, then ϕ is a contradiction and ψ is a contradiction
c. If $\phi \vee \psi$ is a contingency, then ϕ is a tautology or ψ is a contingency

Exercise 8 Prove the following general assertion:

a. If ϕ and ψ have no proposition letters in common, then $\phi \vee \psi$ is a tautology iff ϕ is a tautology or ψ is a tautology

7.4 VALIDITY

The concepts of equivalence, tautology, contradiction and contingency tell us a lot about the nature of the formulas of a propositional language and the relations between them. There is, however, one additional concept that deserves special attention, and that is the concept of validity.

Validity applies to argument schemes, and we adopt the following notation:

Definition 5 (Argument scheme)
An argument scheme is a sequence of formulas $\phi_1, \ldots, \phi_n/\psi$, where $\phi_1, \ldots, \phi_n$ are called the 'premises' and ψ the 'conclusion'.

Note that argument schemes are finite.

Definition 6 (Validity)
An argument scheme $\phi_1, \ldots, \phi_n/\psi$ is valid iff for all V: $V(\phi_1) = \cdots = V(\phi_n) = 1 \Rightarrow V(\psi) = 1$

An argument scheme is valid if the truth of the premises entails the truth of the conclusion. Or, to put it differently, if it is not possible for the premises to be all true while the conclusion is false. Validity is indicated by the following notation: $\phi_1, ..., \phi_n \models \psi$. If a scheme is not valid we use: $\phi_1, ..., \phi_n \not\models \psi$

Note that the validity of $\phi_1, \ldots, \phi_n/\psi$ reduces to ψ being tautologous if $n = 0$, and that the notation $\models$ is therefore no more than an expansion of the notation introduced above.

As was the case with showing that two formulas are equivalent, or that a formula is a tautology, etc., the validity of an argument scheme in proposition logic can also be shown both by means of a truth table, or by means of reasoning about the truth definition and the definition of validity.

By way of example consider the argument scheme $p \to (q \wedge r), q \to \neg r/\ \neg p$. The composite truth table is given in 7.9. For reasons of perspicuity, we add a column marked / to indicate the division between premises (to the left) and conclusion (to the right). We use this column also to mark with $*$ those rows in which all premises are 1. For it is only those rows that we need to check. If the conclusion also has 1's on all those rows, the scheme is a valid one. What the truth value of the conclusion is in other cases, i.e., those where the premises are not all true, is immaterial.

Reasoning about the truth definition provides another way of establishing the validity of this scheme (reference is to clauses in definition 2:

p	q	r	$q \wedge r$	$p \to (q \wedge r)$	$\neg r$	$q \to \neg r$	/	$\neg p$
1	1	1	1	1	0	0		
1	1	0	0	0	1	1		
1	0	1	0	0	0	1		
1	0	0	0	0	1	1		
0	1	1	1	1	0	0		
0	1	0	0	1	1	1	⋆	1
0	0	1	0	1	0	1	⋆	1
0	0	0	0	1	1	1	⋆	1

Table 7.9: Composite truth table for $p \to (q \wedge r),\ q \to \neg r / \neg p$

Proof. Suppose the argument is not valid. Then there is a V such that:

$$
\begin{aligned}
V(p \to (q \wedge r)) = V(q \wedge \neg r) = 1, V(\neg p) &= 0 \text{ (assumption)}\\
\text{then } V(p) &= 1\ (\neg)\\
\text{so } V(q \wedge r) &= 1 \text{ (first premise, } \to)\\
\text{then } V(q) = V(r) &= 1\ (\wedge)\\
V(q) = 1 \text{ implies that } V(\neg r) &= 1 \text{ (second premise, } \to)\\
\text{so } V(r) &= 0\ (\neg)\\
\text{That contradicts } V(r) &= 1
\end{aligned}
$$

So the assumption must be rejected. □

Now we turn to a simple example of an argument scheme that is not valid; $p \to q, q/p$. (This is also known as the 'fallacy of affirming the consequent'). First the truth table 7.10.

p	q	$p \to q$	/	p
1	1	1	⋆	1
1	0	0		
0	1	1	⋆	0
0	0	1		

Table 7.10: Composite truth table for $p \to q, q/p$

There are two rows in which both premises are assigned 1, and in one of those the conclusion is 0. That row represents a situation in which the premises are true yet the conclusion is false. We call such a situation 'a counterexample'.

Composite truth tables are an efficient and effective way of finding counterexamples. Showing that an argument scheme is invalid by reasoning is usually somewhat more cumbersome, as the following example of a proof that shows that $p \to q, q \not\models p$:

Proof. Suppose $p \to q, q \models p$. Then every $V\colon V(p \to q) = V(q) = 1$ should be such that also $V(p) = 1$. Consider a $V\colon V(p) = 0$. That V is such that $V(p \to q) = 1$. The assumption that it is also such that $V(q) = 1$ is consistent with that. But then we have a $V\colon V(p \to q) = V(q) = 1$ and $V(p) = 0$, which contradicts the assumption, hence has to be rejected. □

Exercise 9 Determine whether the following argument schemes are valid. If a scheme is not, give a counterexample.

a. $p \wedge q/p$
b. $p,\ \neg p/q$
c. $p \wedge q/q$
d. $p \to (q \wedge \neg q)/\neg p$
e. $p \vee q/p$
f. $p \vee q, p \to r,\ q \to r/r$
g. $p,\ q/p \wedge q$
h. $p \vee q,\ (p \wedge q) \to r/r$
i. $p/p \vee q$
j. $p \vee q,\ p \to q/q$
k. $q/p \vee q$
l. $p \vee q,\ p \to q/p$
m. $p/p \wedge q$
n. $p \to q, \neg q/\neg p$
o. $p,\ p \to q/q$
p. $p \to q/\neg p \to \neg q$
q. $p,\ q \to p/q$

Exercise 10 Consider the following arguments and prove whether it is valid or not.

a. If Ann and Bill are murderers, then Carol is innocent; if Carol is guilty, then Donald's testimony is correct; if Donald's testimony is correct, then Bill is the murderer. So Bill is the murderer.
b. If Ann attends the party, then Bill, Carol, and Donald all attend the party; Bill did not attend the party and Carol attended the party. Therefore, Ann did not attend the party.

7.5 Truth functions and functional completeness

Proposition logic is about the validity of argument schemes that depend on truth-functional connectives. In the preceding chapters we have introduced the languages of proposition logic, given the semantic interpretation of such languages, and, in the present chapter, we have defined the central concept of validity, which establishes proposition logic proper. With that we can determine for every argument scheme that can be formulated in a propositional language whether it is valid or not.

Our choice of connectives, i.e., the set $\{\neg, \wedge, \vee, \to, \leftrightarrow\}$, is certainly intuitive, as they function as representations of very commonly used expressions found in natural languages. For sure, we have also seen that languages often have a variety of ways of expressing the same truth-functional connective, often ones that have different communicative functions. But from the perspective of logic that is immaterial.

What is a relevant question, however, is whether our set of choices is adequate. First of all, do we need all these connectives? And second, and more important, can we express any truth-functional connection between sentences with their help?

This is typically a question not within a logical system but about that system itself. It, therefore, belongs to what is also called 'meta-logic', the investigation of properties of logics as formal systems. We will encounter some other central meta-logical questions later, in chapter 21.

The question whether we need all the connectives in our set has actually already been answered, albeit partially and implicitly, when we looked at equivalence. The fact that we have, e.g., the following equivalence:

$$\phi \to \psi \Leftrightarrow \neg\phi \vee \psi$$

shows that as long as we have $\neg$ and $\vee$ we do not need $\to$: we can use the equivalence to replace every occurrence of a formula of the form $\phi \to \psi$ by a corresponding one of the form $\neg\phi \vee \psi$. The question then becomes which elements of our set of choices are sufficient to define the others.

Where the first question is whether our set of choices is too big, the second question addresses a more important issue, viz., whether our set of connectives is big enough, i.e., whether it allows us to express any possible truth-functional connective? Only if that question can be answered in the positive can we say that our logic represents 'the' logic of propositions.[1] This question is the question of 'functional completeness'.

7.5.1 *Connectives as truth functions*

In order to answer the question of functional completeness, it is convenient to look at connectives from a different perspective, viz., that of truth functions. As the definitions by means of truth tables make clear a connective can be considered as a function that takes one (negation) or two (the other connectives) truth values as arguments and delivers a truth value as value.

Thus we can write the corresponding truth functions as follows. Our connectives $\neg$, $\wedge$, $\vee$, $\to$, and $\leftrightarrow$ are interpreted by the functions $f_{\neg}$, $f_{\wedge}$, $f_{\vee}$,

$f_{\rightarrow}$, and $f_{\leftrightarrow}$ respectively:

$$f_{\neg}(1) = 0 \text{ and } f_{\neg}(0) = 1$$
$$f_{\wedge}(1,1) = 1 \text{ and } f_{\wedge}(1,0) = f_{\wedge}(0,1) = f_{\wedge}(0,0) = 0$$
$$f_{\vee}(1,1) = f_{\vee}(1,0) = f_{\vee}(0,1) = 1 \text{ and } f_{\vee}(0,0) = 0$$
$$f_{\rightarrow}(1,1) = f_{\rightarrow}(0,1) = f_{\rightarrow}(0,0) = 1 \text{ and } f_{\rightarrow}(1,0) = 0$$
$$f_{\leftrightarrow}(1,1) = f_{\leftrightarrow}(0,0) = 1 \text{ and } f_{\leftrightarrow}(1,0) = f_{\leftrightarrow}(0,1) = 0$$

Then, for every V we have

$$V(\neg\phi) = f_{\neg}(V(\phi))$$

and if $\circ$ is any one of our binary connectives, then for every V we have

$$V(\phi \circ \psi) = f_{\circ}(V(\phi), V(\psi))$$

.

7.5.2 *Functional completeness*

If we view connectives semantically as truth functions, then the question of truth-functional completeness is the question of whether we can express any truth function with the help of the functions that correspond to our set of choices. Two observations are in order.

First of all, note that corresponding to equivalences such as:

$$\phi \rightarrow \psi \Leftrightarrow \neg\phi \vee \psi$$

which we can use to eliminate $\rightarrow$ from our set of choices, we have definitions such as:

$$f_{\rightarrow}(x,y) = f_{\vee}(f_{\neg}(x), y)$$

that define truth functions in terms of others.

Second, note that truth functions can be of any -arity: there are three-place functions, four-place functions, ... These would correspond to three-place, four-place, ... connectives that operate on three, four, ... formulas. Given that formulas are of finite length, connectives have a finite number of places, and hence we need to look at n-ary truth functions, for arbitrary n.

The question of function completeness then is the question whether the set of truth functions $\{f_{\neg}, f_{\wedge}, f_{\vee}, f_{\rightarrow}, f_{\leftrightarrow}\}$ is sufficient to define all n-ary truth functions, i.e., all functions $f\colon \{0,1\}^n \rightarrow \{0,1\}$.

As an example of what is required, consider unary truth functions. Of these there are just four, which are displayed in tabel 7.11

x	$f_1(x)$	$f_2(x)$	$f_2(x)$	$f_4(x)$
1	1	1	0	0
0	1	0	1	0

Table 7.11: The unary truth functions

f_1, f_2, f_3 and f_4 are all unary truth functions, and as such they are the only candidates for serving as the interpretation of a truth-functional unary connective. We have only one in our set, viz., $\neg$, but all of f_1, f_2, f_3 and f_4 can be expressed in our language: $p \vee \neg p$, p, $\neg p$ and $p \wedge \neg p$ have truth tables that correspond to f_1, f_2, f_3 and f_4.

That takes care of the unary truth functions. But what about the general case? The number of n-ary truth functions is 2^{2^n}. Can all these functions be expressed by means of the connectives in our set of choices? The answer is given by theorem 2.

Theorem 2 (Functional completeness of proposition logic)
For all n-ary truth functions f, there is a formula ϕ with n proposition variables $p_1, \ldots, p_n$ such that for every valuation V of $p_1, \ldots, p_n$, $V(\phi) = f(V(p_1), \ldots, V(p_n))$

We do not give a full proof of the theorem, but illustrate the general method of finding a suitable ϕ for any n-ary f by showing how it works in the case of the ternary truth function specified in table 7.12.

x	y	z	$f(x, y, z)$
1	1	1	1
1	1	0	0
1	0	1	1
1	0	0	0
0	1	1	0
0	1	0	1
0	0	1	0
0	0	0	1

Table 7.12: Example of a ternary truth function

The task is to construct a formula ϕ with proposition variables p, q, and r that has a truth table that corresponds to this function. We can get such a formula ϕ by systematically constructing sub-formulas $\phi_1 \ldots \phi_n$ such that each ϕ_i is true in exactly one situation in which the function f yields 1. The disjunction of those sub-formulas will be a formula that has the truth table that corresponds to the function f.

As we can see $f(x, y, z) = 1$ in exactly four cases:

$$\begin{aligned} x = y = z = 1 \\ x = z = 1, y = 0 \\ x = z = 0, y = 1 \\ x = y = z = 0 \end{aligned}$$

The first case corresponds to $p \wedge q \wedge r$, the second to $p \wedge \neg q \wedge r$, the third to $\neg p \wedge q \wedge \neg r$ and the fourth to $\neg p \wedge \neg q \wedge \neg r$.[2]

Their disjunction:

$$(p \wedge q \wedge r) \vee (p \wedge \neg q \wedge r) \vee (\neg p \wedge q \wedge \neg r) \vee (\neg p \wedge \neg q \wedge \neg r)$$

then is the formula ϕ that expresses the ternary truth function in table 7.12.

Some reflection shows that this method can be applied to the specification of any n-ary truth function f.

Note that this method uses a subset of our set, viz., $\{\neg, \wedge, \vee\}$. So these three connectives by themselves form a set that can express all truth functions, i.e., that is functionally complete. Obviously any superset of a functionally complete set of connectives is functionally complete as well.

But $\{\neg, \wedge, \vee\}$ is not the only such set, nor is it the smallest. For example, given the equivalence:

$$\phi \vee \psi \Leftrightarrow \neg(\neg\phi \wedge \neg\psi)$$

we can eliminate all occurrences of $\vee$, which means that $\{\neg, \wedge\}$ by itself is also a functionally complete set. In the exercises another functionally complete set is specified, as well as a functionally complete set of connectives with just one element.

Exercise 11 Give a formula with only $\vee$ and $\neg$ which is equivalent to $(p \wedge \neg q \wedge r) \vee (\neg p \wedge q \wedge r) \vee (\neg p \wedge q \wedge \neg r)$

Exercise 12 Show that $\{\neg, \vee\}$ and $\{\neg, \rightarrow\}$ are functionally complete sets of connectives. (The last combination was Frege's choice in his *Begriffschrift*.)

Exercise 13 The connective $|$ (the 'Sheffer stroke')[3] can be defined according to the truth table given in 7.13.
Show that $|$ by itself is already a complete set of connectives.

Exercise 14 Determine the maximal number of non-equivalent formulas that can be constructed from two proposition letters p and q using only material implication.

ϕ	ψ	$(\phi \mid \psi)$
1	1	0
1	0	1
0	1	1
0	0	1

Table 7.13: Truth table for the Sheffer stroke

Exercise 15 We call a binary truth function f 'conservative' if $f(x,\ y) = f(x,\ f_{\wedge}(x,\ y))$. And we call a truth function 'truly binary' if its truth table cannot be defined using unary truth functions only. Determine all propositional formulas with two proposition letters p and q with truly binary conservative truth functions.

7.6 Conclusion

This completes the introduction to the first system of logic that is treated in this book: proposition logic. It is a system in which we can represent arguments that are based on truth-functional connectives and check their validity. Since the set of connectives is functionally complete, we can be sure that any form of propositional argument in any language is covered by proposition logic. In that sense it is 'the' logic of propositional reasoning.

However, in setting up proposition logic a number of choices have been made that could be disputed. For example, the semantics treats all formulas as either true or false. I.e., our semantics satisfies the principle of excluded middle: $\phi \vee \neg\phi$ is a proposition logical tautology.

When it comes to setting up a system of logic this is a choice that we can make. But if we look at sentences and arguments in natural language, it is not a matter of choice but a matter of fact whether the principle of bi-valence holds. As we shall see in chapter 22 there are reasons to assume that the principle does not hold unqualified.

And then there is the concept of validity. It is defined in semantic terms, i.e., in terms of truth and falsity of premises and conclusion: the argument is valid iff whenever the premises are all true, the conclusion is true as well. That is certainly an intuitive way of interpreting validity, but it is not the only one. We can look for an entirely different way of proving validity, viz., by making actual inferences, i.e., by constructing a proof in which the conclusion is derived from the premises. That gives a different way of dealing with arguments and checking validity. It will be explored in detail in chapter 9.

8

Excursus: reasoning and logical validity

8.1 The topic

As was already indicated in the introduction (see 1.1) the conception of logic as 'the science of reasoning', though intuitively appealing, is complicated and raises important questions concerning the very phenomenon of reasoning as such. For reasoning is a rich concept and the question whether logic can capture all of it, or at least its core features, is very much an open question. Here are some considerations.

First of all, reasoning is an act, it is something we do: we reason on the basis of premises that we entertain and draw conclusions from those premises employing rules.[1] 'Entertain', 'draw', 'employ' all indicate activities. These are not necessarily ones that we undertake consciously, as much reasoning seems to take place at an unconscious level. But they are activities nonetheless. If we consider the notion of validity that we have defined and studied in the previous chapter, being an activity is an aspect of reasoning that is not obviously captured. Of course, if we do the exercises and test whether a particular scheme is valid or not, we do things: we draw up a complex truth table and check the lines in the final column for occurrences of 0. But the semantic notion of validity as such is not connected in any way with action. That changes when we look at another way of defining validity, one that concerns proofs in natural deduction. As we shall see, a proof is a more 'active' concept in itself, it is something that is constructed on the basis of rules for using expressions. (That is a connection that is central in the excursus following the exposition of natural deduction in chapter 10).

A second consideration concerns the role of context. At least in everyday situations, reasoning as an act is something we do in a specific context, pursuing a particular goal. We do not 'infer q from p and if p then q' just for the fun of it, we do so in the context of realising some goal. That can be everyday and practical, such as deciding what to buy for dinner, or when to leave home to meet friends. Or it can be more theoretical, as when we wonder about what could explain an unexpected outcome of an experiment in the lab, or when we are trying to predict the outcomes on the economy of the central bank's decision to raise interest rates. But in each case, reasoning is something that is done in a context, with a particular purpose. It is quite clear that the concept of validity abstracts away from such contextual considerations.

These are just two considerations that have been reasons for some authors to question the relationship between logic and reasoning. Others have focussed on the role of argumentation in debate, following a distinction between logic as 'the science of reasoning' and rhetoric as 'the art of persuasion'. Debates about the scope and limitations of logic have a long history in the western tradition. Aristotle distinguished between dialectic (i.e., logic) and rhetoric. In other traditions, too, various conceptions of reasoning and argument, and of the role that logic plays in that, have been circulating. It would go too far to go into that here, but suffice it to say that in all traditions the debate is long from settled.

The author of the text that is the topic of this excursus takes up a clear position. Reasoning in the various forms in which we encounter it in everyday life, in science, and in philosophy, does not have a formal logic as its core. Logic does not account for a stable core of reasoning patterns, that can be found across various forms of reasoning. Logical argument and reasoning are principally different: 'It may be a mistake to expect principles of reasoning to take the form of a logic.' (Harman, 1986a, p. 6).

At this point it is important to note that such a view seems based on a particular view of what logic is. Logic, it appears, is assumed to be classical logic, i.e., the propositional logic that we have studied so far and the predicate logic that is the topic of the second part. In the third part of this book we will encounter a number of extensions and modifications of classical logic. Arguably, some of the logical apparatus that is developed in these non-standard logics can be used to incorporate aspects of reasoning that were outlined above, such as its act-like character and its intimate relation with practical goals.

But if logic is viewed strictly as standard, classical logic there is no justification for developing such additions and modifications of it. If reasoning is categorically different from what logic accounts for it would be like painting stripes on a horse in order to turn it into a zebra. If done cleverly it may look like one, but it remains a horse.

8.2 The author

Gilbert Harman (1938–2021) was an American philosopher who taught for most of his career at Princeton University. Harman studied philosophy and got his PhD from Harvard under the supervision of W.V.O. Quine. He has worked in a broad range of fields, from philosophy of language and philosophy of mind to epistemology, philosophy of science, and ethics. In ethics, Harman worked on moral relativism, virtue ethics and related topics. His work in epistemology and philosophy of science centres around topics such as statistical learning theory and induction, psychology of reasoning, and the distinction between entailment and inference.

One of Harman's main contributions to philosophy of language and philosophy of mind, and the one that is most relevant in the present context, is a perspective on natural language meaning that goes by the name of 'conceptual role semantics' (a.k.a. 'inferential role semantics').This is a view that associates the meaning of an expression with the function it has in reasoning and decision-making. It is related to the inferentialism of Brandom (see Brandom (1994)), to Horwich's use theory of meaning (see Horwich (1998)), and also bears some resemblances with proof-theoretic semantics, which will be the focus of chapter 10.

Conceptual role semantics comes in various shapes and forms, and various authors have contributed to it, among whom Ned Block and Hartry Field are the most well-known. Conceptual role semantics also provides a bridge between philosophy of language and philosophy of mind, as it is usually presented, not just as a theory of meaning of natural language expression, but also as a theory of conceptual content. The relative priority of the two is then a matter of debate. In both cases though, conceptual role semantics is characterised by a commitment to some form of holism and a rejection of the idea that features of the external environment have a significant role to play.[2]

8.3 The text

The text consists of the first two chapters of Harman's 1986 book *Change in View. Principles of Reasoning*. The book is devoted to the development of a theory of belief revision that functions as an account of an important form of everyday reasoning. The first two chapters are devoted to the connection between reasoning and belief revision (the focus of chapter 1), and to the relation between reasoning and logic (the main topic of chapter 2).

That reasoning essentially involves beliefs and changing of beliefs, which Harman often refers to as 'change in view,' is illustrated with an example: Mary wants to have Cheerios (a kind of cereal) for breakfast, finds out that there aren't any left, and then opts for Rice Krispies (another kind of cereal) instead. This everyday piece of reasoning starts with someone entertaining certain beliefs, then finding out that some of them are false, and hence having to change them. And these changes in belief are connected with changes in plans, in intentions. According to Harman this shows that everyday reasoning involves both 'practical reasoning', i.e., reasoning that is related to action, as well as 'theoretical reasoning', i.e., reasoning that is related to facts in the world.

A crucial observation is that when one finds that one's beliefs do not fit the facts, there are often different ways of making changes to make them fit, and classical logic does not tell us which one to choose. A simple example is provided by the logical rule of Modus Ponens. Suppose I believe that p, that $p \rightarrow q$, and thus that q. Now I observe that $\neg q$. Then I cannot maintain q, obviously, but I also need to make a change with respect to p and $p \rightarrow q$. At least one of them has to give way in order for my beliefs to remain consistent.[3] But the logical rule in question does not provide justification for any choice.

Thus, Harman concludes, reasoning is about belief revision, and since logical rules do not tell you how to revise your belief set, what is needed in order to account for reasoning is a different type of rule: principles of revision.[4] At this point Harman points out, first of all, that what he calls 'maxims of reflection', such as the maxim that one should take into account all alternatives, are different from principles of change: the former do not bring about change, the latter do. Secondly, Harman notes that we should distinguish between what he calls 'principles of change' and principles of revision. The former are empirical regularities that describe how people actually change their beliefs, the latter are normative: they concern how they should change them. On similar grounds Harman dismisses the idea that inductive logic might stand a better chance than standard, deductive logic of accounting for key features of reasoning, in particular of belief revision.

The account that Harman is after is thus a normative theory that tells us how to revise our beliefs, how to 'change our view'.[5] Harman acknowledges that the two are 'intimately related', but maintains that nevertheless the concept of a normative theory can be maintained given the fact that we have intuitions about mistakes in reasoning. He then goes on to distinguish and discuss four ways of doing so, concluding that it is only cases where someone revises their view 'in accordance with an incorrect rule of revision, thereby violating the correct rules' that are genuine instances of reasoning mistakes.

In that way, Harman suggests, we can build a normative theory of principles of revision: 'One way to try to discover the right principles of revision might be to consider actual cases in which people make mistakes of type 4 [= the above type] to see why they are mistakes.' Harman (1986a, p. 7).[6] But how should one go about doing that? Harman argues that analysis of other types of mistakes is of no use. There are mistakes that are logical fallacies, such as that of 'affirming the consequent', i.e., concluding p from $p \rightarrow q$ and q, but:

> If we distinguish clearly between argument and reasoning, we must agree that only arguments and proofs can be valid or invalid and that the notions of validity and invalidity have no clear application to changes in view, except in the sense that one can make a mistake about what validly implies what, a mistake that affects one's reasoning. [*Harman (1986a, p. 8)*]

Another example Harman discusses is the 'gambler's fallacy', which is concerned with inductive reasoning.

The upshot of the discussion is that looking at an argument, in particular at mistakes with argument will not deliver a theory of reasoning, since it does not provide proper principles of revision. The best shot we have, Harman concludes, is to work with Rawls' concept of 'reflective equilibrium': we start with intuitions about what proper principles of revision could be; then we check their working against actual practices of revision; in case of mismatches we adjust our principles; rinse and repeat, until a state of equilibrium is reached.

In the second chapter Harman discusses and defends in more detail his position that logic has no special relation with reasoning. His first argument concerns the role of implication and consistency as putative revision principles. The Implication principle holds that if p follows from one's beliefs (one's 'view'), that is a reason to accept p as one of one's beliefs. And the Inconsistency principle states that inconsistency is to be avoided.

As reasoning principles, Harman argues, these do not work. For instance, the Implication principle does not apply across the board, as we have seen above with modus ponens example: if one believes p and $p \rightarrow q$, then this is not a reason to accept q in a situation where one observes that q is not the case. A modification, which Harman calls the Closure principle, does not work either. Closure requires one's belief to be closed under logical implication. So if a proposition is not believed, yet implied by one's beliefs there is something wrong, and one should either add it or give up one or more of the implying beliefs. However, Harman observes, there are many implications of what one believes that are not all interesting or useful to maintain as beliefs themselves. A simple example is weakening, i.e., the fact that p implies an infinite number of weaker formulas, such as $p \vee q, p \vee q \vee r, \ldots$

An appeal to a distinction between implicit beliefs and explicit beliefs when it comes to Closure does not help: explicit beliefs are not closed under implication because, Harman maintains, we only ever entertain a finite number of explicit beliefs that have an infinite number of logical consequences. But neither are implicit beliefs, because recognising an implication may require a complex proof. Anyway, the distinction as such, Harman argues, is not strictly relevant to the discussion, and thus can be avoided.

What does seem to be a reasonable principle, Harman states, is 'Clutter Avoidance': we should maintain only those beliefs that are 'of use' to us, not each and any triviality that follows from those beliefs.[7] Clutter avoidance itself is not a principle of revision, for it does not tell us how to avoid clutter concretely. Rather, it is meta-principle that governs actual principles of revision: these should operate in such a way as to avoid clutter.

As for the Inconsistency principle, which rules that inconsistency is to be avoided, Harman maintains that, just like Implication, it is not something that applies in each and every situation. Harman illustrates this with an extensive discussion of the Liar-paradox, a paradox that occurs whenever a language has a truth predicate and means for self-reference.[8] When the Liar-paradox occurs we have what Harman calls 'unavoidable inconsistency', so the Inconsistency principle is not a proper principle of revision for everyday reasoning.

Although as such not proper principles of reasoning, the Implication principle and the Inconsistency principle do point in the right direction. Harman proposes to replace them with the 'Recognised Implication principle' and the 'Recognised Inconsistency principle'. These are principles that use the concepts of logical implication and logical inconsistency, but give them a dispositional twist. Consider the Recognised Implication Principle. It states that 'one has a reason to believe *P* if one recognises that *P* is implied by one's view.' Harman suggests that we need to read this principle in a dispositional way:

> Someone who is disposed to treat beliefs in *P* and in 'if *P* then *Q*' as reasons to believe *Q* has, by virtue of that very disposition, an appropriate ability to recognise this sort of implication, at least if this disposition is also accompanied by the disposition not to believe *P*, 'if *P* then *Q*, and 'not-*Q*'. And the latter sort of disposition might reflect an appropriate ability to recognise that sort of inconsistency. [*Harman (1986a, p. 18)*]

So given such a dispositional reading these principles are proper revision rules. The concepts of 'immediately implying' and 'immediate being inconsistent' are thus key elements in Harman's quest for an account of everyday reasoning as a form of belief revision:

> So, I am inclined simply to assume one has certain basic dispositions to take some propositions immediately to imply other propositions and to take some propositions as immediately inconsistent with each other. More generally, I assume one can have general dispositions with respect to certain patterns of immediate implication and inconsistency even if some instances of the patterns are so long or complex or otherwise distracting that one has no particular disposition to take those particular instances to be immediate implications or inconsistencies. [*Harman (1986a, p 19)*]

It is on that basis, and not on that of formal logic, that an account of reasoning can, and should be, based.

8.4 Study and discussion questions

Study questions

- What are principles of revision?

- Why do logical principles, such as the rule of modus ponens, not qualify as principles of revision?
- What is the distinction between 'principles of change' and 'principles of revision'?
- Why does Harman claim that 'Obviously, there is deductive argument, but it is not similarly obvious that there is deductive reasoning.' (p. 6)?
- What is wrong, according to Harman, with the requirement that one's beliefs be closed under logical consequence?
- Why are only mistakes of type 4 relevant for determining the principles of revision?
- What is the distinction between implicit and explicit belief?
- What is the Liar-paradox? And why does it occur in natural language?
- Why does Harman appeal to a dispositional reading of the 'Recognised Implication Principle' and the 'Recognised Inconsistency Principle'?

Discussion questions

- Rawls' conception of 'reflective equilibrium' allows room for 'facts' to determine 'norms'. Is that a reasonable stance with respect to every kind of norm?
- Try to identify some situations in which a formal reconstruction of some informal reasoning is beneficial. What are the benefits of switching to formal logic in these cases? Do these have something in common?
- Consider the passage from p. 8, quoted above: Can that be constructed as saying that a valid argument is a necessary condition for correct reasoning? If so, how does that affect Harman's view on the disconnect between logic and reasoning?

8.5 Further reading

A short paper in which Harman defends a similar position as in the text discussed here is Harman (1986b). For a critical appraisal of Harman's position, see e.g., Besson (2009, 2012); Allo (2016); Steinberger (2017). Reviews of *Change in View* are Bach (1988); Browne (1988).

9
Natural Deduction

Introduction

In this chapter a different perspective on the validity of arguments is introduced, which takes the form of an argument, rather than the meaning of premises and conclusion, as its starting point. What makes an argument valid, or not, is not analysed in terms of truth, but in terms of derivability.

There are a number of ways in which such an approach can be worked out. What is presented here is the system of natural deduction, which, as its name suggests, aims to mimic a natural way of deriving a conclusion from a set of premises.

9.1 Validity and derivability

Before we present the details of the system of natural deduction for propositional logic, we first look at the general approach that this system instantiates, viz., the idea that what makes an argument valid is a matter of its form.

Broadly speaking, there are two ways of looking at the validity of an argument schema $\phi_1, \ldots, \phi_n/\psi$. One is the semantic view, which we already encountered in chapter 5. It centers around the question: given what $\phi_1, \ldots, \phi_n$ and ψ mean, is the conclusion entailed by the premises? The other view is often called 'syntactic', since it proceeds in terms of form: given the form of $\phi_1, \ldots, \phi_n$ and ψ, can we derive the conclusion from the premises?

As we have seen in the previous chapter, the semantic view proceeds in terms of meaning, and thus extensionally in terms of reference and truth. Then validity is defined as follows: whenever the premises are all true, the conclusion must be true as well. The syntactic view proceeds in terms of form. In the case of propositional logic the relevant aspects of form are the occurrences of logical constants. And then validity is characterised in terms of derivability: if the premises are given, we can derive the conclusion using the connective-specific rules for manipulating formulas in which these connectives occur.

Both the semantic view and the syntactic view can be made concrete in a variety of ways. In the previous chapter we have used truth-tables as the means to, first, define the meanings of logical constants, and, second, check the validity of arguments. Other approaches are available as well. For example, we can use valuations for propositional languages to do the same. These are all just different ways of reaching the same goal: to specify the meaning of the logical constants and give the means to define and check the validity of arguments

For the syntactic view, which proceeds in terms of form and derivability, the same holds. It, too, can be operationalised in a number of ways. The most common ones are axiomatic systems, sequent calculi, and natural deduction systems. For certain programming languages, such as Prolog, another method, that of resolution, is often used. And there are also methods that are in a way in between the semantic and the syntactic view, such as the semantic tableaux method.[1]

The semantic and the syntactic views focus on the two different sides of the same coin: the intuitive validity of an argument. The semantic view starts from a definition of the meaning of logical constants and defines validity in terms of that. The syntactic view starts at the other end: it defines a set of rules for making valid inferences and thus indirectly defines the meanings of the constants. Take $\wedge$ as an example. In the semantic approach we explicate the consequences of the definition of the meaning of $\wedge$: given the truth table for $\wedge$, ϕ follows from $\phi \wedge \psi$, as does ψ. On the syntactic approach we first specify what inferences can be made with $\wedge$, e.g., by stipulating that from $\phi \wedge \psi$ one may derive both ϕ and ψ, and then take that as an implicit definition of the meaning of $\wedge$.

9.2 Natural deduction

9.2.1 *Preliminary*

Before we start with defining the key components of the natural deduction system for propositional logic, viz., the rules for the connectives, we first need to say something about derivations.

A derivation of a formula χ is a finite, numbered list of formulas which has χ as its last element:

$$\begin{array}{ll} 1. & \chi_1 \\ \vdots & \\ m. & \chi_m \\ \vdots & \\ n & \chi \end{array}$$

Each row in a derivation indicates how the formula on that row has been obtained. Formulas can be obtained in one of two ways: first, by application of one of a finite number of rules; and second, by assumption. In order to indicate the status of a formula in a given step in a derivation we mark each step either by the name of the rule used and the row number(s) of formula(e) to which the rule has been applied; or by using 'A' to indicate it is an assumption.

Thus, a specified derivation has the following form:

$$\begin{array}{lll} 1. & \chi_1 & \mathtt{A} \\ \vdots & & \\ m. & \chi_m & R_k, j \\ \vdots & & \\ n & \chi & R_l, h, m \end{array}$$

A word about assumptions. The main distinction that needs to be made is between assumptions that are 'active', and those that are 'withdrawn'. We return to withdrawn assumptions later on, when we discuss the rules for implication. Here we note that the premises of an argument schema are always active assumptions and, by convention, are listed at the beginning of a derivation.

So, a derivation of ψ from premises $\phi_1 \ldots \phi_n$ has the following form:

$$\begin{array}{lll} 1. & \phi_1 & \mathtt{A} \\ \vdots & & \\ n. & \phi_n & \mathtt{A} \\ \vdots & & \\ n+m & \psi & \end{array}$$

We write $\phi_1 \ldots \phi_n \vdash \psi$ to indicate that there is a derivation for the argument schema $\phi_1 \ldots \phi_n/\psi$.

The basic idea of a natural deduction system is that for each connective we have two rules:

- An *introduction* rule: how do I get something of a certain form?
- An *elimination* (or: 'use') rule: how can I use something of a certain form?

Thus, the introduction rule for a connective c tells us what we already need to have established in the course of a derivation to be able to derive a formula with c as its main connective. Conversely, the elimination rule for c specifies what we can do when we have such a formula as part of our derivation.

Let us illustrate this by specifying the introduction and elimination rules for the binary connectives $\wedge, \vee, \rightarrow$ first.

9.3 Conjunction

Introduction rule $I_\wedge$:

$$\begin{array}{ll} 1. & \\ \vdots & \\ m_1. & \phi \\ \vdots & \\ m_2. & \psi \\ \vdots & \\ n. & \phi \wedge \psi \quad I_\wedge, m_1, m_2 \end{array}$$

$I_\wedge$ says that in order to derive a conjunction $\phi \wedge \psi$ one needs to have derived, or have available as an assumption, both conjuncts, ϕ and ψ.[2]

Here is a simple example that shows that $p, q, r \vdash q \wedge (p \wedge r)$:

$$\begin{array}{lcl} 1. & p & \mathtt{A} \\ 2. & q & \mathtt{A} \\ 3. & r & \mathtt{A} \\ 4. & p \wedge r & I_\wedge, 1, 3 \\ 5. & q \wedge (p \wedge r) & I_\wedge, 2, 4 \end{array}$$

Of course, we can also apply the introduction rule to the same premises to show that $p, q, r \vdash p \wedge (q \wedge r)$

$$\begin{array}{lcl} 1. & p & \mathtt{A} \\ 2. & q & \mathtt{A} \\ 3. & r & \mathtt{A} \\ 4. & q \wedge r & I_\wedge, 2, 3 \\ 5. & p \wedge (q \wedge r) & I_\wedge, 1, 4 \end{array}$$

The introduction rule shows how to obtain a conjunction as a derived result. The elimination rule tells us how conjunction can be used in a derivation of other formulas.

Elimination rule $E_\wedge$:

$$\begin{array}{ll} 1. & \\ \vdots & \\ m. & \phi \wedge \psi \\ \vdots & \\ k. & \phi \quad E_\wedge, m \end{array}$$

and:

$$
\begin{array}{lll}
1. & & \\
\vdots & & \\
m. & \phi \wedge \psi & \\
\vdots & & \\
k. & \psi & E_{\wedge}, m
\end{array}
$$

$E_{\wedge}$ is specified in two parts, but it is one rule: a conjunction $\phi \wedge \psi$ can be used to derive both of its conjuncts, ϕ and ψ.

A simple example shows both rules in action. It is a derivation for the argument scheme: $p \wedge q / q \wedge p$ (an instance of 'commutativity of conjunction'):

$$
\begin{array}{lll}
1. & p \wedge q & \mathtt{A} \\
2. & p & E_{\wedge}, 1 \\
3. & q & E_{\wedge}, 1 \\
4. & q \wedge p & I_{\wedge}, 3, 2
\end{array}
$$

Exercise 1 Make derivations that show that the following argument schemes are valid:

a. $(p \wedge q) \wedge r \vdash p \wedge (q \wedge r)$ ('associativity of conjunction')
b. $p \vdash p \wedge p$
c. $p \wedge (q \wedge r) \vdash r \wedge p$
d. $p \wedge (q \wedge r) \vdash (p \wedge q) \wedge (p \wedge r)$
e. $(p \wedge q) \wedge (p \wedge r) \vdash p \wedge (q \wedge r)$

9.4 Implication

We start with the elimination rule, which tells us how to use an implication in a derivation.

Elimination rule $E_{\rightarrow}$:

$$
\begin{array}{lll}
1. & & \\
\vdots & & \\
m_1. & \phi \rightarrow \psi & \\
\vdots & & \\
m_2. & \phi & \\
\vdots & & \\
k. & \psi & E_{\rightarrow}, m_1, m_2
\end{array}
$$

The elimination rule for the implication is straightforward. If an implication $\phi \rightarrow \psi$ is available, either as an intermediate result or as an assumption, then it can be used to derive ψ provided the antecedent ϕ is also available.

Here is an example of the use of $E_{\rightarrow}$, that shows that $p \rightarrow (q \wedge r), r \rightarrow s, p/s$ is valid :

1.	$p \rightarrow (q \wedge r)$	A
2.	$r \rightarrow s$	A
3.	p	A
4.	$q \wedge r$	$E_{\rightarrow}, 1, 3$
5.	r	$E_{\wedge}, 4$
6.	s	$E_{\rightarrow}, 2, 5$

Exercise 2 Make derivations that show that the following argument schemes are valid:

a. $p \wedge r, r \rightarrow q \vdash p \wedge q$
b. $p \wedge q, p \rightarrow r, q \rightarrow s \vdash r \wedge s$
c. $p, q, p \wedge q \rightarrow r \vdash r$
d. $p \wedge q, p \rightarrow (q \rightarrow r) \vdash r$

The introduction rule for the implication, that tells us how to derive a formula of the form $\phi \rightarrow \psi$ is as follows.

Introduction rule $I_{\rightarrow}$:

1.		
$\vdots$		
$m.$	ϕ	A
$\vdots$		
$n-1.$	ψ	
$n.$	$\phi \rightarrow \psi$	$I_{\rightarrow}$

In order to derive an implication $\phi \rightarrow \psi$, one starts by introducing the antecedent ϕ as an assumption, derives the consequent ψ, and then derives the implication at the same time withdrawing the assumption ϕ.

In such a derivation the assumption ϕ is made in some step m, is withdrawn in a later step n, and is active in the intermediate steps $m+1$ to $n-1$.

Here is a simple example in which both rules for implication are used, a case of 'strengthening the antecedent':

1.	$p \rightarrow q$	A
2.	$p \wedge r$	A
3.	p	$E_{\wedge}, 2$
4.	q	$E_{\rightarrow}, 1, 3$
5.	$(p \wedge r) \rightarrow q$	$I_{\rightarrow}$

Another example shows that $p \rightarrow q, q \rightarrow r/p \rightarrow r$ is valid ('transitivity of implication'):

1.	$p \to q$	A
2.	$q \to r$	A
3.	p	A
4.	q	$E_{\to}, 1, 3$
5.	r	$E_{\to}, 2, 4$
6.	$p \to r$	$I_{\to}$

Assumptions need some further discussion. The last example illustrates that a derivation can have both active and withdrawn assumptions: in this derivation $p \to q$ and $q \to r$ are active assumptions (they are the two premisses of the argument), and p is a withdrawn assumption. It is active when it is made (in step 3) and remains so until it is withdrawn (in step 6). The part of the derivation in which an assumption that gets withdrawn is active is indicated by drawing a line from the step in which the assumption is made to the step in which it is withdrawn.

The following conditions guarantee a proper use of assumptions:

1. An assumption that is withdrawn can not be used later in the derivation
2. What depends on an assumption that is withdrawn can also not be used later
3. When more than one assumption is made, the last one made is to be the first one that is withdrawn

Here are illustrations of what goes wrong when these conditions are not met.

Condition 1:

	1.	$p \wedge q$	A
	2.	p	$E_{\wedge}, 1$
	3.	$(p \wedge q) \to p$	$I_{\to}$
*	4.	q	$E_{\wedge}, 1$

The fourth step in this derivation applies a rule to a formula, $p \wedge q$, that is a withdrawn assumption and hence no longer available. If this were allowed, we would have a derivation of q without any assumptions, i.e., a proof of the validity of q as such.

Condition 2:

	1.	$q \to r$	A
	2.	$p \wedge q$	A
	3.	q	$E_{\wedge}, 2$
	4.	$(p \wedge q) \to q$	$I_{\to}$
*	5.	r	$E_{\to}, 1, 3$

In step 5 we make use of a formula, q, that was derived under an assumption, $p \wedge q$, that at that point in the derivation has been withdrawn.

Condition 3:

$$\begin{array}{rlll} & 1. & p \to q & \texttt{A} \\ & 2. & p & \texttt{A} \\ & 3. & q & E_{\to}, 1, 2 \\ \hline * & 4. & (p \to q) \to q & I_{\to} \end{array}$$

Step 4 withdraws an assumption, $p \to q$, and thereby discards another assumption, p, that was made later and that at that stage is still active. If we withdraw the assumptions in the right, i.e., reverse order, the result is correct, and clearly shows where the assumptions do their work:

$$\begin{array}{lll} 1. & p \to q & \texttt{A} \\ & \begin{array}{lll} 2. & p & \texttt{A} \\ 3. & q & E_{\to}, 1, 2 \\ \hline 4. & p \to q & I_{\to} \end{array} & \\ \hline 5. & (p \to q) \to (p \to q) & I_{\to} \end{array}$$

Exercise 3 Make derivations that show that the following argument schemas are valid:

a. $\vdash (p \to (q \to r)) \to ((p \wedge q) \to r)$
b. $\vdash (p \to (p \to q)) \to (p \to q)$
c. $p \to q, p \to r \vdash p \to (q \wedge r)$
d. $p \to (q \to r) \vdash (p \wedge q) \to r$

9.5 Repetition

The Repetition rule allows one to repeat material that has already been derived so it can be used again:

$$\begin{array}{lll} 1. & & \\ \vdots & & \\ m. & \phi & \\ \vdots & & \\ n & \phi & Rep, m \end{array}$$

Condition:

- The repeated formula is not an assumption that is withdrawn, or dependent on such an assumption

Here is a simple example where Repetition comes in handy, a derivation that shows that $\vdash p \to (q \to p)$:

1.	p	A
2.	q	A
3.	p	Repetition, 1
4.	$q \rightarrow p$	$I_{\rightarrow}$
5.	$p \rightarrow (q \rightarrow p)$	$I_{\rightarrow}$

The following derivation illustrates what can go wrong if the condition is not met:

	1.	$p \wedge q$	A
	2.	p	$E_{\wedge}$
	3.	q	$E_{\wedge}$
	4.	$(p \wedge q) \rightarrow q$	$I_{\rightarrow}$
*	5.	p	Repetition, 2

The Repetition rule does not add any expressive power to the system, its effects can also be had with the rules that are already there. For example, we can get a 'repetition' of ϕ by applying $I_{\wedge}$ to just ϕ, and then derive ϕ from the result by application of $E_{\wedge}$:

1.		
$\vdots$		
$m.$	ϕ	
$\vdots$		
$m+k.$	$\phi \wedge \phi$	$I_{\wedge}, m, m$
$\vdots$		
$n.$	ϕ	$E_{\wedge}, m+k$

Exercise 4

a. Show how to mimic the effects of Repetition using the rules for implication.

b. Make two derivations that show that $\vdash q \rightarrow ((p \rightarrow q) \rightarrow q)$, one using the Repetition rule, and one without.

9.6 Disjunction

Like conjunction and implication, disjunction is characterised by an introduction rule, which tells when we can derive a disjunction, and an elimination, that spells out how we can use a disjunction in a derivation. We start with the introduction rule.

Introduction rule $I_\vee$:

$$\begin{array}{lll} 1. & & \\ \vdots & & \\ m. & \phi & \\ \vdots & & \\ n. & \phi \vee \psi & I_\vee, m \end{array}$$

and:

$$\begin{array}{lll} 1. & & \\ \vdots & & \\ m. & \psi & \\ \vdots & & \\ n. & \phi \vee \psi & I_\vee, m \end{array}$$

This rule will speak for itself: to derive a disjunction $\phi \vee \psi$, it suffices to have derived one of the disjuncts.

Slightly more complicated is the elimination rule. How do we use a disjunction in a derivation? If we have, e.g., $p \vee q$, either as an assumption or as a derived result, what can be derived from it? Obviously, neither p nor q can be inferred from $p \vee q$, so what use can we make of it? Its use is indirect: if we could derive some formula from each of the disjuncts, then having the disjunction would allow us to derive that formula. This is what the elimination rule states.

Elimination rule $E_\vee$:

$$\begin{array}{lll} 1. & & \\ \vdots & & \\ m_1. & \phi \vee \psi & \\ \vdots & & \\ m_2. & \phi \rightarrow \chi & \\ \vdots & & \\ m_3. & \psi \rightarrow \chi & \\ \vdots & & \\ k. & \chi & E_\vee, m_1, m_2, m_3 \end{array}$$

So a disjunction $\phi \vee \psi$ can be used in a derivation of some formula χ by deriving χ from both the assumption ϕ as well as the assumption ψ. If these two results are available, then the availability of the disjunction warrants the derivation of χ.

Here is an example, a derivation that shows that $p \vee q \vdash ((p \rightarrow q) \rightarrow q)$:

1.	$p \vee q$		A
2.	p		A
3.	$p \rightarrow q$	A	
4.	q	$E_{\rightarrow}, 2, 3$	
5.	$(p \rightarrow q) \rightarrow q$	$I_{\rightarrow}$	
6.	$p \rightarrow ((p \rightarrow q) \rightarrow q)$		$I_{\rightarrow}$
7.	q		A
8.	$p \rightarrow q$	A	
9.	q	Repetition, 7	
10.	$(p \rightarrow q) \rightarrow q$	$I_{\rightarrow}$	
11.	$q \rightarrow ((p \rightarrow q) \rightarrow q)$		$I_{\rightarrow}$
12.	$(p \rightarrow q) \rightarrow q)$		$E_{\vee}, 1, 6, 11$

Exercise 5 Make derivations that show that the following argument schemes are valid:

a. $p \vee q \vdash q \vee p$
b. $p \vee (p \wedge q) \vdash p$
c. $p \vee (q \vee r) \vdash (p \vee q) \vee r$
d. $(p \vee q) \rightarrow r \vdash p \rightarrow r$
e. $p \wedge (q \vee r) \vdash (p \wedge q) \vee (p \wedge r)$

9.7 Negation

The rules for negation are more complicated than those for the binary connectives. And this complexity is connected with the strength of the resulting logic.

First we present the elimination rule, which governs the use one can make of $\neg\phi$.

Elimination rule $E_{\neg}$:

$$\begin{array}{lll} 1. & & \\ \vdots & & \\ m. & \neg\phi & \\ \vdots & & \\ k. & \phi & \\ \vdots & & \\ n. & \bot & E_{\neg}, m, k \end{array}$$

$\bot$ is a special atomic formula, called *Falsum*, which plays the role of a contradiction. What motivates $E_{\neg}$ is that if a derivation makes available both $\neg\phi$ and

ϕ, something is wrong. So, the basic idea is that a formula of the form $\neg\phi$ can be used to derive $\bot$ if we have a derivation for both ϕ and $\neg\phi$.

Here is a simple example that shows that $p, q \to \neg p, q \vdash \bot$:

$$
\begin{array}{lcl}
1. & p & \mathtt{A} \\
2 & q \to \neg p & \mathtt{A} \\
3. & q & \mathtt{A} \\
4. & \neg p & E_{\to}, 2, 3 \\
5. & \bot & E_{\neg}, 1, 4
\end{array}
$$

Note that we have added $\bot$ as a new expression to the language of propositional logic. That is for the sake of convenience. Instead of using $\bot$ we could also use any arbitrary contradiction, e.g., $q \wedge \neg q$.

$\bot$ also plays a role in the Introduction rule $I_{\neg}$:

$$
\begin{array}{lcl}
1. & & \\
\vdots & & \\
\hline
m. & \phi & \mathtt{A} \\
\vdots & & \\
n-1 & \bot & \\
\hline
n. & \neg\phi & I_{\neg}
\end{array}
$$

$\neg\phi$ can be derived if the assumption that ϕ allows a derivation of $\bot$, intuitively, if that assumption leads to a contradiction.

Note that this treats $\neg\phi$ as $\phi \to \bot$, i.e., if we add $\bot$ to the language, we do not need $\neg$ as a basic expression: we can introduce it by definition.

An example of the use of both $E_{\neg}$ and $I_{\neg}$ is the following derivation that shows that $\vdash \neg(p \wedge \neg p)$:

$$
\begin{array}{lcl}
\hline
1. & p \wedge \neg p & \mathtt{A} \\
2 & p & E_{\wedge}, 1 \\
3. & \neg p & E_{\wedge}, 1 \\
4. & \bot & E_{\neg}, 2, 3 \\
\hline
5. & \neg(p \wedge \neg p) & I_{\neg}
\end{array}
$$

Exercise 6 Make derivations that show:

a. $\vdash \neg((p \to q) \wedge (p \wedge \neg q))$
b. $p \to q, p \to \neg q \vdash \neg p$
c. $\vdash p \to \neg\neg p$
d. $\vdash (p \to q) \to (\neg q \to \neg p)$
e. $\neg p \vee q \vdash p \to q$
f. $\neg p \vee \neg q \vdash \neg(p \wedge q)$

Note that $\neg(p \wedge \neg p)$ is an instance of $\neg(\phi \wedge \neg\phi)$, which is also known as the 'principle of non-contradiction'. It is a valid principle in the logic with just $E_{\neg}$ and $I_{\neg}$ (and the introduction and elimination rules for $\wedge, \rightarrow, \vee$).

This logic is called 'minimal logic.' As the name suggests, minimal logic is a rather weak system: some intuitively valid formulas that depend on the meaning of $\neg$ and that come out as valid in the semantics used in chapter 5, cannot be derived in it. So, the introduction and elimination rules that we have defined thus far do not characterise the same logic, viewed as the set of valid inferences, as the semantics gives us. It is essentially weaker.

Stronger logics can be obtained from minimal logic by adding further rules involving negation.

The first strengthening is illustrated by the formula $p \rightarrow (\neg p \rightarrow q)$. This characterises the nature of a contradiction: if a contradiction were true, anything would follow. This principle is called 'Ex Falso Sequitur Quodlibet', which is Latin for: 'From a contradiction one may derive whatever one wants.'

It is added to the natural deduction system as a separate rule.

EFSQ-rule ('Ex Falso Sequitur Quodlibet'):

1.		
⋮		
$n-1.$	$\bot$	
$n.$	ϕ	EFSQ, $n-1$

The EFSQ-rule thus embodies an important aspect of $\bot$ as contradiction in the system.

The following example, $p \vee q, \neg p \vdash q$, illustrates the use of EFSQ:

1.	$p \vee q$	A
2.	$\neg p$	A
3.	p	A
4.	$\bot$	$E_{\neg}, 2, 3$
5.	q	EFSQ, 4
6.	$p \rightarrow q$	$I_{\rightarrow}$
7.	q	A
8.	$q \rightarrow q$	$I_{\rightarrow}$
9.	q	$E_{\vee}, 1, 6, 8$

Exercise 7 Make derivations that show that the following formulas are valid:

a. $\neg p \rightarrow (p \rightarrow q)$
b. $(p \wedge \neg p) \rightarrow q$
c. $\vdash (p \rightarrow q) \rightarrow ((p \rightarrow \neg q) \rightarrow (p \rightarrow r))$
d. $\vdash ((p \rightarrow q) \rightarrow p) \rightarrow p$

There is one more type of valid formula that is left unaccounted, viz., $\phi \vee \neg\phi$, the principle of excluded middle (a.k.a. the law of bi-valence). It states that for every formula ϕ either that formula itself or its negation is true. This is not derivable, and that is connected with a derivation step that depends on negation, but that cannot yet be made. What is needed is the step from a formula of the form $\neg\neg\phi$ to ϕ, the law of double negation.

Like in the EFSQ case, the required additional power is added in the form of an additional rule involving negation.

Double negation rule $\neg\neg$-rule:

$$
\begin{array}{lll}
1. & & \\
\vdots & & \\
m. & \neg\neg\phi & \\
\vdots & & \\
n. & \phi & \neg\neg\text{-rule}, m
\end{array}
$$

The following derivation of $q \to p, \neg q \to p \vdash p$ illustrates the use of the double negation rule:

1.	$q \to p$	A
2.	$\neg q \to p$	A
3.	$\neg p$	A
4.	q	A
5.	p	$E_{\to}, 1, 4$
6.	$\bot$	$E_{\neg}, 3, 5$
7.	$\neg q$	$I_{\neg}$
8.	p	$E_{\to}, 2, 7$
9.	$\bot$	$E_{\neg}, 3, 8$
10.	$\neg\neg p$	$I_{\neg}$
11.	p	$\neg\neg$-rule, 10

The logic we now have, i.e., with $\neg\neg$-rule added to $E_{\neg}$, $I_{\neg}$ and EFSQ, satisfies the principle of excluded middle:

1.	$\neg(p \vee \neg p)$	A
2.	p	A
3.	$p \vee \neg p$	$I_{\vee}, 2$
4.	$\bot$	$E_{\neg}, 1, 3$
5.	$\neg p$	$I_{\neg}$
6.	$p \vee \neg p$	$I_{\vee}, 5$
7.	$\bot$	$E_{\neg}, 1, 6$
8.	$\neg\neg(p \vee \neg p)$	$I_{\neg}$
9.	$p \vee \neg p$	$\neg\neg$-rule

The natural deduction system that comprises all of the above rules characterises exactly the same logic as the semantics that was introduced in chapter 5, viz., classical logic.

It is worth noting that minimal logic, and the logic that results from adding only the EFSQ-rule, are coherent and sensible systems in and of themselves. The latter is called 'intuitionistic logic', and it has a special place in a wide range of areas. It originated as the logic that formalises so-called 'constructive reasoning' in mathematics. Constructivists accept the existence of a mathematical entity only if there is a way to construct that entity. They reject the double negation rule that is needed when one wants to prove the existence of an entity by showing that the assumption that it does not exist leads to a contradiction. Note that $\phi \to \neg\neg\phi$ is a constructive principle, it is satisfied in minimal logic, i.e., it can be derived without the EFSQ-rule and the $\neg\neg$-rule:

1.	p	A
2.	$\quad \neg p$	A
3.	$\quad \bot$	$E_\neg$, 1, 2
4.	$\neg\neg p$	$I_\neg$
5.	$p \to \neg\neg p$	$I_\to$

The differences between minimal, intuitionistic and classical logic are summarised in table 9.1

	Minimal logic	Intuitionistic logic	Classical logic
Rules	$E_\neg$, $I_\neg$	$E_\neg$, $I_\neg$, EFSQ	$E_\neg$, $I_\neg$, EFSQ, $\neg\neg$-rule
Not derivable	$\neg\phi \to (\phi \to \psi)$, $\phi \vee \neg\phi$	$\phi \vee \neg\phi$	—

Table 9.1: Negation and different logics

9.8 Concluding remarks

The natural deduction system is characterised by its intuitive character. That can perhaps best be appreciated if it is compared with an example of an axiomatic deductive system, such as Łukaciewicz' axiomatisation of proposition logic.

That system consists of the following axioms:

A1 $(\phi \to (\psi \to \phi))$
A2 $(\phi \to (\psi \to \chi) \to ((\phi \to \psi) \to (\phi \to \chi)$
A3 $(\neg\phi \to \neg\psi) \to (\psi \to \phi)$

And it has one rule of inference, *Modus Ponens*:

MP From ϕ and $\phi \to \psi$, conclude ψ.

A derivation of ψ from $\phi_1 \ldots \phi_n$ is, as usual, a finite sequence of formulas, each of which is either an instantiation of one of the axioms, one of the premises $\phi_1 \ldots \phi_n$, or a formula that can be derived using Modus Ponens from two preceding formulas, and which has ψ as last element.

Here is an example, a derivation of $p \to p$:

1. $p \to (p \to p)$ (A1)
2. $p \to ((p \to p) \to p)$ (A1)
3. $(p \to ((p \to p) \to p)) \to ((p \to (p \to p)) \to (p \to p))$ (A2)
4. $(p \to (p \to p)) \to (p \to p)$ (MP 2, 3)
5. $p \to p$ (MP 1, 4)

The axioms cover only negation and implication, the other connectives can be covered using the usual definitions.

This axiomatisation and the natural deduction system both capture the same concept, that of derivability in standard propositional logic. That is to say, both characterises exactly the same propositional logical arguments as valid. But they do so in strikingly different ways.

First of all, where the natural deduction system has rules for all the connectives, Łukaciewicz' axioms only mention implication and negation. That such an approach is possible comes as no surprise since $\{\neg, \to\}$ form a functionally complete set of connectives.

Also, the axiomatic method does not tell us anything directly about how to actually go about making a derivation for an argument, it relies more on intuition than the natural deduction method, where the 'rules of thumb' can be applied in a great many cases to guide us to the construction of a derivation.

Finally, although Łukaciewicz' axioms can be seen to be safe (the system is what is called 'sound' in a technical sense that will be explored in chapter 21) it is not intuitively clear that these are the axioms one needs.[3] Per contrast the natural deduction method deals directly with intuitively relevant aspects of formulas of a certain form. Thus it answers such questions as: given a conjunctive formula, how can it be put to use in constructing a derivation? And if the goal is to derive a conjunctive formula, what would allow one to do so?

It is in this sense that many have argued that natural deduction actually captures a particular philosophical outlook on meaning, viz., that meaning can best be viewed in terms of use. The idea goes back to work by Ludwig Wittgenstein, in particular his *Philosophical Investigations* (Wittgenstein, 2009). The connection with natural deduction has been explored by various authors.[4] The idea is intuitively appealing: the introduction and elimination rules for a connective do indeed seem to tell one all that one needs to know in order to be able to use the connectives in accordance with their meaning.

This explains the intuitive appeal of natural deduction, and it also gives rise to an interesting question: does any combination of an introduction rule and an elimination rule define a meaningful new connective? This question is directly relevant for one of the deep and perennial questions in the philosophy of logic: What is a logical constant? It is the subject of the philosophical excursus of this chapter.

10

Excursus: proof-theoretic semantics

10.1 The topic

As was explained in the exposition of the natural deduction rules for the logical constants, one idea in the background is that there is a sense in which knowing what an expression means is knowing what to do with, and how to use it. This is a conception of meaning that in the analytic tradition is often connected with the later work of Ludwig Wittgenstein, in particular his *Philosophical Investigations* (Wittgenstein, 2009).

A bit of history. Until well into the twentieth century the distinction between semantic and syntactic approaches to validity as it is commonly conceived of today had not yet emerged. The early logical systems, such as those of Frege, Peano, Peirce, Russell & Whitehead, followed the role model of classical mathematics and were axiomatic. A fixed number of axioms, combined with one or more deduction rules, defines a set of theorems that constitute the logic of a certain system. An early dissenting voice was that of the young Wittgenstein, who in his *Tractatus Logico-Philosophicus* (Wittgenstein, 1960) rejected the reliance on axioms and explored what we would now call a semantic approach, including a truth-table method for determining the logical status of propositions (tautology, contingency, contradiction) and, by extension, the relationship of entailment.[1]

It was with the seminal work of Tarski from the early 1930s on the concept of truth in formalised languages that the conceptual distinction between a 'semantic' and a 'syntactic' approach to the characterisation of validity became more commonplace. We will come back to Tarski's ideas, as he formulated them in Tarski (1944), in chapter 14. In the canonical texts in mathematical logic after the 1930s the distinction is accepted more or less in the form in which it is still with us today.

A semantic characterisation of validity proceeds in terms of truth; truth preservation from premises to conclusion is what defines entailment; and a valid argument is one where the premises entail the conclusion. A syntactic characterisation, on the other hand, relies solely on the form of expressions, and proceeds in terms of rules (axioms and/or inference rules) that allow one to infer one expression provided others are available. A prominent proponent of this view was the German mathematician David Hilbert (1862 – 1943), whose aim (a.k.a. 'Hilbert's Program') was to formalise all of mathematics using axiomatic methods and prove the consistency of the resulting axiomatisations. Meaning does not enter into the process at all.

Once the syntax – semantics distinction is made, it makes sense to ask such questions as: If a formula is syntactically derivable from a given set of formulas, is the argument that has that formula as a conclusion and the given set of formulas as premises semantically valid? And reversely, if an argument is semantically valid, does that mean that the conclusion can indeed be derived from the premises? As we will see later on (in chapter 21), the first question concerns the correctness of the syntactic method and the second its completeness.

Although this view is indeed canonical, that does not mean it is undisputed. Already in the 1930s Gerhard Gentzen (1909 – 1945), a German mathematician and logician, formulated a different view. Gentzen's main work was in proof theory. He established a distinct approach as an alternative to the axiomatic method, of which natural deduction, along with the so-called 'sequent calculus', are the two most prominent forms. What is important in the current context is that Gentzen viewed his proof-theoretic systems not as 'syntactic' in the canonical sense described above. Rather, he insisted that his systems defined the meaning of logical constants, albeit not in a referential way.[2] Rather, it is the rules that govern the ways in which logical constants can be introduced and eliminated that provide an account of their meaning.

This is the basic idea of a 'proof-theoretic semantics'. It has been worked out by different authors in different ways. Gentzen, Dag Prawitz, Michael Dummett, Per Martin-Löf, and others, all present their own accounts of the connection between rules and meaning. But what all these accounts have in common, despite their differences, is a commitment to the idea that the meaning of an expression is captured by the way in which the expression is used. This is a fundamentally different way of looking at meaning than the one that lies at the heart of model-theoretic semantics.

In model-theoretic semantics it is the relation between an expression and reality, or a suitable model that represents reality's relevant features, that grounds meaning. That relation is one of reference.[3] In proposition logic, where atomic formulas are the smallest meaning units, this referential relation is simple: a formula is associated with a truth value, 1 or 0. Atomic formulas are assumed to have truth values and then the truth values of complex formulas can be derived from these using the truth functions that are associated with the logical connectives. In chapter 5 we have used truth tables to define these functions, but we have also seen that we can formulate them as functions directly. In the next chapters, where we will be introducing predicate logic, we will see that the truth values of atomic formulas are not stipulated, but are defined in terms of what the sub-sentential expressions that make up these formulas refer to. So, it's reference again, only one level deeper.

From the perspective of proof-theoretic semantics, meaning is determined, not by reference, but by use, and so the meaning of a connective can be considered to be specified by its introduction and elimination rules. Both rules determine aspects of the use of an expression. For example, the introduction rule for conjunction specifies what needs to be established in order for a conjunction to be used justifiably; and the elimination rule for the implication tells us what legitimate consequences can be connected with an implication. A broad concept of 'use' covers both kinds of cases, and in that sense one can indeed say that the system of natural deduction conforms with a use conception of meaning.

The precise role that is played by introduction and elimination rules is one factor that differentiates approaches that share this common perspective. Gentzen's idea was that introduction rules fix the meaning and that elimination rules spell out the consequences. Martin-Löf promoted the opposite idea, according to him it is the elimination rules that determine the meaning, as the meaning of an expression is conveyed most clearly by what one can do with it. As discussed in detail the paper by Ruy de Queiroz, various positions have been defended, by Gentzen, Martin-Löff, Prawitz, and Dummett. As de Queiroz explains, according to Dummett the differences correspond to different ways of spelling out the general idea of 'meaning is use'.

For Dummett an important additional consideration is a metaphysical one, and has to be with the idea that truth must be conceptualised in terms of verification, which is connected with a specific conception of realism: we need to acknowledge as real that about which we can make statements the truth of which is, in principle, verifiable. Prawitz was inclined to think more in terms of use as what an expression can be used for, an idea that is more akin to a certain form of pragmatism and its conception of truth: 'Truth is what works', as William James once put it. Both conceptions are, of course, fundamentally different from the semantic conception of truth that Tarski advocated.

10.1.1 The Wittgenstein connection

To what extent these discussions can be settled by going back to Wittgenstein's later work is not an easy matter to decide. The paper by de Queiroz gives a detailed and informative overview of various connections that can be made between proof-theoretic semantics in logic and Wittgenstein's work. But some further background with regard to the latter's ideas about meaning as developed in his later work may be in order.

It is interesting to note that Wittgenstein starts *Philosophical Investigations* (Wittgenstein, 2009) with a long quote from Augustine's *Confessions*.[4] In the passage Augustine describes how as a small child learned his first language. By observing people and their linguistic utterances, Augustine claims, he learned what the words they used stand for and thus what thoughts they expressed with their utterances.

To Wittgenstein, Augustine's description suggests the following idea:

> These words, it seems to me, give us a particular picture of the essence of human language. It is this: the words in language name objects a sentences are combinations of such names. – In this picture of language we find the roots of the following idea: Every word has a meaning. This meaning is correlated with the word. It is the object for which the word stands. [*Philosophical Investigations 1*]

This is in essence a referential conception of meaning, one in which every type of expression functions basically in the same way: by standing for some extra-linguistic entity.

Wittgenstein then invites us to look at the following example:

> Now think of the following use of language: I send someone shopping. I give him a slip of paper marked 'five red apples'. He takes the slip to the shopkeeper, who opens the drawer marked 'apples'; then he looks up the word 'red' in a chart and finds a colour sample next to it; then he says the series of elementary number-words – I assume that he knows them by heart – up to the word 'five', and for each number-word he takes an apple of the same colour as the sample out of the drawer. — It is in this and similar ways that one operates with words. — 'But how does he know where and how he is to look up the word 'red' and what he is to do with the word 'five'?' — Well, I assume that he acts as I have described. Explanations come to an end somewhere. – But what is the meaning of the word 'five'? – No such thing was in question here, only how the word 'five' is used. [*ibid.*]

In this example, one could say that 'apples' functions in accordance with the referential conception of meaning: it is attached to a box of apples. But with 'red' this is not obviously the case: the shopkeeper uses the word to identify a color sample on a chart and then uses the color sample to select apples. Does 'red' refer here? If so, to what? To the colour red? To all things that are red? No, it is used to select red apples from a box and the colour sample is a means to do so. In the case of 'five' the question of a referential meaning becomes even more obtuse: 'five' is used in counting out five apples, nothing more, nothing less.

This simple example contains a number of ideas that are subsequently worked out and discussed in much more detail in the following sections of *Philosophical Investigations*. It is very difficult to describe Wittgenstein's complex conception of meaning in a few lines. But key is, as the example of 'five red apples' illustrates, that the meaning of an expression is closely associated with how it is used. Two things are important to note. First, the Wittgensteinian conception does not imply that language is never used in a referential manner, it is one of the possibilities of using language, but it is not the only one. Second, how an expression is used depends on context. Wittgenstein introduces the famous concept of a 'language game' to indicate that. The concept of a language game is not confined just to linguistic behaviour: as Wittgenstein states in section 7: 'I shall also call the whole, consisting of language and the activities into which it is woven, a "language-game".' This broadens the Wittgensteinian conception in many directions. What we use language for, what purposes it serves, how those purposes relate to other forms of action, how that may change over time, how we learn to participate in such language games, . . . , these are aspects that Wittgenstein subsequently analyses and the resulting conception is one that can be applied and modified in many directions.

That makes the Wittgensteinian conception philosophically rich and versatile, but it also makes it difficult to turn into a 'theory', i.e., into something that is clearly defined and well-delineated. For Wittgenstein that is not a problem, on the contrary. He explicitly rejects the idea of theory in philosophy: 'If someone were to advance theses in philosophy, it would never be possible to debate them, because everyone would agree to them.' (*Philosophical Investigations* 128). There is no doubt that Wittgenstein analyses meaning by looking at use, and at learning and teaching. But a theory that defines meaning as use seems not in his spirit. At best logical approaches such as natural deduction can claim Wittgenstein as a source of inspiration.[5]

10.2 The author

Ruy J. Guerra B. de Queiroz (born 1958) is a professor at the Department of Informatics of the University of Pernambuco in Brazil. Initially, de Queiroz studied electrical engineering, but then switched to computer science, and obtained a PhD in that field at Imperial College, London in 1990. His dissertation was entitled *Proof Theory and Computer Programming. An Essay into the Logical Foundations of Computation.*

De Queiroz is a very active and prolific researcher in the interdisciplinary area between logic, computer science and philosophy. In the 1980s de Queiroz started his investigations into a reformulation of a particular approach in deductive systems, Per Martin-Löf's type theory, as an instance of a Wittgenstein-inspired 'meaning is use' theory. Later, he collaborated with Dov Gabbay on the development and application of the theory of labeled natural deduction, and with Anjolina de Oliveira on a geometric formulation of natural deduction.

De Queiroz is active in various organisations in the field of logic, such as the *Foundation for Logic, Language and Information*, and has initiated the WoLLIC series of workshops that brings together logicians, computer scientists, linguistics and philosophers. He is also active as editor of various journals in the field of logic and computer science.

10.3 The text

The paper by Ruy de Queiroz, 'On Reduction Rules, Meaning-as-Use, and Proof-theoretic Semantics' (Queiroz, 2008), is a rich investigation into the various ways in which different interpretations of what a proof-theoretic semantics can, or should look like can be connected with Wittgenstein's observation regarding the relationships between meaning and use. De Queiroz uses a variety of sources on both sides, using work by Gentzen, Prawitz, Dummett, and drawing from various works by Wittgenstein.

The paper starts with a characterisation of the main elements of a proof-theoretic semantics, which is followed by an overview of some of the main controversies that have arisen in that paradigm, in particular the different roles that have been assigned to introduction rules and elimination rules vis à vis the meaning of logical connectives. These topics are covered in section 1 of the paper.

The next section is devoted to a detailed exploration of the relationships between the concepts of 'meaning', 'use' and 'consequence', The attention to the role of the consequences that can be connected with the use of an expression is motivated by the main thesis of the paper, viz., that the views of both Dummett and Prawitz can be improved upon by paying more attention to the role of immediate consequences: they are what define the meaning of a logical connective.

In support De Queiroz claims that in his later work Wittgenstein did not completely abandon the strict atomism of his early *Tractatus Logico-Philosophicus* but rather replaced it by what de Queiroz calls a functional, 'manageable' holism, in which the concept of 'consequence' plays a crucial. De Queiroz illustrates this with a number of references to Wittgenstein's work, of which the extensive quote from the *Lectures on the Foundations of Mathematics* from 1939 is a telling example.

In section 3 de Queiroz enters into a discussion about meaning and use. The concept of use, de Queiroz notes, is very vague, and taking this vagueness at face value would lead one to believe that according to Wittgenstein no systematic account of language is possible. However, he argues that we can construct a concept of use that is systematic. Here, he refers to game-theoretic semantics, such as those proposed by Konrad Lorenzen and Jaakko Hintikka in support of this claim.[6] The key feature, de Queiroz argues, is that of intentionality, this what distinguishes 'usefulness' from 'use', and it is in terms of the concept of usefulness that we can give a systematic account of meaning. De Queiroz then continues to argue that this is indeed, although not explicitly stated, a key element in Wittgenstein's writings as well.

Along the same lines, sections 4–6, are devoted to showing that the close connection between meaning and consequences can be ascribed to Wittgenstein. Here, de Queiroz draws on a large number of Wittgenstein's writings, ranging from his latest work, *On Certainty*, to the early *Tractatus Logico-Philosophicus*. The discussion of the latter, in section 6, is interesting because it reinforces the point that de Queiroz made earlier on, viz., that the change from Wittgenstein's early work to his later writings is not a complete breach, but a matter of continuous change. The main point here is that logical constants are to be regarded as instruments, things that can be put to use, and not as expressions that refer. (De Queiroz adds a long discussion about the relationship between connectives and quantifiers; at this point that can be skipped.)

In the last section, 'Concluding remarks', de Queiroz returns to the initial question, concerning the role that various kinds of rules in natural deduction are assumed to play with regard to the definition of the meaning of logical connectives. He also includes Lorenzen's dialogue games and Hintikka's semantic games at this point. Disregarding the many technical details for the moment, the main claim that de Queiroz wants to defend is contained in the following passage:

> The general underlying principle is that of the logical principle of inversion [...]: the elimination procedure is the exact inverse of the introduction, therefore all that can be asked from an assertion is what is indicated in the explanation of the elimination procedure.

This principle of inversion, de Queiroz maintains, can be found in a wide variety of formal systems, and thus seems to capture best the initial idea that the meaning of logical constants can be explained in terms of their use.

10.4 Study and discussion questions

Study questions

- Try to find the common point of view in the quotes from Kahle & Schroeder-Heister (page 211–212), Gentzen (page 212), Martin-Löf (page 213), Dummett (page 214), and Prawitz (page 214).

- The two passages from Dummett's *The Logical Basis of Metaphysics* (Dummett, 1991b) that are quoted on page 215 and 216 contains the core of the issue that de Queiroz is engaged with: what is that?
- What is the difference between his own position and that of Prawitz that Dummett notes in the passage quoted on page 216–217?
- What alternative to the Dummett–Prawitz approach does de Queiroz want to explore?
- Why does de Queiroz think that the passage from Wittgenstein's *Lectures on the Foundations of Mathematics* that he quotes on page 223 – 224 supports his argument? (NB: $(x).fx$ is Wittgenstein's notation for the universal quantifier; read this as 'for all objects x it holds that x has the property f'; analogously, fa means 'object a has the property f.)
- What distinction does de Queiroz make between 'use' and 'usefulness'? And why is this distinction important for de Queiroz' argument?
- Why are the remarks that Wittgenstein makes about 'consequences' important for the argument that de Queiroz wants to develop?
- How does the discussion of Wittgenstein's remarks that are quoted on page 232 illustrate the need for a 'workable' holism?
- Can you connect this with the way that de Queiroz interprets the passage from 1912 that is quoted at the end of section 6?

Discussion questions

- Try to find examples of expressions and/or modes of speech in natural language for which it can be argued that their meaning is most naturally explained in terms of use, rather than in terms of reference (denotation).
- Why would the concept of 'usefulness', unlike that of 'use', involve intentionality? Give examples to illustrate the difference.
- The concept of a 'workable' holism is key to de Queiroz reading of Wittgenstein, and to his own project. Explain.
- The semantics of propositional logic as we use it is atomistic, not holistic. Explain. What is the role of the principle of compositionality?
- Does an absolute conception of logic fit an approach that relies on the explanation of meaning in terms of use? If so, how? If not, why not?

10.5 Further reading

References to the main contributions to this debate, of Gentzen, Prawitz, Dummett, and others, can be found in the paper by De Quiroz; see Schroeder-Heister (2018) for a recent overview and extensive bibliography.

Proof-theoretic semantics bears resemblance to inferentialism, an approach to natural language semantics, advocated by Robert Brandom. The key reference is Brandom (1994); see also Peregrin (2012).

Part II

Predicate Logic

11

Predicate Logic: Syntax

11.1 Introduction

In this chapter we introduce first-order predicate logic. This logical system occupies a very special place and can be regarded as something like the 'queen bee' of logical systems. There is a great variety of logical systems around, each with its own characteristics and applications. But predicate logic is special. Other systems are generally conceived of as modifications or extensions of it, or they are presented as such. It is a system with sufficient expressive power to allow for a large number of applications in a wide variety of settings, while at the same it has a number of 'meta-properties'[1] that makes it attractive from a theoretical perspective. It also has respectable historic credentials: the development of predicate logic is what lies at the basis of modern logic.[2] And it has been applied with great success, first in the foundations of mathematics, somewhat later in philosophy, and in recent times in theoretical computer science, artificial intelligence, linguistics, and so on. The philosophical excursus in this chapter , which is devoted to Quine's famous paper 'On What There Is', will provide an illustration of its use in philosophy.

11.1.1 Beyond the sentence level

In proposition logic what we study is the validity of arguments that is based on truth-functional sentential connectives. I.e., proposition logic gives an account of negation, conjunction, disjunction, material implication and material equivalence determine which inference patterns give rise to valid arguments and which do not. The logic of connectives is, of course, an important part of logic as such, but it is only a part of what is going on. It takes into account what happens between sentences but many arguments center around what happens beyond the sentence level.

In predicate logic we are concerned with arguments that depend on the structure of sentences as such, i.e., the ways in which these are constructed from sub-sentential expressions and the meanings of these expressions themselves. Here we will see some of the differences between grammatical form and logical form that modern logic relies on that were central to the considerations of Frege and Russell which were discussed in the introductory chapter.

Predicate logic centers around a small set of linguistic concepts: predicates and relations; names and variables; quantified expressions. These are the subject matter of the current section. Identity, as a special kind of relation, will be added to that later on.

Before we turn to the formalities, we first examine a number of examples to illustrate what predicate logic is all about. In doing so, we also identify what expressive means a predicate logical language should provide.

Examples

Consider the following example:

(1) France is bigger than Germany, and Germany is bigger than the Netherlands. So, France is bigger than the Netherlands

In proposition logic this argument can only be represented in the following way:

- $p, q/r$
- Key: p: France is bigger than Germany; q: Germany is bigger than the Netherlands; r: France is bigger than the Netherlands

A counterexample is easily constructed, but intuitively the argument is valid. So, proposition logic fails to account for it.

The reason is clear: the validity of the argument depends on the meanings of the words occurring in the premises and the conclusion. More specifically, it is the meaning of the relation 'is bigger than' that occurs in all three and the way in which the names are related by this relation that makes the argument valid.

In order to account for examples such as these we need:

Needed 1:
ways to refer to entities and relations between them

Here is what an analysis roughly looks like if we have that at our disposal:

(1′) Bigger-than(France, Germany)
Bigger-than(Germany, Netherlands)
So, Bigger-than(France, Netherlands)

Note that in order to account for the validity an additional premise is needed, one that spells out a particular property of the relation 'is bigger than':

- If Bigger-than(x, y) and Bigger-than(y, z), then Bigger-than(x, z)

Here, x, y and z stand for arbitrary objects that the relation might hold between. Note that this spells out a pattern, one that plays a role in many arguments, not just in this one.

Let's look at another example:

(2) All students work hard. Zhang San is a student, so he works hard

Again, in proposition logic there is no way that we can represent this argument in such a way that we can account for its validity. Each of the two premises and the conclusion can only be represented as an elementary sentence, which is inadequate.

And again, the validity depends on the meanings of the expressions occurring in the sentences used: properties, names, and what is called a 'quantified noun phrase', in this case, 'all students'. So, what we also need is:

> *Needed 2:*
> ways to refer to properties and to groups of entities that share a property

In this particular example, we need to be able to state that all individuals who are students have the property of working hard:

(2′) For all x it holds that if Student(x), then Work-hard(x)
Student(Zhang San)
So, Work-hard(Zhang San)

We use x to refer to an arbitrary individual; the phrase 'for all x' turns what follows it into a universal claim.

A final example shows the role of type of another quantified expressions, exemplified in the following example by 'some teacher':

(3) Some teachers are foreign and some are friendly. So at least one foreign teacher is friendly

As before, the expressive power of a language of proposition logic is insufficient to deal with this example. It is not a valid argument, but that is beside the point: we want to be able to represent premises and conclusions correctly and then show why the argument does not hold. In order be able to do that we need:

> *Needed 3:*
> ways to refer to unidentified entities that have a property

If we have that, we can provide a representation along the following lines:

(3′) There is a x such that Teacher(x) and Foreign(x)
There is a x such that Teacher(x) and Friendly(x)
So, there is a x such that Teacher(x) and Foreign(x) and Friendly(x)

Using the same device as before, i.e., variables, the phrase 'there is a x' turns what follows it into an existential statement.

11.1.2 *Patterns*

These are concrete examples of arguments, with concrete premises and conclusions. Like in the case of proposition logic, what is at stake in predicate logic are not concrete arguments, but the patterns that they exemplify. And like in the case of propositional arguments, these patterns reveal themselves if we look at what can and what cannot be changed in order to preserve the logical status of the argument in question.

Thus, if in the first example we replace 'The Netherlands' with 'Belgium' the argument still goes through. And if we switch the roles of 'France' and 'Germany', the argument also remains valid. (Recall that the premises and conclusion do not have to be actually true for the argument to be valid.) And the same holds if we replace 'bigger than' by 'smaller than', or 'is the same size'.

All that matters is that we have an argument scheme of the following form:

(4) Rab, Rbc, so Rac

as long as R satisfies the condition that for all x, y, z: if Rxy and Ryz, then Rxz.

In a similar way we can discern that the second example exemplifies the following pattern:

(5) All P are Q, c is a P, so c is a Q

And the third example is one that conforms to this pattern:

(6) Some P are Q, some P are R, so some P are both Q and R

It is these patterns that are the subject matter of predicate logic.

11.2 Ingredients of a predicate logical language

Now let's look in a more general way at the kind of symbols that would make a good language for predicate logic. (The formal definition can be found in section 11.4.)

11.2.1 *Symbols for properties and relations*

First of all, we have relation symbols with a specified number of arguments:

- 1-place relation symbols (a.k.a. property symbols)
- 2-place relation symbols
- 3-place relation symbols
- ...
- [0-place relation symbols: proposition letters]

We already encountered example of 1-place relations (properties) and of 2-place relations. Examples of 3-place relations would be 'lie between, 'give to', ... An example of an expression of natural language that needs to be represented as a 4-place relation is more difficult to come by. But from a logical point of view there is no reason to put an upper limit to the number of argument places.

Note that 0-place relations are typically a logical category: proposition letters do not have natural language counterparts as such. But again, from a logical point of view there is no reason to exclude them. Note also that since the truth-functional connectives will be part of a language of predicate logic as well, this means that any such language subsumes a language of proposition logic.

11.2.2 *Terms*

Next, there are expressions that fill the argument places:

- individual constants: names that refer to entities
- individual variables: expressions that stand for arbitrary entities

Collectively we refer to individual constants and variables as 'terms'.

At this point it is good to note that the way in which the vocabulary is introduced is completely neutral as to what kinds of entities constants refer to, variables stand for, and relational symbols express properties of and relations between. That is to say, a predicate logical language is completely agnostic as to what it is about. That is a matter of application. When we apply predicate logic we choose a particular domain of entities (a.k.a. the 'domain of discourse', or the 'universe of discourse') and interpret expressions with reference to that domain. Such a domain can be basically anything, and it is the application that determines what makes a good domain. From the point of view of the logical language, any set will do as long as it is not the empty set. (More on the why of that later.). The language provides means of representation, application takes care of the actual substance that is represented.

11.2.3 *Atomic formulas*

Combining relation symbols and terms we form what are called 'atomic formulas':

- An n-place relation symbol combined with n terms forms an atomic formula

Atomic formulas are the counterparts in predicate logic of the proposition letters in proposition logic. Like proposition letters, atomic formulas do not contain occurrences of connectives. However, unlike them, they do have an internal structure that can be exploited to determine the validity of arguments in which they occur.

11.2.4 *Quantifiers*

Finally, we have quantifiers to deal with quantified expressions. In our examples we encountered two standard form, i.e., expressions of the form 'all P' and 'some P'. But there are a lot more. Here is a sample of expressions that on their own, or in combination with a noun, constitute a quantified expression:

- everyone, someone, anyone, no-one
- determiners: every, any, each
- numerals: one, two, three, ...
- definite article: the; indefinite article: a
- possessives: my, yours, his/hers, ours, theirs
- qualified numerals: at most n, at least n, exactly n
- ...

Although we will introduce only two quantifiers, and we could even make do with just one of them as we shall see, we can represent all these forms of quantified expressions in a language of predicate logic, in some cases with the help of identity, which will be added later.

But there are limits, there are also quantified expressions that defy adequate expression in a language of first-order predicate logic. Notable examples are quantified expressions of the form 'most P' and 'few P'.

Excursus

In order to understand how quantifiers work in predicate logic, it is useful to take a step back in history, and look at Aristotle's way of dealing with arguments involving quantified expressions in his theory of syllogisms.

Aristotle's approach uses statements that exemplify a basic grammatical pattern, that of subject (S) – predicate (P). A subject term is a quantified expression containing a predicate, and a predicate term is one that indicates a property. This enables Aristotle to analyse these statements as indicating relations between properties.

Here are our two examples:

(7) All students work hard = the property of being a student implies the property of working hard
(8) Some teachers are friendly = the property of being a teacher and that of being friendly do not exclude one another

The first is what is called a 'universal affirmative' statement ('SaP'), the second is a 'particular affirmative' statement, ('SiP'). In addition Aristotle recognised also 'universal negative' statements ('SeP'), such as:

(9) No student is lazy

and 'particular negative' statements ('SoP')::

(10) Some teachers are not foreign

These four types of statements together form the substance of Aristotle's theories of syllogisms: arguments that contain two such statements as premises and one as conclusion.

Syllogisms can be tied to patterns, some of which are valid, and others are not. For example:

- $PaQ, QaT/PaT$

is a valid pattern, i.e., every substitution of property-indicating expressions for P, Q and T will deliver a valid argument. For example:

- All students work hard. Everyone who works hard passes. So, all students pass

End excursus

The Aristotelian approach works well as long as we are dealing with statements that have the grammatical form of a subject – predicate statement, or that can be transformed into statements of that form without loss of meaning.

However, this is where the concerns that led Frege, and later Russell, to deviate from the Aristotelian model, come in.[3] To illustrate what the problem is, consider statements such as:

(11) Some people admire anyone who flatters them
(12) Every two non-parallel lines have a point in common

The special feature of such 'multiple quantified statements' is that they cannot be reduced to something that fits the Aristotelian mold of a subject – predicate statement without loss of information that may be central to deciding the validity of an argument in which they occur.

Predicate logic takes another route. First of all, it considers relational expressions as being on an equal footing, logically speaking, with predicates. That means that there is no logically relevant distinction between a sentence of the form At and one of the form Rtt'. But for obvious reasons, it cannot treat a quantified expression, such as 'every man' as a direct argument of a predicate or relation symbol. Those arguments are terms, and terms denote individuals. But there is no such thing as an individual that is 'every man'.[4] So, secondly, it regards quantified expressions not as denoting term, but analyses them as expressions that take a formula with a specific variable, and turn it into a formula that expresses that some quantity of individuals satisfy that formula at that argument.

The two standard quantifiers are the universal quantifier and the existential quantifier:

- Universal quantifier: $\forall x\phi$: for all entities it holds that ϕ
- Existential quantifier: $\exists x\phi$: there is at least one entity for which it holds that ϕ

As we shall indicate later, one could make do with just one of them, but having both at our disposal simplifies things.

11.3 Representation

Armed with these ingredients, how do we put them to use in representing statements and arguments?

First we lay down some requirements on our procedures, and then we will illustrate them by revisiting the examples discussed earlier and providing some additional ones.

11.3.1 Requirements

Here are the requirements that need to be met if we represent natural language sentences and arguments into predicate logic:

1. Specify the domain
2. Specify a representation key
3. Explicate as much logical structure as possible

The first requirement is needed to guarantee that the meaning of quantifiers and variables is determined. As indicated above, we read '$\forall x\phi$' as 'for all entities it holds that ϕ'. But that leaves undetermined what entities we are talking about, since the language of predicate logic is agnostic about that. Specification of the domain is part of application, and representing natural language expressions is one type of application.

So, the specification of the domain is a part of that. And it is an important part, since the choice of domain makes a difference. For example, if Px stands for 'x is pleasant,' then $\forall xPx$ on the domain of cities means something different from what it means if the domain consists of pastimes, or of people, or of natural numbers.

The second requirement should not need much clarification: we need to indicate what relational symbols and individual constants are supposed to represent if we aim to represent a specific sentence by means of a predicate logical formula.

An important aspect of a representation key is that by the use of variables it determines how exactly a relational symbol applies to its arguments, specifically, in which order the arguments fit in the relation.

Suppose we had the following key:

- B: lies between; b: Beijing; s: Shijiazhuang; t: Taiyuan

Then the meaning of $Bbst$ is underspecified, as it could be taken as a representation of each of the following two sentences:

(13) Beijing is between Shijiazhuang and Taiyuan.

(14) Shijiazhuang is between Beijing and Taiyuan.

The trick is to use variables to specify in which order the arguments are intended:

- $Bxyz$: x lies between y and z

represent the meaning of (13), whereas:

- $Bxyz$: y lies between x and z

represents that of (14).

Note that variables are used in representation keys, but they themselves are not declared. Variables do not have a meaning of their own, they function as placeholders.

The third requirement means that we should try to avoid hiding relevant logical structure and make as much of it explicit as we can. The following simple example illustrates this:

(15) All Dutch people are blond

We could represent this as follows:

- Domain: Dutch people
- Key: Bx: x is blond
- Representation: $\forall x Bx$

This is adequate. But problems arise if we follow the same strategy for this example:

(16) All square circles are square

We cannot stipulate that the domain consist of square circles, for there aren't any. Rather we need to specify a larger domain:

- Domain: mathematical entities
- Key: Cx: x is a circle; Sx: x is square
- Representation: $\forall x((Sx \wedge Cx) \rightarrow Sx)$

Given that the domain does not contain any entities that meet the condition that they are both square and circles, we get an adequate representation. This hinges on the fact that $\forall x(\phi \rightarrow \psi)$ does not come with a presupposition that there are entities that satisfy ϕ. For more discussion on that, see section 2.

11.3.2 Examples revisited

Now let's return to the examples. We repeat them for the sake of convenience. First up:

(1) France is bigger than Germany, and Germany is bigger than the Netherlands. So, France is bigger than the Netherlands

- Domain: Countries

- Key: Bxy: x is bigger than y; f: France; g: Germany; n: the Netherlands
- Representation: $Bfg, Bgn/Bfn$

In order to make the entire argument explicit we also represent the implicit premise that it relies on:

- Bfg, Bgn, $\forall x \forall y \forall z((Bxy \wedge Byz) \to Bxz)$ / Bfn

Onto the second example:

(2) All students work hard. Zhang San is a student, so he works hard

- Domain: People
- Key: Sx: x is a student; Wx: x works hard; c: Zhang San
- Representation: $\forall x(Sx \to Wx)$, Sc / Wc

Note that because variables do not have an independent meaning $\forall y(Sy \to Wy)$ would do just as well: it expresses the same assertion, only by a different choice of variable.

Cases such as $\forall x(Sx \to Wx)$ and $\forall y(Sy \to Wy)$ are called 'alphabetic variants'. We will give a formal definition of that concept later.

The third example:

(3) Some teachers are foreign and some are friendly. So at least one foreign teacher is friendly

- Domain: People
- Key: Tx: x is a teacher; F_1x: x is foreign; F_2x: x is friendly
- Representation: $\exists x(Tx \wedge F_1x)$, $\exists x(Tx \wedge F_2x)$ / $\exists x(Tx \wedge F_1x \wedge F_2x)$

Note that the use of x in both $\exists x(Tx \wedge F_1x)$ and in $\exists x(Tx \wedge F_2x)$ does not imply they are about the same entity. If we want to prevent any confusion we can use different variables, e.g., write $\exists y(Ty \wedge F_2y)$, but strictly speaking this is not necessary.

Exercise 1 Represent the following sentences by formulas of predicate logic; specify the domain and give the key:

a. Anyone who lives in Beijing is happy
b. Not all people who live in Beijing are born there
c. Some numbers are odd, some numbers are even
d. No number is both odd and even
e. Prime numbers are odd
f. Everyone hates someone who admires everyone
g. If Zhang San admires everyone, he admires himself
h. If you don't do anything, you don't do anything wrong
i. Everything Zhang San does, he does well

11.3.3 Things to note

Let us end this section on using predicate logical languages for representation of natural language with a word or warning concerning the representation of phrases containing an indefinite article.

Some cases are straightforward: the indefinite article is adequately represented using an existential quantifier. Examples:

(17) A man entered the shop
(18) Every number has a divisor

These are clearly existential statements: the first one states that at least one man entered the shop, and the second claims that every number is divisible by at least one number.

But in other cases the definite article has a different import, which is better represented using a universal quantifier:

(19) If a farmer owns a donkey, he feeds it lots of hay
(20) If a number is even, it is divisible by 2

Consider (19): it is not about some farmer and some donkey that he owns, it is a claim about all farmers and all donkeys that they own. This should be clear from the fact that it suffices to identify just one farmer who does not feed one donkey that he owns lots of hay to show that the claim is false.

And then there are cases where the indefinite article is definitely not used as an existential quantifier, but also not exactly as a universal one:

(21) A lion is a fierce animal

While it is true that in general lions are fierce, one example of a tame lion does not falsify that claim. So, it is not strictly speaking a universal statement, but what is called a 'generic statement'. The proper analysis of generics is a fascinating and longstanding problem in natural language semantics, but it is beyond the scope of this introduction to delve deeper into it.[5]

11.4 Syntax: definition

In this section we will give precise definitions of the ingredients and the syntax of a predicate logical language and introduce a number of concepts that will be relevant for a definition of the semantics, which will be the subject of the following section.

11.4.1 Vocabulary

Here is a definition of the basic expressions from which a predicate logical language is built:

Definition 7 (Vocabulary)
The vocabulary of a language of predicate logic L consists of:

1. A set of predicate letters $A_1^i, \ldots, A_n^i, \ldots, A_1^k, \ldots, A_n^k, \ldots$ of arbitrary -arity $i, k, \ldots$; indicated as PRED$_L$
2. A set of individual constants $c_1, \ldots, c_n, \ldots$; indicated as CON$_L$
3. A set of variables $x_1, \ldots, x_n, \ldots$; indicated as VAR$_L$

Definition 8 (Terms)
The terms of L consists of the individual constants and the variables of L; indicated as TERM$_L$

Note that for mnemonic purposes we will also use:

- $P, Q, \ldots R, S, \ldots,$ as symbols for predicate letters
- $a, b, \ldots, p, s, \ldots$ as symbols for individual constants
- $x, y, z, \ldots v, w, \ldots$ as symbols for variables

Also we leave out the indication of the -arity of a predicate letter when this is clear from the context.

11.4.2 *Formulas*

In terms of vocabulary the set of formulas of a predicate logical language can be defined as follows:

Definition 9 (Syntax)
Given a vocabulary for L, the set of formulas of a language of predicate logic L is the smallest set such that:

1. If A_i^n is an n-ary predicate letter and $t_1, \ldots, t_n$ are terms, then $A_i^n t_1 \ldots, t_n$ is a formula.
2. If ϕ is a formula, then so is $\neg\phi$.
3. If ϕ, ψ are formulas, then so are $(\phi \wedge \psi), (\phi \vee \psi), (\phi \rightarrow \psi), (\phi \leftrightarrow \psi)$.
4. If ϕ is a formula and x_j is a variable, then $\forall x_j \phi, \exists x_j \phi$ are formulas.

As in the case of the languages of proposition logic, we leave off the outer brackets.

Here are some examples of well-formed atomic formulas:

- $A_1^1 x_3$, $A_6^2 c_2 c_4$, $A_1^3 c_1 x_4 x_1$,...

The notation is not very perspicuous, hence we use more readable formulations, leaving out the indication of the -arity:

- Px, Rcd, $Tsxy$,...

And here are some examples of quantified formulas:

- $\forall x_3 A_3^2 x_3 c_6$, $\exists x_2(A_2^1 x_2 \wedge \forall y_1(A_8^1 y_1 \rightarrow A_5^2 y_1 x_2))$, $\exists x_1 A_5^1 c_2, \ldots$

Again, to improve readability we use mnemonic notations and leave out the -arity:

- $\forall x Rxc$, $\exists x(Px \wedge \forall y(Qy \rightarrow Syx))$, $\exists z Pc, \ldots$

Note the last example: it is an instance of so-called 'vacuous quantification', i.e., of a formula in which an occurrence of a quantifier does not do any work, in this case because there is no occurrence of the variable z in Pc.

Another example involving vacuous quantification is $\forall x \exists x Px$. Here the occurrence of $\forall x$ is vacuous, but that of $\exists x$ is not. In order to explain this difference we need the concept of 'scope' of a quantifier occurrence, and that of 'free and bound occurrences' of a variable

11.4.3 Construction trees

The syntactic structure of a formula of predicate logic is unique, and can be represented in a construction tree in a straightforward manner. An example is given in Figure 11.1:

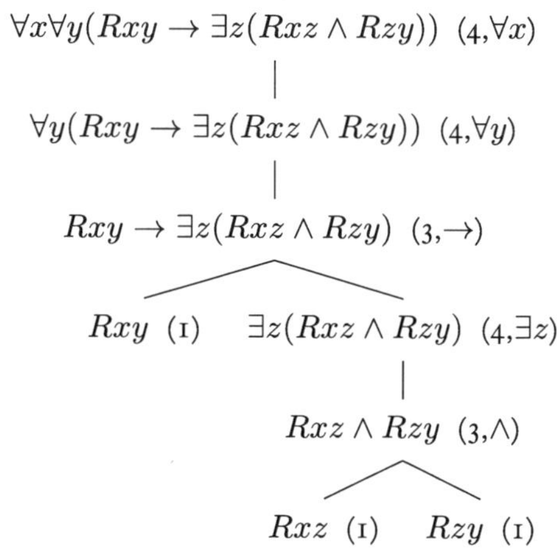

Figure 11.1: Construction tree $\forall x \forall y(Rxyx \rightarrow \exists z(Rxz \wedge Rzy))$

Just like in the case of proposition logic, we can use the unique structure of formulas of predicate logic as the basis of inductive proofs.

11.4.4 Scope

Definition 10 (Scope of quantifier occurrence)
If $\forall x \psi$ is a sub-formula of ϕ, then ψ is called the scope of the occurrence of the quantifier $\forall x$ in ϕ.

Exercise 2 Determine the scope of the quantifier occurrences in the following formulas:

a. $\forall x(\exists yRxy \to Px)$
b. $\forall x\exists y(Rxy \to Px)$
c. $\exists xPx \wedge \exists yRcy$
d. $\exists x(Px \wedge \exists yRcy)$
e. $\forall xPx \to \forall yQy$
f. $\forall xPx \to \forall xQy$

11.4.5 *Free and bound variables*

Definition 11 (Free and bound occurrences)

- An occurrence of a variable x in a formula ϕ which is not part of a quantifier is said to be free in ϕ if this occurrence of x is not in the scope of the occurrence of a quantifier $\forall x(\exists x)$ in ϕ
- If $\forall x\psi$ $(\exists x\psi)$ is a sub-formula of ϕ and an occurrence of x is free in ψ, then that occurrence of x is said to be bound by the occurrence of the quantifier $\forall x(\exists x)$ in $\forall x\psi$ $(\exists x\psi)$.

Exercise 3 Determine which occurrences of variables are free and which are bound:

a. $\exists x(Px \wedge Qx)$
b. $\exists xPx \wedge Qx$
c. $\forall x(Px \to \exists yRxy)$
d. $\forall x(Px \to \exists xRxx)$
e. $\exists x\forall xRxy$
f. $\exists y\forall xRxy$

11.4.6 *Sentences*

Now that we have definitions of the concepts of scope and of free and bound occurrences we can define one more notion, that of a 'sentence':

Definition 12 (Sentence)
A sentence is a formula of L which lacks occurrences of free variables.

Exercise 4 Determine which of the following formulas are sentences:

a. Pc
b. Rcy
c. $\exists xRxc$
d. $\forall zPx \to Scz$
e. $\forall xPy$
f. $\forall z(Px \to Scz)$

12

Excursus: logic and ontology

12.1 The topic

The question 'What is there?' is the central question that is asked in ontology. It has been around in the Western tradition ever since philosophy started out as an independent intellectual enterprise. The Greek philosophers of classical antiquity (Heraclitus, Plato, Aristotle, . . .) wrestled with it, as did a great many of their predecessors. Ontological disputes were central to the Scholastic schools of thought in the Middle ages, and the modern period saw the rise of traditions (rationalism and empiricism) that provide new answers. Locke, Hume, Berkeley, Descartes, Leibniz, and many others provided different answers to this central question. In their approaches ontological and epistemological considerations are mixed. Subsequently, Immanuel Kant made the epistemological question central and pushed ontological concerns into the background. And in the early twentieth-century, Martin Heidegger gave the question what there is a new twist and placed what he called 'the question of Being' center stage again. Under the influence of the so-called 'linguistic turn' in twentieth century analytical philosophy ontological questions were often dismissed as 'pseudo-questions. Linguistic analysis of our ways of speaking, often using logic as a tool, took their place. But in recent years there has been a rise of 'analytic metaphysics' that does try to tackle at least some aspects of these issues with new methods, also often using logic.

Classical ontological questions are: What kinds of entities are there? What are their properties? How are they related? Are some entities more basic than others? Is their existence necessary or contingent? and so on. The answers that one might want to consider are in part determined by the methods that one deems legitimate. If one considers sensory perception of the external world the primary source of knowledge these questions may receive different answers than if one also counts purely rational deliberations and intuitions as a source of insight. And, of course, if one includes divine inspiration as well, yet other answers become possible.

This shows that the question of how we know what there is and the question of what there is are very closely connected. This means that depending on what one considers to be reliable sources of knowledge the range of acceptable answers to these questions might differ. In particular, if one embraces naturalism, as Quine does as we shall see, the ultimate arbiter about what there is, is science. And if one's form of naturalism is thoroughly physicalistic, it is physics that has the ultimate say.

However, naturalism, and certainly physicalism, are themselves philosophical positions, so this reduction is not philosophically neutral. And it faces a number of difficulties as it is hardly evident what kind of reductionism is needed for a satisfactory analysis of all entities in terms of the ultimate components of the physical universe (whatever these turn out to be). The problems start already with medium and large-sized biological entities, and the complexity of the issues increases substantially when one attempts to reduce social entities and cultural phenomena.

Thus, the age-old question 'What is there?' is still with us, despite the many attempts of philosophers and scientists to answer it. In that sense, it is a perfect corroboration of the thesis that progress in philosophy does not consist in its core problems being solved but in the ever-increasing sophistication of the solutions proposed.

12.2 The author

Willard Van Orman Quine (1902 – 2000) is one of the most influential philosophers of the twentieth century, and a major innovator in American philosophy in this period. His work combines insights from logical positivism, that originated in Europe, with American pragmatism. He applied formal logic as a central instrument in philosophical analysis. And he can be counted as one of the founding fathers of naturalism in philosophy, a way of thinking that dominates much of Anglo-Saxon analytic philosophy to this very day.

Quine studied mathematics and philosophy and completed a PhD under the supervision of Whitehead at Harvard in 1932. Before the second world war he travelled to Europe, and got in touch with logicians in Poland (Tarski was still there at the time), and with the members of the Vienna Circle in Austria, whose ideas about logical positivism turned out to have a marked influence on his own philosophical development.

After serving as a navy intelligence officer during the war, Quine returned to Harvard, where he supervised a number of students that became very influential in their own time, among whom are such luminaries as David Lewis, Daniel Dennett, Gilbert Harman, Dagfinn Føllesdal and Hao Wang. Quine was also a major influence of a number of his contemporaries: Wilfrid Sellars, Nelson Goodman, Donald Davidson, Noam Chomsky.

Quine worked in a broad range of areas: mathematical logic, philosophy of science, epistemology, ontology, and philosophy of language. Although these are quite different subject areas, Quine's work is characterised by a strong unity, that can be summed up in a few keywords: holism, empiricism, behaviourism, and naturalism.

The influence of logical positivism on Quine's philosophical approach is unmistaken, but there are also marked differences. What the logical positivists and Quine agree on is the 'linguistic turn': questions about epistemology, ontology, and so on, can only be answered through linguistic analysis. They also agree that formal logic is an important instrument for such an analysis, and that (natural) science is the only reliable source of knowledge.

Where Quine and the logical positivist differ is on matters of implementation: where the logical positivists thought of meaning in terms of verification, Quine holds a behaviouristic view. And instead of the sense data empiricism that they espoused (at least during a certain period), Quine was thoroughly naturalistic with respect to epistemological issues, and often defended a physicalistic version of naturalism.

Quine was a prolific author and quite a number of his articles and books have become classics in their areas. 'Two Dogmas of Empiricism' is a classic text in philosophy of science, as are 'On What There Is' and 'Ontological Relativity' in ontology, and 'Epistemology Naturalised' in epistemology; *Word and Object* is a hall-mark work in philosophy of language; 'New Foundations for Mathematical Logic' and *Mathematical Logic* are major contributions to mathematical logic and the foundations of mathematics, and *Philosophy of Logic* is a key contribution to philosophy of logic; *The Roots of Reference* and *Pursuit of Truth* are accessible overviews of the various strands of thought in Quine's philosophical project.

12.3 The text

'On What There Is' (Quine, 1948) is one of the most famous papers of Quine, and, dating from 1948, it is also one of his earliest. Methodologically, it is a representative example of linguistic analysis in the tradition of logical positivism, but Quine's conclusions go off on a tangent, and bear clear naturalistic traces. Also, at various points one can discern seeds of later ideas, such as a behavioural conception of language and meaning (set out later in great detail in *Word and Object* from 1960), and a rejection of the analytic – synthetic distinction (a key element of the 'Two Dogmas of Empiricism' paper from 1951).

It is a characteristic feature of linguistic analysis that it does not address questions directly, but starts from a meta-perspective, i.e., from how we speak about the issue. Thus Quine's analysis asks what the question 'What is there?' itself means by investigating how we would answer this question.

Quine starts with an analysis of a classical problem: the meaning of so-called 'negative existential statements', i.e., statements such as 'Pegasus does not exist', 'There is no such thing as ether', 'Vulcan does not exist',[1] There is no largest prime', . . . These constitute an apparent problem: in order to truthfully claim that some thing a does not exist, one needs to be able to use the name 'a' in a meaningful way. And that seems to imply that one needs to assume that a exists after all: if 'a' does not refer, then how can it be meaningful?[2]

A number of possible reactions are then discussed. The first, which is almost immediately dismissed, is that 'Pegasus' in 'Pegasus does not exist' refers, not to a physical entity (because there is no such entity), but to an idea of such an entity. This, Quine observes, is a confusion that only muddies the waters.

Then there is the reaction that accepts that a reference is required for any meaningful use of a name, and that postulates that in the case of a non-existent the name refers to something that subsists, rather than exists. Thus it postulates an ontology that recognises, next to actually existing entities, also non-existing, possible entities.[3] Quine's main objections are two. First of all, there is the problem of a lack of identity criteria for possible entities: we lack criteria for judging whether two possible entities are identical or not. And secondly, there is the problem posed by impossible entities, such as entities of which the defining features are internally contradictory.

Quine then goes on to outline the analysis that Russell has proposed for definite descriptions, that is, phrases of the form 'the X'. We will deal with Russell's analysis later on in chapter 17, where we will also discuss 'On Denoting', Russell's famous paper on this topic. The key idea of Russel is that we need to analyse such phrases contextually, i.e., we need to analyse not the phrase as such, but the phrase as it occurs in a sentence. This idea can be extended to names, given that we can define a general way to turn any name into a corresponding description.

In that way we end up with logical representations that only contain variables and predicates, but no names. And the meaningfulness of variables and predicates does not come with existence presuppositions. In case there is no object that satisfies a certain set of conditions, the statement that there is such an object is simply false, but not meaningless.

The problem of existence does not, of course, apply just to the question of what individual entities there are. It extends also to properties and relations. In traditional parlance: there is an issue with respect to the existence of particulars, and there is one with respect to universals. Quine's argumentation with respect to the latter follows the pattern displayed earlier when he was discussing the former.

One may take the existence of properties such as 'redness' as a trivial consequence of one's conceptual scheme. But then the obvious objection is that there are other conceptual schemes that do not have such entailments built in. So this does not settle the issue.

Taking recourse to the meaning of property expressions needs another type of rebuttal. Here Quine rejects the hypostasis of meanings, i.e., the supposition that meanings are entities in their own right, and points out that meaningfulness (or 'significance' as he prefers), can also be accounted for in behavioural terms.

At this point Quine turns to the formulation of a positive answer to the question 'What is there?'. The core idea is that ontological commitments can be determined by looking at what the bound variables of the language that we use, range over. 'Something', 'nothing', 'everything': it is how we use these expressions that determine what we are committed to accept as entities.

Thus, if we analyse 'There are white dogs' as 'Something is a dog and something is white', we are committed to the kind of entities that 'something' ranges over: individual entities, such as dogs. And if we would analyse 'Chong and Yun are both from Jiangsu province' as 'There is a property that Chong and Yun have in common and that is the property of being from Jiangsu province' we would be committed to the existence of properties. But unlike in the first case, here we have a choice: we can also simply analyse 'Chong and Yun are both from Jiangsu province' as 'Chong is from Jiangsu province and Yun is from Jiangsu province'. And then the ontological commitment to properties disappears.

Quine proceeds with a short, but to-the-point discussion of the traditional approaches to the existence of universals, viz., nominalism, conceptualism and realism, and adds a twentieth century one, viz. formalism, and notes that it is the bound variables of the logical representations that we give of a certain part of our language that determine ontological commitments.

This introduces an element of choice: the conceptual scheme that we choose to adopt, and that guides our logical representation, determines our ontology. So additional factors need to weigh in. Ontological parsimony, a.k.a. 'Occam's Razor', is one that Quine embraces. And physicalistic naturalism is another one.

'To be is to be the value of a variable' summarises Quine's approach, but he is quick to warn us not to mistake it for an answer to the question 'What is there?' It serves to determine the commitments in a formal fashion, but it does not determine what, if anything, meets the requirements that are set out. In the end that is determined by the conceptual scheme, i.e., the language of the scientific theory that one accepts: in the end, nature makes the final call.

12.4 Study and discussion questions

Study questions

- What is the problem with negative existential statements?
- What is Quine's main argument against the position of McX?

- On what grounds does Quine reject the position that contradictory statements are meaningless?
- How does Russell's analysis avoid the problem of negative existential statements?
- How does Quine extend Russell's analysis of descriptions to proper names?
- What is the distinction between particulars and universals?
- What role do conceptual schemes play in determining our ontological commitments w.r.t. universals?
- Why do bound variables carry the brunt of ontological commitment?

Discussion questions

- Try to identify the epistemological presupposition in Quine's argument against the analysis proposed by 'McX'.
- Quine's main objection against Wyman's position is that possible entities lack identity criteria. Explain. Can you think of reasons to relax the requirement that only if we have identity criteria for them we can speak of entities of a particular kind?
- There is a short discussion on page 23 about the relation between 'existence' and 'being located in space-time'. What is Quine's take on this? Does one run into problems if one equates the two? If so, what kind of problems?
- As mentioned in the introduction, reliance on natural science as the sole source of knowledge about what there is, implies a strong form of reductionism. Discuss.

12.5 Further reading

Some of Quine' most influential papers, including 'On What There Is' and 'Two Dogmas of Empiricism' are collected in Quine (1953). For Quine's behaviouristic account of meaning, see Quine (1960). More general philosophical treatments of various intertwined themes can be found in Quine (1974, 1992). Many studies devoted to Quine's ideas exist; older, but still insightful and accessible is Romanos (1983).

As for ontology, it would be impossible to supply a comprehensive yet representative list of references. After a long decline during much of the twentieth century, interest in ontology among analytic philosophers has seen a veritable surge in the last twenty years. For an overview of recent debates and approaches focussed on the relation between logic and ontology, see Hofweber (2020).

13

Predicate Logic: Semantics

In this chapter we will provide the semantics for predicate logical languages. It uses some basic set-theoretic concepts and notations. If you are not familiar with them, or want to brush things up, consult the appendix for a brief exposition.

The semantics that is provided is the one that specifies classical first-order logic. As in the case of many logical languages, the languages of predicate logic can be interpreted in a variety of ways as well. But these different semantics are usually characterised and motivated as variations of, or deviations from, the standard semantics that is the subject matter of this chapter.

As will become clear, the same semantics can be specified in two ways that differ as to how the semantics of the quantifiers is defined. We will specify both, and also add a bit of discussion with respect to the relevance of the differences.

13.1 Extending referential semantics

Standard semantics of predicate logic is a referential semantics.[1] It analyses the meanings of expressions in terms of what these expressions refer to. In the case of propositional logic that is slimmed down to just two categories of referents: truth values and truth functions. What the sentences of a language of propositional logic refer to, are truth values, and the connectives that combine them refer to truth functions.[2]

The languages of predicate logic are richer. The atomic formulas have internal structure, and besides the sentential connectives there are also quantifiers that build new sentences from given ones. These two call for an extension of the semantics as well. Like in the case of proposition logic, atomic formulas will be assigned truth values, but whereas this is an arbitrary assignment in the case of proposition logic, here we want those truth values to be determined by the components from which the atomic formulas are built.[3] Forgetting about variables for the moment (more about them later), this means that we want truth values of atomic sentences of the form $A^i c_1 \ldots c_i$ to depend on what A^i and $c_1 \ldots c_i$ refer to.

A simple example will illustrate what is meant here. Suppose the domain consists of people. Suppose further that we have the following predicates: Bx: x is bald, and Lxy: x loves y, and the following individual constants b: Bill; j: John; m: Mary. Then we want Bb to be true iff the property that is referred to by B applies to the individual that is referred to by b, i.e., iff Bill is bald. Likewise, our semantics should specify that Lmj is true iff the relation that is referred to by L holds between the individuals referred to by m and j, respectively, i.e., iff Mary loves John.

What about sentences with quantifiers? As we shall see, technically there are different ways to account for their semantics. But both exemplify the same core idea, viz., that quantified formulas have truth conditions that are determined by the truth conditions of the sub-formula they are formed from. Thus, the truth values of quantified sentences $\forall x\phi$ and $\exists x\phi$ depend on which elements in the domain satisfy ϕ.[4] It is this notion of 'satisfaction' that can be analysed in different ways. Intuitively, though, the idea is simple: a formula with a free occurrence of a variable can be viewed as expressing a (complex) property. $\forall x$ turns that into the claim that every entity in a domain has that property, and $\exists x$ into the claim that at least such entity exists.

Again a simple example. Let domain and predicates be as above. Example $\forall x\exists yLxy$ is true iff for every individual in the domain there is an individual in the domain such that the relation that is referred to by L holds between the first one and the second one, i.e., iff everyone loves someone.

So what is needed for a semantics for a predicate logical language are three things: a way of saying what we use the language to talk about; interpretations that specify what the expressions in the vocabulary refer to and thus what the truth values of atomic formulas are; and a specification of how the truth values of complex formulas depend on that of their component parts. The latter will contain the specification of the truth-functional connectives of proposition logic in addition to those for the quantifiers.

Let us now turn to a formal definition of these ingredients.

13.2 Ingredients

13.2.1 Models

As we have seen a predicate logical language can be used to talk about a wide variety of things: about people, numbers, places, material objects, points in time, . . . , and about any combination of these entities. As long as it is non-empty and does not contain everything[5] any set will serve as the 'domain of discourse', in short: the domain. And a suitable interpretation of the predicate letters and individual constants will be a function that specifies what these expressions refer to given a choice of domain by linking them to entities that are elements of the domain, or constructed from it.

A domain D and an interpretation function I form a model M:

Definition 13 (Model)
A model M for a predicate logical language L is an ordered pair $\langle D_M, I_M \rangle$ such that:

- D_M is a non-empty set
- I_M is a function such that:
  - $I_M(A_i^n) \subseteq D_M^n$, for all predicate letters A_i^n of L
  - $I_M(c_i) \in D_M$, for all individual constants c_i of L

An individual constant is linked with an element of the domain as its referent. A 1-place predicate refers to a set of such elements, a 2-place relation refers to a set of ordered pairs, and in general an n-place relation refers to a set of n-tuples of elements of the domain.[6]

13.2.2 *Truth definition: first step*

Given a model M we can give a semantics for a part of a language of predicate logic, viz., its atomic sentences and the formulas that can be constructed from them. Note that we do not cover atomic formulas in general, i.e., atomic formulas with one or more occurrences of variables are left out. For now at least.

Definition 14 (Valuations)
Let M be a model $\langle D_M, I_M \rangle$ for L. A valuation V_M is a function with the sentences in L as its domain and $\{0, 1\}$ as its range, such that:

1. $V_M(A_i^n c_1 \dots c_n) = 1$ iff $\langle I_M(c_1) \dots I_M(c_n) \rangle \in I_M(A_i^n)$
2. $V_M(\neg\phi) = 1$ iff $V_M(\phi) = 0$
3. $V_M(\phi \wedge \psi) = 1$ iff $V_M(\phi) = 1$ and $V_M(\psi) = 1$
4. as usual for $\vee, \rightarrow, \leftrightarrow$

13.2.3 *Atomic sentences*

The only new element in the definition just given is the first clause, which gives the semantics of atomic sentences. The clause states that an atomic sentence consisting of a n-place predicate followed by n (not necessarily different) constants is true in a model iff the references of the constants form an n-tuple that is an element of the set of n-tuples that the predicate refers to.

By way of illustration consider the following simple examples:

- $V_M(Bb) = 1$ iff the entity $I_M(b)$ is an element of the set of entities $I_M(B)$

- $V_M(Ljm) = 1$ iff the ordered pair $\langle I_M(j), I_M(m)\rangle$ is an element of the set of ordered pairs $I_M(L)$

Another way of illustrating how the semantics of atomic sentences works is by doing some 'model checking': given a model we can investigate whether a given atomic formula is true or false in that model. An example:

- $D_M = \{\texttt{john,bill,mary}\}$; $I_M(B) = \{\texttt{john,bill}\}$; $I_M(L) = \emptyset$
- Then $V_M(Bb) = 1$, since $I_M(b) \in I_M(B)$; and $V_M(Ljm) = 0$, since $\langle I_M(j), I_M(m)\rangle \notin I_M(L)$

And another example:

- Let D_M be as above and suppose $I_M(L) = \{\langle\texttt{john,mary}\rangle, \langle\texttt{mary,bill}\rangle\}$
- Then $V_M(Ljm) = 1$, since $\langle I_M(j), I_M(m)\rangle \in I_M(L)$

13.2.4 *Quantifiers*

So far so good, but what about the quantifiers $\forall x\phi$ and $\exists x\phi$? How do we extend the truth definition to assign truth conditions to formulas of the form $\forall x\phi$ and $\exists x\phi$.

There are two main options. The first is the so-called 'substitutional interpretation', and the second goes by the name 'objectual interpretation'. We will present both. The differences between the two are part technical, and part conceptual. The technical differences will become clear as we go along. We will note some conceptual differences later on. We start with the substitutional interpretation.

13.3 Substitutional interpretation

13.3.1 *Basic idea*

One way of introducing the substitutional interpretation is by starting from the observation that there is an intuitive connection between the quantifiers and sentential connectives.

The universal quantifier is connected with conjunction. For example, $\forall xPx$ means that Pc_1 is true and Pc_2 is true and ... and Pc_n is true and .... Analogously, the existential quantifier is connected with disjunction: $\exists xPx$ means that Pc_1 is true or Pc_2 is true or ... or Pcs_n is true or ....

The connection is, of course, not always as direct as in these two examples. The scope of a quantifier occurrence can be an arbitrarily complex formula, so we cannot directly define the semantics of the quantifiers in terms of that of atomic sentences. But given the fact that the complexity can be diminished in a step-by-step fashion, the suggestion is that ultimately all we need for determining the truth value of a quantified formula is the truth values of a range of atomic sentences and suitable truth functional combinations thereof.

There is one crucial caveat: for this to work everything in the domain has to have (at least one) name. For in a situation in which P holds only of one entity and that entity happens to be nameless, we could not account for the truth of $\exists xPx$ in terms of the truth of an atomic sentence of the form Pc_i. Nor would we be able to do so for the falsity of $\forall xPx$ in a situation in which P fails to hold of just one, nameless entity.

13.3.2 *Additional requirement*

So we add to the definition of a model the following requirement:

- I_M is a function of CON_L onto D_M

f is a function from A onto B iff for all $b \in B$ there is at least one $a \in A$ such that $f(a) = b$ ('No b's left behind')[7]

This additional requirement on I_M ensures that every entity in the domain is the referent of at least one individual constant in the vocabulary of L. And that guarantees that if we talk about the referents of all the individual constants, we are indeed talking about all the entities.

13.3.3 *Substitution*

Before we can state the clauses in the truth definition for the quantifiers, we need one additional notion, that of substitution.[8]

Definition 15 (Substitution)
$[c/x]\phi$ is the formula ϕ' that results from substituting c for every free occurrence of x in ϕ.

The definition is straightforward, but do note that we need to take care that we are only concerned with free occurrences of the relevant variable. By way of illustration consider the following examples:

- $[c/x]Px = Pc$
- $[c/x](Px \wedge Qx) = Pc \wedge Qc$
- $[c/x](Px \rightarrow \forall xQx) = Pc \rightarrow \forall xQx$

13.3.4 *Truth definition*

Now we have all the ingredients in place to define the truth conditions for the quantifiers. For ease of reference we repeat the clauses for atomic sentences and connectives that were already formulated above.

Definition 16 (Truth definition)
Let M be a model $\langle D, I\rangle$ for L. A valuation V_M is a function with the sentences in L as its domain and $\{0, 1\}$ as its range, such that:

1. $V_M(A^n_i c_1 \ldots c_n) = 1$ iff $\langle I_M(c_1) \ldots I_M(c_n)\rangle \in I_M(A^n_i)$

2. $V_M(\neg\phi) = 1$ iff $V_M(\phi) = 0$
3. $V_M(\phi \wedge \psi) = 1$ iff $V_M(\phi) = 1$ and $V_M(\psi) = 1$
4. as usual for $\vee, \rightarrow, \leftrightarrow$
5. $V_M(\forall x\phi) = 1$ iff $V([c/x]\phi) = 1$ for all c in CON_L
6. $V_M(\exists x\phi) = 1$ iff $V([c/x]\phi) = 1$ for at least one c in CON_L

The clauses for $\forall x$ and $\exists x$ implement the basic idea mentioned above. $\forall x\phi$ is true iff every constant c that one substitutes for all the relevant occurrences of x in ϕ, i.e., the ones that are bound by $\forall x$, result in a formula that is true. Analogously for $\exists x\phi$. Given the additional requirement on models, viz., that every entity is the referent of at least one constant, this defines the appropriate semantics.

Let us illustrate this with a couple of simple examples. First, $\exists xBx$:

- $V_M(\exists xBx) = 1$
  iff there is a c: $V_M([c/x]Bx) = 1$,
  iff there is a c: $V_M(Bc) = 1$
  iff there is a c: $I_M(c) \in I_M(B)$

The second example, $\forall x\exists yLxy$, has multiple quantifiers:

- $V_M(\forall x\exists yLxy) = 1$
  iff for all c: $V_M([c/x]\exists yLxy) = 1$,
  iff for all c: $V_M(\exists yLcy) = 1$,
  iff for all c there is a c': $V_M([c'/y]Lcy) = 1$,
  iff for all c there is a c': $V_M(Lcc') = 1$
  iff for all c there is a c': $\langle I_M(c), I_M(c')\rangle \in I_M(L)$

Model checking also illustrates what is at stake. Suppose M is the following model:

- $D_M = \{\texttt{j},\texttt{b},\texttt{m}\}$
- $I_M(j) = \texttt{j}; I_M(b) = \texttt{b}; I_M(m) = \texttt{m}; I_M(B) = \{\texttt{j},\texttt{b}\}; I_M(L) = \{\langle\texttt{j},\texttt{m}\rangle, \langle\texttt{m},\texttt{b}\rangle\}$

We can check that $V_M(\exists x(Bx \wedge \exists yLyx)) = 1$:

- $V_M([b/x](Bx \wedge \exists yLyx)) = V_M(Bb \wedge \exists yLyb)) = 1$, since
- $I_M(b) = \texttt{bill}$ and $\texttt{bill} \in I_M(B)$ and
- $V_M([m/y]Lyb) = V_M(Lmb) = 1$ since
- $I_M(m) = \texttt{mary}$ and $\langle\texttt{mary}, \texttt{bill}\rangle \in I_M(L)$

13.3.5 *Observations*

The substitutional interpretation of the quantifiers works: it assigns the right truth conditions. However, it also has some odd features.

For one thing, the assumption that the language has a name for all elements in the domain seems awkward. The only motivation for it is that it allows us to deal with quantifiers in terms of (ultimately) atomic sentences. However, apart from that there seems to be no other reason to make this assumption.[9]

A second, and more important observation is that the truth definition only interprets sentences. No interpretation is supplied for atomic formulas with variables, such as Px or Ajy. And that means that quantified formulas $\forall x\phi$, $\exists x\phi$, need to be interpreted, not in terms of their actual scope ϕ, but in terms of $[c/x]\phi$. That is a breach of the principle of compositionality, which dictates that the meaning/reference of a complex expression is a function of the meanings/references of its parts. But $[c/x]\phi$ is not a part of $\forall x\phi$, only ϕ is.

Finally, there is a conceptual issue: on the substitutional interpretation the meaning of the quantifiers is explained in terms of formulas, i.e., linguistic objects. This seems counterintuitive: what we intend to express with a quantified formula is not something about the truth of other formulas, but something about objects in the domain. That is what the second method, a.k.a. 'objectual interpretation', captures.[10]

13.4 Objectual interpretation

The basic idea behind the second method for giving the semantics for a predicate logical language is to provide all expressions with an interpretation, so also variables, and formulas that contain free occurrences of them. In order to be able to do use, we need an additional concept, that of an assignment.

13.4.1 Assignments

Assignments are functions that assign references to variables. The set of assignments is defined in terms of the vocabulary of a language L and depends on a model M, since that provides the domain in which the references are to be located.

Definition 17 (Assignments)
Given a model M, the set of assignments G is the set of all functions g from VAR_L to D_M

In addition to this definition we also need the following notation:

- $g[x/d]$ is g except for the possible difference that $g(x) = d$

Thus, $g[x/d](y)) = g(y)$ for all $y \neq x$. And if $g(x) = g[x/d](x)$ (i.e., $= d$) , then $g[x/d] = g$

When needed we extend the notation to more than one variable as follows:

- $g[x_i/d_k, \ldots, x_n/d_l]$

Let us now see how assignments are used.

13.4.2 *Interpretation of terms*

The terms of L are the individual constants and variables of L: $\text{TERM}_L = \text{CON}_L \cup \text{VAR}_L$. If we want to define truth conditions for atomic formulas in general, not just for atomic sentences, we need to specify the interpretation of all terms. And this is where assignments come in:

Definition 18 (Interpretation of terms)
Given a model M and an assignment g, the interpretation of a term t, written as $[\![t]\!]_{M,g}$, is defined as follows:

$$[\![t]\!]_{M,g} = \begin{cases} I_M(t) & \text{if } t \text{ is a constant} \\ g(t) & \text{if } t \text{ is a variable} \end{cases}$$

Armed with this we can then tackle the truth definition.

13.4.3 *Truth definition*

Definition 19 (Valuations)
Let M be a model $\langle D, I \rangle$ for L and G the set of assignments. A valuation $V_{M,g}$ is a function from the set of formulas of L to $\{0, 1\}$ such that:

1. $V_{M,g}(At_1 \ldots t_n) = 1$ iff $\langle [\![t_1]\!]_{M,g}, \ldots, [\![t_n]\!]_{M,g} \rangle \in I(A)$
2. $V_{M,g}(\neg\phi) = 1$ iff $V_{M,g}(\phi) = 0$
3. $V_{M,g}(\phi \wedge \psi) = 1$ iff $V_{M,g}(\phi) = 1$ and $V_{M,g}(\psi) = 1$
4. as usual for $\vee, \rightarrow, \leftrightarrow$
5. $V_{M,g}(\forall x\phi) = 1$ iff for all $d \in D$: $V_{M,g[x/d]}(\phi) = 1$
6. $V_{M,g}(\exists x\phi) = 1$ iff there is a $d \in D$: $V_{M,g[x/d)]}(\phi) = 1$

Valuations are now based on a model M and an assignment g. The latter comes into action at two points. In clause 1, which defines when an atomic formula is true, and in clauses 5 and 6, which deal with the quantifiers.

Atomic formula may contain occurrences of variables, and via the definition of the interpretation of terms, the assignment g that is a parameter of $V_{M,g}$ takes care of that, as the following example shows:

- $V_{M,g}(Rxc) = 1$ iff
- $\langle [\![x]\!]_{M,g}, [\![c]\!]_{M,g} \rangle \in I_M(R)$ iff
- $\langle g(x), I_M(c) \rangle \in I_M(R)$

And then there are the clauses for the quantifier. The clause for $\forall x\phi$ states the truth conditions directly in terms of the interpretation of ϕ: for $\forall x\phi$ to be true it should hold that for every entity d in the domain ϕ is true if x refers to d.

The assignment function takes care of that. Starting from some function g, we check for every d whether ϕ holds with respect to $g[x/d]$, i.e., with respect to the assignment that keeps everything as it is, except that it assigns d to x. If that succeeds for every d, $\forall x\phi$ is true.

The existential quantifier works in a similar fashion. For the sake of illustration we write out a simple example in full:

- $V_{M,g}(\exists x(Px \wedge Qx)) = 1$
- iff there is a $d \in D$: $V_{M,g[x/d)]}(Px \wedge Qx) = 1$
- iff there is a $d \in D$: $V_{M,g[x/d)]}(Px) = 1$ and $V_{M,g[x/d)]}(Qx) = 1$
- iff there is a $d \in D$: $[\![x]\!]_{M,g[x/d)]} \in I_M(P)$ and $[\![x]\!]_{M,g[x/d)]} \in I_M(Q)$
- iff there is a $d \in D$: $g[x/d)](x) \in I_M(P)$ and $g[x/d)](x) \in I_M(Q)$
- iff there is a $d \in D$: $d \in I_M(P)$ and $d \in I_M(Q)$

And model checking also illustrates how semantic interpretation of the quantifiers works. Let M be as defined above (page 130). We check $\exists x(Bx \wedge \exists y Lxy)$:

- $V_{M,g}(\exists x(Bx \wedge \exists y Lxy)) = 1$ since $V_{M,g[x/\mathtt{j}]}(Bx \wedge \exists y Lxy) = 1$:
  - $V_{M,g[x/\mathtt{j}]}(Bx) = 1$ since
    $[\![x]\!]_{M,g[x/\mathtt{j}]} = g[x/\mathtt{j}](x) = \mathtt{j}$ and $\mathtt{j} \in I_M(B)$
  - $V_{M,g[x/\mathtt{j},y/\mathtt{m}]}Lxy = 1$ since
    $\langle [\![x]\!]_{g[x/\mathtt{j},y/\mathtt{m}]}, [\![y]\!]_{g[x/\mathtt{j},y/\mathtt{m}]} \rangle = \langle g[x/\mathtt{j}, y/\mathtt{m}](x), g[x/\mathtt{j}, y/\mathtt{m}](y) \rangle$
    $= \langle \mathtt{j}, \mathtt{m} \rangle$ and $\langle \mathtt{j}, \mathtt{m} \rangle \in I_M(L)$

These examples illustrate not only that the objectual interpretation using assignments is adequate, they also indicate that this interpretation does indeed overcome the problems that we noted with respect to the substitutional interpretation.

The additional requirement that everything in the domain have a name, is no longer needed. In that sense the objectual interpretation is also more general as it works perfectly for a predicate logical language that does not have any individual constants, just variables. The substitutional interpretation simply cannot be used in such a (limit) case.

The objectual interpretation is also more in accordance with the intuitive principle of compositionality, since it makes it possible to determine the truth value of a quantified formula directly from the interpretation of the quantifier and the interpretation of its scope, i.e., it embodies the 'step-by-step' philosophy that informs compositionality.

The broader scope of the objectual interpretation compared to the substitutional interpretation also comes to the fore if we look at how truth and validity are defined.

13.5 Truth and validity

Since the substitutional interpretation and the objectual interpretation have a different range, we need to define truth and validity for both separately.

Definition 20 (Truth, substitutional)
A sentence ϕ is true w.r.t. M iff $V_M(\phi) = 1$

Definition 21 (Truth, objectual)
A formula ϕ is true w.r.t. M and g iff $V_{M,g}(\phi) = 1$

Definition 22 (Validity, substitution)
A sentence ϕ is valid iff $V_M(\phi) = 1$, for all M

Definition 23 (Validity, objectual)
A formula ϕ is valid iff $V_{M,g}(\phi) = 1$, for all M and g

These definitions will speak themselves. Truth is defined relative to a model M, c.q., a model M and an assignment g. And validity is truth in all models M, c.q., all models M and assignments g.

The substitutional interpretation requires that we restrict truth and validity to sentences only, as formulas with free variables do not get an interpretation. The objectual method is broader and covers these cases, and thus requires also reference to an assignment. Apart from that, the definitions are the same.

That is an important observation as it means that in all cases where both interpretations apply, they will give the same results. More specifically, whenever both interpretations are defined, they will characterise exactly the same formulas, and by extension also the same argument schemes, as valid. I.e., both interpretations give rise to the same logic for the domain of formulas and argument schemes that they have in common. In that sense they do specify the same semantics for predicate logical languages.

The difference is simply that the range of application of the objectual interpretation is broader and also covers formulas with free variables, and thus will be able to also qualify a formula such as $Px \vee \neg Px$ as valid.

The next chapter is devoted to a closer look at validity in predicate logic. It will use only the objectual interpretation, but, in view of the observation just made, that is not a restriction.

13.6 Model checking

A final remark concerns model checking, in particular model representation.

As was already hinted at above, model checking is a good way to explicate the interpretation of predicate logical formulas, in particular more complex ones. It is therefore a very useful tools for developing skills that are needed to construct and to interpret representations of complex statements and arguments. As we shall see in the next chapter it also prepares for the task of constructing counterexamples, i.e., models that proof that a given formula or a given argument scheme is not valid. For this reason we have included a number of exercises that involve model checking.

Concerning model representations: especially when the domain of a model becomes larger, and one or more relations are defined on it, specifying the model in purely set-theoretic terms becomes quite cumbersome, and the resulting specification becomes less and less survey-able. Graphical representations improve on that, as the following example shows:

Let M be the following model:

- $D_M = \{1, 2, 3, 4\}$
- $I_M(P) = \{1, 3\}$; $I_M(R) = \{\langle 1,2\rangle, \langle 2,1\rangle, \langle 1,3\rangle, \langle 3,3\rangle\}$

Then M is represented by the following graph:

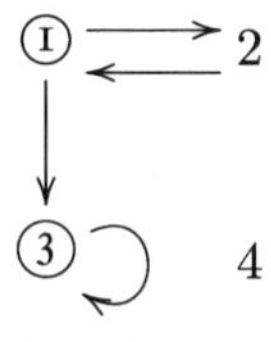

In such a graphical representation the elements from the domain are represented by points, arrows between points are used to indicate relations, and properties are represented by marking on the points being encircled.

Exercise 1 Consider the following model for a predicate logical language with a 1-place predicate letter A, and 2-place predicate letter R:

$$D = \{1, 2, 3, 4\}$$
$$I(A) = \{1, 4\}$$
$$I(R) = \{\langle 1,1\rangle, \langle 1,2\rangle, \langle 1,3\rangle, \langle 1,4\rangle, \langle 3,3\rangle, \langle 4,1\rangle, \langle 4,2\rangle, \langle 4,3\rangle, \langle 4,4\rangle\}$$

a. Draw a graph of the model
b. Which of the following formulas are true in the model? Motivate your answer.
   i. $\forall x(Ax \leftrightarrow \forall y Rxy)$
   ii. $\forall x \forall y(Rxy \rightarrow Ryx)$
   iii. $\exists x \exists y(Rxy \wedge Ryx)$

Exercise 2 Let the domain D be the set of all people. Use the following key: Lx: x is late; Bx: x is in a bad mood; Wxy: x is waiting for y, to determine what the following formulas state:

a. $\forall x(Lx \rightarrow \neg\exists y Wyx)$
b. $\forall x \forall y((Wxy \wedge Ly) \rightarrow Bx)$
c. $\forall x(\exists y(Wxy \wedge Ly) \rightarrow Bx)$

Exercise 3 Consider the following model for a predicate logical language with a 1-place predicate letter A, and 2-place predicate letter R:

$$D = \{1, 2, 3, 4, 5\}$$
$$I(A) = \{1, 2, 5\}$$
$$I(R) = \{\langle 1,2\rangle, \langle 1,3\rangle, \langle 1,4\rangle, \langle 2,1\rangle, \langle 2,4\rangle, \langle 2,5\rangle, \langle 3,4\rangle, \langle 4,4\rangle, \langle 5,4\rangle\}$$

a. Draw a graph of the model
b. Which of the following formulas are true in the model? Motivate your answer.
   i. $\exists x \forall y Ryx$
   ii. $\forall x \forall y (((Ax \wedge Ay) \wedge Rxy) \rightarrow Ryx)$
   iii. $\forall x (Ax \rightarrow \exists y (Rxy \wedge Ryy))$

14
Excursus: truth

14.1 The topic

The question after the nature of truth, whether truth can be defined, and if so, in what way, has occupied philosophers and logicians throughout the ages, in particular in the Western tradition.

Aristotle's famously defined truth as 'to say of what is that it is not, or of what is not that it is, is false, while to say of what is that it is, and of what is not that it is not, is true' (*Metaphysics*). This is often construed as an instance of the so-called 'correspondence view' on truth: what makes a statement true (or false) is whether it corresponds with how reality is. Commonly one distinguishes between metaphysical version and semantic one. A metaphysical view on correspondence can be found in the formulation of Thomas Aquino, who defined truth as follows: 'veritas est adaequatio rei et intellectus', i.e., truth is the agreement between things and thought. A metaphysical correspondence view thus relies on the availability of a category of entities in the world that make a statement true (or false, as the case may be). In modern parlance these are called 'truth makers'. Examples of truth makers are facts, states of affairs, situations, and so on. A classical example of a fact-based correspondence view is the logical atomism espoused by Russell in the 1910s.[1] The correspondence view can also be construed in a less metaphysical, more semantic way, and Aristotle and Tarski are often interpreted in this way.

There are also those who deny that truth can be defined. And there are those who hold that the very concept of truth is superfluous. A famous example of the first is Gottlob Frege, who in the opening sections of his paper 'The Thought' ('Der Gedanke', (Frege, 1918–1919a)) from 1916, states that although truth is the leading concept for logic, any attempt to define it in terms of correspondence runs into insurmountable problems. First of all, Frege notes that 'truth' signifies a property whereas 'correspondence' signifies a relation. But, secondly and more importantly, the key problem, Frege states, lies in defining what 'correspondence' means. It would be unproblematic to define correspondence as actual coincidence. However, that cannot account for the fact that a whole range of entities of different kinds, viz., thoughts, statements, pictures, ideas, etc, can be said to be true. So the notion of coincidence must be relativised to a certain respect: a thought and a fact, for example, cannot actually coincide, they can only share certain features. But that, Frege states, means we need to decide whether it is true that different entities coincide in a certain respect, and that leads us inevitably into a regress.

Another rejection of the idea that it makes sense to search for a definition of truth stems from the view that the concept itself is vacuous. To say that it is true that Beijing is the capital of the P.R.C, so the argument goes, means nothing over and above saying that Beijing is the capital of the P.R.C. The qualification 'It is true that A' may have a rhetoric or a pragmatic function, but it does not by itself add any semantic content to that of A. This is often called the 'deflationary view' on truth.[2]

And then there are other approaches to truth that focus, not on the semantic or metaphysical roles of truth, but on its epistemological and practical roles. If a given statement is coherent with a body of statements that we accept, that might be sufficient reason for calling it true: the coherence view on truth. Or, if accepting a statement allows us to solve a problem, that might also be a reason for accepting it as true: the pragmatist view, 'truth is what works'. In these approaches truth becomes much less a matter of fact, i.e., something that is determined independently of us, but much more a matter of how reasonable or practical it is for us to accept something as true.[3]

14.2 The author

Alfred Tarski (1901 – 1983) was born in Poland and initially studied biology at the University of Warsaw. Under the influence of Leśniewski, who took up the chair of logic there in 1918, he switched to mathematics and logic. He was connected to the Łwow - Warsaw school of logic and the school of mathematics at the University of Warsaw.

In 1939, just before the outbreak of the Second World War, he travelled to the United States. He stayed in the US, and, after holding a number of temporary positions, he moved to the department of mathematics at the University of California, Berkeley, where he remained for the rest of his life. At Berkeley, Tarski supervised a large number of talented mathematicians and logicians who would become prominent researchers in their own right, among whom Andrzej Mostowski, Bjarni Jónsson, Julia Robinson, Robert Vaught, Solomon Feferman, Richard Montague, Haim Gaifman, Chen Chung Chang, and Jerome Keisler.

Throughout his career Tarski worked both in mathematics and in logic. His mathematical work was on a wide range of topics in the areas of algebra, arithmetic, geometry, and set theory. He worked on the axiomatisation of Euclidean geometry, on Peano arithmetic, on the (un)decidability of theories in, among others, group theory and lattice theory, and on relational algebra and cylindric algebra.

Tarski's contributions to logic have been decisive in shaping the questions, methods and theories in mathematical logic of the twentieth century, and Robert Vaught has ranked Tarski as one of the four most important logicians of all time, along with Aristotle, Gottlob Frege and Kurt Gödel. Tarski contributed to a wide range of areas in mathematical logic, especially on the interface with foundations of mathematics. Very influential have been Tarski's ideas on how to characterise what he called 'logical notions', i.e., the basic elements including logical operators that a logic is built from. Tarski's ideas about the concept of truth have also been immensely influential. His research on the concept of truth has given rise to model theory as a separate branch of mathematical logic. It has also shaped the ways in which philosophers, and later on linguists, have thought about truth and meaning. The latter can be traced in two ways. First of all there are those, most prominently Donald Davidson, who claim that a Tarski-style theory of truth can function directly as a theory of meaning for natural language: a specification of the truth conditions for the sentences of a given natural language is a specification of their meanings. But the link can also be more indirect: any semantic theory that describes the meaning of natural language expressions using a formal language that has semantics that consists of a Tarskian truth definition, in effect applies the same ideas.

14.3 The text

Tarski's paper 'The Semantic Conception of Truth and the Foundations of Semantics' (Tarski, 1944) dates from 1944, and is an informal presentation of ideas that Tarski had been working on already in the early 1930s and that were first published in a 1935 paper called 'Der Wahrheitsbegriff in den formalisierten Sprachen' ('The concept of truth in formalised languages', (Tarski, 1935)). Although Tarski makes clear in the text that the application of his theory to natural language is not at all straightforward, he does claim that it is of interest to philosophy. The original work is highly technical and not easily accessible for non-mathematicians, which is why he wrote this more informal exposition.

The opening sections (1 – 3) of the paper are devoted to a specification of what Tarski considers to be the key questions that a theory of truth has answer: what are the things that truth is predicated of? and what is the general meaning of truth? After that Tarski enters into a long discussion of how to formulate requirements that an adequate definition of truth should meet. Section 4 is devoted to the 'material adequacy criterion', which is that an adequate definition should allow us to derive so-called 'T-sentences' for all and only the sentences of the language for which the definition is given. A T-sentence gives the truth conditions of a sentence in the language for which truth is being defined, the so-called 'object language'. The language in which that definition is phrased is called the 'meta-language'. Note that this terminology is only introduced in section 9. In section 5 Tarski then argues why his definition can be properly characterised as semantic.

Section 6 is devoted to the discussion of a requirement that a language needs to meet in order for it to be possible to formulate a truth definition for it: it has to have a formally specifiable structure. Via a discussion of the 'antinomy of the liar', also known as 'the paradox of the liar', in section 7, Tarski introduces another requirement, 'the formal adequacy criterion'. A general formulation is given in section 8. It requires that a language for which a truth definition is constructed not be semantically closed, i.e., not contain its own truth predicate and allow self-reference. If a language allows that, then, assuming the laws of logic hold, it can be shown to be inconsistent.

Ruling out semantically closed languages means that we always need to formulate a truth definition for a given language in another one, viz., one which contains the truth predicate for the first language and allows us to refer to its sentences. This is the hierarchy of object languages and metalanguages, which is discussed in section 9. The consequences are spelled in section 10.[4] Section 11 then provide further details of the way in which a truth definition can be set up. It introduces the concept of a sentential function and the notion of satisfaction. Sections 12 and 13 are devoted to a discussion of the general nature of the theory and of its consequences for other semantic notions, such as consequence (entailment), synonymity and meaning.

Sections 1 – 13 form the first part of the paper, and are devoted to the core elements of Tarski's view on what constitutes an adequate semantic definition of truth. The second part of the paper, consisting of sections 14 – 23, is more polemical and speculative in nature. Most of the discussion take the form of dealing with a possible objection: that the theory is circular (section 15); that semantic terms, including 'true', are redundant (section 16); that the definition does not concur with ordinary language use (section 17); that it is not relevant for 'the philosophical problem of truth' (section 18); or, rather conversely, that it is not philosophically neutral, but metaphysically loaded (section 19). Sections 20 – 22 discuss the potential for the application of a semantic definition of truth in the sciences. Especially these last remarks show that Tarski saw a great potential for the application of his ideas on truth. And as we already noted above, in linguistics, in particular in formal semantics, Tarski's semantic conception of truth has been, and indeed still is, used extensively.

14.4 Study and discussion questions

Study questions

- What is the philosophical conception of truth that Tarski wants his theory to model?
- Why does Tarski claim that 'truth' is a semantic concept?
- When does it mean for a definition of truth to be 'materially adequate'? What criterion does Tarski formulate for material adequacy?
- Why is it necessary for for formal structure of a language to be specified in order for us to be able to give a truth definition for that language?
- What is a 'semantically closed language'? And why is it problematic to define truth for such a language?
- What is the distinction between object language and metalanguage? How many metalanguages are there for Mandarin? Which are they?
- What requirements should be met by a metalanguage for it to allow for the formulation of a truth definition in that language?
- What is 'satisfaction'? What role does satisfaction play in Tarski's theory of truth?
- Why does Tarski define truth in terms of satisfaction and not in terms of truth of atomic sentences?

Discussion questions

- Is Tarski's theory incompatible with other philosophical conceptions of truth than the one he mentions in the paper? If so, why? If not, what other conceptions could be modelled by Tarski's theory?
- Would it be possible to dismiss the concept of satisfaction and formulate a truth definition that defines truth of complex sentences in terms of truth of atomic ones?
- Natural languages appear to be semantically closed. Does that mean that it is impossible to formulate a truth definition for them?
- Suppose we are convinced that truth for natural languages cannot be defined in the same way as is done for formal languages. What would be the consequence for how we view the relationship between logic and philosophy? (Recall the views of Frege and Russell, for instance.)

14.5 Further reading

On Tarski's semantic conception of truth, see Field (1972). Davidson's uptake of Tarski can be found in Davidson (1967). A detailed analysis of problems with semantically closed languages is given in Shapiro (2013).

15

Predicate Logic: Validity

In this chapter we delve a little bit deeper into truth, validity and counter-examples in predicate logic. The semantics that will be used is the one that is based on the objectual interpretation of the quantifiers, i.e., the one that is formulated in terms of assignments.

15.1 Truth

For ease of reference we first repeat the definition of the interpretation or terms and the truth definition. (Note: in what follows we use v to indicate an arbitrary variable.)

Definition 24 (Interpretation of terms)
Given a model M and an assignment g, the interpretation of a term t, written as $[\![t]\!]_{M,g}$, is defined as follows:

$$[\![t]\!]_{M,g} = \begin{cases} I_M(t) & \text{if } t \text{ is a constant} \\ g(t) & \text{if } t \text{ is a variable} \end{cases}$$

Definition 25 (Truth definition)
Let M be a model $\langle D, I\rangle$ for L and G the set of assignments. A valuation $V_{M,g}$ is a function from the set of formulas of L to $\{0,1\}$ such that:

1. $V_{M,g}(At_1 \dots t_n) = 1$ iff $\langle [\![t_1]\!]_{M,g}, \dots, [\![t_n]\!]_{M,g}\rangle \in I(A)$
2. $V_{M,g}(\neg\phi) = 1$ iff $V_{M,g}(\phi) = 0$
3. $V_{M,g}(\phi \wedge \psi) = 1$ iff $V_{M,g}(\phi) = 1$ and $V_{M,g}(\psi) = 1$
4. as usual for $\vee, \rightarrow, \leftrightarrow$
5. $V_{M,g}(\forall x\phi) = 1$ iff for all $d \in D$: $V_{M,g[x/d]}(\phi) = 1$
6. $V_{M,g}(\exists x\phi) = 1$ iff there is a $d \in D$: $V_{M,g[x/d)]}(\phi) = 1$

We now take a look at some facts that follow from the truth definition.

An immediate consequence of the truth definition is the following fact:

Fact 8 If $g(v) = g'(v)$ for every variable v that occurs free in ϕ, then:

$$V_{M,g}(\phi) = 1 \text{ iff } V_{M,g'}(\phi) = 1$$

Proof. By induction on the construction of ϕ. Here are three of the cases:

1. $\phi = At_1 \ldots t_n$:
   $V_{M,g}(At_1 \ldots t_n) = 1$ iff $\langle [\![t_1]\!]_{M,g} \ldots [\![t_2]\!]_{M,g}\rangle \in I(A)$.
   By assumption it holds that $g(v) = g'(v)$ for every variable v that occurs freely in $At_1 \ldots t_n$.
   So it holds that $[\![t_i]\!]_{M,g} = [\![t_i]\!]_{M,g'}$ for every t_i in $At_1 \ldots t_n$.
2. $\phi = \neg\psi$:
   $V_{M,g}(\neg\psi) = 1$ iff $V_{M,g}(\psi) = 0$.
   From the induction hypothesis it follows that:
   $V_{M,g}(\psi) = 0$ iff $V_{M,g'}(\psi) = 0$ for all g, g' s.th. $g(v) = g'(v)$ for every variable v that occurs free in ψ.
   So it also holds that:
   $V_{M,g}(\neg\psi) = 1$ iff $V_{M,g'}(\psi) = 0$ for all such g, g' (clause $\neg$)
   and hence that $V_{M,g}(\neg\psi) = 1$ iff $V_{M,g'}(\neg\psi) = 1$ for all such g, g'.
3. $\phi = \exists x\psi$:
   Consider g, g' s.th. $g(v) = g'(v)$ for every v that occurs free in $\exists x\psi$. The variable that occur free in ψ are the same as those that occur free in $\exists x\psi$ with the possible addition of x.
   From that it follows that $g[x/d](v) = g'[x/d](v)$ for every v that occurs free in ψ.
   From the induction hypothesis it follows that :
   $V_{M,g[x/d]}(\psi) = V_{M,g'[x/d]}(\psi)$, and thus that:
   $V_{M,g}(\exists x\psi) = V_{M,g'}(\exists x\psi)$ (clause $\exists$).

□

Exercise 1 Do the remaining cases.

From Fact 8 it follows that the truth value of a sentence, i.e., a formula in which no variables occur free, does not depend on the assignment. This is expressed in the following fact, which thus is a direct consequence of the previous one:

Fact 9 If ϕ is a sentence, then for all g, g':

$$V_{M,g}(\phi) = 1 \text{ iff } V_{M,g'}(\phi) = 1$$

Fact 9 allows us to leave out mention of assignments when dealing with sentences.

Exercise 2 Show that Fact 8 implies Fact 9.

Another fact that holds on the basis of the truth definition is the following:

Fact 10 For all M and g: $V_{M,g}([c/x]\phi) = V_{M,g[x/I(c)]}(\phi)$

Proof. By induction on the construction of ϕ. Note that if x does not occur free in ϕ, $[c/x]\phi = \phi$, and the relevant result follows right away. Therefore we leave that case out of consideration.

1. $\phi = At_1 \ldots t_n$:
   Suppose $t_i = x$. We know that:
   $V_{M,g[x/I(c)]}(At_1 \ldots x \ldots t_n) = 1$ iff
   $\langle [\![t_1]\!]_{M,g[x/I(c)]} \cdots [\![x]\!]_{M,g[x/I(c)]} \cdots [\![t_n]\!]_{M,g[x/I(c)]} \rangle \in I(A)$,
   and that:
   $V_{M,g}(At_1 \ldots c \ldots t_n) = 1$ iff
   $\langle [\![t_1]\!]_{M,g} \cdots [\![c]\!]_{M,g} \cdots [\![t_n]\!]_{M,g} \rangle \in I(A)$.
   Since $g[x/I(c)](v) = g(v)$, for all $v \neq x$ and $g[x/I(c)](x) = I(c)$ the result follows immediately.
   Note that the case where x occurs more than once is not relevantly different.
2. $\phi = \psi \wedge \chi$:
   Note that $[c/x](\psi \wedge \chi) = [c/x]\psi \wedge [c/x]\chi$. The induction hypothesis tells us that for all M and g:
   $V_{M,g}([c/x]\psi) = V_{M,g[x/I(c)]}(\psi)$,
   and the same holds for $[c/x]\chi$ and χ.
   On the basis of the truth definition (clause $\wedge$) the required results follow.
3. $\phi = \forall y \psi$:
   Note that $[c/x]\forall y \psi = \forall y[c/z]\psi$.
   The induction hypothesis states that for all M and g:
   $V_{M,g}([c/x]\psi) = V_{M,g[x/I(c)]}(\psi)$.
   That means that for arbitrary d:
   $V_{M,g[y/d]}([c/x]\psi) = V_{M,g[x/I(c),y/d]}(\psi)$.
   And we have (clause $\forall$) the required result.

□

Exercise 3 Do the remaining cases.

We extend the notation for syntactic substitution, given in chapter 13, as follows:

$[v'/v]\phi$ and $[t/v]\phi$, where v, v' variables, and t a term.

Note that if we substitute a variable for another one, it may happen that occurrences of the new variable become bound even when the occurrences of the original variable were free.

Example: although x occurs free in $\exists y Rxy$, y in $[y/x]\exists y Rxy$ becomes bound: $[y/x]\exists y Rxy = \exists y Ryy$.

Often we want to avoid such cases, or minimally take good notice of them, and hence we define the following notion:

Definition 26 (free for)
y is free for x in ϕ iff there is no free occurrence of x in ϕ that is within the scope of an occurrence of $\exists y$ or $\forall y$

Exercise 4 Let x, y, z, and w be different variables, and consider the formula

$$\exists x Rxy \wedge (\forall y Ryx \vee Rzz)$$

Is y free for x? for z? Is w for x? Is x free for y?

Armed with the definition of when a variable is free for another one in a formula we can state the following generalisation of Fact 10:

Fact 11 For all M and g:
$V_{M,g}[t/x]\phi = V_{M,g[x/[\![t]\!]_{M,g}]}\phi$, if t is free for x in ϕ

Exercise 5 Prove Fact 11.

15.2 Validity

We continue with the definition of the validity of formulas, notation: $\models \phi$, and that of the validity of an argument scheme, notation: $\phi_1 \ldots \phi_n \models \psi$.

Definition 27 (Validity)
ϕ is (universally) valid iff for all M and g: $V_{M,g}(\phi) = 1$

Notation: $\models \phi$

Definition 28 (Validity of argument scheme)
$\phi_1 \ldots \phi_n \,/\, \psi$ is valid iff for all M and g: if $V_{M,g}(\phi_1) = \ldots = V_{M,g}(\phi_n) = 1$, then $V_{M,g}(\psi) = 1$

Notation: $\phi_1 \ldots \phi_n \models \psi$

The validity of of formulas and that of validity of argument schemes is connected, as is expressed in the following theorem:

Theorem 3 (Deduction theorem)

$$\phi_1 \ldots \phi_n \models \psi \text{ iff } \phi_1 \ldots \phi_{n-1} \models \phi_n \rightarrow \psi$$

As an instance of the Deduction theorem we have:

$$\phi \models \psi \text{ iff } \models \phi \rightarrow \psi$$

Repeated application of the deduction theorem delivers the following general form:

Theorem 4 (Deduction theorem, general form)

$$\phi_1 \ldots \phi_n \models \psi \text{ iff}$$

$$\models \phi_1 \to (\phi_2 \to (\ldots \to (\phi_n \to \psi) \ldots) \text{ iff}$$
$$\models (\phi_1 \wedge \phi_2 \wedge \cdots \wedge \phi_n) \to \psi$$

15.3 PROVING VALIDITY

Now how do we prove that a formula is valid, or that an argument scheme is valid?

One way is by reasoning in the meta-language, using the truth definition and the definitions of validity. By way of illustration we provide a couple of examples.

We start with an extended and informal reasoning that shows that:

$$\models \exists x(Ax \wedge Bx) \to (\exists x Ax \wedge \exists x Bx)$$

By the definition of validity, $\models \exists x(Ax \wedge Bx) \to (\exists x Ax \wedge \exists x Bx)$ says that for all M and g, $V_{M,g}(\exists x(Ax \wedge Bx) \to (\exists x Ax \wedge \exists x Bx)) = 1$. Now take an arbitrary M and g. Given the clause of the truth definition for $\to$ it is sufficient to show that if $V_{M,g}(\exists x(Ax \wedge Bx)) = 1$, also $V_{M,g}(\exists x Ax \wedge \exists x Bx)) = 1$. Assume that $V_{M,g}(\exists x(Ax \wedge Bx)) = 1$. On the basis of the clause for $\exists$ it follows that there is a d in D is such that $V_{M,g[x/d]}(Ax \wedge Bx) = 1$. Given the clause for $\wedge$ this means that $V_{M,g[x/d]}(Ax) = 1$ and $V_{M,g[x/d]}(Bx) = 1$, which, given the clause for atomic formulas and the definition of the interpretation of terms, means: $d \in I(A)$ and $d \in I(B)$. Hence, from the assumption that $V_{M,g}(\exists x(Ax \wedge Bx)) = 1$ it follows that there is a d such that $d \in I(A)$ and $d \in I(B)$. How can we conclude from this that $V_{M,g}(\exists x Ax \wedge \exists x Bx)) = 1$? On the basis of the clause for $\wedge$ this is the case if $V_{M,g}(\exists x Ax) = 1$ and $V_{M,g}(\exists x Bx) = 1$, which, given the clause for $\exists$, demands that there be a d such that $V_{M,g[x/d]}(Ax) = 1$, and that there be a d such that $V_{M,g[x/d]}(Bx) = 1$. If we apply the clause for atomic formulas and the definition of the interpretation of terms, this boils down to the demand that there be a d such that $d \in I(A)$, and a d such that $d \in I(B)$. But this condition is fulfilled given the assumption that $V_{M,g}(\exists x(Ax \wedge Bx)) = 1$. For from the latter we have concluded that there is a d which is both an element of $I(A)$ as well as an element of $I(B)$, which guarantees that there is a d in $I(A)$ and a d in $I(B)$. Since M and g are arbitrary we can conclude that this holds for *all* M and g, which means that we have shown that $\models \exists x(Ax \wedge Bx) \to (\exists x Ax \wedge \exists x Bx)$.

Of course this is a much too cumbersome and at one point also unnecessarily complicated way to write down a proof. But we have written it out in full detail to show what the reasoning behind such a proof looks like.

But we can, and should, formulate the same reasoning in a more concise and standardised way, and then the proof looks like this:

Proof. Suppose $V_{M,g}(\exists x(Ax \wedge Bx)) = 1$ for arbitrary M and g. Then there is a d such that $V_{M,g[x/d]}(Ax \wedge Bx) = 1$ (clause $\exists$), i.e., such that $V_{M,g[x/d]}(Ax) = 1$ and $V_{M,g[x/d]}(Bx) = 1$ (clause $\wedge$). From $V_{M,g[x/d]}(Ax) = 1$ it follows that $V_{M,g}(\exists xAx) = 1$ (clause $\exists$). Analogously we have that $V_{M,g}(\exists xBx) = 1$. Thus it follows that (clause $\wedge$) $V_{M,g}(\exists xAx \wedge \exists xBx)) = 1$. □

Note that we have taken a shortcut: instead of reasoning as we did in the informal proof above to the conclusion that $d \in I(A)$ etc, we directly conclude from $V_{M,g[x/d]}(Ax) = 1$that $V_{M,g}(\exists xAx) = 1$.

As a second example consider:

$$\models (\forall x\phi \vee \forall x\psi) \rightarrow \forall x(\phi \vee \psi)$$

Proof. Suppose $V_{M,g}(\forall x\phi) = 1$ for arbitrary M and g. Then it holds for all d: $V_{M,g[x/d]}(\phi) = 1$ (clause $\forall$). For arbitrary d it follows from $V_{M,g[x/d]}(\phi) = 1$ that $V_{M,g[x/d]}(\phi \vee \psi) = 1$ (clause $\vee$), which shows that $V_{M,g}(\forall x(\phi \vee \psi)) = 1$. □

Note that this proves that every formula of this form is valid.

Of course in constructing a proof one may use facts that have already been proved. The last example illustrates this:

$$\models \forall x\phi \rightarrow [c/x]\phi$$

Proof. Suppose $V_{M,g}(\forall x\phi) = 1$ for arbitrary M and g. Then it holds for all $d \in D$: $V_{M,g[x/d]}(\phi) = 1$ (clause $\forall$). Since $I(c) \in D$, it follows that $V_{M,g[x/I(c)]}(\phi) = 1$, and on the basis of Fact 11, that $V_{M,g}([c/x]\phi) = 1$. □

Exercise 6 Prove that the following formulas are valid:

a. $[c/x]\phi \rightarrow \exists x\phi$
b. $(\forall x\phi \wedge \forall x\psi) \rightarrow \forall x(\phi \wedge \psi)$
c. $\forall x\phi \rightarrow \exists x\phi$
d. $\exists x\forall yRxy \rightarrow \exists xRxx$

Now we discuss a few examples of proofs of the validity of argument schemes. As a first example consider:

$$\forall x(Ax \rightarrow Bx), Aa \models Ba$$

Proof. Suppose for arbitrary M and g that $V_{M,g}(\forall x(Ax \rightarrow Bx)) = V_{M,g}(Aa) = 1$. From the first assumption it follows (clause $\forall$) that for all d: $V_{M,g[x/d]}(Ax \rightarrow Bx) = 1$. So (clause $\rightarrow$): for all d, if $d \in I(A)$ then $d \in I(B)$. The second assumption says that (clause atomic formulas) $I(a) \in I(A)$, hence $I(a) \in I(B)$, which (same clause) means that $V_{M,g}(Ba) = 1$. □

A second example:

$$\exists y \forall x \phi \models \forall x \exists y \phi$$

Proof. Suppose for arbitrary M and g that $V_{M,g}(\exists y \forall x \phi) = 1$. Given the clause for $\exists$ this means that there is a d such that $V_{M,g[y/d]}(\forall x \phi) = 1$. With the clause for $\forall$ it follows that for d it holds that for every d': $V_{M,g(y/d,x/d')}(\phi) = 1$. Since $y \neq x$ it holds that $g[y/d, x/d'] = g[x/d', y/d]$. Then it follows from the clause for $\exists$ that for all d': $V_{M,g[x/d']}(\exists y \phi) = 1$, and with the clause for $\forall$ that $V_{M,g}(\forall x \exists y \phi) = 1$. □

Exercise 7 Prove:

a. $\forall x \phi \models [y/x]\phi$, if y is free for x in ϕ
b. $\exists y \forall x Rxy \models \forall x \exists y Rxy$
c. $\forall x(\phi \to \psi), \exists x \phi \models \exists x \psi$
d. $\neg \forall x \phi, \forall x(\psi \to \phi) \models \exists x \neg \psi$

15.4 Equivalence

We define logical equivalence of predicate logical formulas as follows:

Definition 29 (Logical equivalence)
ϕ and ψ are (logically) equivalent iff for all M and g: $V_{M,g}(\phi) = V_{M,g}(\psi)$

Notation: $\phi \Leftrightarrow \psi$. It is easy to see that the following three assertions are equivalent:

Fact 12

1. $\phi \models \psi$ and $\psi \models \phi$
2. $\phi \Leftrightarrow \psi$
3. $\models \phi \leftrightarrow \psi$

Let us now turn to the matter of proving equivalences. We first give a number of equivalences that can be used in proofs:

a. $\forall x \neg \phi \Leftrightarrow \neg \exists x \phi$
b. $\forall x \phi \Leftrightarrow \neg \exists x \neg \phi$
c. $\neg \forall x \phi \Leftrightarrow \exists x \neg \phi$
d. $\neg \forall x \neg \phi \Leftrightarrow \exists x \phi$
e. $\forall x(\phi \wedge \psi) \Leftrightarrow \forall x \phi \wedge \forall x \psi$
f. $\exists x(\phi \vee \psi) \Leftrightarrow \exists x \phi \vee \exists x \psi$
g. $\forall x(\phi \vee \psi) \Leftrightarrow \phi \vee \forall x \psi$, if x not free in ϕ
h. $\exists x(\phi \wedge \psi) \Leftrightarrow \phi \wedge \exists x \psi$, if x not free in ϕ
i. $\forall x(\phi \to \psi) \Leftrightarrow \phi \to \forall x \psi$, if x not free in ϕ
j. $\forall x(\phi \to \psi) \Leftrightarrow \exists x \phi \to \psi$, if x not free in ψ
k. $\forall x \forall y \phi \Leftrightarrow \forall y \forall x \phi$

l. $\exists x \exists y \phi \Leftrightarrow \exists y \exists x \phi$
m. $\forall x \phi \Leftrightarrow \forall y [y/x]\phi$, provided y free for x in ϕ
n. $\exists x \phi \Leftrightarrow \exists y [y/x]\phi$, provided y free for x in ϕ

When proving equivalences it comes in handy to make use of equivalences that have already been proven. That we can do so is because the following theorem holds:

Theorem 5 (Extensionality)

$$\forall x_1 \ldots x_n(\phi \leftrightarrow \psi) \models \chi \leftrightarrow [\psi/\phi]\chi$$

where $x_1 \ldots x_n$ are the variables that occur free in ϕ and ψ

Given that we have:

Fact 13
$\phi \Leftrightarrow \psi$ iff $\models \forall x_1 \ldots x_n(\phi \leftrightarrow \psi)$

the Extensionality theorem allows us to replace a formula by an equivalent one in a bigger formula.

Now let's turn back to equivalences. By way of illustration we show a proof of the validity of equivalence f.:

$$\exists x(\phi \vee \psi) \Leftrightarrow \exists x \phi \vee \exists x \psi$$

Proof. $\exists x(\phi \vee \psi)$ is equivalent with $\neg\forall x \neg(\phi \vee \psi)$, given d. The latter is equivalent with $\neg\forall x(\neg\phi \wedge \neg\psi)$, given the proposition logic equivalence $\neg(\phi \vee \psi) \Leftrightarrow \neg\phi \wedge \neg\psi$ (one of De Morgan's laws). Given e. we conclude that this is equivalent with $\neg(\forall x \neg\phi \wedge \forall x \neg\psi)$. Applying De Morgan again, we get $\neg\forall x \neg\phi \vee \neg\forall x \neg\psi$. And given d. that is equivalent with $\exists x \phi \vee \exists x \psi$. □

Exercise 8 Prove the other equivalences listed above.

15.5 Invalidity

In order to show that a formula ϕ is *not* valid, it suffices to show that there is at least one model M and assignment g such that $V_{M,g}(\phi) = 0$. Analogously, we prove that an argument scheme $\phi_1 \ldots \phi_n \,/\, \psi$ is not valid by specifying an M and g such that $V_{M,g}(\phi_1) = \ldots = V_{M,g}(\phi_n) = 1$ and $V_{M,g}(\psi) = 0$. Such a model plus assignment we call a 'counterexample'. In what follows we only treat the construction of counterexamples to show invalidity of argument schemes, since that subsumes the invalidity of formulas.

Unlike in the case of proposition logic there is no decision procedure for predicate logical validity. That is to say, there is no mechanical method that for every argument scheme will tell us in a finite number of steps whether it is valid or not.

In the case of proposition logic there is such a decision procedure because in order to determine the truth value of a formula we always only need to take into account the finite number of truth values of a finite number of proposition letters. These can be listed in a mechanical way in a complex, but also finite truth table. If we do so for the finite number of formulas that make up an argument scheme, we get a mechanically constructed finite truth table that can be checked, again in a completely mechanical way, for counterexamples.

In the case of predicate logic this is not the case. This is what Church's Theorem, one of the most celebrated results of modern logic, says.[1] To actually prove that would take us way too far afield, but we can intuitively grasp why predicate logical validity is different. The difference is not one of syntax: predicate logical formulas and argument schemes are, like their propositional logical counterparts, finite syntactic objects. The difference is in the semantics. For a propositional argument scheme we can determine a priori on the basis of the syntactic structure of premises and conclusion which finite number of interpretations might be relevant. For predicate logical argument schemes this is different: an infinite number of possible models (and assignments, in case there are variables that occur free) might need to be checked, and moreover some of these models might themselves be infinite, because they contain an infinite number of objects. That means that we cannot expect that there is a method that will always tell after a finite number of steps whether a scheme is valid or not.

It is the finiteness of a decision procedure that is the problem, not so much the mechanical nature. In fact there are systematic ways of looking for counterexamples, such as the semantic tableaux method, but these are not guaranteed to give a definite answer after a finite number of steps.

In what follows we approach the matter of constructing counterexamples in a slightly more intuitive manner, but note that the argument scheme itself usually suggests a more or less systematic way of doing so.

By way of illustration we describe in some detail how we can show that the following argument scheme is invalid by constructing a counterexample:

$$\forall x(Ax \to Bx), \exists x \neg Bx \,/\, \neg \exists x Ax$$

There are a few things to note before we start the construction. First of all, the formulas do not contain free occurrences of variables. So we do not need to bother about the specification of an assignment g, and we will therefore leave reference to assignment out, whenever possible. The counterexample will in this case thus consist of just a model M that makes the premises true and the conclusion false. Secondly, note that the scheme only contains the predicate constants A and B, which means that we only need to specify the interpretation of these two constants, i.e., $I(A)$ and $I(B)$. Finally, because the semantics assumes that domains are not empty, we also know that D contains at least one element, i.e., $D = \{d_1, \ldots\}$. So what will an adequate M look like? We need to make sure that $V_M(\forall x(Ax \to Bx)) = V_M(\exists x \neg Bx) = 1$ and $V_M(\neg\exists x Ax) = 0$. To start with the latter, $V_M(\neg\exists x Ax) = 0$ iff $V_M(\exists x Ax) = 1$ (clause $\neg$) iff there is a d such that $V_{M,g[x/d]}(Ax) = 1$ (clause $\exists$) iff there is a d such that $d \in I(A)$ (clause atomic formulas and definition of interpretation of terms). So in order to make the conclusion false we need to choose the interpretation of A in such a way that it is not empty. The easiest way to do this is to combine this requirement with the fact that D already contains d_1, and thus to stipulate that $I(A) = \{d_1, \ldots\}$. On to the premises. $V_M(\forall x(Ax \to Bx)) = 1$ demands (via a number of steps that we will not write out) that for all d it holds that if $d \in I(A)$, then $d \in I(B)$. As for $I(B)$ we conclude from this that $d_1 \in I(B)$. Now we need to make sure that $V_M(\exists x \neg Bx) = 1$, which boils down to the condition that there is a d such that $d \notin I(B)$. The only way to do that is to add a second element d_2 to D but to keep that out of both $I(B)$ and $I(A)$.

Summing up, the counterexample looks as follows:

$$D = \{d_1, d_2\}, I(A) = I(B) = \{d_1\}$$

It is easy to check that for every entity in the domain it holds that if it has property A it also has property B; that there is an entity in the domain that does not have property B; and that it nevertheless is not true that nothing has property A.

Of course, one would not write out the construction of a counterexample in such detail in each and every case. Usually one confines oneself to a specification of the counterexample as such, if needed with a short commentary. The description just given was meant to illustrate how by systematically reasoning about premises and conclusion one can construct a counterexample in a more or less structured way.

Three remarks are in order at this point. First of all, the counterexample above is, of course, not the only one. On the contrary, it is easy to see that there is an infinite number of them: one can simply keep on adding elements to the domain in such a way that the first premise remains true (which can always be done). So there is, in general, no such thing as 'the counterexample'. However, the model we constructed is the smallest and simplest. And usually these are the ones that one comes up with by systematically reasoning about premises and conclusion using the truth definition.

Secondly, note that our counterexample is completely abstract. Given that the only thing we have said about the domain is that it contains two elements d_1 and d_2, one could in fact look at the counterexample as a proxy for a whole range of concrete counterexamples: the domain could consist of two people, two numbers, two birds, two countries, ... Abstract counterexamples are not better than concrete ones. But constructing concrete counterexamples can be more tricky because a choice for a particular concrete domain might come with additional conditions that might go unnoticed. By letting oneself be guided by the relevant clauses of the truth definition one ends up with sufficiently abstract counterexamples.

Third, as was already mentioned constructing a counterexample is not something that guarantees a result: if we fail to come up with a counterexample, that does in no way prove that it does not exist. In fact more or less mechanically constructing one, i.e., by increasing the domain with one element at a time will fail to produce a counterexample in cases where the only counterexamples that exist have an infinite domain. To see that that is needed requires a certain amount of insight that cannot be mimicked by a mechanical finite procedure.

We conclude with a second example. The following argument scheme is not valid:

$$\forall x \exists y Rxy, \forall x(Rxx \leftrightarrow Ax) \,/\, \exists x Ax$$

Proof. Consider the following model:

$$D = \{d_1, d_2\}, I(R) = \{\langle d_1, d_2\rangle, \langle d_2, d_1\rangle\}, I(A) = \emptyset$$

Since $I(A) = \emptyset$ we have that $V_M(\exists x Ax) = 0$. Since there is no pair $\langle d, d\rangle$ in $I(R)$, we also have that $V_M(\forall x(Rxx \leftrightarrow Ax)) = 1$. And for every d in D there is indeed a d' such that $\langle d, d'\rangle \in I(R)$ (for d_1 this is d_2 and for d_2 it is d_1), so $V_{M,g}(\forall x \exists y Rxy) = 1$. □

Note that a counterexample such as this one can be very well specified in a graphical manner, by means of the kind of diagrams that we discussed earlier.

Exercise 9 Prove that the following argument schemes are invalid by constructing a counterexample:

a. $\exists x Ax, \exists x Bx \,/\, \exists x(Ax \wedge Bx)$
b. $\forall x(Ax \vee Bx), \exists x \neg Ax, \exists x \neg Bx, \forall x((Ax \wedge Bx) \rightarrow Cx) \,/\, \exists x Cx$
c. $\forall x \exists y Rxy \,/\, \exists x Rxx$
d. $\exists x \forall y Rxy, \forall x Rxx \,/\, \forall x \forall y(Rxy \vee Ryx)$
e. $\forall x \exists y Rxy, \forall x \forall y(Rxy \vee Ryx) \,/\, \forall x \forall y \forall z((Rxy \wedge Ryz) \rightarrow Rxz)$
f. $\forall x \exists y Rxy, \forall x \forall y \forall z((Rxy \wedge Ryz) \rightarrow Rxz) \,/\, \exists x Rxx$

16

Predicate Logic: Identity

In this chapter we expand the expressive power of the language of predicate logic by adding a new logical constant that allows us to deal with arguments in which the notion of identity plays a crucial role.

16.1 Why?

There are a great number of phenomena that illustrate the usefulness of such an addition. We will briefly discuss a few of them.

16.1.1 Other

The first kind of case has to do with the fact that variables in the language of predicate logic do not have a meaning of their own. As a a consequence quantifiers that use different variables, also do not have a different meaning. Whether we use $\exists x$ or $\exists y$ does not really matter, as the use of different variables does not result in a difference in meaning. $\exists x Px$ and $\exists y Py$ mean the same thing, different variables do not necessarily pick out different objects in the domain.[1] This creates a problem if we want to represent the distinction between the claims made by (1) and (2):

(1) John loves someone and Bill loves someone
(2) John loves someone and Bill loves someone else

The representation that we can give:

(3) $\exists x Ljx \wedge \exists y Lby$

is adequate for (1), but not for (2), as is illustrated by the following simple model:

- $D_M = \{\mathtt{j}, \mathtt{b}, \mathtt{m}\}$
- $I_M(j) = \mathtt{j}$; $I_M(b) = \mathtt{b}$; $I_M(m) = \mathtt{m}$; $I_M(L) = \{\langle \mathtt{j}, \mathtt{m}\rangle, \langle \mathtt{b}, \mathtt{m}\rangle\}$

It is easy to see that $V_{M,g}(\exists x Ljx \wedge \exists y Lby) = 1$, since $V_{M,g[\mathtt{m}/x]}(Ljx) = V_{M,g[\mathtt{m}/y]}(Lby) = 1$.

The ability to distinguish between different objects without having to refer to them 'by name', i.e., without having to use distinguishing identifiers, is, of course, crucial for the way in which we speak and reason, not just in everyday contexts, but also in the context of science.

16.1.2 Only

Another kind of example has to do with (implicit) claims of exclusiveness. In English this is often expressed using the modifier 'only'. Consider the following examples:

(4) John loves Mary
(5) John loves only Mary
(6) Only John loves Mary

The translation we can give is:

(7) Ljm

However, where (7) is adequate as a representation of (4), it does not express what is claimed in (5), since (7) is consistent with John loving also Sue, which is excluded by (5). Analogously, (7) also fails to capture the meaning of (6), since (7) does not exclude that Mary is also loved by Bill, which (6) does rule out.

Again a simple model illustrates what is at stake here: :

- $D_M = \{\mathtt{j}, \mathtt{b}, \mathtt{m}, \mathtt{s}\}$
- $I_M(j) = \mathtt{j}; I_M(b) = \mathtt{b}; I_M(m) = \mathtt{m}; I_M(s) = \mathtt{s}$
  $I_M(L) = \{\langle \mathtt{j}, \mathtt{m}\rangle, \langle \mathtt{j}, \mathtt{s}\rangle, \langle \mathtt{b}, \mathtt{m}\rangle\}$.

As is easily checked, in this model (4) is true, but (5) and (6) are not.

Exclusiveness can also be present more implicitly, for example in the way answers to questions are interpreted. If A asks B whether he knows which students got a passing grade, and B answers that he does, and he tells A that it were student X, Y, and Z, then A will interpret this answer as giving an exhaustive specification of the students with a passing grade. I.e., A will interpret 'X, Y, and Z got a passing grade' as 'Only X, Y, and Z got a passing grade.' For if, unbeknownst to B, also a fourth student, W, would have gotten a passing grade and A would learn this, then A would regard B's claim that he knows which students got a passing grade as false.

16.1.3 Numerals

An important class of expressions that cannot be adequately represented in the language of predicate logic as we have defined it so far are numerals. Again, we can illustrate what is at stake with a few simple examples:

(8) Mary loves someone
(9) Mary loves two people

For (8) we have an adequate representation:

(10) $\exists x\ Lmx$

But what about (9)? For reasons that have been explained already above, the following will not do:

(11) $\exists x\ Lmx \wedge \exists y\ Lmy$

since (11) is also true if Mary loves only one person. Again, a small model illustrates what is going on:

- $D_M = \{\mathtt{m}, \mathtt{j}\}$
- $I_M(m) = \mathtt{m}; I_M(j) = \mathtt{j}; I_M(L) = \{\langle \mathtt{m}, \mathtt{j} \rangle\}$.

$V_{M,g}(\exists x\ Lmx \wedge \exists y\ Lmy) = 1$ for $V_{M,g[\mathtt{j}/x]}(Lmx) = V_{M,g[\mathtt{j}/y]}(Lmy) = 1$

No matter how many instances of the existential quantifier we use in our representation, we will not be able to express the distinctness of individuals because different variables do not necessarily refer to different objects.

The use of numerals in reasoning and argumentation is essential in a great variety of contexts. Without an adequate system of numerical expressions we would not be able to do arithmetic, or engage in other forms of quantitative reasoning.

16.1.4 *Descriptions*

A final category of examples has to do with the way in which definite descriptions are used to pick out individuals. We start again with a simple example from natural language, one that actually has a prominent philosophical pedigree, as we shall see later on:

(12) The King of France is bald

If we represent this as:

(13) $\exists x(KFx \wedge Bx)$

we do not adequately capture the meaning of (12) since (13) does not exclude that there is more than one King of France.

Another inadequacy is illustrated by the following model:

- $D_M = \{\mathtt{b}, \mathtt{j}\}$
- $I_M(b) = \mathtt{b}; I_M(j) = \mathtt{j}; I_M(KF) = \{\mathtt{b}, \mathtt{j}\}; I_M(B) = \{\mathtt{j}\}$

In this model:

$$V_{M,g}(\exists x(KFx \wedge Bx) = 1 \text{ since } V_{M,g[(j)/x]}(KFx \wedge Bx)) = 1; \text{ but also}$$
$$V_{M,g}(\exists x(KFx \wedge \neg Bx) = 1 \text{ since } V_{M,g[(b)/x]}(KFx \wedge \neg Bx)) = 1$$

However, this is at odds with the fact that

(14) The King of France is bold and the King of France is not bold

seems to be a contradiction.

Definite descriptions abound in all kinds of contexts. Their usefulness resides in the fact that they allow us to identify an object in terms of its properties and/or its relations with other objects. If two lines l_1 and l_2 intersect, we can designate the intersection with a name, say P_1. But we can also use a description: 'the intersection of l_1 and l_2'. This is much more informative since it is the description by itself that allows us to determine the object, something that the use of a mere name cannot do.

It is the versatility of definite descriptions, which can make use of all the expressive resources of a language, that makes them an indispensable part of any language that is used to talk about a complex and partly unknown reality. It is simply impossible to set up an adequate reservoir of names prior to our investigations. But we need to be able to talk about what we want to investigate, formulate hypotheses, and speculate about possible outcomes beforehand. Definite descriptions provide us with the means to do that.

16.2 How?

The conclusion that can be drawn from these examples is that we need a way to distinguish different objects in the language of predicate logic. That we currently do not have. As we have seen, using different variables does not work. And using different constants does not work straightforwardly either. Since there are no constraints in the interpretation function that link constants with objects using different constants does not ensure that we refer to different objects.

So we need to extend the expressive power of the language. We do so by adding a constant that allows us to state that what two (or more) expressions refer to is, or is not, the same object. It is (non-)identity that is key to the various examples we discussed.

16.3 Adding identity

First, we amend the syntax of a language of predicate logic by adding a designated 2-place constant to the vocabulary of L:

- '$=$' is a two-place predicate letter of L

This allows for the formation of additional atomic formulas, such as:

- $a = b$, $x = y$, $a = x$

Note: instead of $\neg(s = t)$, we write: $s \neq t$

Then we add the following clause to the semantics:

- In all models M: $I_M(=) = \{\langle d, d\rangle \mid d \in D\}$

In words: identity is the relation that every object has to itself and only to itself.

Note that the interpretation of identity is fixed: in all models M it has the same reference. This makes $=$ different from other constants" their reference can vary across models. In other words, $=$ is treated like a logical constant.

Adding $=$ in this way extends the expressive power of the language. An abstract, but simple example serves to illustrate this. We set up two simple models M_1, M_2:

- $D_{M_1} = \{1, 2\}$
- $I_{M_1}(R) = \{\langle 1, 1\rangle, \langle 2, 2\rangle\}$
- $D_{M_2} = \{1, 2\}$
- $I_{M_2}(R) = \{\langle 1, 1\rangle, \langle 2, 2\rangle, \langle 1, 2\rangle\}$

Now we evaluate the following two formulas in each of these models :

(15) $\exists x \exists y Rxy$
(16) $\exists x \exists y(x \neq y \wedge Rxy)$

As is easily checked, (15) is true in both M_1 and M_2, whereas (16) is true only in the latter. I.e.:

$$\{M|V_{M,g}(16) = 1\} \subset \{M|V_{M,g}hbox(15) = 1\}$$

which means that (16) $\models$ (15) but (15) $\not\models$ (16).

16.4 Examples revisited

Let us now quickly check how the addition of $=$ helps to solve the problems we noted above with certain classes of expressions.

16.4.1 *Other*

(17) John loves someone and Bill loves someone
$\exists x Ljx \wedge \exists y Lby$
(18) John loves someone and Bill loves someone else
$\exists x \exists y(Ljx \wedge Lby \wedge x \neq y)$

As was noted, the representation of (17) is adequate, since the sentence does not exclude that John and Bill love the same person, and neither does the predicate logical representation. That is what differentiates (18) from (17), and with the help of the identity constant we can now make that explicit in the logical representation as well.

Let's consider the model given above:

- $D_M = \{\mathtt{j}, \mathtt{b}, \mathtt{m}\}$
- $I_M(j) = \mathtt{j}; I_M(b) = \mathtt{b}; I_M(m) = \mathtt{m}; I_M(L) = \{\langle \mathtt{j}, \mathtt{m}\rangle, \langle \mathtt{b}, \mathtt{m}\rangle\}$

It's easy to see that (15) is true and (16) is false in this model.

A model that satisfies both is:

- $D_M = \{\mathtt{j}, \mathtt{b}, \mathtt{m}\}$
- $I_M(j) = \mathtt{j}, I_M(b) = \mathtt{b}, I_M(m) = \mathtt{m}$
- $I_M(L) = \{\langle \mathtt{j}, \mathtt{m}\rangle, \langle \mathtt{b}, \mathtt{b}\rangle\}$

Generally, we have that (18) $\models$ (17), and (17) $\not\models$ (18).

16.4.2 Only

Let's consider the examples given above, along with representations that make use of the expressive power of =:

(19) John loves Mary $\rightsquigarrow Ljm$
(20) John loves only Mary $\rightsquigarrow Ljm \land \forall x(Ljx \to x = m)$
(21) Only John loves Mary $\rightsquigarrow Ljm \land \forall x(Lxm \to x = j)$

As we saw above, the following model:

- $D_M = \{\mathtt{j}, \mathtt{b}, \mathtt{m}, \mathtt{s}\}$
- $I_M(j) = \mathtt{j}; I_M(b) = \mathtt{b}; I_M(m) = \mathtt{m}; I_M(s) = \mathtt{s};$
  $I_M(L) = \{\langle \mathtt{j}, \mathtt{m}\rangle, \langle \mathtt{j}, \mathtt{s}\rangle, \langle \mathtt{b}, \mathtt{m}\rangle\}$

verifies (19), but falsifies (20) and (21). If we change the model into:

- $D_{M_1} = \{\mathtt{j}, \mathtt{b}, \mathtt{m}, \mathtt{s}\}$
- $I_{M_1}(j) = \mathtt{j}; I_{M_1}(b) = \mathtt{b}; I_{M_1}(m) = \mathtt{m}; I_{M_1}(s) = \mathtt{s};$
  $I_{M_1}(L) = \{\langle \mathtt{j}, \mathtt{m}\rangle, \langle \mathtt{b}, \mathtt{m}\rangle\}$

both (19) and (20) are true, but (21) is not. And if we change the original model into:

- $D_{M_2} = \{\mathtt{j}, \mathtt{b}, \mathtt{m}, \mathtt{s}\}$
- $I_{M_2}(j) = \mathtt{j}; I_{M2}(b) = \mathtt{b}; I_{M2}(m) = \mathtt{m}; I_{M_2}(s) = \mathtt{s};$
  $I_{M_2}(L) = \{\langle \mathtt{j}, \mathtt{m}\rangle, \langle \mathtt{j}, \mathtt{s}\rangle\}$

the result verifies (19) and (21), but not (20).

These observations show that (20) $\Vdash$ (19) and that (21) $\Vdash$ (19), but that (20) and (21) are independent: (20) $\not\Vdash$ (21) and (21) $\not\Vdash$ (20), i.e., neither implies the other.

Multiple occurrences of 'only' can also be handled, as illustrated in (2)):

(22) Only John loves only Mary $\rightsquigarrow$
$Ljm \land \forall x(Ljx \to x = m) \land \forall x(Lxm \to x = j)$

16.4.3 Numerals

The added expressive power provided by = also allows us to deal with numerals:

(23) There is at least one $P \rightsquigarrow \exists x Px$
(24) There is at most one $P \rightsquigarrow \forall x \forall y((Px \land Py) \to x = y)$
(25) There is exactly one $P \rightsquigarrow \exists x(Px \land \forall y(Py \to x = y))$

The existential quantifier guarantees the existence of at least one object with a certain property, which is illustrated by the case of 'at least one'.

The universal quantifier really means something like: 'Take an arbitrary object from the domain, inspect it, and then put it back.' The last part is crucial. To illustrate this, look at the case of 'at most one'.

We can paraphrase the formula in (24) as: 'Take an arbitrary object, see whether it has the property P; put it back, take another arbitrary object, inspect it: if in both cases the object has property P, it was the same object. This holds for all the objects that can be picked.'

The case of 'exactly one' can be treated a simple combination of 'at least one' and 'at most one', as is illustrated by (25).

The other numerals simply generalise the way in which 'one' is treated. Here is 'two':

(26) There are at least two Ps $\rightsquigarrow \exists x \exists y(x \neq y \wedge Px \wedge Py)$
(27) There are at most two Ps $\rightsquigarrow$
$\forall x \forall y \forall z((Px \wedge Py \wedge Pz) \rightarrow (x = y \vee x = z \vee y = z))$
(28) There are exactly two Ps $\rightsquigarrow$
$\exists x \exists y(x \neq y \wedge Px \wedge Py \wedge \forall z(Pz \rightarrow (z = x \vee z = y)))$

Exercise 1

a. Give a representation of 'There are at least two and at most three Ps'
b. Consider 'There is an infinite number of Ps'. Can that be represented? If not, why not? If yes, how?

16.4.4 Descriptions

Finally, definite descriptions. Consider once more the traditional example:

(29) The King of France is bald
$\exists x(KFx \wedge \forall y(KFy \rightarrow x = y) \wedge Bx)$

The representation of a sentence containing a definite description contains three elements:

1. Existence claim: $\exists x KFx$
2. Uniqueness claim: $\forall y(KFy \rightarrow x = y)$
3. Predication: Bx

So we can paraphrase the representation of (29) along the following lines: 'There is someone who is the King of France, there is at most one King of France, and he is bald.'

It is the uniqueness claim that is contained in a statement containing a description that takes care of the problem that was noted above: there cannot be two Kings of France, one bold, and one with hair.

This is basically the analysis that Bertrand Russell gives of definite descriptions. More on Russell's definition, and on the alternatives that have been proposed, in the philosophical excursus that follows this chapter.

16.4.5 Compressed formulations

Sometimes translations can be stated in a more compressed form, e.g.:

(30) John loves only Mary $\rightsquigarrow$
$Ljm \wedge \forall x(Ljx \rightarrow x = m) \Leftrightarrow \forall x(Ljx \leftrightarrow x = m)$

(31) King of France is bald $\rightsquigarrow$
$\exists x(KFx \wedge \forall y(KFy \rightarrow x = y) \wedge Bx) \Leftrightarrow \exists x \forall y((KFy \leftrightarrow x = y) \wedge Bx)$

(32) There is exactly one P $\rightsquigarrow$
$\exists x(Px \wedge \forall y(Py \rightarrow x = y)) \Leftrightarrow \exists x \forall y(Py \leftrightarrow x = y)$

As for (30) note that $\forall x(Ljx \leftrightarrow x = m)$ is equivalent to $\forall x((Ljx \rightarrow x = m) \wedge (x = m \rightarrow Ljx))$ and that Ljm is equivalent to $\forall x(x = m \rightarrow Ljx)$.

Exercise 2 Translate the following sentences. Specify the domain and the translation key.

a. There is no greatest number
b. If everything has a cause, then there is something that is a cause of everything
c. Everyone has two parents
d. Parallel lines do not intersect
e. If you only admire yourself, then nobody will admire you

16.5 Models and validity

As we have seen, the addition of $=$ is taken care of by giving it a fixed interpretation as the smallest reflexive relation on a domain D. I.e., we stipulate that

$$I_M(=) = \{\langle d, d\rangle \mid d \in D_M\}$$

for every M.[2] In all other respects the semantics of predicate logical languages remains the same.

16.6 Model checking

Let M be the following model:

- $D_M = \{1, 2, 3, 4\}$
- $I_M(P) = \{1, 3\}; I_M(R) = \{\langle 1, 2\rangle, \langle 2, 1\rangle, \langle 1, 3\rangle, \langle 3, 3\rangle\}$

Then M is represented by the following graph:

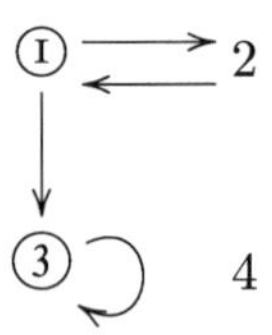

Using '$M \models \phi$' as notation for 'ϕ is true in model M', we can check that in this model M the following holds:

1. $M \models \exists x(Rxx \wedge \forall y(Rxy \rightarrow x = y))$
2. $M \models \forall x(Px \rightarrow \exists yRyx)$
3. $M \models \exists x\forall y(\neg\exists zRzy \leftrightarrow x = y)$
4. $M \not\models \forall x\forall y(Rxy \rightarrow Ryx)$
5. $M \not\models \forall x(\exists yRyx \rightarrow Px)$
6. $M \not\models \forall x(\exists yRxy \rightarrow \exists y(x \neq y \wedge Rxy))$

By way of example, consider case (1). The formula asserts that there exists a point x that stands in the R-relation to itself and only to itself. I.e., there is a point in the graph that has an arrow to itself, and only to itself: x has an arrow to x, and if x has an arrow to a point y, then $x = y$. That is true: (3) has an arrow to itself, but not to any of the other points, 1, 2 and 4.

As a second example consider case (5). This states that if a point has an arrow arriving in it, it is encircled. This is falsified by the existence of point 2: in 2 an arrow arrives, viz., from 1, but 2 does not have a circle around it.

We can also give a more formal account by reasoning with the truth definition. Here is what that would look like for case (4):

$$\langle 1,2\rangle \in I_M(R) \quad \text{(a)}$$
$$\text{so } V_M([1/y][2/x]Ryx) = 1 \quad \text{(b)}$$
$$\text{hence } V_M([2/x]\exists yRyx) = 1 \quad \text{(c)}$$
$$2 \notin I_M(P) \quad \text{(d)}$$
$$\text{hence } V_M([2/x]Px) = 0 \quad \text{(e)}$$
$$\text{so } V_M([2/x]\exists yRyx \rightarrow Px) = 0 \quad \text{(f)}$$
$$\text{hence } V_M(\forall x(\exists yRyx \rightarrow Px)) = 0 \quad \text{(g)}$$
$$\text{thus } M \not\models \forall x(\exists yRyx \rightarrow Px) \quad \text{(h)}$$

Exercise 3 Do the remaining cases.

Exercise 4 Consider the following model for a predicate logical language with a 1-place predicate letter A, and a 2-place predicate letter R:

$$D = \{1,2,3,4,5\}$$
$$I(A) = \{1,2,5\}$$
$$I(R) = \{\langle 1,2\rangle, \langle 1,3\rangle, \langle 1,4\rangle, \langle 2,4\rangle, \langle 2,5\rangle, \langle 4,4\rangle, \langle 5,3\rangle, \langle 5,5\rangle\}$$

a. Draw a graph of the model
b. Which of the following formulas are true in the model? Motivate your answer.
    i. $\forall xRxx$
    ii. $\exists x\exists y\exists z(x \neq y \wedge x \neq z \wedge y \neq z \wedge \forall w(Aw \leftrightarrow (w = x \vee w = y \vee w = z)))$

iii. $\forall x \forall y(Rxy \vee Ryx \vee x = y)$
iv. $\forall x \forall y \forall z((Rxy \wedge Ryz) \rightarrow Rxz)$
v. $\forall x \forall y(Rxy \leftrightarrow \neg Ryx)$
vi. $\forall x(Ax \rightarrow \exists y(Ay \wedge Rxy))$

16.6.1 Validity

Like the semantics, the definition of validity does not change either. A formula ϕ is universally valid iff it is true in every model under every assignment, and an argument scheme $\phi_1, \ldots, \phi_n / \psi$ is valid iff every model and very assignment that makes all the premisses true, also makes the conclusion true.

Proving that a formula or an argument scheme is valid be done by reasoning in the meta-language about the truth definition. An example:

$$\models \forall x \forall y(x = y \rightarrow (Px \rightarrow Py))$$

This formula is also known as Leibniz's 'law of indiscernibility of identicals': identity implies that all properties are shared.[3] Here is a proof:

Proof. Take arbitrary $d, d' \in D$. If $V_{M,g[x/d,y/d']}(x = y) = 1$, then $d = d'$, and thus $g[x/d, y/d'] = g[x/d, y/d]$. Suppose $V_{M,g[x/d,y/d]}Px = 1$; then $V_{M,g[x/d,y/d]}Py = 1$ follows immediately. Since d, d' were arbitrarily chosen, the result follows. □

Exercise 5 Prove the following:

a. $\models \exists x\, x = a$
b. $\models \forall x \forall y((x = a \wedge y = a) \rightarrow x = y)$
c. $\models \exists x \exists y\, x = y$
d. $\forall x(Px \rightarrow Qx), \exists x(x = a \wedge Px) \models Qa$
e. $\exists x(Px \wedge \forall y(Py \rightarrow x = y), \exists x(Qx \wedge \forall y(Qy \rightarrow x = y) \models \forall x \forall y((Px \wedge Py \wedge Qx \wedge Qy) \rightarrow x = y)$

Proving that an argument scheme is not valid also proceeds in the usual way, i.e., by constructing a counterexample. By way of illustration we show that:

$$\forall x \exists y(x \neq y) \not\models \exists x \exists y \exists z(x \neq y \wedge x \neq z \wedge y \neq z)$$

The premise states that for every entity there is a different one. The conclusion is that therefore there are at least three entities. A counterexample should make the premise true, and the conclusion false. The latter requirement means that the domain should contain at most two elements, so $D = \{1\}$ or $D = \{1,2\}$. (Recall that $D = \emptyset$ is not allowed.) In the first case the premise is false, but in the second case it is true: for every element one can find an element that is different. For 1 this is 2 and for 2 this is 1.

This means that any M such that $D_M = \{1,2\}$ is a counterexample, since in such M we have:

- $V_{M,g}(\forall x \exists y (x \neq y)) = 1$
- $V_{M,g}(\exists x \exists y \exists z (x \neq y \land x \neq z \land y \neq z)) = 0$

Exercise 6 Prove that the following argument schemes are invalid by constructing a counterexample:

a. $\forall x Rxx \,/\, \forall x \forall y Rxy$
b. $\forall x \forall y (Rxy \to Ryx), \forall x \forall y \forall z ((Rxy \land Ryz) \to Rxz) \,/\, \exists x Rxx$
c. $\forall x \exists y (Rxy \land x \neq y), \forall x \forall y \forall z ((Rxy \land Ryz) \to Rxz) \,/\, \forall x \forall y (x = y \lor Rxy \lor Ryx)$
d. $\exists x \exists y \forall z (x = z \lor y = z) \,/\, \forall x \forall y (x = y)$
e. $\forall x (Ax \leftrightarrow \forall y Rxy), \exists x \forall y (Ay \leftrightarrow x = y) \,/\, \forall x \forall y ((Rxx \land Ryy) \to x = y)$

17
Excursus: more on descriptions

17.1 The topic

As was already mentioned in the chapter on identity, definite descriptions abound in all kinds of contexts. In natural languages, obviously, but also in more specialised forms of discourse, such that of mathematics and the various sciences. Their usefulness resides in the fact that they allow us to identify an object in terms of its properties and/or its relations with other objects.

To repeat an example given in the previous chapter: If two lines l_1 and l_2 intersect, we can designate the intersection with a name, say P_1. But we can also use a description: 'the intersection of l_1 and l_2'. This is much more informative since it is the description by itself that allows us to determine the object, something which the use of a mere name cannot do.

It is the versatility of definite descriptions, which can make use of all the expressive resources of a language, that make them an indispensable part of any language that is used to talk about a complex and partly unknown reality. It is simply impossible to set up an adequate reservoir of names prior to our investigations. But we need to be able to talk about what we want to investigate, formulate hypotheses, and speculate about possible outcomes beforehand. Definite descriptions provide us with the means to do that.

In logic descriptions occupy a special place since the seminal work of Frege and Russell, who developed different ways of dealing with definite descriptions in the context of a logical language. In the chapter on identity we have embraced Russell's contextual analysis of definite descriptions, which was presented in Russell (1905). Certainly in the context of logic, this analysis has become a de facto standard. But as our reading of Strawson's paper (Strawson, 1950) will make clear, that does not mean that it has gone unchallenged.

In order to provide a bit more background for the Russell – Strawson debate we will begin with a brief sketch of the work of Frege on descriptions, which inspired Russell to define his alternative.

Frege on identity

In what is one of the most influential papers in analytic philosophy, the 1892 paper 'On Sense and Reference' (Frege, 1948), Frege starts with a conundrum with regard to identity statements. Suppose the identity statement $a = b$ is true, then what is the difference between $a = a$ and $a = b$?

Intuitively we assign a quite different status to these two statements: $a = a$ is analytic (i.e., true solely on the basis of its meaning and thus not something that gives us information about the world) and a priori (i.e., its truth can be recognised without any need for empirical evidence). $a = b$ on the other hand is synthetic (i.e., it does tell us something about the way the world is) and a posteriori (i.e., its truth can be recognised only on the basis of empirical evidence).

How are we to account for this? First of all, we need to ask the question what identity is a relation between? Is it a relation between signs? Or one between objects? These seem to be the only two options we have, but they are both not satisfactory.

If we regard identity as a relation between signs, then identity statements do not say anything about objects in the world. After all, the relation between sign and object is arbitrary, so the fact that two signs are identical says nothing about identity or non-identity of objects. However, if we construe identity as a relation between objects it seems that we lack a way of accounting for the intuition mention above, viz., that the cognitive status of $a = a$ and $a = b$ is different.

Frege's solution proceeds in terms of a distinction between what he calls 'sense' (German: 'Sinn') and 'reference' (German: 'Bedeutung').[1] The reference of an expression is what it stands for, in the case of a name, it is an object. The sense is 'the way in which the reference is given'. i.e., a descriptive content that picks out what a name refers to. In this way, Frege can maintain that identity is a relation between objects, and account for the intuition regarding the difference in cognitive status in terms of a difference in sense.[2]

Descriptions

Crucial for this to work is Frege's conception of 'name'. Anything that refers to an individual counts as such: proper names, descriptions, a functional expressions applied to an argument, ... All have sense, and that means that Frege de facto analyses proper names as definite descriptions. And that gives the problem of non-referring names a definite twist: if all names are descriptions, everything hinges on how we deal with descriptions that fail to refer.[3]

Note that the problem of failure of reference can have two sources: a description may lack reference (existence failure), or it may refer to more than one entity (uniqueness failure).

From a general point of view there are two ways of dealing with the relation between descriptions and reference.[4] There is Russell's analysis: which maintains that descriptions assert existence and uniqueness. And there is Frege's approach that holds that descriptions presuppose existence and uniqueness. The difference shows up in what is assumed to be the consequence when a description fails on existence and/or uniqueness. For Russell a statement containing such a description is false, for Frege it lacks a truth value.

In other words the challenge that failing descriptions pose is directly connected with a fundamental principle of logic, viz., the principle of excluded middle $\phi \vee \neg\phi$. Russell's analysis opts to maintain excluded middle, whereas Frege's analysis accepts truth-value gaps and thus abandons the principle. As we shall see this difference corresponds directly with two different views on how descriptions are analysed syntactically, and hence also semantically.

Compositionality

The principle of compositionality plays a key role in this:

> The meaning (reference) of a complex expression is determined by the meanings (references) of its component parts and the way in which these are combined

It allows us to give a finite characterisation of syntax and semantics of (potentially) infinite sets of expressions of a language. Also it is often invoked as a principle that accounts for the ability of language users use and understand new expressions.

How does it affect the way we analyse descriptions? From an intuitive point of view quantified phrases are constituents:

(1) Every man is happy
(2) Some men who like to dance are happy
(3) The man wearing a hat is happy

According to compositionality the meaning (reference) should be a function of the meaning (reference) of the respective constituent parts.

However, whereas 'John' in 'John is happy' can be analysed in terms of an expression that refers, viz., j in Hj, no such analysis is forthcoming for 'Every man is happy': that cannot be represented as $H(\text{every man})$. The reason is obvious: whereas 'John' refers to an individual 'Every man' does not.[5]

But what about definite descriptions? Descriptions are complex phrases, like 'some man' and 'every man', but unlike them they do refer to individuals, just like proper names do. So descriptions share characteristics both with quantified phrases and with constants and variables.

Russell's choice is to treat them in the same way as other quantified phrases. But an alternative is to analyse them in the same way as other individual-denoting phrases, such as constants and variables.

Adding descriptions as terms

We give a brief sketch of the second way of dealing with description in a language of predicate logic, because Russell's analysis is in part motivated by concerns about the consequences of this way of going about.

Recall that expressions with a free occurrence of a variable express properties: Px can read as 'being P'.[6] The basic idea is to treat the definite article as an expression that turns such an expression into an individual denoting expression. This is done by means of a new logical expression, called the 'iota-operator':

If ϕ is a formula, then $\iota x\phi$ is a term

Thus, the term ιxPx stands for 'the P', the term $\iota x(Px \wedge Rcx)$ stands for 'the P that stands in the relation R to c', and so on.

As terms, descriptions operate in the same way as constants and variables: $Q(\iota xPx)$ represents 'the P is Q', and $S(a, \iota x(Px \wedge Rxc))$ expresses 'a stands in the relation S to the P that stands in the relation R to c'.

The definition of the syntax becomes slightly more complicated. Since terms are formed from formulas but also occur in formulas, the syntax is now a simultaneous inductive definition of two classes of expressions, viz., that of terms and that of formulas.

What about the semantics of the ι-operator? That is given by the following clause:

$$[\![\iota x\phi]\!]_{M,g} = \text{the unique } d \in D_M : V_{M,g[d/x]}(\phi) = 1$$

Note that if there is no individual that satisfies ϕ, or if there is more than one, then $[\![\iota x\phi]\!]_M$ is undefined. Compositionality dictates that if a subexpression of an expression is undefined then so is the expression itself. And hat means that excluded middle, i.e., $\phi \vee \neg\phi$, fails as a general principle.

The nil-element

Frege acknowledged this and provided a way out. He maintains that lacking a reference is a shortcoming of natural language expressions, a proper (logical) language always supplies a reference for any name (including descriptions).[7]

In the context of a formal language Frege introduces a distinguished 'nil-element' d_0 for descriptions that do not refer. In that way the principle of excluded middle can be saved. This requires two moves.

First, we define:

$[\![\iota x\phi]\!]_M$ = the unique $d \in D_M : V_{M,g[d/x]}(\phi) = 1$ if such d exists; $= d_0$ otherwise

And second, we exclude d_0 from the interpretation of all n-ary predicate constants and individual constants:

$$\text{For all } c, P^n, M\colon d_0 \neq I_M(c), \notin I_M(P^n)$$

Now this is a purely formal solution, but in a formal context such moves are not uncommon. One could maintain that the formal nature of the solution is an objection only in the context of natural language. And that would mean that in the context of natural language giving up bi-valence should be an option.

The Russell – Strawson debate

This sets the stage for the debate between Russell and Strawson: Russell motivates his analysis in part by objecting to Frege, and Strawson can be read as taking a Fregean stance, but accepting the consequences w.r.t. bi-valence when it comes to natural language. Strawson does not, however, fall back to Frege's position, since his concern is natural language as such. And as we shall see, that leads him to make an important distinction, viz., that between meaning and use, between semantics and pragmatics.

Russell's theory of description has been very influential. It had gone basically unchallenged until Strawson published his paper in 1951. The main reason why getting descriptions right is so important for Russell is the epistemological distinction between what he calls 'knowledge by acquaintance' and 'knowledge by description'. The first arises from direct (unmediated) relation between knower and object and its properties; i.e., knowledge of one's own sense data and mental states. The second, on the other hand, depends on identification of objects in terms of description; i.e., all knowledge of the physical world and the mental life of other people. This highlights that descriptions are the primary means of identifying objects in the external world.

Strawson concerns, on the other hand, are largely motivated by the relationship between logic and natural language. He takes issue with the dominance of referentialism in semantics. It is the assumption, he claims, that reference, and by extension truth and falsity, need to be ascribed to expressions (sentences) that creates the problem that Russell then attempts to solve by diverging from the grammatical structure of natural language. But if we accept that it is not expressions that refer, but that it is our use of them that establishes reference, and that truth and falsity are not properties of sentences but of utterances of sentences, then the problem disappears.

This debate is important, not only because it concerns a key category of expressions, viz., descriptions, but also because it points to an important discussion, viz., what are the limits of the application of logic to natural language? We will come back to that issue in a later excursus, when we discuss the approach of H.P. Grice.

17.2 The authors

Bertrand Russell

For more information on Russell we refer to the sketch that was given in the introductory chapter.

Peter Strawson

Peter Strawson (1919 – 2006) was an English philosopher who spent almost his entire academic life at Oxford University. He studied Philosophy, Politics and Economics there, under supervision of, among others, H.P. Grice. After a period of service in the army during the Second World War, he was appointed at Oxford University, first as a lecturer, then as a fellow. In 1968 he become the successor of Gilbert Ryle as Waynflete professor of metaphysics. He retired in 1987 but remained academically active until his death in 2006.

Strawson counts as one of the most important English philosophers in the second half of the twentieth century. He was a contemporary of J.L. Austin, whose ordinary language philosophy was highly influential in the fifties and early sixties. Austin emphasised a descriptive approach to natural language as a philosophical method and generally eschewed the big abstract questions of the philosophical tradition. Strawson, on the other hand, was very much a systematic thinker, who was convinced that it was the task of philosophy to tackle these questions. What Strawson and the philosophers in the ordinary language school did have in common was a deeply felt conviction that natural language was too complex and/or too unsystematic to allow for any strict, logical account. As we shall see this is also the core of his criticism of Russell.

Strawson work is broad, and ranges from philosophy of language, logic and epistemology to metaphysics and moral philosophy. He did not write much on issues in the latter field but his discussion of the problem of free will in 'Freedom and Resentment' (Strawson, 1962) has been very influential and remains one of the most cited and discussed papers on this issue to this very day. Strawson also wrote on logic and defended a deflationary view on truth, arguing against Austin's form of a correspondence conception. In later work he also wrote on scepticism and naturalism.

The main body of Strawson's work was in metaphysics, where he practised what he called 'descriptive metaphysics', i.e., a metaphysics that tries to come up with substantial answers to the core metaphysical questions. Two books in particular are important, *Individuals* (Strawson, 1959) and *The Bounds of Sense* (Strawson, 1966). In the first book Strawson explores various issues concerning properties and individuals, the way in which they can referred and described, thought and imagined. The second book is a critical engagement with Kant and Kantian themes.

There are various themes that occur and re-occur throughout Strawson's extensive oeuvre. For our concerns, what is the most relevant one is his insistence that natural language cannot be captured by means of formal logic, but has to be studied and appreciated on its own terms. Thus for Strawson a detailed analysis of the basic subject – predicate structure of natural languages is both starting point and end point: there is no point in departing from that.[8] The way in various types of expressions that fit into this scheme and the variety of ways in which they refer and thus contribute to meaning are the real substance of a philosophical engagement with natural language.

17.3 The texts

Russell, 'On Denoting'

Russell starts with a brief indication of why the analysis of denoting phrases is important: the distinction between knowledge by acquaintance and knowledge by description. By 'denoting phrases' Russell means quantified expressions and the basic principle of his theory of denoting he expresses as follows:

> [that] denoting phrases never have any meaning in themselves, but [that] every proposition in whose verbal expression they occur has a meaning (page 482)

Basic denoting phrases 'everything', 'something', 'nothing' are dealt with as syncategorematically defined operations on what he calls 'propositional functions', i.e., expressions with a free occurrence of a variable. Thus 'C(everything)' means '$C(x)$ is always true', 'C(something)' means '$C(x)$ is not always false', and so on.

The definitions of complex quantified phrases, 'every P, some P, no P', follow the same pattern. 'C(every P)" means ' "If $P(x)$ then $C(x)$ is true" is always true', 'C(some P)' means 'It is false that "$P(x)$ and $C(x)$" is always false', and so on.

It is important to note that Russell's definitions are contextual. Denoting phrases do not have an independent interpretation, they are defined in the context of a propositional function. I.e., the theory does not tell you what, e.g., 'everything' means, it tells you what the meaning is of a formula in which 'everything' occurs.

Descriptions are also treated contextually. 'C(the P)' means 'It is not always false of x that Px and that Cx and that "if Px then y is identical to x" is always true of y'. Note that this entails that there exists something that is P and that there is at most one thing that is P

Russell continues with providing arguments to support his analyses. Some of these argument are indirect: other approaches fail. Other arguments are direct: his approach 'solves puzzles'.

The indirect arguments center concern two answers to the key question of how to deal with non-referring descriptions. viz., those of Meinong and Frege.

Meinong assumes that non-referring descriptions do denote, but that their denotations are non-actual objects.[9] Frege, as we have seen, assumes that non-referring descriptions do denote and introduces a special 'nil-element' to act as such.

Russell then goes on to criticise both. Against Frege, Russell's main argument is that his solution is artificial. And against Meinong, his argument is that his solution violates principle of non-contradiction $\neg(\phi \wedge \neg\phi)$.

Russell's direct arguments in favour of his approach concern three what he calls 'puzzles'.

The first is concerned with 'substitution of identicals' and is illustrated as follows:

(4) George IV wished to know whether Scott was the author of *Waverley*
(5) Scott is the author of *Waverley*
(6) George IV wished to know whether Scott was Scott

This is an invalid argument, but if we take descriptions to function the same way as names, it would appear valid.

Because descriptions have scope, Russell can solve this. A description may have what he calls a 'primary occurrence' and 'a secondary occurrence'. In our predicate logical terms this looks like:

- $\exists x(\text{AW}x \wedge \forall y(\text{AW}y \rightarrow y = x) \wedge \text{WK}(g4, x = s))$: primary occurrence
- $\text{WK}(g4, \exists x(\text{AW}x \wedge \forall y(\text{AW}y \rightarrow y = x) \wedge x = s))$: secondary occurrence

In order to show that the argument above does not go through we need to analyse the description as having a primary occurrence, i.e., as being outside the scope of the term 'wished to know'.

The same mechanism allows for two ways of reading 'The King of France is not bald':

- $\exists x(\text{KF}x \wedge \forall y(\text{KF}y \rightarrow y = x) \wedge \neg Bx))$: false
- $\neg\exists x(\text{KF}x \wedge \forall y(\text{KF}y \rightarrow y = x) \wedge Bx))$: true

And this solves the puzzle concerning the principle of excluded middle.

A third argument is concerned with the distinction between meaning and denotation. It uses as an example the description 'The meaning of the first line of Grey's Elegy', and is therefore know in the literature as 'The Grey's Elegy argument'. The exact point of the argument is highly controversial, and a number of very complex arguments have been proposed that argue for wildly different interpretations. [We will therefore not go into further here and skip this part of the paper.][10]

Strawson, 'On Referring'

Strawson's paper starts with a short introduction to Russell's theory of descriptions. He emphasises that it is based on a rejection of the assumption that the grammatical subject – predicate form is reflected in the logical form of sentences that contain descriptions as their subject term: a grammatical subject need not be a logical subject, and in this case it is not.

He continues by pointing out that Russell did accept that in some cases grammatical subjects are also logical subjects, viz., when we deal with what he called 'logically proper names'. These are expressions that are meaningless when they lack a reference, and that distinguishes them from descriptions, which can be meaningful despite lacking a reference.

This is what Strawson takes issue with. In order to distinguish his position from that of Russell he prefers to use the term 'expression used in the uniquely referring way ' to indicate the class of expressions that we are dealing, and reserves 'description' to what is analysed in accordance with Russell's theory. So for Strawson there are no descriptions.

Note the reference to use in Strawson's terminology. Strawson develops his alternative theory, in the second part of the paper, in terms of that. He makes a distinction between a sentence, the use of a sentence, and the utterance of a sentence. The distinction between the latter two is explained as follows. Utterances are unique, no two utterances, even simultaneously, are the same. Uses, however, can be different or the same. If two people utter 'The King of France is bald' at the same time to refer to a particular king, their different utterances correspond to the same use. However if the two utterances are made at different to refer to different kings, not only the utterances but also the uses are different.

Strawson then continues to spell out the consequence: reference and truth are not to be associated with expressions and sentences, but are connected with uses made of them. Thus:

> Generally, as against Russell, I shall say this. Meaning (in at least one important sense) is a function of the sentence or expression; mentioning and referring and truth or falsity, are functions of the use of the sentence or expression. (page 327)

Meaning is analysed by Strawson as giving 'general directions' for use. But it is distinct from any particular concrete use, so an expression can be meaningful ('significant' is the term Strawson uses) without a particular use being successful in referring.

Strawson continues with a diagnosis of Russell's mistake in these terms, and in the course of that points out that the verb 'to mean' in English is ambiguous.

[The first three parts contain both the core of Strawson's arguments against Russell and the essence of his alternative. The following sections work out a number of details. For completeness sake a brief indication of their contents follows, but for the discussion in class they can be skipped.]

In the third part of the paper Strawson enters into a detailed discussion of various situations. Upshot of that is the claim that existence of a referent of a uniquely referring expression is not something that is asserted by a sentence containing that expression, but something that is presupposed: if it fails 'the question of whether [the sentence] is true or false simply does not arise.' (page 330).

Uses of sentences with expressions that fail to refer are called 'spurious', and cover a wide range of cases, including fiction, imagination, and so on. In such cases the existence presupposition is, so to speak, 'suspended'. Without an explicit indication that such a use is intended, however, Strawson maintains that using a uniquely referring expression comes with the presupposition of reference.

The attempts, such as Russell's, to 'reduce' this to explicit assertion is misguided:

> The general moral of all this is that communication is much less a matter of explicit or disguised assertion than logicians used to suppose. (p. 333)

The fourth part of the paper is devoted to a discussion about the role of referring and ascribing as part of what it is to make an assertion. Subject terms refer, predicates ascribe (or classify). Both act are needed in order to make an assertion, i.e., to state a fact. The difference resides in the conventions for their use. In the case of ascriptive expressions these are simple: it can be applied to an entity provided the entity has the relevant characteristics, and that is what is contained in its use. In the case of referring expressions things are more complex: fulfilment of the existence and uniqueness conditions is not contained in the use, but presupposed by it.

Strawson then goes on to diagnose the failure to recognise this distinction, and finds fault with logicians, who, he claims, are too much occupied with definitions and are led astray by the use of formal languages. Strawson then continues by illustrating the importance of the distinction.

The last part of the paper contains a short description of three further problems about referring uses of expressions: indefinite reference; identification statements; and subjects and predicates.

17.4 Study and discussion questions

Study questions

Russell

[Not including the 'Grey's Elegy argument', i.e., pp. 486–488]

- What are 'denoting phrases'?
- What is the distinction between knowledge by acquaintance and knowledge by description? And why is it important here?
- What is a propositional function?
- Translate Russell's representation on p. 480 in predicate logic.
- *Idem* for the representations on p. 481
- *Idem* for the representations on p. 482
- Why does Meinong's theory breach the law of non-contradiction?
- What is Russell's first problem with Frege's approach in terms of meaning and denotation (i.e., what was called 'sense' and 'reference' in the introduction)?
- And what is his second objection?
- Why is the puzzle of substitution of identicals a problem?
- And the puzzle of excluded middle?
- What are primary and secondary occurrences ? How does the distinction help to solve the identicals problem?
- What is Russell's view on the usefulness of identity statements?

Strawson

[Only parts I – III]

- What are 'expressions with uniquely referring use'?
- Strawson claims that Russell's theory was based on his rejection of two 'obviously bad arguments'; what are these arguments?
- What is the distinction between a grammatical subject and a logical subject?
- Why does Strawson think it is an important distinction?
- What are logically proper names?
- Why are descriptions not logically proper names?
- What is the distinction between the use of an expression and an utterance of it?
- What is 'refers to *a*' a property of? And 'is true?
- What is meaning according to Strawson? How are meaning and use related?
- How does Strawson argue that existence of a referent is *not* logically implied (entailed)?
- And what is the connection with the use of an expression?

- Strawson says that the definite article 'acts as a signal'. What does it signal? And what accounts for the signalling function?

Discussion questions

- How much difference between the syntactic structure of a given natural language and that of a formal language is unproblematic? Discuss with reference to Strawson's views on the logical relevance of the grammatical subject – predicate distinction.
- Can you think of a way to *decide* between the Russell and the Strawson analyses? What kind of observations, thought experiments, arguments, . . . might do the trick?
- Strawson claims (p. 329) that 'knowing the meaning hasn't anything to do with knowing about any particular use of the sentence to talk about anything'. Discuss.
- Quine relies on Russell's description theory. Could his ontological criterion also be formulated using (something like) Strawson's approach?

17.5 Further reading

The analysis of definite descriptions continues to be a topic in philosophy of language, and in natural language semantics. Much debated topics center around the distinction between referential and attributive use of description, originally proposed by Keith Donnellan (Donnellan, 1966), and that between semantic reference and speaker's reference, that goes back to Saul Kripke (Kripke, 1979). For more on that see also chapter 26. For an overview of semantic issues, see Abbott (2008).

18
Relations and orderings

18.1 Introduction

In this chapter we introduce a number of general, systematic properties of relations that play a key role in a large variety of arguments. And we will introduce some standard way of using relations with certain properties to order sets.

18.1.1 Reasoning with relations

In many argument schemes in which relations figure in premises and/or conclusion, the properties of those relations play a key role in determining whether the argument is valid or not.

As usual we start by illustrating what is at stake by looking at a couple of simple examples. As a first example consider the following piece of reasoning:

(1) John is bigger than Bill
(2) Bill is bigger than Tom
(3) So, John is bigger than Tom

This is a valid argument, and its validity depends on the meaning of the 'bigger than' relation. For the same argument with 'is bigger than' replaced by 'admires' is not valid:

(4) John admires Bill
(5) Bill admires Tom
(6) So, John admires Tom

Here is a slightly more complicated example with the 'bigger than' relation:

(7) John is bigger than everyone else except Bill
(8) Bill is bigger than everyone else except John
(9) So, Johan and Bill are equal in height

Again, this is a valid argument, and it is so because of the properties of the 'bigger than' relation.

Another examples involve family-relations:

(10) Sue is Mary's mother
(11) So, Mary is not Sue's mother

The validity of this argument depends on the 'mother of' relation. And here is a slightly more complicated example of an argument involving the 'brother of' relation:

(12) John is Robin's brother
(13) Robin is not John's brother
(14) So, Robin is a woman

But it is not always only the properties of relations that play a role, the domain may also have a say in what comes out as holding. I.e., the same argument when interpreted in different domains may hold in one, but not the other:

(15) x is not bigger than y
(16) y is not bigger than x
(17) So x and y are identical

This is a valid argument if we take x and y to range over natural numbers, but it is not if they range over people.

So, the validity of an argument may be determined by systematic properties of relations, and in some cases also by the nature of the domain on which they are interpreted.

18.1.2 Assigning order

Relations and their properties are also key elements of orderings: systematic ways of arranging the elements in a set. By way of illustration we look at two different ways to analyse the structure of time.

First of all, we can conceptualise time as a straight line, as something that progresses linearly from the past, through the present, into the future, as visualised in figure 18.1.

$$\ldots \longrightarrow t_{-2} \longrightarrow t_{-1} \longrightarrow t_0 \longrightarrow t_1 \longrightarrow t_2 \longrightarrow \ldots$$

Figure 18.1: Linear time

Here the arrow represents the relation 'is earlier than', t_0 indicates the present, with to its left the past stretching out indefinitely, and to its right the future. The core feature of this picture of time is that points in time are conceptualised as lying on a straight line connected, which means that for every two points it is determined how they are related, i.e., which precedes which. And thus, from any given point in time t, the past with respect to t is fixed: it consists of the points lying to its left on the straight line, as is the future: all the points lying to its right.

Another conception of time is that of branching time, as visualised in figure 18.2.

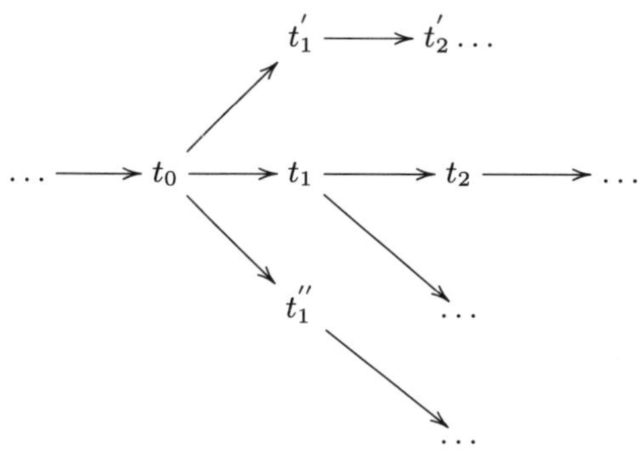

Figure 18.2: Branching time

Time is conceptualised here as having a branching structure: at every point there are a number of ways in which time can proceed. Again. the arrow represents the 'earlier than' relation but in this picture it has different properties: it no longer is the case that any two points are connected by the 'earlier than' relation. For example, t_1, $t_1^{'}$, $t_1^{''}$ are simultaneous and represent different continuations of the immediately preceding point $t_{)}$. Interpreting the latter as the present, these points and the branches on which they lie, thus represent different futures.

Whether a similar conceptualisation of the past of any given point t makes sense is another matter, that we can leave out of consideration here. That requires a separate modelling decision. And the same goes for whether one wants to allow for an infinite number of branches.

It is clear that these two conceptualisations of time embody all kinds of assumptions, some philosophical, and some physical. And these manifest themselves also in the (in)validity of temporal arguments. For example, whether one accepts an argument of the form: 'Some event e will happen. Therefore, it has always been the case that e will happen.' is closely connected to one's conceptualisation of the structure of time.

This example illustrates that the ordering of a given domain, in this case, that a relation, in the case 'earlier than' gives rise to, can be characterised in terms of the properties we assume that hold of the relation. Again, it is systematic properties of relations that play a key role.

18.2 Some core properties of relations

In this section we review a number of systematic properties and illustrate them with some simple examples.

18.2.1 Symmetry

The first property is that of symmetry. It is defined as follows:

Definition 30 R is symmetric iff $\forall x \forall y(Rxy \rightarrow Ryx)$

Symmetry requires that if a relation holds between two arbitrary points x and y it also holds between y and x.

We can use a simple diagram by way of illustration.

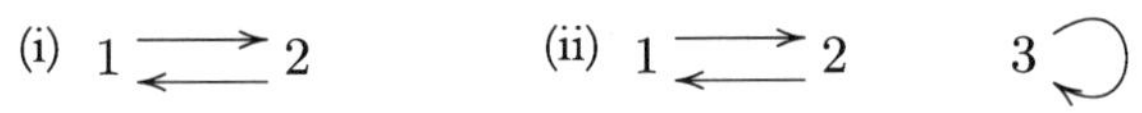

Figure 18.3: Cases of symmetry

Examples of symmetric relations are identity, 'as big as', 'related by blood', ...

As was already noted earlier, whether a relation has a certain property may depend on the domain. In the case of symmetry we can observe that for example the relation 'brother of' is not symmetric on the domain of people, but that it is symmetric on the domain of all male people.

18.2.2 Asymmetry

The opposite of symmetry is asymmetry:

Definition 31 R is asymmetric iff $\forall x \forall y(Rxy \rightarrow \neg Ryx)$

Asymmetry requires that if a relation holds between two arbitrary points x and y it does not hold between y and x.

Again, we can use a simple diagram by way of illustration.

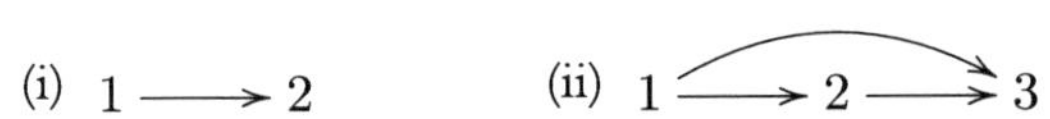

Figure 18.4: Cases of asymmetry

Examples of asymmetric relations are 'bigger than', 'parent of', ...

Note that asymmetry is not just 'not being symmetric': it is a much stronger requirement. Thus in the following diagram the relation is not symmetric, but also not asymmetric:

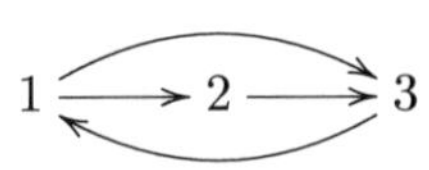

18.2.3 Anti-symmetry

A third property that has to do with symmetry is that of anti-symmetry:

Definition 32 R is anti-symmetric iff $\forall x \forall y(x \neq y \rightarrow (Rxy \rightarrow \neg Ryx))$

A relation is anti-symmetric if for any two different points it is asymmetry.

Again a pictorial illustration:

Figure 18.5: Cases of anti-symmetry

Examples of anti-symmetric relations are 'greater than or equal to', 'at least as big as' (on the domain of numbers), ...

Note that anti-symmetry is a restricted form of asymmetry, and thus a weaker requirement: asymmetry $\Vert\!\models$ anti-symmetry. The difference is that asymmetry rules out a case like this:

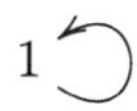

which does not violate anti-symmetry.

An equivalent definition of anti-symmetry is this:

$$\forall x \forall y((Rxy \wedge Ryx) \rightarrow x = y)$$

Exercise 1 Prove that $\forall x \forall y(x \neq y \rightarrow (Rxy \rightarrow \neg Ryx)) \Leftrightarrow \forall x \forall y((Rxy \wedge Ryx) \rightarrow x = y)$

18.2.4 Reflexivity

The difference between asymmetry and anti-symmetry that was noted above concerns another property of relations, viz., reflexivity. It is defined as follows:

Definition 33 R is reflexive iff $\forall x Rxx$

A relation is reflexive if it (also) holds between every element of the domain on which it is defined and that element itself.

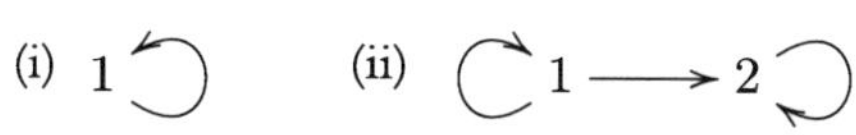

Figure 18.6: Cases of reflexivity

Examples of reflexive relations are identity, 'of the same age as', ...

18.2.5 *Irreflexivity*

Just as symmetry has a counterpart in asymmetry, reflexivity also has such a counterpart, which is irreflexivity:

Definition 34 R is irreflexive iff $\forall x \neg Rxx$

Irreflexivity rules out any graph with a point like this:

Examples of irreflexive relations are 'bigger than', 'parent of', ...

Note that irreflexivity is not merely the negation of reflexivity. A relation R can be neither reflexive, nor irreflexive, viz., if some entities may stand in the R-relation to themselves, whereas others do not.

As was already hinted at above, asymmetry entails irreflexivity, whereas anti-symmetry does not.

Exercise 2 Prove that:

a. asymmetry $\Vdash$ irreflexivity
b. anti-symmetry $\nVdash$ irreflexivity

18.2.6 *Transitivity*

Another important systematic property of relations is that of transitivity. Its definition runs as follows:

Definition 35 R is transitive iff $\forall x \forall y \forall z((Rxy \land Ryz) \rightarrow Rxz)$

Transitivity requires that if x is related to y and y to z, then x is also related to z. We can say that a transitive relation is a relation that allows one to 'skip the middle man'.

A simple diagram illustrates what is at stake:

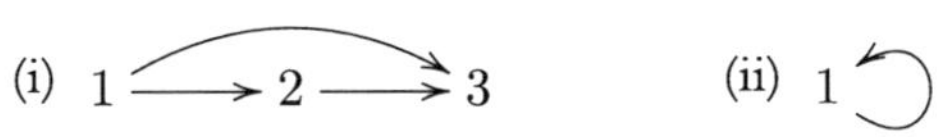

Figure 18.7: Cases of transitivity

Examples of transitive relations are 'ancestor of,' 'greater than', identity ...

18.2.7 *Intransitivity*

Like symmetry and reflexivity, transitivity, too, has its counterpart, viz., intransitivity:

Definition 36 R is intransitive iff $\forall x \forall y \forall z((Rxy \wedge Ryz) \rightarrow \neg Rxz)$

I.e., for an intransitive relation it holds that if x is related to y and y to z, x is not related to z.

Here is an illustration:

$$1 \longrightarrow 2 \longrightarrow 3$$

Figure 18.8: Case of intransitivity

Examples of intransitive relation are 'mother of', 'differs exactly 1 from', ...

18.2.8 Connectedness

A final systematic property that relation may have, or lack, is that of connectedness. The definition runs as follows:

Definition 37 R is connected iff $\forall x \forall y(x \neq y \rightarrow (Rxy \vee Ryx))$

Connectedness tells us something about the scope of a relation on a domain: a relation R is connected on a domain iff every two distinct elements x and y are related, one way or the other (or both ways, of course).

By way of illustration, in this diagram the relations are connected:

Figure 18.9: Cases of connectedness

whereas in this diagram they are not:

Figure 18.10: Cases of non-connectedness

An example of a connected relation is 'smaller than' on the domain of numbers; note that it is not connected on the domain of people.

Another, equivalent definition of connectedness defines R to be connected iff $\forall x \forall y(Rxy \vee Ryx \vee x = y)$

Exercise 3 Prove that $\forall x \forall y(x \neq y \rightarrow (Rxy \vee Ryx)) \Leftrightarrow \forall x \forall y(Rxy \vee Ryx \vee x = y)$

18.3 Orderings

As was illustrated by the informal examples discussed above, an ordering is a way to arrange the elements of a set by means of a relation that has certain properties. So it is the properties of the relation that define the ordering.

In this section we look at a few standard orderings that have applications in a wide variety of domains.

18.3.1 Partial ordering

The first ordering is a partial ordering. Its definition runs as follows:

Definition 38 R is a partial ordering iff R is

- reflexive
- anti-symmetric
- transitive

A relation with these properties orders the elements of the set partially, as the name suggests: not every two elements of the set are ordered with respect to each order, i.e., they may be not connected by R and thus remain unordered with respect to each other.

Examples of partial orderings are the subset-relation on sets of sets, divisibility on the natural numbers, and 'causally affecting' on the set of events in special relativity.

Partial orderings give rise to a great many mathematical structures by adding additional conditions.

18.3.2 Strict partial ordering

So-called strict partial orderings are defined as follows:

Definition 39 R is a strict partial ordering iff R is

- asymmetric
- transitive

Note that, as we have seen above, asymmetry implies irreflexivity.

Examples of strict partial orderings are 'smaller than' on the domain of people, the proper subset relation (i.e., $\subset$, not $\subseteq$) on a set of sets, ...

The diagram in figure 18.11 illustrates how $\subset$ induces a strict partial ordering of the power set of the set $\{\texttt{x},\texttt{y},\texttt{z}\}$.

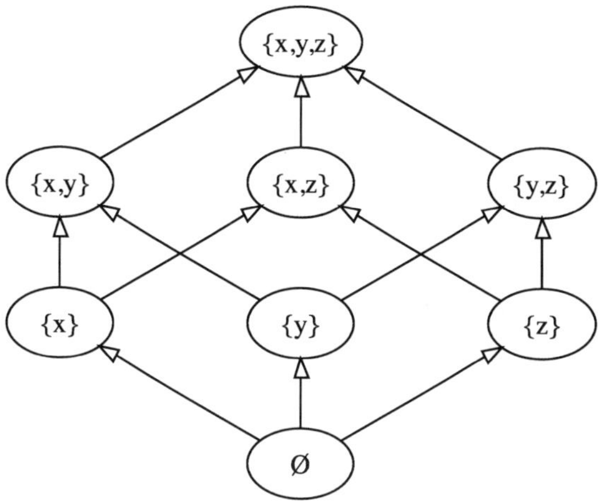

Figure 18.11: Example of a strictly partially ordered set

18.3.3 Linear ordering

The 'partial' in 'partial ordering' refers of course to the fact that not any two elements of a set are ordered with respect to each other. That is the case with a linear ordering.

We get a linear ordering from a partial ordering by adding the property of connectedness, as the following definition shows:

Definition 40 R is a linear ordering iff R is

- a partial ordering
- connected

An example of a linear orderings is $\leqslant$ on the natural numbers $\mathbb{N}$. If R is a strict partial ordering we get strict linear ordering, e.g., $<$ on $\mathbb{N}$

18.3.4 Equivalence relations

A final example of an important type of ordering is that of an equivalence relation.[1] It is defined as follows:

Definition 41 R is an equivalence relation iff R is

- reflexive
- symmetric
- transitive

Examples of equivalence relations are identity, 'as big as', 'having the same two parents', ...

An equivalence relation on a set induces a partition of that set:

Definition 42 A partition of a set A is a set of non-empty subsets of A such that every element of A belongs to exactly one subset

The elements of a partition that is induced by an equivalence relation are also called 'equivalence classes'.

Thus the relation 'having the same two parents' on a set of people divides that set into subsets that each contain all and only those people who have the same parents.

Exercise 4

a. Show that the identity relation is an equivalence relation on any set
b. What are the elements of the partition induced by the identity relation?

18.4 Use of orderings

In this section we briefly discuss two uses of orderings. The first one concerns the analysis of time, which we already discussed informally at the beginning of this chapter. The second concerns the relationship between properties and relations.

18.4.1 Temporal orders

The first application concerns the distinction between linear time and branching time that we referred to earlier on.

How do we define these two temporal structures? We start by assuming that T is an infinite set of discrete temporal points, and that Ett', read as 't is earlier than t'', is a relation defined on T. The point is now to lay down properties of E that will characterise these two temporal structures.

The first one is easy: we want time to be a linearly ordered structure, so we stipulate that E is a strict linear ordering on T:

∘ $\langle T, E\rangle$ is a model of linear time iff E is a strict linear ordering

It is easy to check that the properties of a strict linear ordering comply with the intuitions about time as linearly structured: for any two points t, t', if t is earlier than tt' than t' is not earlier than t (asymmetry); for any three points t, t', t'': if t is earlier than t' and and t' is earlier than t'', then t is earlier than t'' (transitivity); and for any two points t, t': either t is earlier than t' or t' is earlier than t (connectedness).

So any infinite set with a linear order is a model for linear time. $\langle \mathbb{N}, <\rangle$ is a natural choice.

What about branching time? This, too, uses a relation E of temporal precedence. As illustrated by figure 18.2, a key characteristic of a conceptualisation of time as having a branching structure is the lack of connectedness: not every two points in time need to be temporally ordered with respect to each other, they can be 'simultaneous'. But the temporal points on each individual branch are linearly ordered.

This is captured by the following stipulation:

- $\langle T, E\rangle$ is a model of (right-branching) branching time iff
  - (i) E is a strict partial ordering, and it holds that:
  - (ii) $\forall t \forall t' \forall t''((Et't \wedge Et''t) \rightarrow (Et't'' \vee Et''t' \vee t' = t''))$

18.4.2 *Temporal orders*

Exercise 5

a. Define left-branching time. How does left-branching time conceptualise the future?
b. What happens if we let time be both left-branching and right-branching?

18.4.3 *Equivalence classes and properties*

Finally, we turn to the properties and relations. As we have seen in the philosophical excursus to the introductory chapter, one of the main arguments for Frege and Russell to deviate from the grammatical structure of natural language is that they felt that the traditional subject – predicate structure that seems to be suggested by that simply is not suited to deal with expressions and arguments in which relational expressions play a role. The various, often ingenious attempts to reduce relational judgements to subject – predicate judgements all had failed, and thus they conclude that from a logical point of view relational expressions form an independent category.

That started the development of modern logic, and at some point it occurred to logicians that in fact some properties can be analysed in terms of equivalence relations. This is done as follows.

Let R be an equivalence relation on some set A, and P a property of elements of A.

Definition 43 We say that P is well-defined (or 'class invariant') under the relation R if and only if $\forall x \forall y(Rxy \rightarrow (Px \rightarrow Py))$.

Recall that every equivalence relation R on a set A induces a partition of A. What the definition of well-definedness of P says is that if one element in an equivalent class defined by R has property P, then all the elements have that property P. Such properties are thus characterisable in terms of relations.

As an example, consider the relation 'as big as' on the domain of people; it defines the property of 'being n tall', i.e., 'having length n', by partitioning the set of people in subsets that consists of all the people that have the same length.

The idea of defining properties in terms of relations is not just of technical interest, there may also be an epistemological, cognitive side to it. At least in some cases, it would seem probable that we learn properties first and foremost by observing relations, of sameness and difference, between the entities that have (or lack) a certain property. That is to say, it seems not at all implausible that an abstract property such as 'having length n' arises only after we have learned to classify people together who are equally tall. And that comes from comparing them, i.e., from applying a relation to order them, not from observing a property in isolation.

18.5 Exercises

Exercise 6

Investigate the following relation as to their reflexivity, irreflexivity, symmetry, asymmetry, anti-symmetry, transitivity, intransitivity, and connectedness:

a. the relation 'ancestor of' on the set of people
b. the relation 'as tall as' on the set of people
c. the relation 'divisible by' on the set of natural numbers
d. the relation 'differs from' on the set of natural numbers

Exercise 7

a. What kind of ordering is induced by the relation of logical consequence ($\models$) on the set of predicate logical formulas?
b. Is the property 'has n connectives' a well-defined property of proposition logic formulas under the relation of logical equivalence? Motivate your answer

18.6 Concluding remarks

This section illustrates primarily the usefulness of predicate logic as a language for talking about abstract properties and structures. Having identity as part of the language is obviously essential for that.

This use of predicate logic has come to the fore initially primarily in the application of logic in the foundations of mathematics. But it has obvious philosophical and even empirical applications as well, as we hope the brief discussion of temporal structure and of class-invariant properties has illustrated.

Can everything be analysed using predicate logic? The answer to that is negative. Although predicate logic is a forceful and rich instrument, with many applications, it is limited in what it can express. This limitation is mainly connected with the fact that quantifiers range only over the elements in a domain. To be sure, that domain can consist of (almost) any set of entities, but once the domain is fixed, the quantifiers range over the elements in that set, and nothing more. This is what is meant by saying that the predicate logic we have introduced is first order logic.

For some applications it turns out that the expressive power of first order logic is not enough, and that we need to be able to quantify not just over the elements in a domain, but also over their properties and relations, over properties of such properties, and so on. A system that allows for that is called higher-order logic.

19

Predicate Logic: Natural Deduction

19.1 Recap

In this chapter we extend the system of natural deduction that was presented in chapter 9 to cover also predicate logic. It is a conservative extension: all the rules for the connectives that were defined there are taken over without change, we just add rules for the quantifiers.[1]

As usual there are two kinds of rules. There are the Introduction rules that answer the question: how do I get something of a certain form? And there the Elimination ('use') rules, that provide an answer to the question: how can I use something of a certain form?

Note that we will only make use of sentences, i.e., we restrict ourselves to derivations in which the formulas do not contain any free occurrences of variables. In this respect, one could say, the rules follow the substitution interpretation in the semantics. But, as we know from facts such as Fact 9, which was discussed in chapter 15, that is not really a restriction: the substitution interpretation and the objectual interpretation characterise the same set of valid arguments.

In doing so we will rely heavily on the notation that was also used in the exposition of the substitution approach in chapter 13, and that we repeat for the sake of convenience:

- $[c/x]\phi =$ the result of substituting c for all free occurrences of x in ϕ

A couple of simple examples by way of illustration:

(i) $[c/x]Rxx = Rcc$
(ii) $[c/x][c'/y]Rxy = [c/x]Rxc' = Rcc'$
(iii) $[c/x]\exists yPy = \exists yPy$
(iv) $[c/x][c'/x]Px = Pc'$

Note example (ii): substitution is applied 'inside out': we apply $[c/x]$ to the result of applying $[c'/y]$ to Rxy. Example (iv) illustrates the relevance of the order in which the substitution is applied: $[c/x][c'/x]Px = Pc'$ and not Pc, which is the result of $[c'/x][c/x]Px$.

As we shall see, the rules for the quantifiers are intuitive, but in two cases there are a number of requirements on derivations that need to be met.

19.2 Existential quantifier introduction

We start with the introduction rule for the existential quantifier (a.k.a. 'existential generalisation').

Introduction rule $I_\exists$:

$$\begin{array}{lll} 1. & & \\ \vdots & & \\ m. & [c/x]\phi & \\ \vdots & & \\ n. & \exists x\phi & I_\exists, m \end{array}$$

The rule is straightforward: if one has a formula in which c occurs we can 'extract' c and replace it by a variable x and thus derive $\exists x\phi$.

The intuition behind the rule is that a formula ϕ containing one or more occurrences of some constant c makes a particular statement about c. From that we can conclude that there is at least one entity for which that statement holds (to wit, whatever it is that c refers to). And that is what $\exists x\phi$ states.

Note that the rule can be applied with any variable v, so it also allows for the derivation of $\exists y\phi, \exists z\phi, \ldots$.

Here are some examples of $I_\exists$ in action:

$$Raa \vdash \exists x Rxx$$

$$\begin{array}{lll} 1. & Raa & \mathtt{A} \\ 2. & \exists x Rxx & I_\exists, 1 \end{array}$$

since $Raa = [a/x]Rxx$

$$Raa \vdash \exists x \exists y Rxy$$

$$\begin{array}{lll} 1. & Raa & \mathtt{A} \\ 2. & \exists y Ray & I_\exists, 1 \\ 3. & \exists x \exists y Rxy & I_\exists, 2 \end{array}$$

since $Raa = [a/y]Ray$ and $\exists y Ray = [a/x]\exists y Rxy$

Exercise 1 Make derivations that show:

a. $Pa, Qa \vdash \exists x(Px \wedge Qx)$
b. $Pa, Qb \vdash \exists x Px \wedge \exists x Qx$
c. $Bb \vdash \exists x \exists z Bz$
d. for each $n \in \omega$, $Ra_0a_1, Ra_1a_2, \cdots, Ra_na_{n+1} \vdash \exists x_0 \cdots \exists x_{n+1}(Rx_0x_1 \wedge Rx_1x_2 \wedge \cdots \wedge Rx_nx_{n+1})$

19.3 Universal quantifier elimination

Next is the elimination rule for the universal quantifier (a.k.a. 'universal instantiation').

Elimination rule $E_\forall$:

$$\begin{array}{lll} 1. & & \\ \vdots & & \\ m. & \forall x\phi & \\ \vdots & & \\ m. & [c/x]\phi & E_\forall, m \end{array}$$

This is another straightforward rule: if you have $\forall x\phi$ you can derive $[c/x]\phi$ for any arbitrary constant *c*.

The intuition behind this rule is the same as that for the truth conditions assigned to $\forall x\phi$ in the substitution method: $\forall x\phi$ applies to all objects, so also to the object referred to by any individual constant *c*.

Some examples to illustrate $E_\forall$:

$$\forall x\forall yRxy \vdash Raa$$

$$\begin{array}{lcr} 1. & \forall x\forall yRxy & \mathtt{A} \\ 2. & \forall yRay & E_\forall, 1 \\ 3. & Raa & E_\forall, 2 \end{array}$$

since $[a/x]\forall yRxy = \forall yRay$ and $[a/y]Ray = Raa$.

$$\forall x\forall yRxy \vdash Rab$$

$$\begin{array}{lcr} 1. & \forall x\forall yRxy & \mathtt{A} \\ 2. & \forall yRay & E_\forall, 1 \\ 3. & Rab & E_\forall, 2 \end{array}$$

since $[a/x]\forall yRxy = \forall yRay$ and $[b/y]Ray = Rab$.

Exercise 2 Make derivations that show:

a. $\forall xPx, \forall xQx \vdash \exists x(Px \wedge Qx)$
b. $\forall x\forall y(Rxy \rightarrow Sxy), \forall x\forall y(Sxy \rightarrow Txy) \vdash Rab \rightarrow Tab$
c. $Qd, \exists xQx \rightarrow \forall xPx \vdash Pd$
d. $\forall x(\exists yRxy \rightarrow Sxx), \forall x\forall y(Sxy \rightarrow Txy) \vdash Rab \rightarrow Taa$

19.4 Universal quantifier introduction

Then we move to the introduction rule for the universal quantifier. This rule comes with requirements.

Introduction rule $I_\forall$:

$$\begin{array}{lll} 1. & & \\ \vdots & & \\ m. & [c/x]\phi & \\ \vdots & & \\ n. & \forall x\phi & I_\forall, m \end{array}$$

provided that:

1. *c does not occur in any active assumptions; and*
2. *c does not occur in ϕ*

This time let's start with the intuition behind the rule. It is one that we make use of when we try to show that some universally quantified formula $\forall x\phi$ is true (or false). Since $\forall x\phi$ says something about each and every entity in the domain of discourse, we can just pick an arbitrary element from the domain and then proceed to check whether ϕ holds of that entity. In the substitution approach, where all the elements in the domain have a name, this means checking whether $[c/x]\phi$ is true or false for some arbitrary constant *c*. If $[c/x]\phi$ turns out to be false, we have a counterexample. If $[c/x]\phi$ turns out to be true, we have established, not just its truth, but also the truth of $\forall x\phi$ precisely because our choice of *c* was arbitrary: nothing was assumed to hold of the entity it refers to that could have made $[c/x]\phi$ come out true in a situation where in fact $\forall x\phi$ was false.

So it is the arbitrariness of an object, c.q. a constant, that is key here. We can derive $\forall x\phi$ from $[c/x]\phi$ provided *c* is arbitrary in the sense just explained. The two conditions take care of that. First of all, *c* may not occur in an active assumption, for if it did, we in fact do assume something about *c*, viz., that it satisfies the assumption. Second, it may not occur in ϕ itself, for then ϕ itself would in fact state something about it, and that makes it non-arbitrary as well.

Before going to some examples, we first show what goes wrong in case the requirements are not met.

We start with a very simple example that illustrates the effect of condition 1 (we mark the offending step with *):

$$\begin{array}{lll} 1. & Pa & \mathtt{A} \\ 2.^\star & \forall x Px & I_\forall, 1 \end{array}$$

Of course, we should have that $Pa \not\vdash \forall x Px$, and this derivation is indeed blocked because a occurs in an active assumption, viz., the premise of the argument, and hence is not arbitrary. Condition 1 thus rules this out, as it should.

Next, an illustration of condition 2:

1.	$\forall xRxx$	A
2.	Raa	$E_\forall, 1$
3.*	$\forall xRax$	$I_\forall, 2$

Clearly this should not go through: $\forall xRxx \nvdash \forall xRax$. And condition 2 indeed correctly blocks the derivation: a occurs in the derived $\forall x\phi$.

Note that condition 2 in effect says that if we apply $I_\forall$ to some formula $[c/x]\phi$ containing an arbitrary c, then all occurrences of c in $[c/x]\phi$ need to be replaced by x and bound by the quantifier $\forall x$ that is introduced. For if not, we are left with a result that destroys the arbitrary nature of c.

Let's look at some examples of derivation in which $I_\forall$ is used.

$$\forall x(Ax \wedge Bx) \vdash \forall xAx \wedge \forall xBx$$

1.	$\forall x(Ax \wedge Bx)$	A
2.	$Aa \wedge Ba$	$E_\forall, 1$
3.	Aa	$E_\wedge, 2$
4.	Ab	$E_\wedge, 2$
5.	$\forall xAx$	$I_\forall, 3$
6.	$\forall xBx$	$I_\forall, 4$
7.	$\forall xAx \wedge \forall xBx$	$I_\wedge, 5, 6$

$$\forall x\forall yRxy \vdash \forall x\forall y(Rxy \wedge Ryx)$$

1.	$\forall x\forall yRxy$	A
2.	$\forall yRay$	$E_\forall, 1$
3.	Rab	$E_\forall, 2$
4.	$\forall yRby$	$E_\forall, 1$
5.	Rba	$E_\forall, 4$
6.	$Rab \wedge Rba$	$I_\wedge, 3, 5$
7.	$\forall y(Ray \wedge Rya)$	$I_\forall, 6$
6.	$\forall x\forall y(Rxy \wedge Ryx)$	$I_\forall, 7$

$$\neg\exists xAx \vdash \forall x\neg Ax$$

1.	$\neg\exists xAx$	A
2.	Aa	A
3.	$\exists xAx$	$I_\exists, 2$
4.	$\bot$	$E_\neg, 1, 3$
5.	$\neg Aa$	$I_\neg$
6.	$\forall x\neg Ax$	$I_\forall, 5$

Note that although a occurs in an assumption at step 2, and thus is not arbitrary as long as that assumption is not withdrawn, a is arbitrary when in step 6 $I_\forall$ is applied, since the assumption made in step 2 is withdrawn in step 5.

Exercise 3 Make derivations that show:

a. $\forall x Px, \forall x Qx \vdash \forall x(Px \wedge Qx)$
b. $\forall x Px \vee \forall x Qx \vdash \forall x(Px \vee Qx)$
c. $\forall x \forall y Rxy \vdash \forall y \forall x Ryx$
d. $\forall x \forall y Rxy \vdash \forall x Rxx$
e. $\forall x \forall y(Rxy \rightarrow \neg Ryx) \vdash \forall x \neg Rxx$
f. $Qd, \exists x Qx \rightarrow \forall x Px \vdash Pd$

19.5 Existential quantifier elimination

Next up is the elimination rule for the existential quantifier. This rule too comes with requirements for its proper application.

Elimination rule $E_{\exists}$:

$$\begin{array}{lll} 1. & & \\ \vdots & & \\ m_1. & \exists x\phi & \\ \vdots & & \\ m_2. & [c/x]\phi \rightarrow \psi & \\ \vdots & & \\ k. & \psi & E_{\exists}, m_1, m_2 \end{array}$$

provided that:

1. *c does not occur in any active assumptions; and*
2. *c does not occur in ϕ; and*
3. *c does not occur in ψ*

Again we start with the intuition behind the rule. How do we make use of $\exists x\phi$? Consider the following example:

(1) If Bill comes, Mary is happy. Someone comes. So, Mary is happy
(2) If anybody comes, Mary is happy. Someone comes. So, Mary is happy

Obviously, the first argument is not valid. But the second is. If we know that there is someone who shows up, and that Mary is happy if anybody comes, then we can conclude that she is happy.

So the use we can make of $\exists x\phi$ is this: to derive some formula ψ from $\exists x\phi$ and $[c/x]\phi \rightarrow \psi$ provided that c is arbitrary. The arbitrariness of c is guaranteed by the three conditions listed above.

Let us illustrate each of them by giving an example of what goes wrong if they are not met.

We start with a simple example that illustrates the effect of condition 1:

1.	$\exists x \exists y Rxy$	A
2.	$\exists y Ray \rightarrow Bb$	A
3.*	Bb	$E_{\exists}, 1, 2$

This derivation should not go through: $\exists x \exists y Rxy, \exists y Ray \rightarrow Bb \nvdash Bb$. Note that since $\exists y Ray = [a/x]Rxy$, the rule can be applied. However, condition 1 is not met, since a occurs in an assumption that is still active in the step in which the rule is applied. So the derivation is blocked, as it should be.

The following example illustrates the effect of condition 2:

1.	$\forall x \exists y Rxy$	A
2.	$\exists y Ray$	$E_{\forall}, 1$
3.	Raa	A
4.	$\exists x Rxx$	$I_{\exists}, 3$
5.	$Raa \rightarrow \exists x Rxx$	$I_{\rightarrow}$
6.*	$\exists x Rxx$	$E_{\exists} 2, 5$

Here condition 2 is not met: a occurs in ϕ, since $[a/y]Ray = Raa$. So the derivation is blocked: $\forall x \exists y Rxy \nvdash \exists x Rxx$.

And then an example to show the workings of condition 3:

1.	$\exists x Rxx$	A
2.	Raa	A
3.	$\exists y Ray$	$I_{\exists}, 2$
4.	$Raa \rightarrow \exists y Ray$	$I_{\rightarrow}$
5.*	$\exists y Ray$	$E_{\exists} 2, 5$
6.	$\forall x \exists y Rxy$	$I_{\forall} 5$

The application of $E_{\exists}$ in step 5. does not meet condition 3: a occurs in $\psi = \exists y Ray$. Thus the derivation is blocked: $\exists x Rxx \nvdash \forall x \exists y Rxy$. (Note that the application of $I_{\forall}$ in step 6 is fine as such.)

To conclude, two examples of proper application of $E_{\exists}$.

$$\forall x(Ax \rightarrow Bx), \exists x Ax \vdash \exists x Bx$$

1.	$\forall x(Ax \rightarrow Bx)$	A
2.	$\exists x Ax$	A
3.	Aa	A
4.	$Aa \rightarrow Ba$	$E_{\forall}, 1$
5.	Ba	$E_{\rightarrow}, 3, 4$
6.	$\exists x Bx$	$I_{\exists}, 5$
7.	$Aa \rightarrow \exists x Bx$	$I_{\rightarrow}$
8.	$\exists x Bx$	$E_{\exists}, 2, 7$

$$\exists x \neg Ax \vdash \neg \forall x Ax$$

1.	$\exists x \neg Ax$	A
2.	$\neg Aa$	A
3.	$\forall x Ax$	A
4.	Aa	$E_\forall, 3$
5.	$\bot$	$E_\neg, 2, 4$
6.	$\neg \forall x Ax$	$I_\rightarrow$
7.	$\neg Aa \rightarrow \neg \forall x Ax$	$I_\rightarrow$
8.	$\neg \forall x Ax$	$E_\exists, 1, 7$

Exercise 4 Make derivations that show:

a. $\exists x(Px \vee Qx) \vdash \exists x Px \vee \exists x Qx$
b. $\exists x Px \vee \exists x Qx \vdash \exists x(Px \vee Qx)$
c. $\exists x(Px \wedge Qx) \vdash \exists x Px \wedge \exists x Qx$
d. $\exists x Px \rightarrow \forall y Qy \vdash \forall x \forall y(Px \rightarrow Qy)$
e. $\exists x \forall y Rxy \vdash \forall y \exists x Rxy$
f. $\forall x(\exists y Rxy \rightarrow Sxx), \forall x \forall y(Sxy \rightarrow Txy) \vdash Rab \rightarrow Taa$

19.6 Identity introduction

The last set of rules concerns identity. Recall that $=$ is treated as a logical constant: its interpretation is fixed across models, in order to account for the role it plays in the semantic validity of arguments. And in a proof system we also want to account for that.

We start with the introduction rule.

Introduction rule $I_=$:

1.		
$\vdots$		
k.	$c = c$	$I_=$

This is the simplest rule of them all: at any point in a derivation we may avail ourselves of a formula of the form $c = c$, for arbitrary c. It comes with no strings attached: there are no requirements to be met and no other formula(s) need to be available.

The intuition behind it directly follows from the interpretation of identity as the smallest reflexive relation.

Here is a simple example to illustrate $I_=$:

$$\vdash \exists x \exists y\, x = y$$

$$\begin{array}{lll} 1. & c = c & I_= \\ 2. & \exists y\, c = y & I_\exists \\ 3. & \exists x \exists y\, x = y & I_\exists \end{array}$$

since $c = c$ is $[c/y]c = y$ and $\exists y\, c = y$ is $[c/x]\exists y\, x = y$.

19.7 Identity elimination

The last rule is the elimination rule for identity.

Elimination rule $E_=$:

$$\begin{array}{lll} 1. & & \\ \vdots & & \\ m_1. & c = d & \\ \vdots & & \\ m_2. & [c/x]\phi & \\ \vdots & & \\ k. & [d/x]\phi & E_=, m_1, m_2 \end{array}$$

The use we can make of having at our disposal $c = d$, for arbitrary c and d, is that we can derive from a formula containing c the corresponding formula that contains d instead of c.

The intuition behind this is clear, if $c = d$ than ϕ and $[d/c]\phi$ are the same statement. Note that this rule can be instantiated in two ways: replacing a by b and vice versa, since c and d are arbitrary.

By way of illustration consider the following examples.

$$a = b, b = c \vdash a = c$$

$$\begin{array}{lll} 1. & a = b & \mathtt{A} \\ 2. & b = c & \mathtt{A} \\ 3. & a = c & E_=, 1, 2 \end{array}$$

since $a = c$ is $[c/b]a = b$.

$$Pa, \neg Pb \vdash a \neq b$$

$$\begin{array}{lll} 1. & Pa & \mathtt{A} \\ 2. & \neg Pb & \mathtt{A} \\ 3. & a = b & \mathtt{A} \\ 4. & \neg Pa & E_=, 2, 3 \\ 5. & \bot & E_\neg, 1, 4 \\ \hline 6. & a \neq b & I_\neg \end{array}$$

since $\neg Pa$ is $[a/b]\neg Pb$

$$\forall x \forall y(Rxy \to x = y), a \neq b \vdash \neg Rab$$

1.	$\forall x \forall y(Rxy \to x = y)$	A
2.	$a \neq b$	A
3.	$\forall y(Ray \to a = y)$	$E_\forall, 1$
4.	$Rab \to a = b$	$E_\forall, 3$
5.	Rab	A
6.	$a = b$	$E_\to, 4, 5$
5.	$\bot$	$E_\neg, 2, 6$
6.	$\neg Rab$	$I_\neg$

Exercise 5 Make derivations that show:

a. $a = b, b = c, Pa \vdash Pb \wedge Pc$
b. $\forall x \neg Rxx, Rab \vdash a \neq b$
c. $\exists x Qx, \exists x \neg Qx \vdash \exists x \exists y(x \neq y)$
d. $Pa \vdash \forall x(x = a \to Px)$
e. $\forall x(x = a \to Px) \vdash Pa$
f. for each $n \in \omega$, $a_0 = a_1, a_1 = a_2, \cdots, a_n = a_{n+1} \vdash a_0 = a_{n+1}$

19.8 Concluding remarks

In combination with the natural deduction rules for the connectives, which were given in chapter 9, the rules given above treat all the logical constants in a language of predicate logic and allow us to construct proofs for argument schemes in which they occur.

In the presentation of the various rules we have often referred to 'the intuition behind the rule', which was usually of a more or less semantic nature. This raises the question of what exactly the relation is between on the one hand the semantics of proposition logic and predicate logic, and on the other hand their natural deduction proof systems. Is what we can derive indeed justified from the point of view of the semantics? And, reversely, if an argument scheme is valid according to the semantics, can we be sure that there is a derivation for it in the natural deduction system?

The first question is the question of the soundness of a proof system vis à vis the semantics, and the second question is the question of its completeness. In the next chapter we will go into more detail for the case of proposition logic and show that the natural deduction system is indeed sound and complete. The same holds for the natural deduction system for predicate logic, but proving that is more complicated and is outside the scope of this introductory book.

20

Excursus: logic and normativity

20.1 The topic

In this philosophical excursus we take up again two discussions that we encountered before, one on what proper logical constants are (the Prior and Belnap papers) and one on the relation between a proof-theoretical account of logical constants and natural language meaning (the papers by de Queiroz and Harman). To this we add a third dimension, viz., the question to what extent logic is normative or rather empirical. As we shall see, these three topics can be discussed in a way that makes them hang together.

For a long time, the question of whether logic is a normative or rather an empirical discipline appeared to have been settled with Frege's forceful defence of the idea that logic is a normative enterprise. What logic describes is not how people actually reason, but how they should reason. The laws of logic are the laws of thought, but of the thought of an ideal thinker, not an actual one.

This point of view appears to have been shared widely throughout the twentieth century up to the early 1960s, when psychologists started to take an active interest in how people actually deal with deductive reasoning tasks.[1] One of the first studies into performance on actual reasoning tasks is that of the so-called 'Wason task', named after its inventor, the psychologist Peter Wason.

The experimental setup is simple. Subjects are informed that each card in a deck has a vowel or a consonant on one side and an even or an uneven number on the other. Then they are presented with the four cards in Figure 20.1 and are asked which cards, and only which cards, should be turned over to check whether the rule 'If a card has a vowel on one side, then it has an even number on the other side' holds. It turns out that only a small minority of less than 25% of subjects (on average over different runs) give the correct answer.[2]

Interestingly, if the test is changed, performance changes as well. In the changed test subjects are told that each card on one side states the drink that a person is having, which is either beer or Coca-Cola, and on the other side states that person's age. Then they are presented with the cards in Figure 20.2 and are asked which cards, and only which cards, should be turned over to check whether the rule 'If a person is drinking beer, they are at least 19 years old' holds.

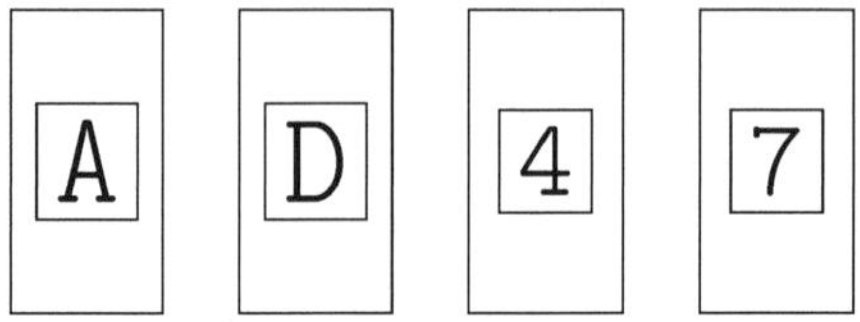

Figure 20.1: The Wason task

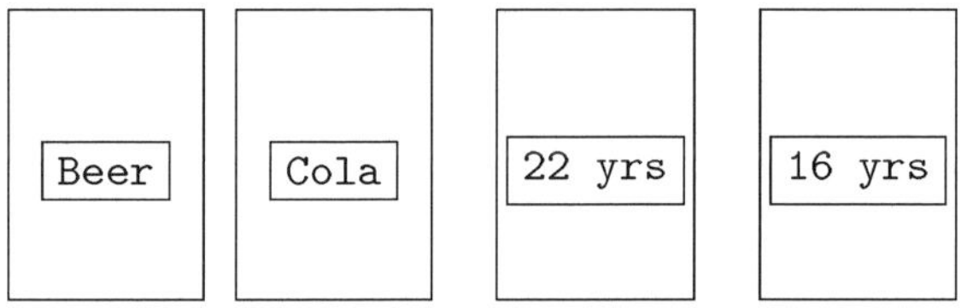

Figure 20.2: The Wason task, now with beer

The results on this second test are remarkably different: more than 75% (again, on average over different runs) give the right answer. But interestingly, from a purely logical perspective the reasoning task in each of these two tests is exactly the same. The only difference is the framing of the task.

Results such as these have spawned a new interest in how logic and actual reasoning relate.[3] Obviously, in Wason's experimental set-up classical logic figured as a norm: it was used to classify answers as 'right' or 'wrong'. But that does not explain the performance difference between the two tests. It leaves open the question of what logic, if any, accurately describes actual reasoning practices of human subjects.

As for the explanation of the difference on the two versions, a fairly commonly accepted idea is that people are more sensitive to concrete rules that are concerned with real life action than to abstract ones. In its turn this feature is often explained in terms of its being evolutionary advantageous.[4]. This would explain the difference in success rates in the two versions.

But that leaves open the second question, viz., what reasoning is employed by subjects who don't give the 'correct' answer. In a follow-up of the Wason experiments the psychologist Keith Stenning and the logician Michiel van Lambalgen found that if the subjects were asked to describe their justification of their reasoning while they were performing the task, they often came up with interpretations of the task setting itself that turned their answer into one that was actually correct given those interpretations.[5]

Stenning and Van Lambalgen conclude that asking someone to perform a reasoning task sets in motion a complex process, that involves two stages. One is what they call 'reasoning to an interpretation', i.e., a process in which the subject tries to make sense of the task that they are asked to perform, by embedding it in an (imagined) context, by adding additional assumptions about the various objects, actions and events that the premisses and conclusion refer to. Once that process has settled on an interpretation of the task, another process starts, 'reasoning from an interpretation. In this process the subject takes the task as they have interpreted it and then tries to reason about its proper answer.

But not only did Stenning and Van Lambalgen find out that the process is more complex, they also noted that people use different kinds of logics to carry it out. This variation occurs not just across subjects, but also within the performance of one subject: he/she may use one kind of logic for reasoning to an interpretation, and another one for reasoning from that interpretation.

This raises a number of questions. First of all, do results such as these have any implications for the question of whether logic is empirical or normative? And second, what are we to make of the pluralism that we see in the results of these empirical investigations?These are the two questions that Engel's paper starts with. But before we turn to Engel's paper we need to make a few comments on the questions as such.

As for the first question, note that even if one sees different subjects use different logics in performing a logical reasoning task, one still needs to assess their results in some way or other. For even relative to the choice of logic that an individual subject makes, they may nevertheless apply it incorrectly. And that is a significant aspect of studying the actual performance, viz., to assess whether it matches the intent of the performer. And normativity is relevant not just for the outside observer/investigator, but for the reasoner as well. For they are concerned with reasoning correctly, i.e., not just to follow some rules, but to follow the right ones. Thus the normative aspect is still there, and normative assessments cannot be avoided.

And then there is the second issue, pluralism in logic. If one looks at the practices of reasoners, those of logicians as well as those of researchers who apply logic in their own fields (philosophers, linguists, computer scientists, ...): pluralism seems to be a given. Despite the 'queen bee' status of classical first order logic, there is an immense variety of logical systems that are being developed and studied for their own sake and that are applied across a wide range of settings. The idea of there being 'one true (correct, ...) logic' seems to have receded into the background once modern formal logic started to come into its own as an independent field of study.[6] However, pluralism complicates the question of normativity. With each choice of logic comes the question of normativity in the application of that particular logic. But there also still remains the question of whether there are good and bad (better and worse) choices to begin with.

The various ways one can answer the question of the normativity of logic and the question of how empirical theories of actual reasoning behaviour relate to logical theories have repercussions for the two issues we discussed before.

The first is the questions of what are proper logical constants, and what are not. This is first and foremost a question about what constitutes a proper logic. Obviously, one's answer to this question and one's attitude towards pluralism are closely intertwined. It also touches on the status and relevance of empirical investigations into actual reasoning practices, as not all the ways in which people reason can be called 'logical' since this depends on what one takes logic, i.e., logical constants, to be.

And, secondly, there is the relation between proof-theory and natural language. Almost all of the reasoning we do in everyday life is informal, i.e., it uses natural language, not some formal language. Proof-theoretic semantics assumes that meaning can be accounted for by a set of proof rules. But from an empirical, cognitive-psychological point of view it appears that humans actually use more 'semantic' methods. The 'mental models' approach of the cognitive psychologist P. Johnson-Laird[7] is a prominent example, one that exemplifies many of the assumptions of the cognitive psychology of the eighties and nineties of the previous century. But also today, many approaches in cognitive science assume that cognitive tasks, including reasoning, involve representations and manipulations thereof. Somehow the referential way of thinking about meaning and information remains deeply ingrained. And that makes the discussion about the relation between logic and empirical theories of reasoning relevant for proof-theoretic approaches to semantics.

20.2 The author

Pascal Engel (1954 – present) is a French philosopher who worked for a long time at the Sorbonne in Paris as professor in philosophy of logic, and who is currently affiliated with the University of Geneva in Switzerland. Engel studied philosophy in Paris and received his PhD with a thesis on identity and reference, which was supervised by Jacques Bouveresse. He became professor in philosophy of logic at the Sorbonne in Paris and then moved to the University of Geneva. During his years in Paris Engel became affiliated with the Institut Jean Nicod, an affiliation that he kept after moving to Geneva. Over the years he held visiting positions at a number of universities in Canada, Hong Kong, and at various universities in Europe.

Pascal Engel's research covers a wide variety of topics, ranging from the philosophy of Wittgenstein to theories of truth, from the works of Donald Davidson and topics in philosophy of language to issues in epistemology and in philosophy of mind. Originally trained in the continental tradition in philosophy he later turned to analytic philosophy, but has been a 'bridge builder' ever since, trying to bring these two major traditions in western 20th century philosophy closer together.

Besides being a prolific writer, who has published not just many academic research articles and books, but who also writes on topics of broader societal relevance aiming at a general audience, Pascal Engel is also an active organiser and editor. He has been editor-in-chief of the journal *Dialactica*, and is secretary-general of the renowned *Institut international de philosophie* in Paris.

20.3 The text

'Logic, Reasoning and the Logical Constants' (Engel, 2006) starts with a short introduction to three questions and their interrelations: (a) how do we reason? (b) how do we ought to reason? (c) what justifies the way we ought to reason?

The first section of the paper is devoted to a discussion of the relation between questions (a) and (b), i.e., to the relevance of logic for reasoning. One distinction that Engel introduces is that between content and logical structure, and he discusses a number of studies that seem to indicate that actual reasoning is much more steered by belief contents, and the associated belief bias effect, than by formal, logical structure. He then reviews how these empirical results have led some authors to reject the relevance of logic for the study of human reasoning, and thus to argue that (a) and (b) are different questions altogether.

Engel goes on to question whether these conclusions are correct, pointing out that mental models (as propagated in Johnson-Laird's account of reasoning) are concerned with truth and obey the requirement of semantic validity.

He then argues that a better way of posing the question about the relation between logic and reasoning needs to be split into two: one dealing with description, the other with prescription. As for the first, he agrees with the authors he has discussed that logic does not describe reasoning, but he maintains that it does not follow from that that logic has no prescriptive role to play. Rather he holds that in reasoning some grasp or rationality, a normative notion, plays a role, albeit usually implicitly and unconsciously. Engel supports this position by making a distinction between the content of norms and the implicit understanding of norms.

The role of the content of norms Engel illustrates by a discussion of the difference between ascribing reasoners with a (tacit) knowledge of a set of formal rules (for connectives), and the weaker kind of implicit understanding that mental model theory presupposes. Engel argues that what we need to ascribe to reasoners is something slightly stronger, and that mental model theory can accommodate that. He illustrates this by reviewing the way in which standard connectives are handled in mental model theory, viz., as regulating the construction of canonical mental models. And he argues that such an approach can handle Prior's 'tonk'-connective.

The implicit understanding of norms is a separate matter from the content of those norms. Engel argues that from the fact that people do not have explicit knowledge of logical rules it does not follow that they do not follow any rules when reasoning. They do not act blindly, but are guided by their implicit understanding of certain reasoning norms.

The second section of the paper is devoted to a discussion of question (c): what justifies the way we ought to reason? This is a more abstract question, viz., how do we justify logical rules and principles? But, Engel notes, it is connected to the first two questions, since the basic distinction between proof-theoretic and semantic justification of logical rules re-occurs at the level of psychological theories. Some are semantic, mental models theory being a prime example. But others are much more akin to a proof-theoretic perspective. Thus meta-logical discussions may have repercussions for how to study actual reasoning.

Engel illustrates this with a discussion of Belnap's diagnosis of Prior's 'tonk'. Belnap argued that the problem with 'plonk' is that adding it to the language of propositional logic is not conservative: it allows derivations that were not allowed before.[8]

Now this is a proof-theoretic notion, but following Peacocke) Engel notes that we can make sense of it from a semantic perspective as well. Truth-preservation is the semantic counterpart that we need here. So Engel does not follow Dummett and Tennant in regarding this as an intrinsically proof-theoretic matter. Rather, in line with his view that the peculiar nature of 'plonk' can be explained in terms of mental model theory, he proposes to analyse the matter in terms of conceptual role semantics.

Accepting the basic outlines of Peacocke's framework, Engel then formulates three conditions that need to be met for ascription of the understanding of a logical constant to a reasoner: (i) rules for basic connectives are obvious; (ii) their normativity is inherent in their conceptual role; and (iii) conceptual roles determine truth conditions. In this way Engel connects meta-normativity with meaning, i.e., truth conditions, and with use, i.e., conceptual role, and through the latter connection links semantics with proof-theory.

The third and final part of the paper is a short discussion of rationality and reflective equilibrium. The latter is Cohen's term to indicate a pre-established harmony between the normativity of logical rules and reasoning competence.[9] The idea is that our intuitions about correct reasoning and our reasoning competence are kept in equilibrium through a series of weighted comparisons. This amounts to an assumption of rationality that has been criticised, mainly because it assumes, rather than proves, that our intuitions are indeed rational to begin with.

Reflective equilibrium is also committed to strong holism and here Engel claims there is a distinction between Cohen's approach and the one who endorses. Conceptual role semantics is not strongly holistic: it only needs to assume that there is a limited set of inferential relations that determine a logical constant and it is not committed to assuming that all inferential relations need to be taken into account.

20.4 Study and discussion questions

Study questions

- What are mental models? And why do they explain the discrepancy between logical validity and the way people actually reason?
- What does Gigerenzer mean when he claims that 'norms have to be "psychologised"' ?
- What does Engel think that the fact that mental models are concerned with truth is an argument against the strict separation of questions (a) and (b)?
- Why does Engel think that empirical results do not necessarily lead to the conclusion that logic has nothing to do with reasoning? Which distinction does he make here?
- What is the distinction between the content of a norm and the understanding of a norm? Are these two somehow dependent?
- What role does the concept of truth play in Engel's explanation of the content of a norm?
- Why does Engel think that mental model theory ascribes too little 'logicality' to reasoners?
- How does Engel explain the peculiar status of Prior's 'tonk' connective?
- For what reason(s) does Engel think that there is such an implicit understanding of rules?
- What relationship does Engel see between questions (a) and (b) on the one hand and question (c) on the other?
- Why is 'conservative extension' not intrinsically a proof-theoretic concept according to Engel?
- What is the function of Engel's appeal to conceptual role semantics?
- What is a 'reflective equilibrium? Why is it connected with strong holism?
- What difference does Engel see between reflective equilibrium approaches and his own conceptual role approach?

Discussion questions

- On page 222 Engel refers to Lewis Carroll's story of Achilles and the Tortoise. What is that story? And what could its upshot be for the question about the relation between logic and actual reasoning?
- Engel claims that 'truth' and 'validity' are normative notions (p. 224). Explain and discuss. Is the normativity in both cases the same?
- On page 228 Engel argues against the idea that if someone does not follow an explicit rule, he therefore 'acts blindly'. Can you think of a way to define the kind of implicit knowledge that Engel seems to rely on here? And do you agree with Engel's (implicit) assumption that 'blind rule following' does not qualify for normative assessment?
- Does Engel's switch from a proof-theoretic to a semantic explanation of conservative extension rely on the fact that there is a completeness theorem for the logic to which it is applied?
- Ultimately, Engel's way of connecting questions (a), (b) and (c) depends on the idea of aspects of logical constants being 'primitively obvious'. Discuss. If someone claims that (a certain aspect of) the meaning of a certain expression is 'primitively obvious', would it be possible to refute that claim?

20.5 Further reading

For an extensive overview of various views on the normative status of logic, see Steinberger (2017). The relation between logic and psychology is the subject of many studies; of particular relevance is the seminal work of Johnson-Laird (Johnson-Laird, 1983), and the alternative approach explored by Stenning and Van Lambalgen (Stenning & van Lambalgen, 2008).

21

Metalogic: a first taste

21.1 Introduction

In this chapter we will give a short introduction to the main ideas behind the soundness and completeness theorems for proposition logic. The soundness theorem states that all proposition logical argument that have a proof are also semantically valid. And, conversely, the completeness theorem states that all semantically valid schemes are provable. These two theorems are what are called 'meta-theorems', i.e., theorems that deal with properties of a formal system.

In § 2 we illustrate the conception of a meta-theorem and meta-proofs using a couple of simple examples. Then in § 3 we turn to the soundness theorem. The completeness theorem is the subject of §4. In § 4.1. we give an informal sketch of the structure of its proof, and in § 4.2 we introduce some important concepts, viz., consistency and maximally consistent sets, that are used and introduce some facts about them that are needed in § 4.3, in which we deal with the proof of the completeness theorem.[1]

Before we turn to the formal treatment of the soundness and completeness theorems, we discuss more informally what it is that these theorems state.

Provability and semantic validity are both formal concepts that are introduced to explicate our intuitive grasp of validity of an argument. The question that is addressed by the soundness and completeness theorems is this: do these two concepts indeed adequately explicate that intuitive notion, i.e., do they both give different explications of the very same notion? The soundness and completeness theorems give a positive answer to this question. The soundness theorem assures us that what is provable is semantically valid. That is one part of the answer. The remainder is given by the completeness theorem, that tells us that what is semantically valid can also be proven.

That provability corresponds to the intuitive notion of validity can be argued by pointing out that all the individual steps in a proof are intuitively correct. Reversely, that what is intuitively valid is also semantically valid can be seen as follows: if an argument is semantically not valid, then it also fails to be intuitively valid since a counter-example will convince of that.

This is not the whole story, of course, two questions are left:

1. Is provability not too restricted, i.e., is everything that is intuitively valid also provable?
2. Is semantic validity not too broad, i.e., is everything that is semantically valid also intuitively valid?

The completeness theorem decides both questions. First of all, completeness states that what is semantically valid is also provable. If we combine that result with the given that what is intuitively valid is also semantically valid, then we can conclude that provability is not too restricted: what is intuitively valid is syntactically derivable. That settles the first question. And, secondly, if we start from the given that what is provable is intuitively valid, then completeness implies that semantic validity is not too broad: what is semantically valid is also intuitively valid. And that settles the second question.

21.2 Proofs about proofs

The correctness and completeness theorems are examples of what are called 'meta-theorems'. Such theorems are not theorems that are formulated in a logical language and proven to be valid. Rather, these are theorems about a logical theory as such. They assert that a logical theory has certain properties, and as such they belong to the theory about that logical theory, i.e., to its 'meta-theory'. The meta-theory of syntactic proof systems is also called 'proof theory' and the meta-theory of semantic validity goes by the name of 'model theory'. In our case, our proof theory is the theory of natural deduction, and the model theory is the theory of truth tables.

Meta-theoretical theorems and proofs are formulated in a meta-language. In our case this will be English enriched with some set-theoretic vocabulary and other jargon. In what follows we will often refer to proofs in the object-language, and in order to facilitate that we introduce in our meta-language variables, written as '$\Pi_1, \Pi_2, \ldots$', to range over proofs.

Note that it is always possible in a natural deduction proof to write it down in such a way that any assumptions that are not withdrawn, which always include the premises of the argument scheme for which we construct a proof, are stated first. Note also that numbering the various steps and indicating on which steps a certain step in the derivation makes use of is not essential to a proof, in this sense that it can always be reconstructed (although not uniquely). We will therefore often leave out the numbering.

A very simple example of a proof-theoretic statement is the following:

Fact 14 $\phi \vdash \psi \;\&\; \psi \vdash \chi \Rightarrow \phi \vdash \chi$

This can be read as follows: if there is a derivation of ψ from ϕ and there is a derivation of χ from ψ, then there is also a derivation for χ from ϕ.

By way of illustration here is a proof of this statement:

Proof. Assume that $\phi \vdash \psi$ and $\psi \vdash \chi$. Then there are two derivations of the form:

$$\begin{array}{ll} \phi & \mathtt{A} \\ \Pi_1 & \\ \psi & \end{array}$$

and:

$$\begin{array}{ll} \psi & \mathtt{A} \\ \Pi_2 & \\ \chi & \end{array}$$

In Π_1 and Π_2 no assumptions appear that are not withdrawn. Out of these two derivations we form a new one that shows that $\phi \vdash \chi$:

$$\begin{array}{ll} \phi & \mathtt{A} \\ \Pi_1 & \\ \psi & \\ \Pi_2 & \\ \chi & \end{array}$$

□

Note that in this derivation ψ is not an assumption.

A second example:

Fact 15 $\neg\phi \vdash \phi \Rightarrow \vdash \phi$

Proof. Assume that $\neg\phi \vdash \phi$. Then there is a derivation that looks like this:

$$\begin{array}{ll} \neg\phi & \mathtt{A} \\ \Pi & \\ \phi & \end{array}$$

in which Π does not contain any assumptions that are not withdrawn. This derivation can be continued as follows:

$$\begin{array}{|ll} \neg\phi & \mathtt{A} \\ \Pi & \\ \phi & \\ \bot & E_\neg \\ \hline \end{array}$$
$$\begin{array}{ll} \neg\neg\phi & I_\neg \\ \phi & \neg\neg\text{-rule} \end{array}$$

Since Π does not contain any assumptions that are not withdrawn, and since the original assumption $\neg\phi$ is withdrawn, this is a derivation that shows that $\vdash \phi$. □

Here are some other facts:

Fact 16 $\Gamma \vdash \psi \Rightarrow \phi_1 \ldots \phi_n \vdash \psi$ for a finite set $\{\phi_1 \ldots \phi_n\} \subseteq \Gamma$

The proof is trivial.

Fact 17 Suppose $\phi_1 \ldots \phi_n \vdash \psi$. Then there is an derivation of ψ that starts with the assumptions $\phi_1 \ldots \phi_n$ in which after step n no assumptions occur that are not withdrawn.

Proof. Given the assumption there is a derivation of the form:

$$\begin{array}{ll} \phi_1 & \texttt{A} \\ \vdots & \\ \phi_n & \texttt{A} \\ \Pi & \\ \psi & \end{array}$$

Drop all active assumptions from Π. □

These facts are used in the proof of the following theorem:

Theorem 6 (Deduction theorem) $\Gamma \cup \{\phi\} \vdash \psi \Rightarrow \Gamma \vdash \phi \to \psi$

Proof. Suppose $\Gamma \cup \{\phi\} \vdash \psi$. Then we know from the facts just mentioned that there is a proof of the following form:

$$\begin{array}{ll} \Pi_0 & \\ \phi & \texttt{A} \\ \Pi_1 & \\ \psi & \end{array}$$

in which Π_0 contains only assumptions and Π_1 does not contain any assumptions that are not withdrawn. It is easy to see that it follows from this that $\Gamma \vdash \phi \to \psi$: simply continue the proof with $I_\to$:

$$\begin{array}{ll} \Pi_0 & \\ \left\lceil \phi \right. & \texttt{A} \\ \left| \Pi_1 \right. & \\ \left| \psi \right. & \\ \hline \phi \to \psi & I_\to \end{array}$$

□

Exercise 1 Prove the following facts:

a. $\phi \vdash \psi \Rightarrow \neg\psi \vdash \neg\phi$

b. $\Gamma \vdash \phi \,\&\, \Gamma \vdash \neg\phi \Rightarrow \Gamma \vdash \psi$
c. $\vdash \phi \vee \psi \& \vdash \neg\phi \Rightarrow \vdash \psi$

Another fact is:

Fact 18 $\Gamma \vdash \phi \,\&\, \Gamma \cup \{\phi\} \vdash \psi \Rightarrow \Gamma \vdash \psi$

Fact 18 is also called the 'Cut rule'. Its proof runs as follows:

Proof. From the assumptions that $\Gamma \vdash \phi$ and $\Gamma \cup \{\phi\} \vdash \psi$ we know that there are derivations of the following form:

$$\begin{array}{l} \Pi_0 \\ \Pi_1 \\ \phi \end{array}$$

and:

$$\begin{array}{ll} \phi & \mathtt{A} \\ \Pi_2 & \\ \Pi_3 & \\ \psi & \end{array}$$

in which Π_0 and Π_2 are the active assumptions from Γ, and Π_1 and Π_3 do not contain any assumptions that are not withdrawn. These we combine to form the derivation:

$$\begin{array}{l} \Pi_0 \\ \Pi_1 \\ \phi \\ \Pi_2 \\ \Pi_3 \\ \psi \end{array}$$

in which ϕ is no longer an assumption, but a derived formula. Since Π_0 and Π_2 contain all the active assumptions from Γ, this shows that $\Gamma \vdash \psi$. □

21.3 The soundness theorem

The soundness theorem for proposition logic states that if ϕ is derivable in the system of natural deduction from a set of premises Γ, then ϕ is also semantically entailed by Γ. To prove this we first of all ascertain that every rule of the natural deduction system as such is sound. The proof of the soundness theorem then follows easily.

As our first example we look at the elimination rule for $\rightarrow$. Suppose that ϕ and $\phi \rightarrow \psi$ are semantically entailed by Γ. With $E_{\rightarrow}$ we derive ψ. Soundness of this rule means simply that ψ is also semantically entailed by Γ. The following fact states this:

Fact 19 $\Gamma \models \phi \,\&\, \Gamma \models \phi \to \psi \Rightarrow \Gamma \models \psi$

Proof. Suppose that $\Gamma \models \phi \,\&\, \Gamma \models \phi \to \psi$. We now need to show that every valuation V that makes (all formulas in) Γ true, also makes true ψ. Take a valuation V that makes Γ true. Given that $\Gamma \models \phi$ this means that V also makes ϕ true, and from $\Gamma \models \phi \to \psi$ we can conclude that V also makes $\phi \to \psi$ true. From this it follows directly that V also makes ψ true. □

The second example is the *EFSQ*-rule:

Fact 20 $\Gamma \models \bot \Rightarrow \Gamma \models \psi$

Proof. For the special proposition letter $\bot$ it holds that $V(\bot) = 0$, for all V. Then it follows immediately from $\Gamma \models \bot$ that there is no V that makes Γ true. And from that it follows that $\Gamma \models \psi$, for all ψ. □

The other rules are left as an exercise to the reader.

Exercise 2 Prove the following facts:

a. $\Gamma \models \phi \,\&\, \Gamma \models \psi \Rightarrow \Gamma \models \phi \wedge \psi$ (*)
b. $\Gamma \models \phi \wedge \psi \Rightarrow \Gamma \models \phi$
c. $\Gamma \models \phi \wedge \psi \Rightarrow \Gamma \models \psi$
d. $\Gamma \models \phi \Rightarrow \Gamma \models \phi \vee \psi$
e. $\Gamma \models \psi \Rightarrow \Gamma \models \phi \vee \psi$
f. $\Gamma \models \phi \vee \psi, \Gamma \models \phi \to \chi \,\&\, \Gamma \models \psi \to \chi \Rightarrow \Gamma \models \chi$ (*)
g. $\Gamma \cup \{\phi\} \models \psi \Rightarrow \Gamma \models \phi \to \psi$
h. $\Gamma \models \phi \,\&\, \Gamma \models \neg\phi \Rightarrow \Gamma \models \bot$
i. $\Gamma \cup \{\phi\} \models \bot \Rightarrow \Gamma \models \neg\phi$ (*)
j. $\Gamma \models \neg\neg\phi \Rightarrow \Gamma \models \phi$

In the proof of the soundness theorem we assemble these separate facts.

Theorem 7 (Soundness Theorem) $\Gamma \vdash \phi \Rightarrow \Gamma \models \phi$

Proof. We prove the following:

$$\text{For every } \phi \text{ and } \Gamma: \text{ if } \Pi \text{ is a deduction of } \phi \text{ from } \Gamma, \text{ then } \Gamma \models \phi$$

The proof is by induction to the number of steps in the deduction Π.

- *Base step:* Π consists of one step. Then Π is of the form :

  1. ϕ A

  and hence ϕ is an element of Γ. Obviously, every V that makes Γ true also makes ϕ true.

- *Induction step:* Π consists of more than one step. The induction hypothesis states that soundness has already been proven for all derivations that are a proper part of Π. What needs to be shown is that the last step in Π is sound. We do that by simply going through all the cases.

As examples we consider $E_\neg$, $I_\rightarrow$, $E_\wedge$ and $I_\neg$.

- $E_\neg$: Suppose ϕ is derived by using $E_\neg$. This means that $\phi = \bot$ and that Π has the following form:

$$\begin{array}{l} \Pi_0 \\ \psi \\ \Pi_1 \\ \neg\psi \\ \bot \end{array}$$

The active assumptions of Π_0 and Π_1 are also active assumptions of Π, and are hence elements of Γ. We apply the induction hypothesis to the derivations:

$$\begin{array}{l} \Pi_0 \\ \psi \end{array}$$

and:

$$\begin{array}{l} \Pi_1 \\ \neg\psi \end{array}$$

This guarantees that $\Gamma \models \psi$ and $\Gamma \models \neg\psi$. And since $\Gamma \models \phi \;\&\; \Gamma \models \neg\phi \Rightarrow \Gamma \models \bot$ (see exercise 2 h), this means that $\Gamma \models \bot$.

- $I_\rightarrow$: Suppose ϕ is derived by application of $I_\rightarrow$. Then ϕ is of the form $\phi_0 \rightarrow \phi_1$ and Π is of the following form:

$$\begin{array}{l|ll} & \Pi_0 & \\ & \phi_0 & \mathtt{A} \\ & \Pi_1 & \\ & \phi_1 & \\ \hline & \phi_0 \rightarrow \phi_1 & I_\rightarrow \end{array}$$

If we leave out the last line, we get:

$$\begin{array}{ll} \Pi_0 & \\ \phi_0 & \mathtt{A} \\ \Pi_1 & \\ \phi_1 & \end{array}$$

To this we apply the induction hypothesis, which gives us that $\Gamma \cup \{\phi_0\} \models \phi_1$. Since $\Gamma \cup \{\phi\} \models \psi \Rightarrow \Gamma \models \phi \rightarrow \psi$ (see exercise 2 g), it follows from that $\Gamma \models \phi_0 \rightarrow \phi_1$.

- $E_\wedge$: Suppose ϕ is derived using $E_\wedge$. Then Π is of the following form:

$$\begin{array}{ll} \Pi_0 & \\ \phi \wedge \psi & \\ \Pi_1 & \\ \phi & E_\wedge \end{array}$$

  in which Π_0 consists of the active assumptions from Γ and Π_1 has no active assumptions. The induction hypothesis tells us that $\Gamma \models \phi \wedge \psi$. Since $\Gamma \models \phi \wedge \psi \Rightarrow \Gamma \models \phi$ (exercise 2 b), it follows that $\Gamma \models \phi$.
- $I_\neg$: Suppose ϕ is derived by $I_\neg$. Then ϕ is of the form $\neg\psi$, and the derivation looks like this:

$$\begin{array}{ll} \Pi_0 & \\ \psi & \mathtt{A} \\ \Pi_1 & \\ \bot & \\ \hline \neg\psi & I_\neg \end{array}$$

  Here Π_0 and Π_1 are as above. If we drop the last step from this derivation we get:

$$\begin{array}{ll} \Pi_0 & \\ \psi & \mathtt{A} \\ \Pi_1 & \\ \bot & \end{array}$$

  Here, the assumption ψ is no longer withdrawn, but active. We apply the induction hypothesis to $\Gamma \cup \{\psi\} \models \bot$, and since $\Gamma \cup \{\phi\} \models \bot \Rightarrow \Gamma \models \neg\phi$ (exercise 2 i) this guarantees that $\Gamma \models \neg\psi$.

□

The other cases proceed in analogous fashion. In each case one of the above facts can be used.

On the basis of the soundness theorem we can now prove that certain formulas are not derivable, by showing that they are not semantically entailed. This is useful because non-derivability is difficult to prove directly, whereas non-entailment can always be decided by specifying a counter-example.

A simple example: in order to show that $p \to q \nvdash q \to p$ it suffices to show that $p \to q \not\models q \to p$, which we do by specifying a valuation V for p and q such that $V(p \to q) = 1$ and $V(q \to p) = 0$.

21.4 The completeness theorem

21.4.1 *A sketch of the proof*

Formulated directly, the completeness theorem reads as follows:

$$\Gamma \models \phi \Rightarrow \Gamma \vdash \phi$$

This says that every formula ϕ that is semantically entailed by a set of formulas Γ, can also be derived syntactically from that set. Although we can prove the completeness theorem in this direct formulation, in the case of predicate logic the proof is complicated. This is because the concept of semantic entailment (semantic validity), although intuitively clear, is difficult to survey because it quantifies over a potentially infinite collection of potentially infinite models. That is why completeness is usually not proven directly, but in the form of its contraposition:

$$\Gamma \nvdash \phi \Rightarrow \Gamma \not\models \phi$$

The insight that completeness can be proven in this way, and the method to do so, is from Leon Henkin. For proposition logic, a proof of the direct version is less complicated, but we give here the indirect one in order to illustrate the basic concepts that are used in the Henkin-construction. We first give an informal sketch of these concepts and then turn to a more precise, formal treatment in the next sections.

The first concept is that of consistency. Intuitively, we call a set of formulas consistent if they do not contradict each other. Now assume that a formula ϕ cannot be derived from some set of formulas Γ. That means that we can add $\neg\phi$ without risk of contradiction to Γ. In other words, if ϕ cannot be derived from Γ, then $\Gamma \cup \{\neg\phi\}$ is consistent. This is easy to see. Suppose that $\Gamma \cup \{\neg\phi\}$ is inconsistent, then it contains a contradiction, and that means that the *Falsum* $\bot$ can be derived from Γ using the $E_{\neg} - rule$. And if that is the case, then we can derive ϕ from Γ as well (see exercise 2 i), which contradicts our assumption.

The second concept is concerned with the relation between consistency and satisfiability. We call a set of formulas Γ satisfiable if there is a valuation V such that $V(\phi) = 1$ for every $\phi \in \Gamma$. The key insight is that if we can show that consistency implies satisfiability, we have in fact proven the completeness theorem in the above, indirect formulation. This can be seen as follows. Consider the consistent set $\Gamma \cup \{\neg\phi\}$. If consistency implies satisfiability, then there is a V such that $V(\psi) = 1$ for every $\psi \in \Gamma$ and $V(\neg\phi) = 1$, i.e., $V(\phi) = 0$. And from that it follows that $\Gamma \not\models \phi$.

In this way, the task of proving the completeness theorem is 'reduced' to the task of proving the so-called 'consistency theorem:

If Γ is consistent, then there is a $V: V(\phi) = 1$ for every $\phi \in \Gamma$

In order to be able to prove the consistency theorem we need one more concept, that of a maximally consistent set. If we are to show that the consistency of Γ implies that there is a valuation that makes every $\phi \in \Gamma$ true, then we would like to be able to 'read off' that valuation from Γ itself. However, for a given consistent Γ there is usually more than one valuation that makes every $\phi \in \Gamma$ true. The idea is then to extend Γ in such a way that we get a *maximally consistent* set Γ': every addition of a formula to Γ' will make it inconsistent. If we can show that every consistent Γ can be extended to a maximally consistent Γ', then our task is reduced to proving that to such a maximally consistent Γ' corresponds a valuation that makes any ϕ true if and only $\phi \in \Gamma'$.

21.4.2 *Consistent and maximally consistent sets*

In this section we provide some more detail concerning the concepts of consistency and maximal consistency and their relation.

We start with consistency:

Definition 44 (Consistency)
A set of formulas Γ is *consistent* iff $\Gamma \nvdash \bot$, otherwise Γ is *inconsistent*

So, Γ is *in*consistent iff $\Gamma \vdash \bot$. Other, equivalent, definitions of consistency are:

- Γ is inconsistent iff there is a formula ϕ such that $\Gamma \vdash \phi$ and $\Gamma \vdash \neg\phi$
- Γ is inconsistent iff for all formulas ψ it holds that $\Gamma \vdash \psi$

Exercise 3 Prove that these definitions are equivalent to definition 44.

Proof. Suppose $\Gamma \vdash \bot$ (= def. 1). From that it follows with the EFSQ-rule that $\Gamma \vdash \psi$, for every ψ (= def. 3). That implies that $\Gamma \vdash \phi$ & $\Gamma \vdash \neg\phi$ (= def. 2). And from that, it follows, with the $E_{\neg}$-rule, that $\Gamma \vdash \bot$. □

Some important consequences are the following:

Fact 21

1. Γ is consistent iff there is at least one formula ϕ such that $\Gamma \nvdash \phi$
2. $\Gamma \cup \{\phi\}$ is inconsistent iff $\Gamma \vdash \neg\phi$
3. $\Gamma \cup \{\neg\phi\}$ is consistent iff $\Gamma \nvdash \phi$
4. If Γ is consistent, at least one of the two sets $\Gamma \cup \{\phi\}$, $\Gamma \cup \{\neg\phi\}$ is also consistent

Proof. We do a couple of cases.

- 1, $\Rightarrow$: suppose Γ is consistent and that for all ϕ: $\Gamma \vdash \phi$. Then $\Gamma \vdash \phi$ and $\Gamma \vdash \neg\phi$, and hence $\Gamma \vdash \bot$, which contradicts the assumption that Γ is consistent.

- 1, $\Leftarrow$: suppose there is a ϕ: $\Gamma \nvdash \phi$ and suppose Γ is not consistent. Then $\Gamma \vdash \bot$, and with *EFSQ*-rule we get $\Gamma \vdash \phi$ for all ϕ, which contradicts the first assumption.
- 2, $\Rightarrow$: suppose $\Gamma \cup \{\phi\} \vdash \bot$. There is a derivation:

$$\begin{array}{ll} \Pi_0 & \\ \phi & \mathtt{A} \\ \Pi_1 & \\ \bot & \end{array}$$

  with Π_0 consisting of all active assumptions from Γ. Continue this derivation as follows:

$$\begin{array}{ll} \Pi_0 & \\ \left\lceil \begin{array}{l} \phi \\ \Pi_1 \\ \bot \end{array} \right. & \begin{array}{l} \mathtt{A} \\ \\ \\ \end{array} \\ \hline \neg\phi & I_\neg \end{array}$$

  This shows that $\Gamma \vdash \neg\phi$.
- 2, $\Leftarrow$: suppose $\Gamma \vdash \neg\phi$. Then there is a derivation:

$$\begin{array}{l} \Pi_0 \\ \Pi_1 \\ \neg\phi \end{array}$$

  in which Π_0, Π_1 are as usual. Continue as follows:

$$\begin{array}{ll} \Pi_0 & \\ \Pi_1 & \\ \neg\phi & \\ \phi & \mathtt{A} \\ \bot & \end{array}$$

  This shows that $\Gamma \cup \{\phi\}$ is inconsistent.
- 3, $\Rightarrow$: suppose that $\Gamma \cup \{\neg\phi\}$ is consistent and also that $\Gamma \vdash \phi$. Then there is a derivation:

$$\begin{array}{l} \Pi_0 \\ \Pi_1 \\ \phi \end{array}$$

  in which Π_0, Π_1 as usual. Continue that derivation as follows:

$$\begin{array}{ll} \Pi_0 & \\ \Pi_1 & \\ \phi & \\ \neg\phi & \mathtt{A} \\ \bot & G_\neg \end{array}$$

This shows that $\Gamma \cup \{\neg\phi\} \vdash \bot$, and hence that $\Gamma \cup \{\neg\phi\}$ is inconsistent, which contradicts the assumption.

- 3, $\Leftarrow$: see 1.
- 4: suppose that Γ is consistent, and that both $\Gamma \cup \{\phi\}$ and $\Gamma \cup \{\neg\phi\}$ are inconsistent. Then there exist derivations:

$$\begin{array}{ll} \Pi_0 & \\ \phi & \mathtt{A} \\ \Pi_1 & \\ \bot & G_\neg \end{array}$$

and:

$$\begin{array}{ll} \Pi_2 & \\ \phi & \mathtt{A} \\ \Pi_3 & \\ \bot & G_\neg \end{array}$$

in which Π_0, Π_2 both contain the active assumptions from Γ. Continue these derivations as follows:

$$\begin{array}{ll} \Pi_0 & \\ \phi & \mathtt{A} \\ \Pi_1 & \\ \bot & \\ \hline \phi \to \bot & I_\to \end{array}$$

and:

$$\begin{array}{ll} \Pi_0 & \\ \neg\phi & \mathtt{A} \\ \Pi_1 & \\ \bot & \\ \hline \neg\phi \to \bot & I_\to \end{array}$$

This shows that $\Gamma \vdash \phi \to \bot$ ànd $\Gamma \vdash \neg\phi \to \bot$. Combine this with $\Gamma \vdash \phi \vee \neg\phi$ and we have that $\Gamma \vdash \bot$, which contradicts the assumption that Γ is consistent.

□

The second concept that of a *maximally consistent* set:

Definition 45 (Maximal consistency)
A set of formulas Γ is *maximally consistent* iff

1. Γ is consistent
2. every Γ' such that $\Gamma' \supset \Gamma$ is inconsistent

So, a maximally consistent set of formulas is a consistent set to which no formula can be added on pain of inconsistency. An alternative definition is:

- Γ is maximally consistent iff Γ is consistent and if $\Gamma \cup \{\phi\}$ is consistent, then $\phi \in \Gamma$

Two properties connected with (maximal) consistency are the following:

- Γ is *syntactically closed* iff Γ is consistent and for every ϕ it holds that $\Gamma \vdash \phi$ or $\Gamma \vdash \neg\phi$
- Γ is *deductively closed* iff if $\Gamma \vdash \phi$ then $\phi \in \Gamma$

A syntactically closed set of formulas contains maximal information in this sense that a decision can be reached on every formula: either that formula itself or its negation can be derived from the set. A deductively closed set already contains everything that can be derived from it. (Note: there is only one inconsistent deductively closed set.)

The following fact specifies some important properties of maximally consistent sets:

Fact 22 Let Γ be a maximally consistent set, ϕ, ψ arbitrary formulas. Then:

1. $\phi \in \Gamma$ iff $\Gamma \vdash \phi$
2. $\neg\phi \in \Gamma$ iff $\phi \notin \Gamma$
3. $\phi \wedge \psi \in \Gamma$ iff $\phi \in \Gamma$ and $\psi \in \Gamma$
4. $\phi \vee \psi \in \Gamma$ iff $\phi \in \Gamma$ or $\psi \in \Gamma$
5. $\phi \rightarrow \psi \in \Gamma$ iff $\phi \notin \Gamma$ or $\psi \in \Gamma$

Proof. We do one part of 2, and one of 5:

- 2, $\Leftarrow$: suppose $\phi \notin \Gamma$. Then $\Gamma \cup \{\phi\}$ is inconsistent. Then it follows that $\Gamma \cup \{\phi\} \vdash \bot$. Suppose that derivation looks like this:

$$\begin{array}{ll} \Pi_0 & \\ \phi & \texttt{A} \\ \Pi_1 & \\ \bot & \end{array}$$

  in which Π_0 consists of the assumptions from Γ. We can continue this derivation as follows:

$$\begin{array}{ll} \Pi_0 & \\ \left\lceil \phi \right. & \texttt{A} \\ \left| \Pi_1 \right. & \\ \left\lfloor \bot \right. & \\ \hline \neg\phi & I_{\neg} \end{array}$$

  which shows that $\Gamma \vdash \neg\phi$. Using fact 21.1 we can conclude that $\neg\phi \in \Gamma$.

- 5, $\Rightarrow$: suppose $\phi \rightarrow \psi \in \Gamma$. If $\phi \notin \Gamma$, we are done. But if $\phi \in \Gamma$, then we need to show that $\psi \in \Gamma$. Since $\phi \rightarrow \psi, \phi \vdash \psi$, and, by assumption,

$\phi \to \psi, \phi \in \Gamma$, we know that $\Gamma \vdash \psi$, from which we can conclude, using 20.1 again, that $\psi \in \Gamma$.
The other cases proceed in analogous fashion.

□

Note that 21.1 states that maximally consistent sets are deductively closed, and that from 21.2 in combination with 21.1 we can conclude that such sets are also syntactically complete.

Exercise 4 Prove the remaining cases of fact 21.

We finish by looking at the relation between consistent and maximally consistent sets of formulas:

Fact 23 (Lindenbaum)
Every consistent set of formulas is contained in a maximally consistent set.

Proof. The formulas of a language of proposition logic can be summed up in an infinitely long sequence of formulas. Let Γ be a consistent set of formulas. Then we define an infinite sequence of sets of formulas $\Gamma_0 \subseteq \Gamma_1 \subseteq \ldots$ as follows:

- $\Gamma_0 = \Gamma$
- $\Gamma_{n+1} = \begin{cases} \Gamma_n \cup \{\phi_n\} & \text{if } \Gamma_n \cup \{\phi_n\} \text{ is consistent} \\ \Gamma_n & \text{otherwise} \end{cases}$

Then define Γ' as $\bigcup_n \Gamma_n$. Claim: Γ' is maximally consistent:

- Γ' consistent: from the consistency of Γ it follows with induction that Γ_n is consistent, for every n. Now assume that Γ' is not consistent. Then $\Gamma' \vdash \bot$, which means that for finite k: $\phi_1 \ldots \phi_k \in \Gamma'$ & $\phi_1 \ldots \phi_k \vdash \bot$ (given fact 22). But that means also that for certain i we already have that $\phi_1 \ldots \phi_k \in \Gamma_i$, and hence that $\Gamma_i \vdash \bot$, which contradicts the consistency of Γ_i.
- Γ' maximal: suppose it is not. then there exists a ϕ such that $\Gamma' \cup \{\phi\}$ is consistent, and $\phi \notin \Gamma'$. However, in the construction of the sequence $\Gamma_0 \subseteq \Gamma_1 \subseteq \ldots$ the formula ϕ must have occurred somewhere, say at Γ_k. Now consider Γ_{k-1}. If $\Gamma' \cup \{\phi\}$ is consistent, then so is $\Gamma_{k-1} \cup \{\phi\}$. But from that it follows that $\phi \in \Gamma_k$, and hence that $\phi \in \Gamma'$. That contradicts the assumption that Γ' is not maximal.

□

At this point we have all the material we need to prove the completeness theorem.

21.4.3 *Completeness*

We repeat the direct formulation of the completeness theorem:

Theorem 8 (Completeness theorem)
$\Gamma \models \phi \Rightarrow \Gamma \vdash \phi$

As indicated earlier, we do not prove the completeness theorem directly, but prove its contraposition:

$$\Gamma \nvdash \phi \Rightarrow \Gamma \not\models \phi$$

We do that as follows. We know that if $\Gamma \nvdash \phi$, $\Gamma \cup \{\neg\phi\}$ is consistent (fact 20.3). If we can show that if a set of formulas is consistent, there is a valuation that makes all its elements true, then we are done. From the consistency of $\Gamma \cup \{\neg\phi\}$ it then follows that there is a valuation V that makes $\Gamma \cup \{\neg\phi\}$ true. Such a V makes both Γ as well as $\neg\phi$ true. But since that V cannot also make ϕ true, it follows that $\Gamma \not\models \phi$.

So our task is reduced to proving the following theorem:

Theorem 9 (Consistency theorem (Henkin)) If Γ is consistent, then there exists a valuation V such that $V(\phi) = 1$, for all $\phi \in \Gamma$

Proof. We know that every consistent Γ is contained in a maximally consistent Γ' (Lindenbaum). Choose a valuation V such that $V(p) = 1$ iff $p \in \Gamma'$. With induction to the construction of ϕ we prove that $V(\phi) = 1$ iff $\phi \in \Gamma'$.

- *Base step*: p atomic. If $p \neq \bot$, then the result immediately follows. If $p = \bot$, then $V(p) = 0$ and $p \notin \Gamma'$, by the consistency of Γ'.
- *Induction step*: we do the cases $\phi = \neg\psi$, $\phi = \psi \to \chi$, and $\phi = \psi \wedge \chi$.
  - $\phi = \neg\psi$: $V(\neg\psi) = 1$ iff $V(\psi) = 0$. From the induction hypothesis it follows that $\psi \notin \Gamma'$. Given fact 21.2 we can then conclude that $\neg\psi \in \Gamma'$.
  - $\phi = \psi \to \chi$: $V(\psi \to \chi) = 1$ iff $V(\psi) = 0$ or $V(\chi) = 1$. The induction hypothesis tells us that $\psi \notin \Gamma'$ or $\chi \in \Gamma'$, and with fact 21.5 it follows that $\psi \to \chi \in \Gamma'$.
  - $\phi = \psi \wedge \chi$: $\phi = \psi \wedge \chi$. $V(\psi \wedge \chi) = 1 \Leftrightarrow V(\psi) = V(\chi) = 1$. The induction hypothesis tells us that $\psi, \chi \in \Gamma'$. And fact 21.3 then gives that $\psi \wedge \chi \in \Gamma'$.

□

The other cases proceed analogously; in each case one of the facts in 21 is used. It will be clear that this also proves the consistency theorem.

Exercise 5 Do the remaining cases.

Part III

Beyond Standard Logic

22
Many-valued logic

In this chapter and the next two we explore the boundaries of classical logic as we have introduced it in the previous chapters. As was emphasised a couple of times, and as has already become clear in some of the philosophical excursus, pluralism is a characteristic of contemporary logic. There is a wide variety of systems, — languages, interpretations —, that logicians develop and study, and that philosophers and scientists use to model conceptual and empirical phenomena.

It will not be possible in the limited scope of this introduction to do justice to the whole gamut of logical systems that are available. We can only illustrate a few aspects. In this chapter we look at many-valued logic, in the next one we introduce some core notions from intensional logic, and in the last chapter we will explore the boundaries between semantics and pragmatics, and the repercussions thereof for the application of logic in the study of natural language.

22.1 Why many-valued logics?

Classical logic knows two truth values: 'true' and 'false', which are commonly represented as '1' and '0', and is therefore a two-valued system. Besides that, classical logic also satisfies the principle of excluded middle, which states that every formula is either true or false: $\phi \vee \neg\phi$ is a valid principle in classical logic. Note that recognising only two truth values as such is not the same as subscribing to excluded middle (bi-valence): one could recognise no other truth values than 'true' and 'false', yet also hold that some statements are neither true nor false.

A many-valued logic is one that recognises more values than 'true' and 'false'.[1] There are three-valued systems and four-valued ones, of which we will meet a couple of examples, but also systems with larger, or even with an infinite number of values.

Before we present some examples, we first look at a couple of cases where logicians have considered that many-valued systems have a role to play. There are actually quite a few reasons for considering many-valued logics.

A well-known and prominent case is the analysis of so-called 'futura contingentia', which are sentences that express a claim about the occurrence of some future contingent event. The logic of vague expressions presents another one. Presupposition and presupposition failure have been analysed with many-valued logics as well. And it has been argued that quantum-phenomena can only be described properly using a language that has a many-valued logic.

Let's look at three of these cases in a bit more detail.

22.1.1 *Futura contingentia*

Futura contingentia sentences are sentences that are concerned with contingent future events. Their analysis presents a challenge that is perhaps best illustrated with the well-known 'sea battle' problem.

Consider the following sentence:

(1) There will be a sea-battle tomorrow

This looks like an ordinary, contingent sentence, i.e., a sentence that could be true, or that could be false. However, consider the following reasoning:

- Premise 1: There will be a sea-battle tomorrow, or there will not be a sea-battle tomorrow.
- Premise 2: If there will be a sea-battle, then it is already true now that there will be one.
- Premise 3: And if there won't be a sea-battle, then it is already true now that will not be one.
- Conclusion: Either case, the future is determined.

But if the future is determined, then (1) is not a contingent statement.

Determinism of the future has substantial consequences, and might not be something that we are willing to accept. Yet the reasoning seems flawless, so what is going on here? There are different strategies open to us, and we will discuss them in more detail in the next chapter, that deals with Aristotle's formulation of the problem and his solution.

For our present purposes it suffices to note that the first premise of the argument is an instantiation of the principle of excluded middle, i.e., ϕ: $\phi \vee \neg\phi$. But that opens up a strategy for avoiding the conclusion: if we are willing to treat sentences about contingent events in the future as lacking a truth value, we can dismiss the argument as being based on a false premise.

22.1.2 *Presupposition failure*

As we have seen in chapter 17 the principle of excluded middle also plays a role in the discussion on how to analyse descriptions. All approaches agree that definite descriptions come with an existence claim.[2] The key question is then how to deal with cases where this fails to be satisfied:

(2) The King of France is bald
(3) France does not have a king

What is the consequence of (3) being true for the truth value status of (2)? This puts the principle of excluded middle on the spot. If we want to maintain excluded middle we are committed to considering (2) to be false. This, as we saw, was Russell's choice. But we can also go with Strawson and say that when (3) is true, the use of the description in (2) fails to refer, and therefore (2) lacks a truth value. Then we jettison excluded middle.

22.1.3 *Vagueness*

Vague expressions, which abound in natural languages, constitute another case in which the principle of excluded middle can be argued to fail.

What is at stake is best illustrated by means of the following argument:

- Premise 1: Someone with no hairs on their skull is bald
- Premise 2: Someone who has one hair more than someone who is bald, is bald
- Conclusion: Everyone is bald

This argument goes by the name of the 'Sorites paradox'.[3] It is clear that something is wrong with this argument. The conclusion is obviously false, and the first premise is basically a definition of what baldness is (i.e., of what 'bald' means). So, one might conclude that premise 2 is the culprit. However, it is not immediately obvious that premise 2 is false.

Again, giving up excluded middles provides a way out: some people are clearly bald, others are clearly not; and then there are some that are neither. To be sure, that still leaves a number of issues to be resolved. The most important of these is how to give an account of where and how the border between the three categories (bold – neither bold nor hairy – hairy) is to be constructed. But suspending excluded middle is a necessary first step if one wants to go that route.

The formulation of the paradox should not mislead one into thinking that these are merely clever tricks from logicians. Vagueness is a pervasive phenomenon, and occurs not just with the meaning of a couple of predicates. Many expressions in natural language have vague boundaries. Also, vagueness has clear perceptual analogues. For example, one can construct colour gradients with clearly distinguishable colours at the two extremes, but where any two adjacent colours are indistinguishable for the human eye.

22.2 But what about logic?

The examples discussed in the previous section seem to provide good reasons for thinking that the principle of excluded middle cannot be maintained as one that applies across the board, to each and every sentence. These are cases where there are good arguments to restrict its application. But is that all there is to it?

That answer is that it is not. Allowing a formula ϕ to be neither true nor false is easy. But the hard question is: what does that mean for formulas in which ϕ occurs as a part? As we have seen above, sentences that are arguably neither true nor false occur in complex pieces of reasoning, in argument schemes of various forms, and as subexpressions of more complex ones.

We take proposition logic as our frame of reference. Then questions that need to be answered are: if ϕ is neither true nor false, what about $\neg\phi$? what about $\phi \vee \psi$? etc. In order to answer these questions we need to look into a redefinition of the truth-tables for the connectives. As we shall see that can be done in different ways, giving rise to different many-valued logics.

22.2.1 *A case in point: negation*

Different many-valued logics are often motivated by different observations that one wants the logic in question to account for. We can illustrate this by looking at two different ways of dealing with negation.

The first case concerns presupposition failure. Suppose (a.) is neither true nor false. Then what about (b.)?

(a.) The King of France is bald
(b.) It is not the case that the King of France is bald

Intuitively, (b.) seems true. So here we have the negation of a sentence that is neither true nor false that itself is a true sentence

The second case concerns 'futura contingentia' sentences. Suppose (c.) is neither true nor false. Then what about (d.)?

(c.) There will be a sea-battle tomorrow
(d.) It is not the case that there will be a sea-battle tomorrow

Intuitively, (d.) seems neither true nor false. So in this case the negation inherits the property of being neither true nor false from the sentence from which it is formed.

This shows that different treatments of negation, and hence different overall logics, are called for in different cases.

22.2.2 *Consequences*

Treating connectives differently has consequences for various logical principles. The principle of excluded middle has already been discussed. But other principles may be affected as well.

An important logical principle is the principle of non-contradiction: $\neg(\phi \wedge \neg\phi)$. In classical logic the principles of excluded middle and non-contradiction are equivalent. But this may not hold in some many-valued logics.

Another key logical principle is the principle of identity: $\phi \rightarrow \phi$.This, too, is a valid principle in classical logic, but that may be different in a many-valued one.

And then there is the inter-definability of connectives. In what follows we will illustrate the effects of many-valued logics in terms of the stock example of the inter-definability of $\wedge$ in terms $\vee, \neg$: $\phi \wedge \psi \Leftrightarrow \neg(\neg\phi \vee \neg\psi)$.

This leads to the following checklist that we can use to chart the properties of various many-valued logics:

excluded middle $\phi \vee \neg\phi$	**non-contradiction** $\neg(\phi \wedge \neg\phi)$	**identity** $\phi \rightarrow \phi$	**inter-definability** $\wedge$ in terms $\vee, \neg$, etc.
?	?	?	?

Figure 22.1: A checklist

As we shall see, in many cases the fact that a particular principle obtains, or fails, is by design. But there are also cases where it is an unintended side-effect.

22.3 Three-valued logics

In this section we look at a number of three-valued logics that illustrate the range of motivations and applications that go into constructing different logics. These are the systems of Łukaciewicz, Kleene (strong), and Bochvar and Kleene (weak).

These systems work in terms of three values which we indicate as $0, 1, \#$. Of these three 0 and 1 are interpreted as usual, viz., as 'false' and 'true', respectively. The value 1 is what is often called the 'designated value', i.e., the value in terms of which the usual concepts of validity, consequence and equivalence are defined. But as we shall see the interpretation of the third value $\#$ is different in different systems.

22.3.1 Łukaciewicz

The system of Łukaciewicz, a Polish logician who was active in the first half of the 20th century, was first proposed in Łukasiewicz (1920). Its inspiration was the sea-battle paradox of Aristotle, about which more in the next chapter. Łukaciewicz adds a third value with the intended interpretation of 'possible', i.e., a formula ϕ that has the value $\#$ is neither actually true (1) nor actually false (0), but could turn out to be either.

Łukaciewicz: truth tables

Let us start with the truth table Łukaciewicz defines for ¬. It looks as follows:[4]

ϕ	$\neg\phi$
1	0
#	#
0	1

Figure 22.2: Łukaciewicz, $\neg\phi$

According to this truth table, the negation of a formula works classically if the formula is true or false, and inherits its third value.

Then we have the truth table for conjunction:

ϕ \ ψ	1	#	0
1	1	#	0
#	#	#	0
0	0	0	0

Figure 22.3: Łukaciewicz, $\phi \wedge \psi$

Conjunction behaves like classical conjunction if the conjuncts are both true and both false, and also returns false whenever one of the conjuncts is, irrespective of the value of the other conjunct. One could say that the classical aspects of the conjunction are followed whenever possible.

A similar behaviour is displayed in the truth table for disjunction that Łukaciewicz proposes:

ϕ \ ψ	1	#	0
1	1	1	1
#	1	#	#
0	1	#	0

Figure 22.4: Łukaciewicz, $\phi \vee \psi$

Like in the case of conjunction, whenever the classical interpretation of disjunction applies, it is used: whenever one of the disjuncts is true, then the disjunction is true, irrespective of the value of the other disjunct; and the disjunction is false only when both disjuncts are false.

Finally, the truth table for the material implication:

ϕ \ ψ	1	#	0
1	1	#	0
#	1	1	#
0	1	1	1

Figure 22.5: Łukaciewicz, $\phi \rightarrow \psi$

Again we see that in all cases that are covered by the classical truth table, this truth table gives the same results. The third value # occurs only when the antecedent is true and the consequent has the third value, and if the antecedent has the third value and the consequent is false.

These truth tables for the various connectives are in accordance with Łukaciewicz's intended interpretation of # as signifying that a formula ϕ is 'possible'.

Thus, a conjunction is assigned # only if one of the conjuncts is true and the other 'possible', or if both are. For in the first two cases it could turn out that both conjuncts are true, and hence the whole conjunction is true; if both are # they could turn out both to be true, in which case the conjunction is true, or one or both of them could turn out to be false, and hence the conjunction as a whole would be false.

And in the case of disjunction we see an analogous pattern. A disjunction is assigned # only if one of the disjuncts is 0 and the other is #, or both are #. For in the first two cases the disjunction could turn out to be true because one of the disjuncts is true, or it could turn out to be false because both disjuncts are false. And in the third case, if one of the disjuncts turns out to be true, then the disjunction is true, and if both turn out the be false, the disjunction is false.

The case of implication is a bit more complicated. An implication $\phi \rightarrow \psi$ gets the value 'possible' if the value of antecedent is 1 and that of the consequent is # since the consequent may turn out to be false, in which case the implication is false. Analogously, if the value of the antecedent is # and that of the consequent is 0, the implication gets the value 'possible ', since the antecedent may turn out to be true, and then, again, the implication as such is false.

The complication is the assignment of 1 to $\phi \rightarrow \psi$ if both ϕ and ψ are assigned #. If ϕ is 'possible and ψ is 'possible', then the implication $\phi \rightarrow \psi$ is considered true. The motivation for this resides in implications of the form $\phi \rightarrow \phi$: if ϕ is 'possible', then this implication intuitively should come as true.

Łukaciewicz: logic

The definitions of validity, logical consequence, and logical equivalence remain as they are in classical logic. A formula ϕ is valid iff it is always assigned the value 1; ψ is a consequence of $\phi_1 \ldots \phi_n$ iff whenever $\phi_1 \ldots \phi_n$ are all assigned 1 so is ψ; and ϕ and ψ are equivalent iff they are always assigned the same value.

Given these definitions and given the truth tables defined above, what are the properties of the resulting logic? Let's check our indicators.

Obviously, excluded middle does not hold: if ϕ is assigned #, then so is $\neg\phi$, and hence also $\phi \vee \neg\phi$.

Non-contradiction does not hold either: if ϕ is assigned #, then so is $\neg\phi$; but then $\phi \wedge \neg\phi$ is assigned # as well, and hence also $\neg(\phi \wedge \neg\phi)$.

The principle of identity $\phi \rightarrow \phi$ does hold, as a check of the truth table for $\phi \rightarrow \psi$ reveals. Note that this is due to the fact that $\phi \rightarrow \psi$ is assigned 1 in case both ϕ and ψ are assigned #. As noted above, this does comply with the interpretation of # as 'possible'. This deviation in the truth table for $\rightarrow$ has consequences for inter-definability.

In classical logic, due to the definability of $\rightarrow$ in terms of $\neg$ and $\vee$, identity and excluded middle come to the same thing. But, as we saw, whereas identity is a valid principle in this three-valued logic, excluded middle is not:

$$\phi \rightarrow \phi \not\Leftrightarrow \neg\phi \vee \phi$$

That case of inter-definability thus fails. But, e.g., the definition of $\wedge$ in terms of $\neg$ and $\vee$ still goes through:

$$\phi \wedge \psi \Leftrightarrow \neg(\neg\phi \vee \neg\psi)$$

Summing up, this is the profile of Łukaciewicz's three-valued logic:

excluded middle	**non-contradiction**	**identity**	**inter-definability**
no	no	yes	partial

Figure 22.6: Properties of Łukaciewicz

Exercise 1 Show that the following hold in Łukaciewicz's three-valued logic:

a. $\neg\neg\phi$ is equivalent with ϕ
b. $\neg\phi$ is not a logical consequence of $\phi \rightarrow \neg\phi$

22.3.2 Kleene (strong)

Kleene (strong): truth tables

In the three-valued system of Kleene[5] the truth tables for $\neg$, $\wedge$, $\vee$ are as in Łukaciewicz's system.

The only point at which Kleene's system differs is in the truth table for material implication $\rightarrow$:

ϕ \ ψ	1	#	0
1	1	#	0
#	1	#	#
0	1	1	1

Figure 22.7: $\phi \rightarrow \psi$

The difference between Kleene's and Łukaciewicz's definition of $\rightarrow$ is in one spot: the case where both ϕ and ψ are assigned the value #. Where Łukaciewicz assigns $\phi \rightarrow \psi$ the value 1, Kleene assigns it the value #.

This is in accordance with another interpretation of #, viz., as signalling 'unknown', or 'undecided'. If both antecedent and consequent are 'unknown', then so must be the implication as a whole. That the antecedent turns out true and the consequent is false, in which case the implication is false, is not excluded, and neither are the outcomes that would make the implication true.

If we look back at the truth tables of the other connectives, we see that they conform with this interpretation of the third value # as well. For example, a conjunction is assigned # only if one of the conjuncts is true and the other 'unknown', or if both are. And a disjunction is assigned # only if one of the disjuncts is 0 and the other is #, or both are #.

Thus we see that the truth tables for the negation, conjunction and disjunction allow for two distinct interpretations: 'possible', as in łukaciewicz' system, and 'unknown' or 'undecided, as in the strong Kleene system. It is in the respective truth tables for the implication that the two interpretations make a difference.

Kleene (strong): logic

This one difference in the truth table for the implication has important consequences for the resulting logic.

As is easy to check, full inter-definability of the connectives is restored:

$$\phi \rightarrow \phi \Leftrightarrow \neg\phi \vee \phi$$

Excluded middle and non-contradiction do not hold, and neither does identity:

excluded middle	**non-contradiction**	**identity**	**inter-definability**
no	no	no	yes

Figure 22.8: Properties of Kleene (strong)

In fact, we can see that the strong Kleene three-valued system does not have any valid formulas: whenever a propositional variable p is assigned the third value # any complex formula ϕ in which p occurs cannot have the value 1. The proof goes by induction on the construction of ϕ.

In the Lukaciewicz system this is different because of the way in which the implication $\rightarrow$ is defined: that generates valid formulas.

Exercise 2

a. Give a truth table in Kleene's strong logic for the bi-conditional $\leftrightarrow$ that preserves definability of $\leftrightarrow$ in terms of $\rightarrow$ and $\wedge$
b. Do the same for the Łukaciewicz system
c. For which bi-conditional does it hold that logical equivalence of ϕ and ψ coincides with the validity of $\phi \leftrightarrow \psi$?

22.3.3 Bochvar–Kleene (weak)

We now briefly look into a different kind of three-valued system in which the third value # behaves differently because a different interpretation is assigned to it. This logic was proposed by Bochvar and also by Kleene.[6]

Bochvar–Kleene (weak): truth tables

The truth table for the negation $\neg$ is as expected:

ϕ	$\neg\phi$
1	0
#	#
0	1

Figure 22.9: $\neg\phi$

The specific nature of the Bochvar–Kleene (weak) system resides in the truth tables for the binary connectives.

This is the truth table for the conjunction $\wedge$:

ϕ \ ψ	1	#	0
1	1	#	0
#	#	#	#
0	0	#	0

Figure 22.10: $\phi \wedge \psi$

Note that the third value # dominates everything: whenever one of the conjuncts is assigned # so is the entire conjunction, irrespective of the value of the other conjunct. This means that falsity of a conjunct is not sufficient for the conjunction to be false as well.

A similar 'contagious' behaviour of # can be observed in the truth table for disjunction:

ϕ \ ψ	1	#	0
1	1	#	1
#	#	#	#
0	1	#	0

Figure 22.11: $\phi \vee \psi$

Here, too, # is dominant: whenever one of the disjuncts is assigned # the entire disjunction is; even is the other disjunct is assigned 1 the disjunction as a whole is still assigned #.

And the pattern repeats in the case of the implication $\rightarrow$:

ϕ \ ψ	1	#	0
1	1	#	0
#	#	#	#
0	1	#	1

Figure 22.12: $\phi \rightarrow \psi$

Again we see that # gets assigned to the whole implication $\phi \rightarrow \psi$ as soon as either the antecedent ϕ or the consequent ψ is assigned #.

The dominant behaviour of # is due to the fact that it is given a different interpretation from the ones that were attached to it in the Łukaciewicz system ('possible') and in the strong Kleene system ('unknown'/'undecided'). The interpretation that fits the patterns displayed in the truth tables of the Bochvar–Kleene (weak) system is 'meaningless'. Meaninglessness is contagious, a meaningless component is sufficient for making a complex formula containing it meaningless as well.

Bochvar–Kleene (weak): logic

If we look at the logic that is generated by the Bochvar–Kleene (weak) truth tables, we note that at the level of our key indicators it behaves like the strong Kleene system, despite having distinctly different truth tables for the connectives (except for negation), and a distinctly different interpretation of the third value $\#$.

Excluded middle, non-contradiction, and identity all fail to hold, and the connectives are inter-definable in the usual way.

excluded middle	**non-contradiction**	**identity**	**inter-definability**
no	no	no	yes

Figure 22.13: Properties of Bochvar–Kleene (weak)

So the differences become apparent only if we look at a more fine-grained level. Take as an example $\neg\phi \rightarrow (\phi \rightarrow \psi)$. This is classically valid, and it is also valid in the Łukaciewicz logic. It is not valid in either the Kleene strong logic or in the Bochvar–Kleene (weak) logic. But in the latter two systems it does have a different status. If we check the truth tables for this formula in the two systems we see that in the former system this formula is stronger than in the latter one.

If we would have a language with four different implication connectives: $\rightarrow_{\text{C}}, \rightarrow_{\text{Ł}}, \rightarrow_{\text{K-s}}, \rightarrow_{\text{B/K-w}}$, we could express this as follows:

$$\phi \rightarrow_{\text{C}} \psi \Rightarrow \phi \rightarrow_{\text{Ł}} \psi \Rightarrow \phi \rightarrow_{\text{K-s}} \psi \Rightarrow \phi \rightarrow_{\text{B/K-w}} \psi$$

22.4 Concluding remarks

The systems introduced above all have three values: $0, 1, \#$. Generalisations to systems with any finite number of values n, or even to an infinite number of values, exist as well. The interpretations of these values differ accordingly.

For example, there is a system defined by Gödel that assigns as values the real numbers in the interval $[0, 1]$. The definition of the values (abbreviated 'v') assigned to the various complex formulas is defined as follows:

- $v(\phi \wedge \psi) = \text{minimum}\ (v(\phi), v(\psi))$
- $v(\phi \vee \psi) = \text{maximum}\ (v(\phi), v(\psi))$
- $v(\neg\phi) = 1$ if $v(\phi) = 0$, $= 0$ otherwise
- $v(\phi \rightarrow \psi) = 1$ if $v(\phi) \leqslant v(\psi)$, $= v(\psi)$ otherwise

A possible interpretation of the values could be the reliability of the information that supports the claim that the formula is true.

Many-valued logics continue to be widely used in quantum logic and in various branches of computer science.[7]

In philosophy, the use of many-valued logics went out of fashion with the rise of modal logic, which deals with a range of similar problems in what appears to be a more intuitive way. However, there has been a revival of the use of many-valued logics recently, especially in the area of formal epistemology, where they are used in, for example, the analysis of the logic of justification.[8]

We end with a note on a cognitive aspect, which relates, albeit indirectly, to an issue that has been discussed before, viz., what is a logical constant? In a two-valued system we have $2^{2^2} = 2^4 = 16$ possible 2-place connectives. In a three-valued system that number is $3^{3^2} = 3^9 = 19.683$. How are we able to distinguish within all these functions which are the ones that correspond to interesting/legitimate/cognitively relevant/ ... connectives? Evidently, we have a need for general principles that identify plausible candidates, irrespective of the logical system that we are considering.

And that suggests strongly that our pragmatic willingness to accept a wide variety of possible logical systems as tools to solve whatever problem at hand, needs to be matched with more principled and cognitively motivated constraints to keep the abundance in check.

23

Excursus: temporal determinism

23.1 The topic

As we have seen in the previous chapter, 'futura contingentia' are sentences that are concerned with contingent future events. Their analysis presents a challenge that is perhaps best illustrated with the well-known 'sea battle' problem. We have already encountered this example in the previous chapter, but repeat it here for convenience's sake:

(1) There will be a sea-battle tomorrow

This looks like an ordinary, contingent statement, i.e., a statement that could be true or that could be false. However, now consider the following reasoning:

- Premise 1: There will be a sea-battle tomorrow, or there will not be a sea-battle tomorrow.
- Premise 2: If there will be a sea-battle, then it is already true now that there will be one.
- Premise 3: And if there won't be a sea-battle, then it is already true now that will not be one.
- Conclusion: Either case, the future is determined.

But if the future is determined, then (1) is not a contingent statement. So what is going on here? There are different strategies open to us.

One is to accept the argument. Contrary to our intuition, we conclude that contingent statements about the future are not possible, since the future is determined. But this raises a number of other questions: if the future is determined, why bother planning our actions? Why consider changing things? In what sense can we be held responsible for what we do? It seems to land us in a counter-intuitive position of absolute fatalism that is strongly at odds with how in fact we lead our lives.

If we decide not to accept the argument, we must find fault with one of the premises. Let's see whether we can reject the second premise.[1] This seems hard to argue against. It seems to be at the core of how we act. Given that a certain thing is going to happen, we prepare for it and act accordingly. If my plane is leaving tomorrow early in the morning, I pack my suitcase tonight. If my friend's birthday is next week, I plan to buy them a present in the coming days and make room for that in my agenda. And so on. A large part of what we do, and what we think about doing, is somehow determined by what is going to happen. The future in that sense plays a crucial part in our lives in the present. From that it appears to follow that we cannot but accept the second premise.[2]

But one could argue that there is a snag here: it seems that the considerations just mentioned depend on a hidden assumption, viz., that we know about the future events. If I don't know that my friend's birthday is next week because, for some reason or other, I think that it is only six months from now, the fact that next week is their birthday will not affect my actions in the way indicated. It appears that it is knowledge about future events, and not the future events per se, that plays a role in action and planning. And we can go one step further and argue that it is not knowledge but belief that is what plays the decisive role. If I believe that there is a general strike in public transport tomorrow, I will call a friend and ask for a ride in their car to get to work. But note that if they then tell me that the strike has been called off, I will adjust my planning accordingly. So 'truth about the future' does play a role, if only in the form of the assumption that contingent statements about the future are possible and that they can be true (or false).

This raises a number of interesting and complex questions: Can we have knowledge about future events? How do we form beliefs about them? What forms of justification for such beliefs are open to us?

We cannot go into these questions here, and neither do we need to, for our problem concerns the underlying ontological assumption about the future itself.[3] In an explanation of how 'futura contingentia' statements inform our actions, we cannot get around the epistemological dimension, but any explanation must be made to rest on a particular view of the structure of time.

For this we take another look at two conceptions of time we already briefly mentioned in chapter 18, viz., that of linear time and that of (right) branching time.

We assume that a temporal model consists of an infinite set T of discrete temporal points, and a relation $<$, read as 'earlier than'.[4] We add operators F, P, H, and G to the language of propositional logic with the following interpretations:

- $V_{M,t}(F\phi) = 1$ iff there exists a $t' > t$ s.th. $V_{M,t'}(\phi) = 1$
- $V_{M,t}(P\phi) = 1$ iff there exists a $t' < t$ s.th. $V_{M,t'}(\phi) = 1$
- $V_{M,t}(G\phi) = 1$ iff for all $t' > t$, $V_{M,t'}(\phi) = 1$
- $V_{M,t}(H\phi) = 1$ iff for all $t' < t$, $V_{M,t'}(\phi) = 1$

Thus $F\phi$ means 'ϕ will be true at some point in the future'; $P\phi$ means 'ϕ was true at some point in the past'; $G\phi$ means 'ϕ is always going to be true in the future'; and $H\phi$ means 'ϕ has always been true in the past. Here, 'future' and 'past' are relative to the time point at which the formula is evaluated.

Now consider the statement 'A sea-battle is going to take place tomorrow', and assume that our time-points are calendar days. Then we can introduce an additional operator $T\phi$, meaning 'ϕ will be true tomorrow', with the following semantics:

- $V_{M,t}(T\phi) = 1$ iff $V_{M,t'}(\phi) = 1$ where $t < t'$ and there is no t'' s.th. $t < t'' < t'$.

If we use a linear model of time, determinism is unavoidable. Let p read as 'A sea-battle occurs', Tp then means 'A sea-battle is going to take place tomorrow'. Furthermore suppose $V_{M,t_1}(p) = 1$. Then we have the situation depicted in Figure 23.1.

$$\begin{array}{ccccccccccccc} & & & & & & Tp & & p & & & & \\ \ldots & \longrightarrow & t_{-2} & \longrightarrow & t_{-1} & \longrightarrow & t_0 & \longrightarrow & t_1 & \longrightarrow & t_2 & \longrightarrow & \ldots \end{array}$$

Figure 23.1: The sea-battle in linear time (1)

It is easy to see that the situation in Figure 23.1 leads to that depicted in Figure 23.2. And since at any point $t < t_1$ Fp is true, it follows that at t_0 and any point preceding it HFp is true as well: if p is going to be true, then that has always already been the case. (Analogously we conclude that GPp is true from t_2 onwards.) Which means that we have the situation as depicted in Figure 23.3.

$$\begin{array}{ccccccccccccc} & & & & & & Tp & & p & & & & \\ \ldots & \longrightarrow & t_{-2} & \longrightarrow & t_{-1} & \longrightarrow & t_0 & \longrightarrow & t_1 & \longrightarrow & t_2 & \longrightarrow & \ldots \\ Fp & & Fp & & Fp & & Fp & & p & & Pp & & Pp \end{array}$$

Figure 23.2: The sea-battle in linear time (2)

The occurrence of a sea-battle tomorrow being a contingent affair, we might also have that $T\neg p$ is true at t_0 because $\neg p$ turns out to be true at t_1. But then we get the analogous deterministic conclusion that $HF\neg p$ is true at t_0 and at all the points preceding it.

If we take branching time as our model, this conclusion can be avoided, as is illustrated in Figure 23.4.[5] Since p is true at $t_1^{'}$ and $\neg p$ is true at $t_1^{''}$, we have both Fp and $F\neg p$ true at t_0, and at all points preceding it. That means that HFp will be false at all such points. Hence no temporal determinism: at

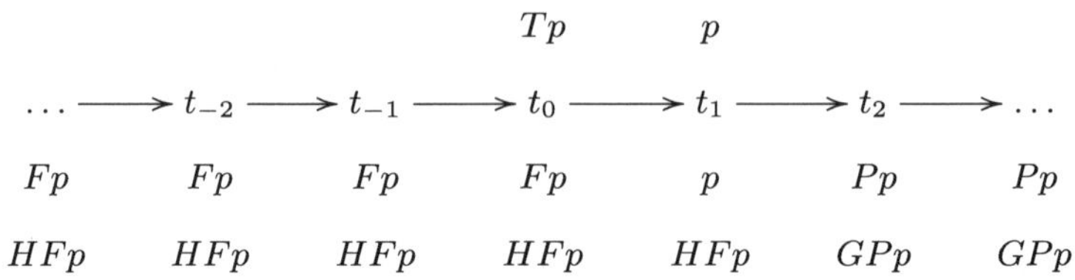

Figure 23.3: The sea-battle in linear time (3)

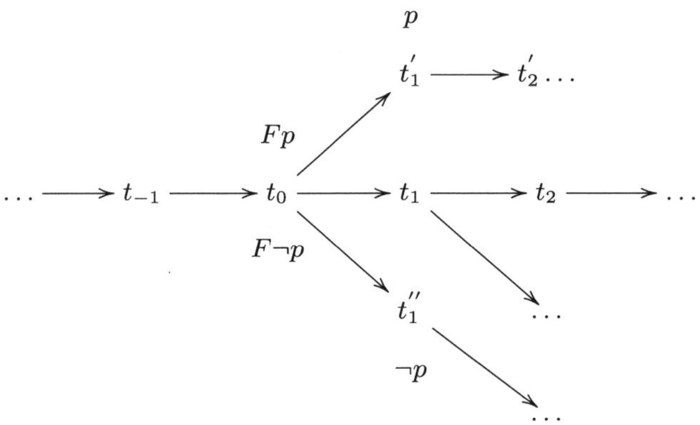

Figure 23.4: The sea-battle in branching time (1)

t_0 and all the points preceding it the future holds two possibilities: p coming out true and $\neg p$ coming out true.

Do note that GPp will be true at all the points on the branch originating in $t_1^{'}$, and that $GP\neg p$ will be true at all the points on the branch originating in $t_1^{''}$. The future is not determined, but in each of the possible futures the past is.

Now what about 'There will be a sea-battle tomorrow', i.e., Tp? If we apply the interpretation of $T\phi$ given above, we find ourselves in an awkward situation: it seems that both Tp and $T\neg p$ are true at t_0. This is illustrated in Figure 23.5.

Now both Fp and $F\neg p$ can be true at some point t. But can Tp and $T\neg p$ also both be true at t? Intuitively, $Tp \Leftrightarrow \neg T\neg p$ but that would rule out Tp and $T\neg p$ being true at the same time. This is one reason to say that Tp, and analogously $T\neg p$, is neither true nor false: the future is indeterminate. This is where the motivation for Łukaciewicz' three-valued logic resides.

However, there is a contravening intuition that starts from the fact if p happens, it seems correct to say that Tp was true. And analogously, of course,

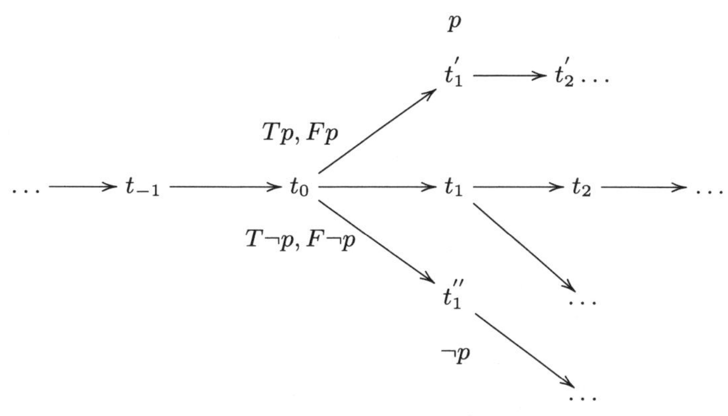

Figure 23.5: The sea-battle in branching time (2)

in case $\neg p$ does, then it would be true to say that $T\neg p$ was true: so, with the help of hindsight, we can assign a truth-value to Tp and $T\neg p$ after all.

But other possibilities are open as well. On a branching time model, we could interpret $T\phi$ as true at t iff there is a possible future, i.e., a branch rooted in t, in which ϕ is true at the 'tomorrow' of t on that branch. On that interpretation, Tp and $T\neg p$ being both true at the same time is no longer counterintuitive. This would give statements about the future the character of statements about possibilities, rather than about (assumed) facts.

A lot more can and should be said about these issues, these remarks just scratch the surface of this complex issue.[6] However, what we hope will be clear is that underlying the various options are distinct views on the structure of time and how those structures interact with the truth conditions of sentences about 'the' future.

23.2 The author

Aristotle (384 – 322 BCE) is one of the towering figures in Western philosophy. His influence in many areas has been enormous, and he continues to be read and discussed to this very day. It is no exaggeration to say that Aristotle's ideas have shaped many aspects of the Western tradition, in philosophy, but also in science, theology, and other areas.

Aristotle was born in Stagira in Macedonia, in the north of Greece, and joined Plato's Academy in Athens in around 367. He stayed there for a prolonged period of time. After Plato's death, Aristotle left Athens in around 347 to return to Macedonia, where in 343 he started tutoring the young son of Macedonia's king Phillipus II, Alexander, who later went on to conquer large parts of the Middle East and Near East and who re-shaped those regions decisively.

Aristotle's oeuvre is large and spans basically any topic that philosophers in that day and age were interested in, and then some. He wrote on poetry, theatre, politics, ethics, epistemology, logic, economics, physics, biology, and other empirical sciences. His views on causation and explanation shaped science until the modern age, when the advent of modern mechanics gave rise to a different model of scientific inquiry. He was honoured in the Muslim world as 'The First Teacher' and in the Christian world simply as 'The Philosopher'.

Among his many contributions, Aristotle's logic stands out as particularly important, certainly in the present context. He was the first to formulate a systematic account of valid reasoning in his syllogistics.[7]

Aristotle's syllogistics is concerned with valid patterns of reasoning involving sentences with a subject – predicate form. Basically these sentences describe relations between properties. For example, 'All A are B' states that the property A is included in the property B. Or, in our extensional, set-theoretical vocabulary, that the set of A-things is a subset of the set of B-things. Similarly, 'Some A are B' says that the set of A-things and the set of B-things have a non-empty intersection; 'Some A are not B' states that the set of A-things is not a subset of the set of B-things; and so on.[8]

Syllogistics was complemented by the Stoics who formulated rules for propositional reasoning. And the scholastic philosophers of the Middle Ages enriched Aristotle's system in various other directions. But Aristotle's logic of the syllogism remained at the core. And so did the subject – predicate form as the basic form of a judgement. It was not that people were not aware of the importance of relational judgments, of course not. But attempts to include them were always guided by the assumption that they somehow had to be reduced to subject - predicate judgements. A lot of ingenuity went into these attempts, but they all failed. It was only in the second half of the nineteenth century, when Peirce and Frege saw that it was necessary to accept relations as a logical category in their own right, that the decisive move forward could be made and Aristotle's syllogistic was replaced by much more expressive and powerful logical systems. But that it lasted for more then two millennia testifies to the enormous importance of Aristotle's logical work.[9]

In contemporary philosophy Aristotle still has considerable influence in certain areas. His views on ethics, as laid down in *Nicomachean Ethics* have seen a remarkable revival in contemporary virtue ethics, as developed by Alistair McIntyre and Philippa Foot. And Aristotle's writing in metaphysics, especially those on causation and explanation, continue to drive debates in analytic metaphysics and epistemology.

23.3 The text

The fragment that we read comes from chapter 9 of Aristotle's *De Interpretatione*.[10] It is the second volume of the *Organon*, in which Aristotle's work on logic, epistemology and methodology is bundled. *De Interpretatione* is arguably the first work ever to contain a systematic and (quasi-)formal analysis of language and logic. It deals with terms, the basic constituents of propositions; with the classifications of propositions in various categories, and with the logical relations between those categories of propositions.

The analysis of 'futura contingentia' statements is part of a discussion about fundamental logical principles: the principle of excluded middle and the principle of non-contradiction. The fragment that we read is densely formulated and the argumentation is complex. It is not always clear what exactly the claims are that Aristotle makes, and how exactly he wants to argue for them.

Aristotle starts with the observation that universal and particular statements about the present and about the past have definite truth conditions and thus are either true or false, depending on what is, or has been the case. But 'with particulars that are going to be it is different' (end of first paragraph).

He goes on to observe that an unlimited application of the principle of excluded middle, i.e., one that includes statements about future contingent events has a remarkable consequence: future determinism. His reasoning seems to run as follows:

- If something is the case or is not the case, then it is necessary that it is the case or it is not the case
- So also if something will happen or will not happen, then it is necessary that it will happen or will not happen
- And hence, if something will happen, then it is necessary that it will happen, and if it will not happen, then it is necessary that it will not happen.

Note that the argument seems to assume that the qualification 'it is necessary that' distributes over a disjunction. If we use $\Box$ to stand for 'It is necessary that', then the argument has the following form:

- $\phi \vee \neg\phi \Rightarrow \Box(\phi \vee \neg\phi)$
- $\phi \Rightarrow \Box\phi$ and $\neg\phi \Rightarrow \Box\neg\phi$

Aristotle then goes on to make a similar point in terms of temporal qualifications:

- If something is the case now, it was also true that it is the case now
- If it was always true that it is the case now, it is not possible for it not be the case
- So, if something is the case now, it is necessary that it is the case now

This rests on a construction that links temporal and modal qualifications. Using temporal and modal operators, we get:

- $\phi \Rightarrow HF\phi$
- $HF\phi \Rightarrow \Box\phi$

So future determinism seems to follow: 'Everything that will be, therefore, happens necessarily' (end of third paragraph).

At this point Aristotle's argument takes an unexpected turn. He (implicitly) seems to reject the conclusion, but then goes on to notice that saying the future contingents are neither true nor false is also not acceptable: it does not account for the contingency as such: 'if it neither will be nor will not be the case tomorrow, then there is no "as chance has it" ' (end of fourth paragraph). This shows that Aristotle main concern is to find a way to maintain that a statement about a future contingent event should be contingently true (or false, as the case may be).

Aristotle continues with his argument by expanding on the absurdity of the conclusion that follows from the unlimited application of the principle of excluded middle. Everything that happens then happens with necessity, and this is a matter of the facts, not of our knowledge of them. But it is obvious to Aristotle that this is absurd: there are things that happen that could not have happened, and vice versa: contingency and possibility are real: 'Clearly, therefore, not everything is or happens of necessity: some things happen as chance has it' (sixth paragraph).

Aristotle sums up his position as follows (beginning of seventh paragraph):

> What is, necessarily is, when it is; and what is not, necessarily is not, when it is not. But not everything that is, necessarily is; and not everything that is not, necessarily is not.

Note the qualification of the necessity: 'What is, necessarily is, when it is'. I.e., if something is true, there is no point in trying to deny it as long as it remains true. But that is insufficient for something to qualify as necessary.

Thus, although it is necessary that either there is a sea-battle tomorrow or there is not (i.e., $\Box(Tp \vee T\neg p)$),[11] it is not necessary that there is a sea-battle tomorrow, nor is it necessary that there is not a sea-battle tomorrow (i.e., $\neg\Box Tp \wedge \neg\Box T\neg p$).

Finally, Aristotle notes that this applies not just to statements and their negation ('contradictories'), but also to statements that exclude one another, i.e., cannot be both true, but that can be both false ('contraries').

23.4 Study and discussion questions

Study questions

- What does Aristotle mean by 'universals' and what does he mean by 'particulars'?
- What is an 'affirmation' and what is a 'negation'?
- How does Aristotle use the term 'chance' ('by chance')?
- 'For what anyone has truly said would be the case cannot not happen': why not?
- What does Aristotle mean by 'possibility' (by something being 'possible')?
- What are 'contraries'? And how do they differ from 'contradictions'?

Discussion questions

- What kind of conception of truth does Aristotle operate with? (Recall the reference to Aristotle in the paper by Tarski (Tarski, 1944))
- If we interpret the third value # in Łukaciewicz's three-valued logic as standing for 'possibility', does Aristotle's objection to 'suspending' the principle of excluded middle for 'futura contingentia' statements still hold?
- At which point in his argumentation does Aristotle make use of an asymmetry between past and future?

23.5 Further reading

The literature on future contingents and on Aristotle's sea-battle argument is extensive. see Øhrstrøm & Hasle (2020) for an overview of the various more technical interpretations, and Shain (2011) for an interpretation from a more philosophical point of view.

24
Intensional logic

This chapter is devoted to a brief exploration of a second example of a different kind of logic, viz., intensional logic. That is a rich field with a wide variety of logical systems that address different types of intensional phenomena. In this short introductory chapter we can only scratch the surface and explain some key concepts. Hopefully, that will give the interested reader enough familiarity with this style of doing logic to further explore this area. Some references to guide the reader will be given at the end of this chapter.

24.1 Extensionality

Classical logic has a number of characteristic properties, the two most prominent of which are perhaps the principle of excluded middle and its extensionality. In the previous chapter we have given an indication of some of the ways in which, and of some of the reasons for which, excluded middle has been questioned as a fundamental characteristic of logic. In this chapter we will take a look at the second one, viz., the extensional character of classical logic.

Note that excluded middle is a characteristic of classical logic that manifests itself in both semantics and proof theory: we have $\models \phi \vee \neg\phi$ and $\vdash \phi \vee \neg\phi$. Per contrast, extensionality seems to be primarily a feature of its semantics. That semantics is reference-based and truth-conditional, and that is what makes it extensional. Concretely, the meanings of individual constants and predicate symbols are what they refer to: individuals and sets of n-tuples of individuals. The interpretation function of a model spells that out. The meanings of formulas are also extensional: they consist in the truth-conditions as specified by the truth definition. And variables, too, are dealt with extensionally: assignment functions assign individuals to variables.

Also note that as far as truth conditions of formulas are concerned there is a difference between those of atomic sentences and those of complex ones.[1] The former differ from model to model as they are solely determined by the references of individual constants and predicate symbols and these are determined by the interpretation function of a given model. Complex sentences are different: their truth conditions are the same across all models. This is because they are determined by the logical constants that occur in them. But the truth conditions of the atomic parts from which complex formulas are ultimately constructed are again model-relative.

The extensional nature of the semantics of classical logic is expressed in the principle of extensionality, which we already encountered before, in chapter 15:

Theorem 10 (Extensionality)

$$\forall x_1 \ldots x_n(\phi \leftrightarrow \psi) \models \chi \leftrightarrow [\psi/\phi]\chi$$

where $x_1 \ldots x_n$ are the variables that occur free in ϕ and ψ

The extensionality principle states that if two formulas ϕ and ψ are materially equivalent, they can be substituted for one another in any formula χ without changing the truth value of χ. Note that since this includes atomic formulas with free variables, the principle also covers extensionality of predicates and relational expressions. The following theorem shows that individual constants, too, are extensional:

Theorem 11 (Extensionality (constants))

$$c = c' \models \chi \leftrightarrow [c/c']\chi$$

Of course, in view of completeness we do have syntactical counterparts of the extensionality principles. Thus corresponding to the extensionality theorem we have:

$$\forall x_1 \ldots x_n(\phi \leftrightarrow \psi) \vdash \chi \leftrightarrow [\psi/\phi]\chi$$

However, intuitively being extensional is first and foremost a property of a semantics.

24.2 Why intensional logic?

Why look beyond extensional logics? There are a number of reasons for that, which we can classify along the following lines. First, there are aspects of the meanings of logical constants that are not adequately covered by an extensional semantics. Second, there are concepts that appear to behave like logical constants in that they have their own set of characteristic inference patterns that we might want to account for. These concepts can be more philosophical or mathematical. Third, if we want to use logic to account for a core part of natural language meaning, we are faced with a range of natural language phenomena that defy adequate characterisation in an extensional framework.[2] Let us look at some examples to make these general considerations more concrete.

24.2.1 *Logical constants*

Note that we talk about 'the meaning of logical constant' here, we do so in a broad sense. Strictly speaking, the meaning of a logical constant is what is defined by a logical system. But in most cases there is an informal meaning attached to it that the system aims to capture. It is this two-sidedness of logical constants, their 'narrow' and their 'wider' senses and the difference between the two, that is what is at stake here.

A first illustration is provided by implication. As we have seen in chapter 6, the meaning of the material implication of classical logic, i.e., the meaning of $\rightarrow$, the logical constant in the narrow sense, captures only part of the meaning of implication as we use it in conditional reasoning, i.e., the meaning of the logical constant in the broader sense. And that lack is due to the extensionality of classical proposition logic. Given the extensional nature of the semantics, no other truth table gives an adequate definition of the meaning of the implication than the one supplied.

But that something is amiss is shown by the so-called 'paradoxes of material implication', certain formulas that come out valid but that intuitively should not. Examples are: $p \rightarrow (q \rightarrow p), \neg p \rightarrow (p \rightarrow q), (p \rightarrow q) \vee (q \rightarrow r)$. Consider the first example: it states that if p is true p follows from any q. Inspection of the truth table reveals that this is indeed a valid principle. But intuitively, 'following from' requires some kind of internal connection between formulas. And precisely because p and q are atomic, no such connection exists.

So the reason that these formulas are intuitively not valid is that in conditional reasoning more plays a role than merely the truth values of antecedent and consequent. In order for a conditional sentence of the form 'If A, then B' to be regarded as true, there should also be a stronger, substantial connection between the contents of what A and B state. And a specification of that content goes beyond 'mere' truth or falsity.[3]

Another interesting case is provided by intuitionistic negation and intuitionistic disjunction. As we saw in chapter 9 the difference between classical logic and intuitionistic logic can be made proof-theoretically by specification of different natural deduction rules. These different sets of rules characterise different properties of negation and disjunction as they occur in deductive inferences. In order to have the semantics reflect this it needs to be changed.[4] The best-known approach to the semantics of intuitionistic logic is the intensional semantics developed by Saul Kripke.[5] More on that below.

Not all discrepancies between the 'narrow' and 'wide' sense of a logical constant call for different logical treatments. One simple example is that of temporal order and conjunction. In many cases, it is natural to read a conjunction 'A and B' as indicating a temporal order, in case A and B describe events, as the following examples illustrate:

(1) John undressed and went to bed

It is natural to read a conjunction like this as implying temporal succession, i.e., to read (1) as (2):

(2) John undressed and then went to bed

But note that this a defeasible aspect of its meaning. Cf.:

(3) John undressed and went to bed, but I don't know what he did first

Someone who utters (3) does not contradict themselves, which they would if the temporal succession were part of the truth conditional meaning.

Aspects of the meaning of connectives such as these are therefore not semantic, but need to be accounted for in other ways. More on that in chapter 26.

24.2.2 *The logic of concepts*

A second source of reasons for going beyond extensional logic is provided by the philosophical and logical analysis of certain concepts. There is a whole range of considerations concerning concepts that have given rise to intensional logic, we restrict ourselves here to a brief discussion of some of the most familiar ones.

First of all, there are concepts of time and temporal notions. We discussed some elementary aspects of that in chapter 23. Recall that different conceptions of time, such as linear time or branching time, can be characterised in terms of temporal orders, i.e., specific sets of properties that can be assigned to the relation 'being earlier than' as defined on a set of temporal points. In order to describe the logical properties of these orders, and hence the time conceptions, we need a language in which we can refer to temporal points and their order. As we have seen, one way of doing so is to add operators to a formal language that express temporal properties of propositions, such as 'being true at some point in the future', 'having always been true', and so on. These operators cannot be defined in an extensional way: the truth value of 'It will be the case that A' at some point in time is not determined by the truth value of A at that point in time, so extensionality fails. We need to have a broader notion of meaning.

A second example is provided by concepts of necessity and possibility, two key modal concepts. These, too, cannot be captured in an extensional manner: that something is necessary is not determined by its being true (or false), and for something to be possible it does not have to be actually true. Note also that there are various logical properties that we can choose to associate with these concepts. For example, if something is necessary, is that necessarily the case? Or if something is in fact true, does it follow that it is necessary that it is possible? Different decisions on such issues result in different conceptions of necessity and possibility. Again, if we add operators to a formal language to characterise them, these cannot be assigned an extensional semantics, for obvious reasons.

A third example, and one with a long history, comes from reasoning in ethics. Concepts of obligation and permission, so-called 'deontic concepts', play a key role in thinking about ethical problems and in formatting ethical principles. For some action to be obligatory is a strong property: it means that the action should be done, not just in the actual situation, but also in others, perhaps even in all. Again, there is a range of logical properties that we can attribute to these concepts, and like in the previous cases, it is clear that if we add operators to our language to express these, their semantics cannot be extensional: other situations than the actual one need to be taken into account.

As a final example, consider epistemic concepts, such as knowledge and belief. Under what circumstances can we ascribe knowledge? What differentiates knowledge from belief? If we solely take the actual truth or falsity of a statement into account, that will underdetermine an ascription of, e.g., knowledge: arguably, in order for something to be knowledge it has to be true, but that is certainly not sufficient. A closely related concept is that of evidence. When does something count as (sufficient) evidence for belief or knowledge? Like in the previous examples, there are a number of options to explore, and in order to do so using a formal language, we need to add operators for the relevant concepts that will have a semantics that cannot be extensional.

Note that there are often interesting connections between these concepts. For example, deontic concepts and modal ones are connected: it seems reasonable to assume that for an action to be obligatory, it should be possible to do it. Or consider the epistemic concept of belief and the modal concept of impossibility: can we ascribe to someone a belief in something that is impossible? Also, in the analysis of causation modal concepts and epistemic concepts both play a role. Modal concepts and temporal ones also have affinities. In fact, some have constructed a very strong relation between the two: according to the so-called 'Diodorean view'[6] something is necessary if and only if it is true throughout time, i.e., in past, present, and future.

24.2.3 Natural language phenomena

And then there is natural language. There is a whole range of constructions and expressions to be found in natural languages that cannot be analysed adequately with an extensional semantics. First of all, there are expressions that correspond to the concepts that we reviewed above. We can qualify events, situations, and actions as necessary or possible; we express and discuss ethical considerations, rules, and prescriptions; we attribute knowledge and belief, discuss evidence; we refer to causal connections in our descriptions and explanations of events; and so on.

Does that mean that the philosophical concepts and the semantics of these natural language counterparts coincide? That is arguably not the case. For one thing, some of these concepts can be analysed in quite different ways, each of them coming with its own, distinct philosophical and logical motivation. But the meanings of natural language expressions, although admittedly sometimes ambiguous, do not correspond one-to-one with these philosophical analyses, of course. There are connections, but also differences. In general, one can say that the meanings of these natural language expressions and constructions underdetermine a specific philosophical or logical analysis. For example, in everyday life we use expressions to refer to causal connections, but we do so in a way that leaves open whether we believe that causal relations only pertain to physical events, or that causality is always only hypothetical, and so on. We can argue such questions using natural language, but generally we cannot argue a particular position solely by pointing to natural language semantics. This is reflected in the fact that in a debate between people who hold opposite views, say on whether causal relations only pertain to events or not, each party will need to sharpen their intended meaning in order to adequately express their different points of view.

That being said, the natural language expressions that correspond, in the above loose sense, to the formal expressions that express these logical concepts do share the key characteristic of not satisfying extensionality. Here are some simple examples of arguments that fail to go through because of that.

A first example is provided by temporal expressions. Natural languages abound in expressions that change their reference along with time, and in expressions that exploit that. Here is a simple example:[7]

(4) The temperature is 90 degrees Fahrenheit
(5) The temperature rises
(6) So, 90 degrees Fahrenheit rises

This obviously invalid argument shows that extensionality fails: even if two expressions are extensionally equivalent they cannot be exchanged in the context created by the verb 'to rise'. Any noun that refers to a function that has different values at different points i time will give rise to this problem. And then there are temporal expressions themselves, such as verb tenses, temporal adverbs, and so on. The meaning of these expressions can only be analysed in a logic that allows reference to time and its structure.

Modal expressions also create a context in which substitution of extensionally equivalent expressions fails:[8]

(7) The number of planets is 9
(8) 9 is necessarily even
(9) So, the number of planets is necessarily even

Suppose there were 9 planets, this would not necessarily be the case: there could have been 10, or 8, if at some point in the development of the solar system things had gone in a different direction.[9] And there are modal expressions themselves: not just phrases such as 'Necessary' and 'Possible', but also constructions such as counterfactuals, such as 'It would have been the case ...' create intensional contexts.

Note that the structure of these examples is quite similar: we have two expressions that happen to have the same extension in a certain situation, and we have predicates that require checking the extension in different situations. In order to ascertain that something rises, we need to compare its values at different points in time; and in order to check whether something is necessarily even we need to ascertain that it is even in every situation. It is predicates that require looking at extensions in different situations in combination with expressions that may have different extensions in different situations that cause the principle of extensionality to fail.

A proper account of the semantics of such expressions and constructions thus requires that we look at their semantics in a parametrised way: semantics assigns, not an extension as such, but an extension relative to a parameter. What these parameters are varies: points in time, possible situations, in the cases just discussed. What also plays a role, is the way in which these objects are structured. In the case of time points, this is by a temporal relation, as we have seen in chapter 23, the case of modality will be discussed later.

Another well-known case of extensionality failure in natural languages is provided by epistemic expressions, such as 'know' and 'believe':

(10) John believes that the trainer of the club is a genius
(11) Ma Jian is the trainer of the club
(12) So, John believes that Ma Jian is a genius

Again, the argument fails, this time because John may not be aware of the identity of the club's trainer.

Besides pointing out concrete expressions and constructions that do not appear to satisfy something like the principle of extensionality, there are also general considerations to support the position that natural language meaning is not extensional. Gottlob Frege famously made the distinction between sense and reference of expressions. More about that distinction and the ways in which it reappears in intensional logic later, in chapter 25. Here we want to point to a general observation that Frege makes in his paper 'On the scientific justification of a concept-script' (Frege, 1964, pp. 155–56):

> Our attention is by nature directed to the outside. Sense impressions surpass memory pictures in vitality to such an extent that at first they practically determine by themselves the course of our mental imagery, as is the case with animals. [...] Nonetheless, our imagery would not with this yet have won its full freedom; it would be limited to that which our hand could form, our voice

> intone, if it were not for the grand discovery of the symbol which calls to our mind that which is absent, out of sight or perhaps even unseeable.[...] Symbols hold the selfsame significance for thinking as did the discovery of using the wind to sail cross-wind for navigation. Let no one be contemptuous of symbols! [...] Without symbols we would further hardly raise ourselves to the level of conceptual thought. In giving the same symbol to similar but different things, we no longer symbolise the individual thing but rather that which they have in common-the concept and the concept itself is first gained by our symbolising it, for, since the concept is of itself imperceptible to the senses, it requires a perceptible representative in order to appear to us. Thus it is that the sensuous opens up for us the world of the non-sensuous.

What Frege observes here is two-fold: that without symbols, i.e., without language, conceptual thought would be impossible, and that this is due to 'the symbol which calls to our mind that which is absent, out of sight or perhaps even unseeable.' The essential function of language is that it enables us to think of what is not present, what we cannot grasp immediately with the senses, because it is absent, or perhaps because it cannot be grasped in that way to begin with. Abstract objects; unrealised, or even unrealisable possibilities; events far in the future or deep in the recesses of time, language allows us to speak and think about all that.[10] Evidently, such language cannot be an extensional one. In order for expressions to be able 'to reach out' beyond the situation in which they are used to identify elutes, properties and relations in other situations, their meaning cannot be simply what they refer to in the situation in which they are used: meaning has to bridge across and bring together different situations, in which expressions may have different extensions, all of which are unified within one and the same meaning.

Thus, in order for logic to be able to capture what seems to be the essence of natural language meaning, viz., its ability to reach across situations of use, it needs to be more expressive than the extensional systems we have seen so far. In what follows we will focus on how that plays out for the semantics of logical languages, but we will come back briefly to proof theoretic aspects at the end of this chapter.

24.3 Relational semantics

So, let's turn to now logics that are designed to cope with these issues. Generally, they go by the name 'intensional logic', a qualification that derives from the venerable distinction between intension and extension. Loosely speaking, extension is what an expression refers to, intension is what determines extension. That distinction is at the heart of every intensional logical system.

Depending on the kind of intensional phenomena that a logic aims to address, more specific monikers are used: tense logics, that deal with time and tense; modal logics, that treat modal concepts such as necessity and possibility, epistemic logics, that concern epistemological notions such as knowledge, belief, evidence and the like; deontic logics, that treat conceptions of obligation and permission.

What all these systems have in common is a particular kind of semantics, which is often called 'relational semantics'. As was already indicated above, the two key features of relation semantics are, first, the adoption of a set of parameters relative to which semantic interpretation is specified, and, two, the addition of structural relations on that parameter set, that define different logical properties of the relevant concepts. In what follows, we will restrict ourselves to a discussion of proposition logic, but a few remarks about quantificational intensional logics can be found in section 24.7.

A pair $\langle \mathcal{S}, \mathcal{R} \rangle$, with $\mathcal{S}$ a parameter set and $\mathcal{R}$ a relation on that set, is called a '(relational) frame'.If we add a valuation V that assigns semantic values to the formulas relative to elements s of $\mathcal{S}$, we get a '(relational) model'.

A more specific interpretation of the parameter set results in specific type of intensional logics, such as tense logics or modal logics. And specific interpretations of the relation define specific instances of such logics.

We already saw an example of that in chapter 23. If we let $\mathcal{S}$ be a set of time points T, and $\mathcal{R}$ some ordering E on that set, we get tense logic. Depending on the specific ordering we get a logic that embodies a specific conception of time. For example, if E is a strict linear ordering, we get linear time; if we loosen the restrictions on E, we characterise other conceptions. The valuation function V assigns truth values to formulas relative to time points $t \in T$, i.e., it is a function $V\colon \textsc{form} \times T \to \{0, 1\}$.

Note that if we just take the language of standard proposition logic and models M as specified above, nothing changes, except that all clauses of the truth definition are parameterised:

- $V_{M,t}(p) \in \{0, 1\}$, for all proposition letters p
- $V_{M,t}(\neg\phi) = 1$ iff $V_{M,t}(\phi) = 0$
- $V_{M,t}(\phi \wedge \psi) = 1$ iff $V_{M,t}(\phi) = V_{M,t}(\psi) = 1$

We now have an intensional semantics, but it becomes useful only if we add expressions to the language that make use of that. In the case of tense logic, these can be operators F and P (already introduced in chapter 23) with the following interpretations:

- $V_{M,t}(F\phi) = 1$ iff there exists a t': Ett' and $V_{M,t'}(\phi) = 1$
- $V_{M,t}(P\phi) = 1$ iff there exists a t': $Et't$ and $V_{M,t'}(\phi) = 1$

If we then also provide a further specification of the relation E on T, for example that it be a strict linear ordering, we obtain a specific logic of tense and temporal expressions.

So, in general, for the definition of a specific intensional logic we need the following:[11]

- A specification of the parameter set: this determines what the logic 'is about'
- A specification of the structure of the parameter set: this allows us to explore variations of the logic
- A set of expressions that are interpreted using the parameter set and its structure
- A truth definition to specify those interpretations

Modal logics form another instantiation of the general scheme of relation semantics, and they illustrate the various components clearly, as the following section will show.

24.4 Modal logics

Modal logics center around the analysis of modal concepts such as necessity and possibility. A language of modal proposition logic is a language of propositional logic with the addition of two operators, viz., $\Box$, a.k.a. 'box', and $\Diamond$, a.k.a. 'diamond'. They turn formulas into formulas:

- If ϕ is a formula, then so are $\Box\phi, \Diamond\phi$

Note that this allows for formulas in which modal operators are nested, such as $\Box\Box p, \Box\Diamond(p \rightarrow q), \neg\Box p \rightarrow \Diamond(p \vee \Diamond q)$, etc.

In a relational semantics for a modal logic the parameter set $\mathcal{S}$ is taken to be some non-empty set W of possible worlds, hence the term 'possible worlds semantics' that is frequently used. From the point of view of modal logics, possible worlds are simply parameters. Philosophically, however, the question what possible worlds are, if there are such things to begin with, is a hotly debated topic. We will not go into that here, but some discussion of the issue can be found in chapter 25.

The relation $\mathcal{R}$ is taken to be a relation of 'accessibility' between possible worlds, denoted as R: Rww' stands for 'world w' is accessible from world w'. Usually, this is written as 'wRw'', and we will follow that convention in what follows. The accessibility relation can have various properties: it can be empty, it can be universal, it can be a relation defined by certain properties. As we will see, different choices result in different modal logics. A valuation function V now assigns truth values to all the formulas of the language relative to worlds w taken from W.

Thus we have:

Definition 46 (Semantics)
A relational model M for a modal proposition language is a triple $\langle W, R, V \rangle$ such that:

- $W_M \neq \emptyset$
- $R_M \subseteq W \times W$
- $V_M \in$ FORM $\times W \rightarrow \{0,1\}$ such that:
  1. $V_{M,w}(p) \in \{0,1\}$, for all proposition letters p
  2. $V_{M,w}(\neg\phi) = 1$ iff $V_{M,w}(\phi) = 0$
  3. $V_{M,w}(\phi \wedge \psi) = 1$ iff $V_{M,w}(\phi) = V_{M,w}(\psi) = 1$
  4. $V_{M,w}(\Box\phi) = 1$ iff $V_{M,w'}(\phi) = 1$ for all w' s.th. wRw'
  5. $V_{M,w}(\Diamond\phi) = 1$ iff $V_{M,w'}(\phi) = 1$ for some w' s.th. wRw'

The clauses for $\vee, \rightarrow, \leftrightarrow$ are left out, as they can be defined in the usual way in terms of $\neg$ and $\wedge$. Note also that given the clauses for $\Box$ and $\Diamond$ we have:

$$V_{M,w}(\Diamond\phi) = 1 \text{ iff } V_{M,w}(\neg\Box\neg\phi) = 1$$

So, if we wish, we can make do with just one modal operator.

The $\Box$-operator amounts to universal quantification over accessible worlds, and the $\Diamond$-operator corresponds to existential quantification over such worlds. This corresponds to an intuitive understanding of necessity and possibility. Something is necessary if it is true in all accessible worlds, and it is possible if it is true in at least one such world.

Finally, validity is defined as expected, viz., as truth in all models in all worlds:

Definition 47 (Validity)
A formula ϕ is valid iff for all M, w: $V_{M,w}(\phi) = 1$

By way of illustration we take a look at some simple examples of models and the evaluation of modal formulas in them.

The diagrams that are used in what follows are not full specification of models, but only represent those features that are needed to illustrate a certain point. Thus, they contain a couple of worlds and specify what holds in them. Circles represent worlds, arrows indicate the accessibility relation. Each world comes with a specification of relevant 'literals', i.e., proposition letters and negations thereof, that hold in that world.

Here is a first example:

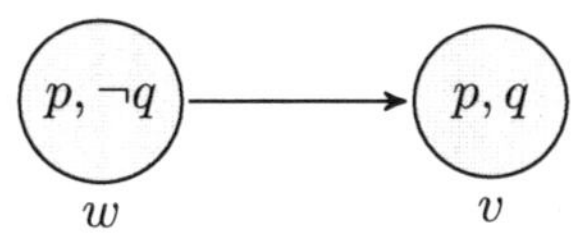

So, in this diagram p is true in w and q is false, whereas in v both are true.

Specification of the truth values of literals in a world determines the truth values in that world of all truth-functional complex formulas composed from them. But that does not hold for modal formulas.

For example, to determine the truth value of $\Box p$ in w we need to look at the truth value of p in all worlds w' that are accessible from w. In this model the only world accessible from w is v, so the truth of $\Box p$ in w is determined by the value of p in v. Given that p is true in v, it follows by the truth definition that $\Box p$ is true in w. And by parity of reasoning, we can also conclude that $\Box q$ is true in w, even though q is false in w.

Now consider the following variation:

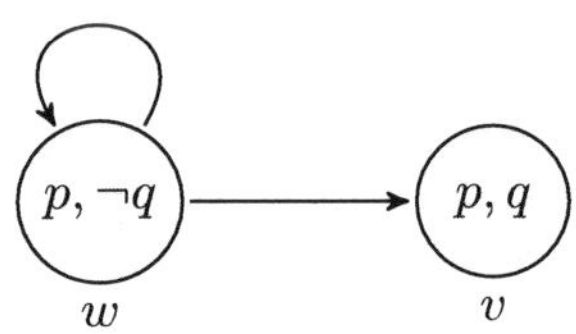

World w is now also accessible from w itself, so for $\Box p$ to be true in w we also need to take into account the truth value of p in w. Since p is true in w, is still true in v and w, v are all the world accessible from w, we have that $\Box p$ is true in w. However, $\Box q$ is now false in w, since w is accessible from w and q is false in w.

Another example:

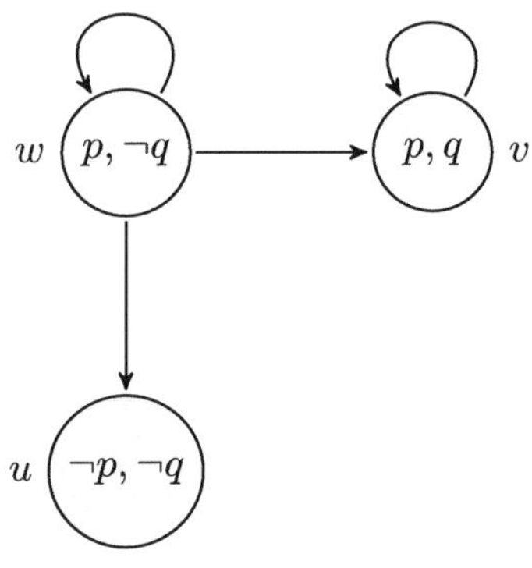

In this model we have a world w from which all worlds are accessible, or, as it is also often expressed: 'w sees all worlds' ; we have a world u from which no worlds are accessible; and a world v that sees only itself.

Now look at $\Box p$: this is false in w, since w sees u and p is false in u. But although p is false in u, $\Box p$ is trivially true in u, since no worlds are accessible from u. And we have that $\Diamond\neg p$ is false in u, even though $\neg p$ is actually true in u.

What this illustrate is that the accessibility relation plays a decisive role for the truth and falsity of modal formulas. But not only that, it also suggests that certain structural properties of that relation are at odds with the intuitive meaning of the modal expressions. If $\Box$ is to stand for necessity, it seems reasonable to require that $\Box p \models p$. Likewise, if $\Diamond$ represents possibility, we would like to have that $p \models \Diamond p$. And that means that the accessibility relation should be reflexive.

We go into such positive requirements on the accessibility relation in more detail in what follows. But let's pause and see what the worlds in the diagram above illustrate.

First consider u; u is a world from which no world is accessible. Now what if that were to hold for all worlds? If no world is accessible from any other world, then R is the empty relation on W, i.e., $R = \emptyset$. In that case every formula of the form $\Box\phi$ becomes a tautology, and thus every formula of the form $\Diamond\phi$ a contradiction. This would annihilate the logic of the concepts of necessity and possibility.

What about v, which only sees itself? If that holds for all worlds, i.e., if worlds have only access to themselves, R is the identity relation on W, i.e., $R = \{\langle w, w\rangle \mid w \in W\}$. If that were the case, the intensional semantics collapses into the standard extensional semantics of proposition logic: $\Box\phi$, $\Diamond\phi$, and ϕ become equivalent. Again, this would destroy the idea of a logic of the concepts in question.

Finally, consider w, which sees all worlds, including itself. If that holds for all worlds, i.e., if all worlds are accessible from all worlds, R is the universal relation on W, i.e., $R = W \times W$. This is arguably more reasonable. It gives a strong interpretation of $\Box\phi$: $\Box\phi$ is true in a world w iff ϕ is true in every world $w \in W$. And conversely, the requirement for $\Diamond\phi$ is weak: $\Diamond\phi$ is true iff there is at least one world $w \in W$ in which ϕ is true.

These considerations illustrate that in order to obtain reasonable formalisations of the modal concepts we need to formulate requirements that the accessibility relation should meet. The next question then is: what are reasonable requirements? And, is there a unique set? As we shall see the answer to the last question is negative, which means that constraining the accessibility in different ways leads to different modal logics.

Before we give a brief sketch of this landscape of logics, we should start by noting that, independently of the specification of R, the following principles hold:

N $\Box\phi$, for all propositional tautologies ϕ
K $\Box(\phi \rightarrow \psi) \rightarrow (\Box\phi \rightarrow \Box\psi)$

That N, also called 'Necessitation', holds is easy to see: if ϕ is a tautology, any valuation V will make it true. Hence ϕ is true in every possible world, and thus also $\Box\phi$. As for K: assume that $\Box(\phi \rightarrow \psi)$ and that $\Box\phi$; then in any world w we have that both $\phi \rightarrow \psi$ and ϕ are true in any world w' that accessible from w. Thus, in every such world w' we have that ψ is true, and hence that $\Box\psi$ is true in w. This system, in which no requirements are imposed on the accessibility relation R, is often called 'modal logic **K**'.

The following illustrates that the validity of other modal principles is connected with properties of the accessibility relation. A first example:

- Reflexive ($\forall x Rxx$): $\Box\phi \rightarrow \phi$

This has intuitive appeal: if something is necessary, it needs to be true. That means that if we evaluate a modal formula $\Box\phi$ in a world w we minimally should always be checking whether ϕ holds in w itself. Reflexivity of the accessibility relation R ensures that. An equivalent formulation is: $\phi \rightarrow \Diamond\phi$.

Other requirements on R can be considered to obtain various concepts of modality. Here are some examples:

- Serial ($\forall x \exists y Rxy$): $\Box\phi \rightarrow \Diamond\phi$
- Symmetric ($\forall x \forall y(Rxy \rightarrow Ryx)$): $\phi \rightarrow \Box\Diamond\phi$
- Transitive ($\forall x \forall y \forall z((Rxy \wedge Ryz) \rightarrow Rxz)$): $\Box\phi \rightarrow \Box\Box\phi$
- Euclidean ($\forall x \forall y \forall z((Rxy \wedge Rxz) \rightarrow Ryz)$): $\Diamond\phi \rightarrow \Box\Diamond\phi$

Some brief observations about these requirements.

Requiring R to be serial means that for every world there is at least one world that it sees. This corresponds to the requirement that what is necessary should be possible: if ϕ is true in every world that is accessible from w and there is at least one such world, then there is a world accessible from w in which ϕ holds, which makes $\Diamond\phi$ true in w. This seems an intuitively acceptable principle, which means that seriality is a reasonable requirement on the accessibility relation. Note that it is weaker than what reflexivity requires.

Symmetry of R means worlds that are accessible are mutually so. This implies that the fact that ϕ holds in a world w is sufficient to sustain the claim that ϕ is possible in every world w' accessible from w: symmetry guarantees that every such world w' sees w. In other words, that something is true does not 'get lost' when looking at other worlds, even if in those worlds it happens to be false.

Transitivity also is about continuity: if we go from w to an accessible world v and from there to a world u that is accessible from v that world u is also accessible from w. That means that if something is necessary in w and thus holds in all worlds accessible from it, it cannot fail to be necessary in those worlds as well: it remains necessary.

Finally, euclidean R: this requires that any two worlds v, u that are accessible from w are also accessible from each other. So, if there is some world accessible from w that makes ϕ true, then that possibility is there to see for all worlds accessible from w. That means this possibility as such is a necessity.[12]

Exercise 1

a. Find a modal principle that corresponds to the following property of R: $\forall x \forall y \forall z((Rxy \wedge Rxz) \rightarrow (Ryz \vee Rzy))$.
b. Which property of R corresponds to $\Diamond\Box\phi \rightarrow \Box\Diamond\phi$?

Finally, let's turn to modal logics. Combinations of properties of the accessibility relation R then lead to a series of different such logics, by validating different (sets of) principles governing the modal operators $\Box$ and $\Diamond$. Table 24.1 lists a number of well-known logics:

Name	conditions on R	valid principles
K	–	–
D	serial	$\Box\phi \rightarrow \Diamond\phi$
T	reflexive	$\Box\phi \rightarrow \phi$
B	reflexive, symmetric	$\Box\phi \rightarrow \phi$, $\phi \rightarrow \Box\Diamond\phi$
K4	transitive	$\Box\phi \rightarrow \Box\Box\phi$
S4	reflexive, transitive	$\Box\phi \rightarrow \phi$, $\Box\phi \rightarrow \Box\Box\phi$
S5	reflexive, symmetric, transitive	$\Box\phi \rightarrow \phi$, $\phi \rightarrow \Box\Diamond\phi$, $\Box\phi \rightarrow \Box\Box\phi$

Table 24.1: Some core modal logics

24.5 Other interpretations of relational semantics

So far we have illustrated the general relational semantics with the case of modal logic. But the general principles underlying relational semantics, including the use of accessibility relations with various properties, can also be used to define logics for different types of operators.

This is a large field, and here we can only illustrate it with a very first look at two examples: deontic logic and epistemic logic.

24.5.1 *Deontic logic*

Deontic logic arises when we read the operator $\Box$ and $\Diamond$ as 'It is required that', and 'It is permitted that', respectively. The accessibility relation between worlds is now intuitively conceived as a relation that is determined by norms: Rwv is read as 'v is in accordance with the norms that obtain in w. The semantics then makes $\Box\phi$ true in w iff in every world v that is in accordance with the norms in w, ϕ is true. And $\Diamond\phi$ will be true in w if there is at least one such world v.

What about principles N and K? Let's start with N. In the deontic setting it states that every propositional tautology represents a situation that is required to be true. That obviously holds.

What about K: $\Box(\phi \to \psi) \to (\Box\phi \to \Box\psi)$? This, too, seems intuitively valid under a deontic interpretation: If it is required that if ϕ, then ψ, and it is required that ϕ, then it follows that ψ is required.

As we have seen, N and K follow on the relational semantics irrespective of the properties of the accessibility relation R. So the next question is, what are intuitive properties of that relation in the deontic setting. It will go too far to discuss this in detail, so we leave that as an exercise for the reader.[13]

Exercise 2 Which of the following are reasonable principles for a deontic logic? Motivate your answer.

a. $\Box\phi \to \Diamond\phi$
b. $\Box\phi \to \phi$
c. $\Box\phi \to \Box\Box\phi$
d. $\phi \to \Box\Diamond\phi$

This gives just a very first indication of what deontic logic is, and leaves out many interesting issues. To mention one: the addition of conditional obligation. Many obligations are not absolute, but relative, they are in force if certain conditions are met: 'On public transport one should wear a face mask.' The same holds for permissions: 'One is allowed to buy alcohol provided one is over 18 years old'.

24.5.2 *Epistemic logic*

Another interpretation reads $\Box$ in an epistemic way, as standing for 'It is known that'. Usually, it is parametrised to individuals. Given a set of individuals D, we have operators $\Box_x$ for each $x \in D$. $\Box_x\phi$ is then taken to mean 'x knows that ϕ'. The interpretation of $\Diamond$ and $\Diamond_x$ on this epistemic reading then becomes something like 'It is compatible with what is known' and 'It is compatible with what x knows', respectively. The accessibility relation R in this setting is likewise parameterised, so we have a set of such relations $\{R_x \mid x \in D\}$. An accessibility relation R_x links a world w to those worlds w' that are compatible with what x considers possible in w. $\Box_x\phi$ is then true in w iff ϕ is true in each world v such that wRv, i.e., in each world that is compatible with what x considers possible in w.

As we have seen, the N-principle holds in the relational semantics independently of the properties of the accessibility relation(s). Is the rule of Necessitation N a reasonable principle for epistemic logic? It amounts to every individual knowing all tautologies, which seems counterintuitive. Similar qualms arise with the K-principle: on the epistemic reading it implies that everyone is able to deduce ψ from $\phi \to \psi$ and ϕ, which, again, seems not warranted. Together, these principles ascribe to individuals the property of 'logically omniscience.' This is admittedly not an intuitive implication of the relation semantics, and there have been many attempts to overcome it.[14]

As for principles that constraint the accessibility relation, we leave it to the reader to ponder their intuitiveness on the epistemic reading.

Exercise 3 Which of the following are reasonable principles for an epistemic logic? Motivate your answer.

a. $\Box_x \phi \to \Box_x \Box_x \phi$
b. $\phi \to \Diamond_x \phi$
c. $\Box_x \phi \to \Diamond_x \phi$

24.6 Proof theory for relational semantics

Our treatment of modal logic so far has been semantic. We have defined a modal language and provided it with a relational semantics. The most important parameter in that semantics is the accessibility relation R. We have seen that it can be constrained in various ways, giving rise to different semantic interpretations of the modal operators, and thus resulting in different modal logics. But what about a syntactic approach to modal validity?

Note that in the discussion above, we have in fact characterised modal logics in two ways: by means of properties of the accessibility relation and in terms of modal principles. The correspondence between the two gives an indication of what a syntactic treatment might look like. The most common way to characterise validity in modal logics in a syntactic manner is by taking an axiomatisation of standard proposition logic with the modal principles added as axioms to characterise modal inferences.

Recall that in chapter 9, section 9.8, we gave the following set of axioms for classical extensional proposition logic:

$A1$. $(\phi \to (\psi \to \phi))$
$A2$. $(\phi \to (\psi \to \chi) \to ((\phi \to \psi) \to (\phi \to \chi)$
$A3$. $(\neg\phi \to \neg\psi) \to (\psi \to \phi)$

along with one rule of inference, MP (Modus Ponens):

- MP: If $\vdash \phi$ and $\vdash \phi \to \psi$, then $\vdash \psi$.

To turn this into an axiomatic modal logic we add the following inference rules:

- N: If $\vdash \phi$, then $\vdash \Box\phi$
- K: If $\vdash \Box(\phi \to \psi)$ and $\vdash \Box\phi$, then $\vdash \Box\phi$

and then further axioms. For example, the modal logic S_4 is axiomatised by:

- $A1 - A3$
- $A4$: $\Box\phi \to \phi$
- $A5$: $\Box\phi \to \Box\Box\phi$

and inference rules MP, N and K.

Using other proof theoretic frameworks, such as the natural deduction system we have introduced in chapter 9 is also possible, but much more complicated, which is why we do not go into it here.[15]

24.7 EXTENDING THE REACH: QUANTIFIED INTENSIONAL LOGICS

Extending the application of relational semantics to quantified languages with intensional operators is straightforward in a way: it requires no substantial new tools. But conceptually it does raise some difficult questions.

Let's start with the easy part. We add modal operators $\Box$ and $\Diamond$ to the vocabulary of a predicate logical language and extend the definition of formulas with clauses that make $\Box\phi$ and $\Diamond\phi$ formulas as well. Note that this allows $\Box$ and $\Diamond$ to be attached to formulas with free occurrences of variables. Thus we have formulas such as $\Box\exists xPx$, $\forall x\Diamond\exists y(Rxy \wedge \neg Ryx)$, $\Box\forall x\exists y(\Diamond Py \to \Box Px)$, etc.

The formulas of this quantified intensional language quantify over individuals, and this is where a conceptual question arises: what do the quantifiers range over? Individuals, of course, but which individuals? Given that interpretation is parameterised, should the domain of individuals be parameterised as well? Or is there rather one big domain?

In everyday use quantified expressions are usually implicitly restricted. If the host of the party asks 'Is everybody happy?' they do not mean to inquire after the well-being of every human being: the context makes clear which group of people is meant. If you see your kid with crumbs on its chin next to an empty cookie jar, and you ask 'Did you eat all the cookies?', you don't mean to ask whether they ate all cookies in the world: the ones in the jar, that's what you mean.

But in other contexts matters are less clear. If one contemplates the finitude of human existence, and states 'All men are mortal, everyone must die', one means, indeed, everyone: past, present and future. On the other hand, if one discusses the possibility for humans to find a way to live forever, one must be able to say 'It might become possible for a human being to live forever' without thereby claiming that such a person exists in the world as it is.

So perhaps there is room for a variety of approaches. Let's briefly consider them for the case of quantified modal logic.

We define a frame F as a triple $\langle W, R, \{D_w \mid w \in W\}\rangle$: we have a set of worlds W, an accessibility relation R on W, and for each world w a set of individuals D_w, the domain of w. A model M is a frame extended with an interpretation I that assigns individuals to constants and sets of (n-tuples of) individuals to predicate and relation symbols. The interpretation function needs to be parameterised, and for each such parameter w it is constrained to pick values from the corresponding domain D_w. So we have $I_w(c) \in D_w, I_w(P) \subseteq D_w$, and so on.

How does this affect the interpretation of formulas in which modal operators and quantifiers occur? Let's look at a few examples. First consider $\Box\forall xPx$. This is straightforward: this formula will be true in a world w iff $\forall xPx$ will be true in every world w' that is accessible from w; i.e., if everything in the domain of each such world has the property P.

Now consider $\forall x\Box Px$. This is more complicated: evaluated in a world w the quantifier ranges over the domain of that world; what the formula claims is that everything in that domain necessarily has the property P, i.e., that in each world w' that is accessible from w everything in D_w has P in w'. Now suppose there is some $d \in D_w$ and some w': Rww' such that $d \notin D_{w'}$. It follows that d does not have the property P in w' since $I_{w'}(P) \subseteq D_{w'}$. But should this mean that therefore $\forall x\Box Px$ is not true in w?[16]

One way of dealing with this problem is to link domains and accessibility: if we make a modal statement about the individuals in a certain world only those worlds need to be taken into account in which these individuals are indeed present. What is often called the 'Increasing Domains Assumption' takes care of this:

- For all w, w': if wRw', then $D_w \subseteq D_{w'}$

This solves the problem we just encountered.

Relations between world-relative domains and the accessibility relation correspond to the validity of certain formulas:

- *BF*: $\forall x\Box Px \to \Box\forall xPx$: this formula is valid iff domains of accessible worlds do not grow, i.e., iff for all w, w': if wRw', then $D_{w'} \subseteq D_w$
- *CBF*: $\Box\forall xPx \to \forall x\Box Px$: this formula is valid iff domains of accessible do not shrink, i.e., iff for all w, w': if wRw', then $D_w \subseteq D_{w'}$

Formula *BF* is 'the Barcan formula': it is named after Ruth Barcan Marcus, a pioneer of modal logic, who first draw attention to its particular status. And *CBF* is 'the converse Barcan formula'.[17]

The Barcan Formula *BF* is often associated with the philosophical position of 'actualism': the conception that only what is actual is possible, i.e., there are no individual that are 'merely possible'. The contraposition of *BF*, $\Diamond\exists xPx \to \exists x\Diamond Px$, expresses this clearly: if it's possible that there is something that is P, then there actually is something that is possibly P. Thus acceptance of the Barcan Formula comes with a commitment to a particular, restrictive view on the nature of what are called 'possibilities', i.e., possible objects of various kinds: individuals, physical objects, ideas, ... For some entities this might make sense, say for mathematical entities on a platonistic view, though not if one is a constructivist. But what about, say, a possible cure for cancer? Does the belief that such a cure is possible commit one to also believing that there actually is some procedure that could be such a cure?

These are deep philosophical questions, and a more in depth treatment of them is far beyond the scope of this first introduction to intensional logic. We just end with mentioning one more possible way of addressing issues of quantification in an intensional setting. This approach simply assumes that there is just one domain of entities D for all worlds, which contains all possible entities. Actuality is taken care of by the introduction of an existence predicate E, which applies in a world w to those entities in D that actually exist in w: $I_w(E) \subseteq D$. Thus $\forall x \Box Px$ means that all entities, possible or actual, necessarily have the property P. If we want to make that claim only about existing entities, we restrict the quantifier: $\forall x(Ex \rightarrow \Box Px)$ will be true in w iff those entities that actually exist in w necessarily are P.

A final issue we need to mention regards the status of possible worlds, points in time, and other entities that can form a parameter set in relational semantics. Are points in time real, is time real? Here, a positive answer seems reasonable, though philosophically not entirely uncontroversial. But what about possible worlds: are they real? This is much less obvious. As David Lewis, a staunch defender of realism with respect to possible worlds once wrote: 'What arguments can be given against realism about possible worlds? I have met with few arguments – incredulous stares are more common.'[18] It's a controversial position.

But does that matter? For the development of tense logics, modal logics, deontic logics, and other intensional systems this question might not be all that important. Obviously, the ability to use concepts that reach across time, that involve the contemplation of possibilities of various kinds (moral, ontological, epistemological), is part of our human nature, and a very essential one. Studying the formal properties of that ability and of the various ways of putting it to use is an important endeavour, one that we can engage with without having to take a stand on these philosophical questions.[19]

24.8 Further reading

The area of intensional logic, especially that of modal logic, is intensively researched. For further exploration, here are some references. One of the early systematic treatments is the work of E. Lemmon, published posthumously in Lemmon (1977); Hughes & Cresswell (1996) is an updated version of Hughes and Cresswell's 1968 classic; strongly focussed on technical aspects are Fitting & Mendelsohn (1998) and Blackburn et al. (2001). Philosophical applications are central in Garson (2006) and in Williamson (2013). For an extensive overview of the history of possible worlds semantics see Copeland (2002). Neighbourhood semantics is an alternative approach to the semantics of modal logics; an early treatment can be found in Chellas (1980), see also Pacuit (2017).

Techniques from intensional logic are also applied in many different fields, such as computer science, artificial intelligence, and linguistics.

25

Excursus: sense, reference, and rigid designation

25.1 The topic

In this excursus the focus is on two classics in intensional semantics. The first is Gottlob Frege's, celebrated 1892 paper 'Über Sinn und Bedeutung' ('On Sense and Reference).[1] This paper has been one of the main sources of intensional semantics, both in philosophy of language, natural language semantics, as well as in logic. The other paper is Saul Kripke's 1971 paper 'Identity and Necessity' (Kripke, 1971), in which he laid down his influential ideas about direct reference and rigid designation.

These two papers highlight a number of key issues about the distinction between sense and reference, about their relation, and about the nature of sense itself. That there is a distinction to be made between what expressions mean and what they refer to, in itself is a natural assumption to make. In various forms it can be found with various authors throughout the ages. However, most of those earlier analyses focussed on the analysis of expressions that stand for concepts. A systematic treatment that not only extends the distinction to other kinds of expressions but also gives an account of how sense and reference of various kinds of expressions are related among themselves came only with Frege's seminal work.

In a series of papers[2] Frege analysed how the distinction between sense and reference[3] applies to concept-expressions, such as nouns, verbs, adjectives; to proper names and define descriptions; and to sentences, both atomic and logically complex. 'Sense' is the core of what we consider to be the meaning of expressions, 'reference' is what expressions refer to. In section 24.2 of the previous chapter we have discussed a number of reasons why an equation of meaning with reference will not do. Quite generally the key issue is change: change over time, over possibilities, over different epistemic states, different normative conditions, ...

Change can be actual, or virtual, i.e., a matter of imagination. The possibility of change, and our ability to perceive it, actual or imaginary, is what creates 'meaning' as a separate concept, i.e., it necessitates a conception of what an expression means that goes beyond its factual reference. Without change meaning is not necessary: a specification of the referential relations between linguistic expressions and non-linguistic entities would suffice for a correct description of the world.[4] If there is change, however, and, equally important, observation of change, then this is no longer true. So we have change, observation of change, but also partial permanence (actual or virtual): if everything would change, there would be no way to anchor meaning. Observation of change is therefore always a relational manner and requires at least two situations that are partially but not completely different. As a consequence meaning, which allows us to describe change, is also relational: meaning reaches from one situation to another. Thus, the meaning of an expression relates different situations by uniting (potentially) different references of that expression in those situations.

On this view there is a natural connection between language and thought. It is meaning that makes thought possible, and it is meaning that links both to reality. In the previous chapter we already quoted extensively from Frege's 1882 'On the scientific justification of a concept-script'[5], here we repeat a key statement that Frege makes there:

> [. . .] our imagery [. . .] would be limited to that which our hand could form, our voice intone, if it were not for the grand discovery of the symbol which calls to our mind that which is absent, out of sight or perhaps even unseeable.

On this view, the primary function of language is to make present what is absent through the use of meaningful symbols. Thus three roles of language come together: the referential relation to reality; the cognitive connection with thought; and, through the assumed intersubjectivity of language, communication. Meaning is supposed to be key in all three, and that means that Frege's notion of sense needs to be able to account for all three as well.

It is exactly this supposed combination of functions that is questioned by the analyses that Kripke presents in his 'Identity and Necessity' paper. Fregean sense determines reference, is what is grasped in thought, and hence forms the content of knowledge and belief, and it is what is being communicated between language users. Kripke aims to show that there is not one conception of meaning that can fulfil all three functions: meaning in the intuitive sense is conceptually heterogeneous. At least some types of expressions refer without an intermediary descriptive content. The acquisition and transmission of knowledge of what such expressions refer to, is a causal process, one that does not rely on shared meanings. And the neat connection between necessity / contingency and a priori / a posteriori that is a characteristic of a Fregean conception of sense breaks down if Kripke's analyses are correct.

This conflict between Frege's attempt to give a unified conception of meaning and Kripke's position that meaning is heterogeneous is what is at stake in this excursus.

25.2 The authors

Gottlob Frege

We already introduced Frege and his importance for logic and philosophy in an earlier chapter, 2, section 2.2. In the current context it would be good to note that while the focus here is on Frege's contributions to philosophy of language and natural language semantics, these disciplinary indications are, of course, anachronisms, and that Frege's interest was first and foremost in logic and its role in a Kantian epistemological framework. Although he was hailed as the founder of modern analytic philosophy[6], other commentators have emphasised Frege's firm commitment to the tradition[7], and have argued that throughout his entire career Frege's primary concern is an investigation of the nature and status of logical notions and logical laws, which, in a Kantian spirit, must be conceived as the laws of thought that enable the acquisition of reliable knowledge about empirical reality. That being said, it is true that Frege's work has been, and continues to be, very influential in philosophy of language and natural language semantics, whether he intended such influence or not.

Saul Kripke

The American logician and philosopher Saul Kripke (1940 – 2022) was without doubt one of the most influential thinkers in logic and analytic philosophy of the last decades. He was educated at Harvard University, and taught logic and philosophy at Rockefeller University from 1968 to 1976, and at Princeton University from 1976 until 1998. In 2001 he was awarded the Rolf Schock Prize, one of the most prestigious awards in the humanities. In 2003 he was appointed as distinguished professor at the Graduate Center of the City University of New York.

Kripke has made significant contributions to a wide variety of areas, including philosophy of language, epistemology, modal logic, set theory, philosophy of logic. His early work, which he started when still in high school, on the semantics of intuitionistic logic was already referred to in chapter 24. This work was an important impetus to the development of relational semantics.[8] He also made significant contributions to the mathematical theory of truth. In 'Outline of a Theory of Truth' (Kripke, 1975) Kripke develops an analysis of truth that allows for languages to that their own truth predicates without thereby becoming inconsistent (as was commonly assumed after Tarski's seminal work on the semantic conception of truth (Tarski, 1944)).

In philosophy of language Kripke is most famous for his view of names as rigid designators, an approach that goes against the prevalent descriptivist theories of names of Frege and Russell. The main source are the 1970 Princeton lectures that were published only in 1980 (Kripke, 1980), under the title *Naming and Necessity*. The paper that is part of the current excursus, Kripke (1971) dates from that period. *Naming and Necessity* embodies ideas that can also be found in work of John Stuart Mill and in earlier work on modal logic of Ruth Barcan Marcus.[9] The rigid designator view of names is an instance of a more general idea, viz., that certain types of expressions are directly referring expressions, i.e. expressions that are linked to their referents without an intermediary meaning. Here, Kripke's work aligns with that of others, notable with the analyses presented by Hilary Putnam (see e.g., Putnam (1975)). The theory of direct reference comes with another take on how meaning is acquired and transmitted, the so-called 'causal theory of reference'. It also dissociates the metaphysical (ontological) notions of necessity and possibility from the epistemological notions of a priori and a posteriori. Kripke also applied these ideas to the problem of identity materialism in philosophy of mind.

Another influential work of Kripke's is *Wittgenstein on Rules and Private Language* (Kripke, 1982), in which he analyses the so-called 'rule following considerations' in Wittgenstein's *Philosophical Investigations* (Wittgenstein, 2009). Although generally considered to fail as an exegesis of Wittgenstein's text, the resulting conception of rule-following has been quite influential, also in philosophy of semantics.

Kripke's lasting influence is mainly through his published work and the many lectures he has given all over the world. The *Saul Kripke Center* (see https://saulkripkecenter.org) is dedicated to the collection and preservation of Kripke's work in this variety of forms.

25.3 The texts

Frege, 'On Sense and Reference'

Frege's paper starts with a question: what is the nature of the identity relation? There appear to be two candidates: it can be a relation between signs, or a relation between what signs refer to, ie., between entities. The former option Frege rejects because of the arbitrariness of the reference relation: that we use this sign to refer to that entity is a conventional matter and on such a view an identity statement of the form $a = b$ would merely tell us something about language, not about the world. But true identity statements are capable of relating substantial knowledge, Frege notes: 'The Morning Star is the Evening Star' formulates a significant astronomical discovery. But that leads to another problem. If 'The Morning Star is the Evening Star' is true and identity is a relation between entities, then there seems to be no difference with 'The Morning Star is the Morning Star': both are true because Venus is Venus. However, whereas the latter is an analytic statement, the truth of which anybody can acknowledge a priori, i.e., irrespective of their knowledge of what 'The Morning Star' refers to, the former, as noted, is synthetic and a posteriori: we learn something about reality if we learn that 'The Morning Star is the Evening Star' is true and we need empirical evidence to reach that conclusion.

So the very problem that Frege formulates at the beginning of the text assumes intrinsic connections between reality, i.e., what expressions refer to; cognitive content, i.e., what potential knowledge is expressed by a statement; and a form of linguistic meaning that ties these together. This aspect of meaning is what Frege calls 'sense' ('Sinn').

The paper continues with an extensive discussion of the nature of sense; its relation with reference; the specific type of sense of names and sentences.[10] Quite generally, sense is 'the way in which the reference is given' ('die Art des Gegebenseins'), i.e., a specific sense is a specific way of determining what an expression refers to. It supplies a criterion for determining reference in different circumstances, e.g., across time, or across possibilities. Thus, sense is a cognitive concept.

As such sense is a key component of meaning. In natural languages, Frege notes, meaning often involves more than sense, and he takes care to mark that sense is to be distinguished from mental associations, which he describes as 'colouring' ('Beleuchtung', 'Färbung'). Expressions often come with certain associations, they may evoke pictures or emotions, but these are not what determine reference. Such associations are subjective, and in a strict sense not communicable. Sense is; it is what determines reference and it does so in an objective manner.[11] The objectivity of sense is what guarantees its communicability. It also sets sense apart in an ontological manner: it does not belong to the sphere of the mental, but it can also not be located in observable, contingent reality: it is on an ontological plane of its own.[12] Frege illustrates the distinctions between reference, sense, and mental association by comparing them to a celestial object, its image in a telescope, and the visual impression on the retina of the observer.[13]

Names, which for Frege include complex expressions such as definite descriptions, have sense, and that sense is what determines their reference. So, a particular sense is a particular way of determining an object. As the considerations with respect to the Morning Star and the Evening Star show, one and the same object, in this case the planet Venus, can be 'given', i.e., characterised in a cognitive sense, in different ways: as the object visible in the sky in the morning, and as the object visible in the sky in the evening.[14] That 'The Morning Star is the Evening Star' is true, means that both senses in the actual world determine the same object. But that need not be the case: under other astronomical configurations the celestial bodies visible in the morning sky and in the evening sky, respectively, might have been different objects. Frege's example to illustrate this point concerns two ways of identifying the common intersection of the bisecting lines in a triangle.

Note that sense here has two aspects: it determines reference and it supplies cognitive content. The two are related, yet distinct: we may know what an expression refers to without knowing its sense; and vice versa we may know the sense of an expression but fail to know what it refers to. And note further that there can be sense without reference: failure to refer does not make an expression meaningless. This failure can be accidental, as is the case with the infamous 'the present King of France', and it can even be necessary, see 'the largest prime'. Frege does note that in a formal language such failures should be avoided, by requiring the introduction of a name to come with a proof of the existence of its referent. Along similar lines, Frege argues, can we avoid the fact that different language users may associate different senses with the same expression. Thus, for some the sense of 'Aristotle' is something like 'the teacher of Alexander', whereas for others it may be 'the author of the Nicomachean ethics'.

Frege extends the sense – reference distinction to sentences in the following way. Every sentence, Frege claims, is associated with a thought. The question now is whether this thought is the reference or the sense of a sentence. That the thought cannot be the reference of a sentence is argued for by an appeal to compositionality. If we replace an expression in a sentence with one that has the same reference but a different sense, then the thought expressed changes. Given compositionality of reference[15], the reference of the sentence does not change, so the thought is not its reference. This suggests that the thought is the sense of a sentence, which is in accordance with the principle of compositionality of sense.

The next question is whether sentences have reference at all, and if they do, what that reference is. Here, Frege starts from the observation that the question of whether a name in a sentence has reference typically occurs when we wonder what the truth value of a sentence is. An example. 'Huangdi invented the oracle bone script': if we want to assess whether this sentence is true or false, we need to assume that the name 'Huangdi' has a referent. Again, with an (implicit) appeal to compositionality of reference, this suggests that the truth value of a sentence is its reference.[16] One consequence is that all true sentences and all false sentences have the same reference: what Frege calls 'the True' and 'the False', respectively. However, since sentences have sense in addition to reference, this does not create a problem.

In the paper Frege goes on to discuss a variety of issues concerning the application of the sense – reference distinction that arise from different constructions in natural language. We mention here briefly only one, the issue of so-called 'intensional contexts', i.e., contexts in which extensionality fails to hold. Familiar examples are the contexts created by modal and temporal operators, epistemic verbs, and so on. In Frege's approach expressions that occur in such contexts do not have their usual reference. However, the sentences containing such intensional contexts usually do have a truth value, i.e., a reference, and thus compositionality dictates that the expressions making up such sentences all have a reference as well. What that reference is, if it's not the usual reference, depends on the context in which the expression occurs. Two examples by way of illustration.

First, so-called 'direct speech' reports:

(1) Peter said "The Morning Star is a celestial body that is illuminated by the Sun"

This is an extreme case: no substitution of expressions in the quotation is allowed, not even of expressions with the same sense. Apparently, what the words in the quotation refer to are the words themselves.[17]

Next, 'indirect speech' reports:

(2) Peter said that The Morning Star is a celestial body that is illuminated by the Sun

Here substitution of expressions with the same reference but different sense is not allowed, but we can replace expressions with the same sense. From this Frege concludes that expressions in such a context refer to what is ordinarily their sense.

Kripke, 'Identity and Necessity'

In 'Identity and Necessity' (Kripke, 1971) Kripke addresses many of the issues that are dealt with more extensively in the famous *Naming and Necessity* lectures (Kripke, 1980), such as the (im)possibility of contingent identity statements; modality *de dicto* and *de re*; proper names as rigid designators; necessity of origin; necessity of material composition.

The paper opens with a proof that identity statements are necessary: necessarily true, when true; and necessarily false, when false. This appears to rule out the possibility of there being contingent identity statements, i.e., statements that are sometimes true, sometimes not. It also appears to be at odds with the idea of their being identity statements that are cognitively substantial, that are able to provide new knowledge. The conclusion has been considered by many authors as paradoxical, and, after having given and defended the proof, Kripke turns to a detailed discussion of some of the considerations that have been brought forward.

In that discussion the distinction between proper names and definite descriptions is crucial. Kripke acknowledges the possibility of contingent identity statements involving definite descriptions, while maintaining that no such statements are possible with proper names. Here he relies on the mechanisms supplied by Russell's analysis of definite descriptions. The fact that definite descriptions have scope allows for that. Kripke does note that we need then also to accept the meaningfulness of modalities *de re* and the concurrent possibility of quantifying into the scope of intensional operators. But this he considers to be unproblematic.

With proper names things are different, Kripke argues. Here we need to accept that an identity statement of the form $a = b$, with a and b proper names, if true, is so necessarily. This is connected with the view of proper names as not having any descriptive content, but being used as 'tags', as arbitrary ways to label an object. This idea, which Kripke traces back to work of Ruth Barcan Marcus, has been criticised because it rules the possibility of informative identity statements involving proper names.

Kripke discusses the objections raised by Quine[18] and notices that if we would analyse proper names as in fact 'abbreviated' definite descriptions, as Russell has proposed, we could deal with the cases Quine brings forward as counterexamples. He goes on to note that the concept of contingent identity statements is not restricted to the case of proper names for objects or individuals. With certain phrases similar issues arise. We take 'Heat is the motion of molecules' to be a true identity statement, but a contingent one. After all, it formulates an important scientific discovery, so it is informative, and the physical fact that it reports might have been different. Other examples involve 'water', 'gold', 'pain'. These are often referred to as 'natural kind terms'.

Kripke then states his own position, which is that we need to accept that true identity statements, both those involving proper names as well as those involving natural kind terms, are indeed necessary. These expressions, he states, are rigid designators, in contrast to definite descriptions such as 'the present King of France', 'the inventor of bifocals', and non-natural kinds terms such as 'tall', 'born in Shanghai', 'married with two children'. Rigid designators are expressions that, whenever they refer, refer to the same thing. That means that also certain definite descriptions meet this condition, Kripke mentions as an example 'the square root of 25, which necessarily refers to the number 5. The rider 'whenever they refer' is important, because rigid designators need not refer to things that necessarily exist.

After this introduction of the concept of rigid designation, Kripke enters into a long discussion of which conception of a possible world, or a counterfactual situation, best fits with it. One objection to the idea of rigid designation is that it is incoherent: in order to determine whether a term refers to the same object in a different world, we need to have a criterion to determine which object in that world is the same as this one. But such criteria are not forthcoming. This is a familiar objection to the very idea of intensional concepts such as possible worlds and possible individuals voiced by Quine.[19] Another objection goes in another direction. It maintains that the very idea of identity across worlds is incoherent, an object does not have an identical in another worlds, it has (at best) only a counterpart: a different object that resembles it in sufficiently many regards.[20]

Kripke thinks both positions rest on a misunderstanding of what possible worlds are. He argues that the very idea that we should be able to give a purely qualitative description of a possible world is what lies at the root of it. Possible worlds are not described as independent entities, they are introduced by partial descriptions. Counterfactuals provide good examples: 'If I had not accepted the invitation, I would never have met you' introduces a situation that is in every respect like the actual one except that in this counterfactual one I did not accept the invitation and consequently did not meet you. This is a situation involving you and me, not counterparts. And it is a non-factual situation that is nevertheless perfectly possible.

Having thus argued for the meaningfulness of the concept of rigid designation, Kripke proceeds to discuss the concepts of necessity and a prioricity. These two concepts are often taken to be co-extensive: whatever is necessary can be known a priori, and vice versa. After all, a prioricity implies independence of whatever can be observed contingently, so must pertain to the necessary. And if something is necessary then knowing it to be so could not really depend on any contingent observation. This equation of a metaphysical concept and an epistemological one is questioned by Kripke. His example is the Goldbach conjecture, that states that every even number is the sum of two prime numbers. This being a mathematical matter, Kripke states, it is certainly something that, if true, is necessarily so. But it being a conjecture it is definitely not something that is known a priori. But can it be known a priori? That really depends on what constitutes knowing a mathematical fact, which is a substantial question that allows for different types of answers.

Another example that Kripke discusses at some length has to do with the essence of material composition. Could something that is actually made of wood have been made of ice instead? Would it be the same object? Or would it merely be a copy executed in a different material? Our intuitive inclination, Kripke states, is to say that it would indeed not be the same object. But then it follows that if an object is made of X is it necessarily made of X. This is another reason to maintain that necessity and a prioricity do not coincide: certainly we do not know a priori what the material composition of most objects is.

The need to distinguish between the metaphysical and the epistemological then provides a way out of some of the problems people have with accepting that identity statements with rigid designators are necessary. That such statements can provide new knowledge, and thus be epistemologically significant, is no longer at odds with their being necessary, as long as we keep in mind that what is necessary need not be knowable a priori.

Additionally, Kripke gives an analysis of why we are inclined to maintain that identity statements are contingent after all. This is because in most cases there is indeed a connection between a name and some descriptive content. The mistake is, Kripke argues, to take this descriptive content to be the meaning of the name. But it plays a different role: descriptive content is (often) used to fix the referent of a name. Names are introduced and taught and learned by describing the referent. But that connection is contingent, which means that the descriptive content cannot be used as a criterion for picking out the referent of the name in different situations.

In the last part of the paper Kripke returns to a detailed discussion of some cases of identity statements involving natural kind terms. That such statements, if true, are necessarily so, has a number of consequences. Kripke focusses on the identity of experiential properties, such as being in pain, and material properties, such as being in a particular brain state. For so-called 'identity theorists', the statement 'Pain is being in brain state *X*' is a true identity. Kripke then argues that 'pain' and 'being in brain state *X*' being rigid designators, the identity theorist then has to accept that this identity is not just true, but necessary. And has to find a way to defend that necessity. The suggestion Kripke leave us with is that such a defence is not forthcoming and that this constitutes a strong argument against the identity theory.

25.4 Study and discussion questions

Study questions

Frege

- Which two analyses of identity does Frege distinguish? And what problems with each of them does he note?
- Consider the following sentences:

  (3) Fred said: 'Beijing is a big city'
  (4) Fred said that Being is a big city

  What do the italicised sentential parts in (3) and (4) refer to according to Frege? (I.e., what is their 'Bedeutung'?) And what is their sense? (I.e., what is their 'Sinn'?)
- Two expressions can have different senses and the same reference. Is it also possible for two expressions to have the same sense and different references? Why (not)?
- How does Frege determine what constitutes the sense and the reference of a sentence? What general principle does he use here (implicitly)?
- What needs to be true, according to Frege, for the sentence 'Odysseus was brought to shore while asleep' to be true or false?

- What analysis of identity does Frege opt for? And how does he solve the problem with that analysis that he notes at the beginning of the paper?

Kripke

- How does Kripke prove that two objects that are identical are identical necessarily? Do you accept the premisses of his argument? And why would someone regard this proof as somehow 'paradoxical'?
- "In Identity and Necessity Kripke investigates whether the proof just mentioned of the necessity of identity statements is valid or not." Is this a good summary of what Kripke does in the paper? Why (not)?
- Kripke argues that a true identity statement with two definite descriptions need not be necessarily true. How does the argument go? And what about an identity statement with a proper name and a definite description?
- If it does not hold that 'Cicero = Tully', if true is necessarily true, what follows about the meaning of 'Cicero' and of 'Tully'?
- Kripke calls proper namers 'rigid designators'. What is a rigid designator? Why are proper names rigid designators according to Kripke? And is 'The China Construction Bank' a rigid designator?
- What distinguishes the pair of concepts 'necessary – contingent' from the pair 'a priori – a posteriori'? How does Kripke argue that necessity does not imply a priority?
- What role do descriptions play in the fixing of the reference of proper names?

Discussion questions

- How does Frege use the principle of compositionality to argue that the reference of the embedded sentence 'that the earth revolves around the sun' in the sentence 'Copernicus believed that the earth revolves around the sun' is not a truth value?
- Does Kripke give convincing arguments that proper names do not have descriptive content?
- Sometimes cultural artefacts are repaired or restored using different materials than those from which the original was made. Evaluate this from the perspective of Kripke's idea of 'necessity of origin'.
- Although he does use natural language examples, at the background of Frege's considerations is always the construction of an 'ideal' formal language. Kripke, on the other hand, is very much focussed on natural language as such. Identify one or more places where that shows in their arguments. And does this make a difference for the way in which and the extent to which Kripke and Frege defend different theories?

25.5 Further reading

Some relevant literature on Frege has already been mentioned in section 2.5. An in-depth study of Frege's concept of 'sense' can be found in Beaney (1996).

For an early critical evaluation of Kripke's analysis of names as rigid designators, see Hintikka & Sandu (1995). For a general introduction to Kripke's Naming and Necessity lectures, see Noonan (2013).

26

Pragmatics

In this chapter we look at logic from a different perspective: not in terms of what it can do and how it can be used, but in terms of what it cannot do, what its limits are. We will do so with a focus on the application of logic to describe natural language meaning.

As we shall see, what the limits, if any, of logic in that area are, is not at all an uncontroversial question, and quite different perspectives on the issue have been worked out and defended.

26.1 Syntax, semantics, pragmatics

Most of the discussions in this area are formulated in terms of a traditional, well-established distinction from the field of semiotics. It was Charles Morris who defined syntax as the study of the form of signs, semantics as the study of the meaning of signs, and pragmatics as that part that deals with the use of signs.[1]

So, syntax : semantics : pragmatics = form : meaning : use. But how are these three domains related among each other?

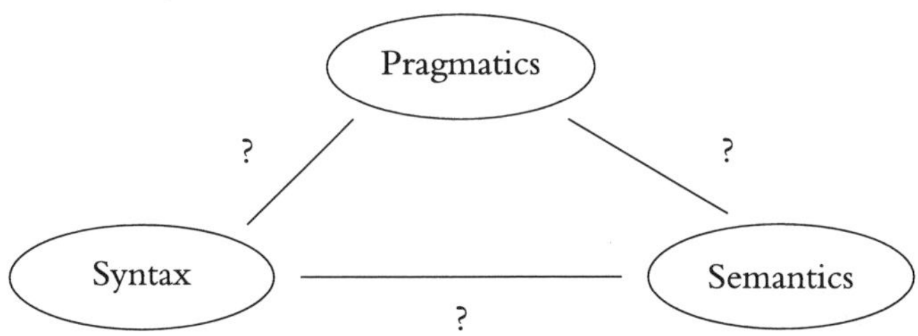

Figure 26.1: Syntax – semantics –pragmatics

More specifically: are there any dependency relations between these three aspects of language, and thus between the three sub-disciplines that study them? What answer one would like to give to this question depends in part also on what exactly one takes the three elements to cover.

Of these three, syntax is probably the least controversial: it deals with the structure of expressions: the way in which they are composed of smaller elements and how the structures of various expressions hang together. Neither meaning, nor use appear to enter into the picture, and that suggests a relative autonomy of syntax.

Semantics is a more complicated affair. At various points we have been confronted with the fact that even in logic there are different ways of looking at what semantics is. That it deals with meaning is a matter of definition, but what meaning is, is not. The dominant conception in logic and in much of analytic philosophy as well as in formal semantics of natural language is referential: meaning is explained in terms of what expressions refer to, culminating in the truth conditions that sentences have. That can still be given different forms, but the core feature of meaning is its referential character.

As we have seen, proof-theoretic semantics starts from quite a different angle: it locates the meanings of expressions in the use we make of them. In the context of logic that use is how logical constants operate in the context of providing proofs. In the context of natural language it develops into a much broader view on meaning.

This indicates that what counts as semantics and what is covered by pragmatics depends very much on what one takes meaning to be. And hence pragmatics, too, can be understood in a variety of ways. The most restricted interpretation has pragmatics deals with a limited number of cases of context-dependence: indexical and demonstrative expressions.[2] And in its widest interpretation it encompasses anything that has to do with how, when, why, where and by whom an expression is used. More on that later.

So the question about what semantics and pragmatics are, and how they relate to one another, depends, at least in part, on what meaning is taken to be. Within the variety of views that result from this, we can identify two extremes: Gricean pragmatics and radical contextualism.

Gricean pragmatics follows the lead of referential semantics. In effect, as we shall see, one of Grice's main aims in developing his ideas was to show that the account of logical connectives that standard logic provides is correct but incomplete: it needs to be augmented. So, on this view syntax provides the basis for a definition of a referential semantics, on top of which sits a pragmatic component that deals with non-referential aspects of meaning, as illustrated in Figure 26.2.

Radical contextualism is, as its name suggests, more radical. In its most extreme form it does away with semantics altogether and only looks at how expressions are used. On this view the relation between syntax and pragmatics is an interactive one: expressions have a certain form that enables a range of uses, but the way we use expressions in its turn in some cases contributes to

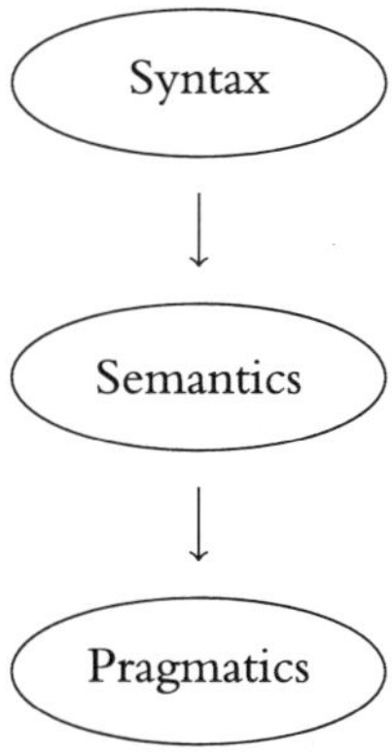

Figure 26.2: Gricean pragmatics

shaping syntactic form. Thus radical contextualism eliminates semantics and makes syntax and pragmatics mutually dependent, as illustrated in Figure 26.3.

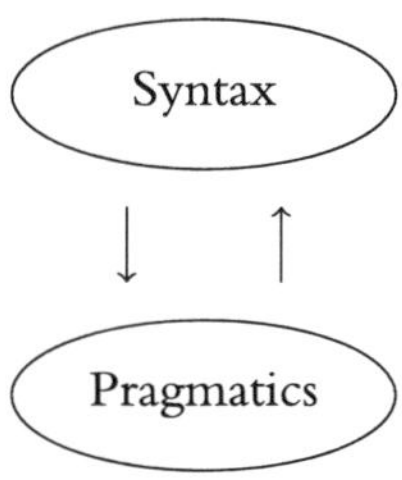

Figure 26.3: Radical contextualism

It will be clear that from the perspective of logic the Gricean picture is the more natural one. Logic provides a syntax and a semantics for its formal languages. This holds also for the case in which one would rely solely on a syntactic account of validity. Although the basic idea of a proof-theoretic semantics relies on the general idea that meaning can be accounted for in terms of use, what such a proof-theoretic semantics does is still providing a semantics that has the same coverage as a referential one: accounting for the validity of argument schemes.

So radical contextualism assigns pragmatics a fundamentally different place than is accorded to it in the Gricean set-up. We do need to note that these two options are not the only ones. A whole range of different points of view can be, and has been, defended. We will have the opportunity to point some of them out later in this chapter.

The remainder of this chapter is primarily devoted to the presentation and discussion of some central phenomena that play a role in the debates concerning the semantics – pragmatics division of labour. We will refer to some key theoretical paradigms along the way, but an extensive treatment of them is beyond the scope of this first introduction.

26.2 Literal meaning

We start with a core concept, that of 'literal meaning'. It does not always go by that name, in many cases it is just referred to as 'meaning', but as a concept it is central to the field of semantics and pragmatics.

Literal meaning has a number of characteristic that can be used to determine whether a particular aspect of the meaning of an expression (sentence) is part of its literal meaning, or is due to other factors, such as the context, speaker's intentions, and so on.

First of all, the literal meaning of an expression is its compositional, linguistic meaning. I.e., it is the meaning that is determined by the meanings of the lexical items, as specified in the lexicon, and by the semantic rules that correspond to the syntactic rules that have produced the expression.

Secondly, literal meaning is often conceived of as what constitutes the semantic competence of the speaker of a language. The idea here is that what constitutes the knowledge of a competent speaker of a language is their knowledge of the language's syntax: they know when an expression is well-formed or not, and their knowledge of the literal meanings of the expressions of the language.

And finally, literal meaning is held to determine the referential import and the semantic content of expressions. I.e., it is what determines what an expression refers to and what the semantic content of the sentences of the language is. This semantic content is then almost always taken to be 'truth-evaluable', i.e., it is content that determines whether a sentence can be said to be true or false. As such literal meaning also forms the starting point for the construction of other, pragmatic aspects of meaning and provides the measure for determining communicative success: if its literal meaning becomes shared a sentence is used successfully in communication.

26.3 Literal meaning and context

This conception of literal meaning applies best to sentences that express content that is not dependent on context. A clear illustration of that is provided by Frege's concept of sense. Frege famously distinguishes sense from reference.[3] He conceived of senses as a kind of platonic entities: they are objective, independent of language, and are also completely independent of context. The sense of a sentence is what Frege calls a 'thought', but this conception of thought has nothing to do with actual human thinking. A thought is an objective content that exists on its own and that is either true or false. But its truth value does not depend on any feature of a context in which it is expressed or grasped. So, if a thought is true, it is always true and if it is false, it is always false. This is called 'eternalism'.

26.3.1 The trouble with eternity

This conception of a thought fits mathematics and logic: 'The square root of 1024 is 32' can indeed be said to be true independently of when or where or by whom it is used.[4] But in natural languages most sentences display an (implicit or explicit) context-dependence that then needs to be paraphrased away.

Consider the following example:

(1) Munich has 800.00 inhabitants
(2) Munich has 800.00 inhabitants in 1897 (on December 14 (at 00.00 hrs))

The truth value of the first sentence depends on the time at which it is used. This time-dependence can be eliminated by making the implicit dependence explicit, as the second sentence illustrates.

Now this raises two questions: Can we always 'eternalise', i.e., can we make all context-dependence explicit in the sentence itself? And supposing we can, should we?

It seems intuitively obvious that a restriction to eternal sentences is too strong. Logic deals with arguments, including arguments in which contingent sentences and the semantics of natural language obviously cannot be confined to only eternal sentences. Moreover, 'eternalising' a sentence changes its meaning, and that is not what we want.

A simple example shows why. Suppose we have the following interaction. *A* says to *B*: 'Munich has 800.000 inhabitants.' And then *B* responds: 'That was true in 1897, but now it no longer is: there are over 5.5 million'. The very possibility of a dispute like this hinges on the fact that sentences are not 'eternalised'. For if they were, this simply would not be a difference in opinion about the matter at hand

So it seems that context-dependence should not be explained away but rather be acknowledged as a characteristic feature of natural language.[5] In what follows we review a couple of examples of types of expressions that introduce context-dependence.

26.3.2 Indexicals

Context-dependence at sentence-level is often the result of the occurrence of explicitly context-sensitive expressions, so-called 'indexicals'. These are personal pronouns, 'I', 'you', . . . , demonstratives 'this', 'that', . . . , temporal expressions 'tomorrow', 'today', . . . , verb tenses, and location-expressions 'here', 'there', . . .

Characteristic features of indexicals are that they are lexical items, that there is only a limited number of them, and that their lexical meaning is not context-dependent, but that their reference is.

The last point needs to be appreciated: the meaning of, for example, 'I' is the same, no matter who uses it. It is the reference that changes with the user. Thus if A says 'I am hungry' his use of 'I' refers to him, A, and if B uses the same sentence her use of 'I' refers to her, B. What they say is the same, what they express is different, in the sense that their respective uses of the same sentence, with the same meaning, have different truth conditions. Here we see how use and meaning interact.[6]

Similar observations can be made with respect to other indexicals. This, 'Tomorrow will be a sunny day' when uttered on a particular day states something about the weather on the following day. It can be used on any day with the same meaning, but makes claims about different days.

26.3.3 Semantics for indexicals

There is a generally accepted way of accounting for the type of context-dependence induced by indexicals in the semantics.indexicals | (It uses the distinction between 'character' and 'content' that was first introduced by David Kaplan in his analysis of demonstratives.[7]

Central to the analysis is the distinction between 'character' and 'content'. The character of an expression is its lexical meaning, which stays the same over different uses that are made of it. The content is what at each particular use the expression contributes to the truth conditional context of the sentence in which it occurs.

An example. The character of 'I' = 'the one who is speaking', which is independent of context. And the content of 'I' in a context of use c = 'the one who is actually speaking in c', which is dependent on context.[8]

The context plays a different role. It may be the context in which we interpret an utterance of a sentence: somebody is saying something, we figure out what they mean. And it may be the context in which we evaluate such an utterance: somebody is saying something, we determine whether what they say is true.

In some cases the difference does not matter, i.e., context of interpretation and context of evaluation coincide. Example: any eternal(ised) sentence. But sometimes it does. A simple example of such 'double indexing' is an utterance of 'I will stop being the speaker'. This is true at c iff the one who is actually speaking at c is not the speaker at some c' later than c. This shows that tense operators (future, past) are 'context-shifters '. Other examples are modal operators, such 'It is possible / necessary that . . . '

26.3.4 Is that all there is?

A lot more can, and needs to be, said about their analysis, but these brief remarks should have made clear that it is possible to account for the context-dependence of indexicals as part of their semantics, that that it can be incorporated in the literal meaning of lexical items in a systematic and descriptively adequate way.

But the main question is, of course: Is that all? I.e., are indexicals the only context-sensitive expressions? If that were the case then we would have no need for pragmatics: indexicals being a finite list of lexical expressions, their incorporation into semantics, along the lines indicated above, would present no challenge. The resulting semantic framework would need to be an extension of classical referential semantics, but the context-dependence that indexicals display, can be accommodated in a suitable extension with various types of operators, such as tense and modal operators.

However, there are several reasons to doubt that this is the case. There are a number of types of context-dependence that seem to defy the kind of analysis that is suitable for indexicals. In what follows we briefly review some prominent examples.

26.3.5 Gradable adjectives

So-called 'gradable adjectives' display a form of context-dependence that it seems cannot be resolved in a 'once-and-for-all' fashion that works with indexicals.

Examples of gradable adjectives are 'tall', 'heavy', 'tasty', ... It is clear that in order to evaluate a sentence such as:

(3) John is tall

we need to know with whom John is being compared: boys of the same age? his family members? basketball players?

Note that this means that 'being tall' is not an absolute property: one can be said to be tall in one sense, but not in another, as the following example illustrates:

(4) John is tall for a 15 year old, but not for a basketball player

So, ascription of a property such as tallness is done relative to a comparison class.

The crucial question then is: Where do comparison classes come from? Are they part of literal meaning? Are they supplied by context? By a combination of both?

Although it may not always make equal sense to do so, it appears that the length of an object can be compared with an open-ended set of classes of objects. That makes it implausible that comparison classes are somehow determined by the lexical meaning of 'tall'. The context in which the expression is used thus seems to be the decisive factor.

26.3.6 Vagueness

And then there are expressions that have inherent vagueness. Examples are such predicates as 'bald', 'empty', . . . , various colour words, terms such as 'heap', 'crowd., . . . , so-called 'predicates of personal taste', such as 'tasty', 'beautiful', 'ugly', 'cheap', 'expensive', . . . , and so on.

We already mentioned the Sorites paradox in the chapter on many-valued logic, and pointed out that it presents a challenge to the principle of excluded middle. But there is also an element of context-dependence. A lot of solutions have been proposed for the problem of providing a satisfactory account of vague predicates. And many of them proceed in terms of parameters (e.g., 'cut off points') that are context-dependent. To given an illustration: what counts as a heap of salt on the kitchen table and what counts as a heap of salt on a site of salt mine are definitely two different things. And that has consequences for the point at which a certain conglomerate of grains of salt ceases to be a heap, or becomes one. What is the appropriate 'cut-off point' depends on the context in which the expression is used.

26.3.7 Speaker's reference

Yet another example concerns referential terms, such as proper names and definite descriptions. It can be argued that the intentions of the speaker are relevant for determining what such a term refers to.

Here is an example.[9] Consider the case where A, pointing to Smith, whom he mistakes for Jones, says 'Jones is raking the leaves.' What is the meaning of A's utterance? Who did A refer to? What are the truth conditions of the sentence used by A given his referential intentions?

It appears that the answer could go either way. One could argue that given the fact that the name 'Jones' refers to Jones, A has said something false, because it is Smith, and not Jones who is raking the leaves. But one could also hold that A said something true of the person whom he intended to refer to, viz., that man over there, Smith.[10] So, semantic reference or speaker's reference?

Clearly, this is not an easy call. Obviously, the semantic reference has a role to play. But the speaker's referential intention cannot be ignored, at least not if we want to understand what it is that someone is trying to say by using an expression or a sentence. The systematic nature and the relevant independence of language from the various contexts in which it can be used, seem to favour the priority of semantic reference. But in order to give an account of success and failure in communicative situations it seems we also need to reckon with the speaker's reference.

Other examples of this phenomenon are produced by the way demonstratives operate along with gestures. Often, if a demonstrative such as 'this' or 'that one' is used, the use is accompanied by pointing or demonstrating gestures (with the hand, the eyes, other body-parts). When used 'bare' it seems that the gestures, which reflect the speaker's referential intentions, are what settles the referent of the demonstrative: it is the object pointed out, gestured towards. But when a demonstrative is used in combination with a descriptive noun, e.g. 'this piece of fish' or 'those mushrooms', we may be confronted with a similar dilemma as above. If *A* points to a piece of white meat and states that he wants 'this piece of fish', what does he want? Fish or meat? In some contexts it may be clear how we would react . For example, if *A* has told us explicitly that he never eats meat, we would interpret his demonstrative act as a mistake, and we would correct him. But if *A* has indicated that he just wants something fried, we can take the demonstrative act as correctly indicating what he wants, and serve him the meat.

Another example of how semantic reference and speakers intentions may be taken into account is Donnellan's distinction between referential and attributive use of definite descriptions.[11] Donnellan's example runs as follows. Suppose *A* is in a courtroom observing *B*, who is on trial, accused of murdering someone called Smith.[12] *A* considers the evidence given against *B* pretty compelling and *B* behaves very erratically, screaming, cursing, giving completely irrelevant answers, which makes *A* say: 'Smith's murderer is insane'. By way of contrast, suppose *A* has never encountered *B*, but utters the same sentence after having looked at pictures of the victim, Smith, who has been murdered in a rather brutal way. Now consider what both uses of the description refer to, in case *B* is indeed Smith's murderer, and in case he is not.

Donnellan takes the first use to be what he calls 'referential' and he suggests that it can be paraphrased as follows: 'That man over there, Smith's murderer, is insane.' In this situation the use of 'Smith's murderer' picks out *B* irrespective of whether *B* is the murderer or not. The second use is what Donnellan calls 'attributive' and that use, he suggests, can be paraphrased as follows: 'Smith's murderer, whoever he is, is insane.' In this case the use of 'Smith's murderer' picks out the actual murderer, which is *B* in case *B* actually did murder Smith, but someone else, if *B* did not do it.

Perhaps more strikingly than the other examples, the speaker's reference highlights the tension between semantic and pragmatic considerations, illustrating that both are needed if we want to account for the effects of using a language.

26.4 Pragmatics

So let us turn to pragmatics and its relation to semantics. Pragmatics is about use, and use always takes place in context. Hence, the preliminary question is: Are all forms of context-dependence semantic? If not, and the various phenomena we have briefly discussed in the previous section strongly suggests that, then the next question is: Where do we draw the line between semantic and pragmatic forms of context-dependence? And are there mechanisms that give a systematic account of pragmatic forms of context-dependence?

These are complicated questions, and there is certainly no consensus among linguists, logicians and philosopher about the answers. In what follows we will therefore take a brief look at some of the main positions.

26.4.1 *Exploring the borders of semantics*

Although there is no consensus, there is something like 'the standard view' on these issues. Generally stated it is something like this: semantics produces expressions with literal meanings, including a fixed set of context-dependence ones (the so-called 'limited set'); then pragmatics derives additional meaning aspects from these literal meanings via various pragmatic mechanisms.

Earlier we called this view 'Gricean pragmatics', and for good reason. The Gricean theory is the best-known and most influential instantiation of the standard view. But it can, and has been, augmented in various ways.

As is explained in more detail in chapter 27 Grice's conception of pragmatics is centred around the Cooperative Principle and the conversational maxims that spell out what requirements speech participants who are engaged in a cooperative information exchange need to meet. On that basis Grice then characterises conversational implicatures as what other speech participants can deduce if the speaker does not conform (intentionally or otherwise) with one or more conversational maxims.

This mechanism with which conversational implicature is 'calculated' is a fairly limited reasoning process that has three inputs: the literal meanings of the expressions used; the conversational maxims (themselves derived from the cooperative principles); and observations regarding the question of whether the conversational maxims are followed or not.

Although the Gricean framework can deal with a fairly wide range of cases, it has its limitations, both in terms of coverage, and in terms of the mechanism it employs.

The latter is considered to be an instance of a more encompassing mechanism, called 'free enrichment'. And besides free enrichment other mechanisms have been proposed as well. In what follows we look at them in a bit more detail.

26.4.2 Pragmatic mechanisms

In the literature one may find the following three basic mechanisms defined, and defended: free enrichment; transfer; and coercion.

We give one or more examples of each and note some characteristic properties of their application.

26.4.3 Free enrichment

Let's start with some examples:

(5) After dinner we were served coffee ⇒ After dinner we were served a cup of coffee
(6) She took out her key and opened the door ⇒ She took out her key and then opened the door with it

The second sentence following the first in each of these two examples seems a straightforward and natural way to interpret the first. It makes explicit, not what is already there in the first sentence, but what is there in our understanding of it.

However, note that the enriched version can be overruled. The following are, perhaps not very plausible, but nevertheless also logical possibilities:

(7) After dinner we were served coffee ⇒ After dinner we were served coffee in the form of frozen espresso granules over vanilla ice cream. Unorthodox but delicious.
(8) She took out her key and opened the door ⇒ She took out her key and opened the door by gently pushing it with her left foot, and then she inserted the key in the alarm system to switch it off. That's how she got in without anybody noticing it.

Free enrichment has the following characteristics. It operates on the literal meaning of the sentences that are generated by the semantics. That means that it is top-down: it works after semantic composition has taken place. It is also a general mechanism, usually some form of Gricean reasoning that starts from literal meaning. It is optional: we do not have to execute the enrichment in any explicit form. It is non-determinate, as the above examples show. And it is cancellable:

(9) *A*: After dinner we were served coffee.
B: A cup of coffee, I presume?
A: No, a whole pot each. (*B*: Weird. But ok.)

The indeterminacy and the general nature of the free enrichment process is both a strength and a weakness. It can account for a wide variety of plausible ways of understanding the use of a sentence in a context. But it seems to over-generate unless it is somehow kept in check.

26.4.4 Transfer

Another ubiquitous mechanism that accounts for a range of pragmatic effects is 'transfer'. Let's start with a few examples.

(10) The ham sandwich asked for the check ⇒ The customer that ordered a ham sandwich asked for the check
(11) There was a stone lion in the court yard ⇒ There was a stone statue of a lion in the courtyard

What these examples illustrate is sometimes also referred to as 'deferred reference'. Take the first example. The idea is that the effect of 'the ham sandwich' referring to a customer and not to a slice of bread with ham on it is not one that comes for an inference on the basis of the literal meaning, because on the basis of the literal meanings of the component expressions the sentence does not have one: there is a category mistake, since the property of asking for a check can only be ascribed to a human subject. That fact triggers the switch from the-ham-sandwich-as-sandwich to the-ham-sandwich-as-customer and that switch occurs during the composition of the meaning of the sentences as a whole. So is not an 'after effect'.

A similar observation can be made with regard to the second sentence: since real lions are not made of stone, the reference of 'stone lion' is transferred to that of 'stature of a lion made of stone'. Again, transfer operates during semantic composition.

Of course, there are ambiguous cases:

(12) The ham sandwich stinks

Here the switch is optional: both a real ham sandwich as well as a customer who has ordered one may stink. So transfer, if it occurs, can operate at sentence-level.

26.4.5 Coercion

The third pragmatic mechanism that is often appealed to is 'coercion'. First some examples:

(13) He finished the chicken and started the desert ⇒ He finished cooking the chicken and started preparing the desert
(14) I can't stand Beethoven's Ninth ⇒ I can't stand listening to a performance of Beethoven's Ninth

Coercion is a process that fills in gaps. It differs from enrichment, which is a process that adds further detail to something that by itself is complete. Coercion, on the other hand, is a process that completes what is still underdetermined. If we learn that 'He finished the chicken' we immediately raise the question: 'He finished doing what to the chicken?' We need an answer to that question in other to be able to assign to the sentences as it is used definite truth conditions. In free enrichment this is not needed: we may raise the what (or why or who) question, but we do not have to. But in cases like this we do. We have to force a definite interpretation on the utterance.

One characteristic of coercion immediately follows: it is not top-down, coercion operates during semantic composition. What the examples also make clear is that coercion is not a determinate process: there are usually many different ways in which we can complete such sentences. Thus, coercion relies very heavily on world-knowledge. And that also indicates the potential problems: there are no clear constraints, and over-generation seems difficult to avoid.

26.5 Varieties of contextualism

After this very incomplete and quick survey of a number of key phenomena and three key mechanisms, let us return to the questions of the semantics – pragmatics relationship.

That a full account of meaning has to involve both semantics and pragmatics is clear. And that a systematic pragmatics can be developed in terms of distinct mechanisms seems also plausible. But then how do semantics and pragmatic relate?

26.5.1 Co-operative varieties

Most approaches to the semantics – pragmatics relationship are cooperative in spirit. They acknowledge the contribution of both and do not see a conflict between the two. Where they differ is at which point the pragmatic mechanisms that they use operate.

A clearly cooperative view is that of what we can call 'pragmatic modesty'. On this view pragmatic modulation of semantic content is optional and always operates after semantic composition. This is the view that underlies the use of free enrichment, including Gricean conversational implicatures, and some forms of transfer. On this view there is a strict separation of steps in the process of generating meaning: starting from syntax, we have first semantics generating literal meanings, and the pragmatics optionally modulating those meanings.

This view was illustrated in Figure 26.4 in the opening section. We repeat it here for the sake of convenience.

Then there is another cooperative view that assigns pragmatics a more independent role. We can call it 'pragmatic composition' and its core feature is that it assumes that pragmatic modulation of lexical meaning is necessary in some case, and thus operates during semantic composition. We can represent it graphically as in Figure 26.5. This is the view that underlies the application of some forms of transfer and of coercion.

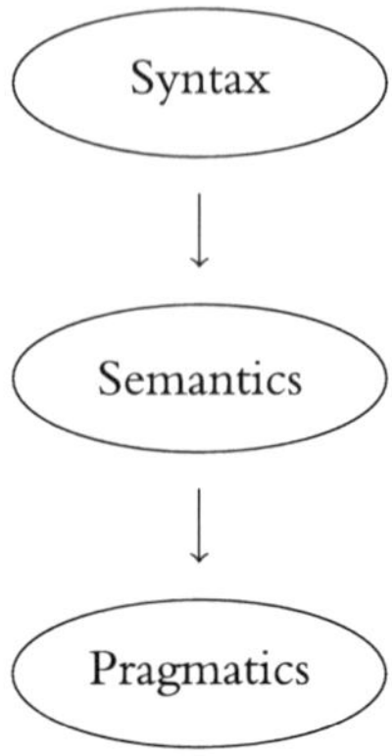

Figure 26.4: Pragmatic modesty

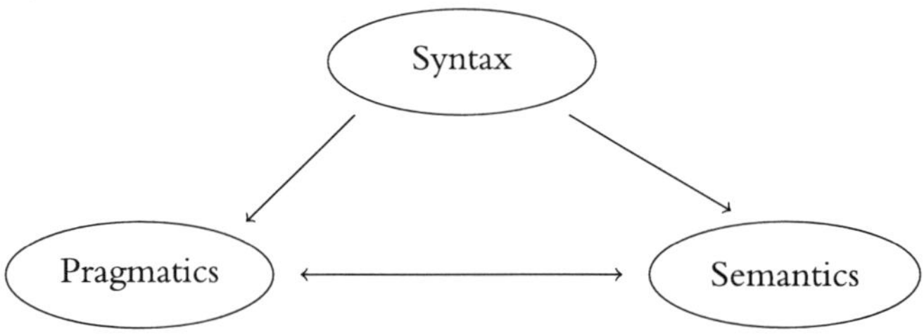

Figure 26.5: Pragmatic composition

26.5.2 A more radical one

But, as was also already noted in the opening section, there are more radical views of the nature of pragmatics, views in which semantics as a separate component is played down, or even disappears.

One example is the view that is often called 'radical contextualism'. Its core ideas are that there is no such thing as semantic content, and that there are no lexical meanings assigned to lexical items that a process of semantic composition operates on. Lexical items are associated with schematic content, and lexical meanings are construed from schematic content in a context of use.

One of the main arguments for this view resides in what is called 'polysemy', the fact that one lexical item may take on a range of different meanings, depending on the expressions it is combined with. A standard example is that of the verb 'to cut', that in different linguistic contexts signifies different things. Compare 'cut the cake', 'cut the grass', 'cut the crap', 'cut someone off', 'Cut!'; . . .

If one holds that all lexical items are polysemous in this sense, then pragmatics plays a role right from the start, and thus there is no such thing as literal meaning. Some of the usual semantic operations may still play a role, but what they operate on is pragmatic through-and-through.

26.5.3 Really radical contextualism

And then there is really radical contextualism, a.k.a. 'meaning eliminativism'. Here it is claimed that there is no semantic content, there are no lexical meanings, there is not even schematic content associated with lexical items. The only thing there is and thus the only things that needs to be accounted for is contextual meaning constructed on each separate occasion on the basis of past uses using various similarity measures.

This form of contextualism uses all available semantic and pragmatic mechanisms in mixed combinations, in order to assign a meaning to an expression used in a particular context. It is illustrated in Figure 26.6.

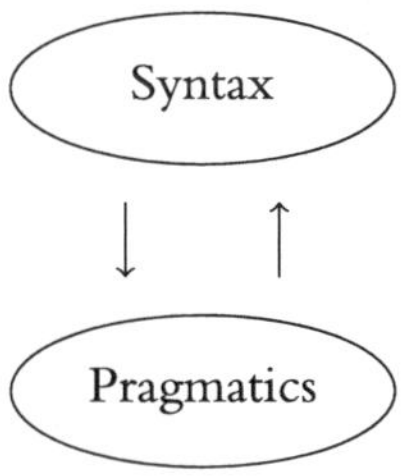

Figure 26.6: Radical contextualism

The motivation for meaning eliminativism comes from considerations about not just the wide range of things an expression can mean in different contexts, but more importantly about the lack of systematic relations between all the things it can mean. Here is an example to illustrate what is meant here. The example comes from Charles Travis, the most outspoken proponent of meaning eliminativism.[13]

Consider a window dresser, *A*, who needs some green leaves to decorate some objects in a shop window. It being winter, he cannot find any, so his friend *B*, always willing to help, takes some brown and red leaves, paints them green and hands them to *A*: 'Here are some green leaves'. *A* is satisfied: 'These are nice green leaves.'

Now *B* has another friend, *C*, who is a botanist who studies chlorophyl reactions and needs some green leaves to experiment with. *B* hands him another set of freshly painted green leaves: 'Here are some green leaves'. But *C* is not satisfied; 'These are not green leaves!'

What examples such as these show, according to Travis, is that the very same sentence can be true and false: A and C are both right. It all depends on context.

26.6 Open questions

What the overview in this chapter hopefully has shown is a number of things. First of all, there is more to meaning than logic provides. There is a range of phenomena that are systematic, meaning-related, and that call for an account that employs pragmatic mechanisms. Second, this does not do away with logic, on the contrary. There is definitely a subset of these phenomena that need literal meaning as part of their explanation. Gricean implicatures and other forms of enrichment seem to provide solid evidence for that claim.

But then what about more radical forms of contextualism? Note that also pragmatic composition needs literal meanings, though perhaps not across the board. In fact it is only with meaning eliminativism that we enter the territory of theoretical approaches that abolish literal meaning altogether, and with that logic.

But radical contextualism, and certainly meaning eliminativism, face a number of serious problems. First of all, here is the cognitive burden they seem to impose on each and every instance of use of language. These theories require potentially elaborate processing of each separate utterance. But is there always an equal amount of processing going on? And what is the nature of the processing? Is it reasoning? What kind? Gricean? Something else?

And note that if it is reasoning, logic is back . . . [14]

27

Excursus: implications and implicatures

27.1 The topic

In the chapter in the syllabus that concerns pragmatics, we have already given a sketch of some of the issues that form the background of the paper by H.P. Grice that is the topic of this excursus.

The core question that is at stake is this: What is the status of the truth-functional semantics that standard logic defines for the logical connectives when it comes to the meaning of their natural language counterparts? Does the truth table for $\wedge$ give an adequate account of the English expression 'and'? Is $\vee$ a good counterpart of German 'oder'? Does the meaning of the material implication $\rightarrow$ correspond to Mandarin 'jiu' conditionals? Is the semantics of the universal quantifiers $\forall x$ that of English 'all'? 'every'? 'each'?[1]

The questions raised above are intentionally formulated with reference to different languages. We know that there is not always a one-to-one relation between the ways in which different languages express, e.g., disjunction, or counterfactuals, or between their respective ranges of quantified expressions. That by itself is a reason to be wary of the idea that the logical expressions provide the meaning of the various natural language counterparts.

But even with respect to one single language there is ample reason to doubt that this is the case. The connectives and quantified expressions in a given natural language usually have meanings that are not fully covered by their counterparts in logic. Some examples have been discussed in chapter 26.

That is an observation. But what conclusion should be drawn from that? One is to discard the idea that logic can play a useful role in the semantics of natural language. The latter being too flexible, contextual, imprecise, or what have you, to be fitted into the mold of a systematic logical analysis. On this view, natural language is simply not amenable to a systematic treatment along those lines. This has been the approach of many in the so-called 'ordinary language school' of analytic philosophy.

But others have taken a different stance. They do not dispute the facts, i.e., they do not try to reason away the differences between the meanings of natural language expressions and their logical counterparts, but they maintain that such differences can be accounted for in a systematic manner. They assume that the logical, truth-functional meaning is a core meaning of these expressions from which other meaning aspects can be derived by means of a small set of intuitive principles that govern the use of these expressions in communicative situations. This approach, which was grounded by H.P. Grice in his work on 'the logic of conversation', thus builds a pragmatic component on top of a truth-conditional semantic component to provide an account of the full range of meanings aspects of natural language expressions. The meanings of the corresponding logical expressions are the basis, the pragmatic principles use them to account for the rest.

This view on how to account for the meaning of natural language has been, and still is, very influential. It is the dominant paradigm in linguistics and has also inspired a lot of research in cognitive science and other disciplines. For multiple reasons, it is an attractive view.

First of all, it is a systematic theory, and one that lends itself to formalisation. That is attractive from a philosophical point of view, since it provides a counterpoint to the approach that holds the intricacies of natural language to be beyond the grasp of systematic theorising. And it greatly enhances the empirical coverage of formal approaches to natural language meaning.

Secondly, from a logical point of view, it gives logic its due: when applied in natural language semantics it is the task of logic to provide an account of the referential, truth conditional aspects of meaning. If it does that adequately, it can then also provide the basis for a further pragmatic analysis of other meaning aspects. Thus the place of logical analysis on this view is clear.

Despite its widespread adoption and successful application the Gricean view has also met with criticism. For one thing, it is built on the idea of communicative exchanges as being essentially cooperative in nature. But that does not seem to fit naturally other goals that such exchanges may have, such as deceit, play, irony and sarcasm, and so on.

Also, the cognitive plausibility of the reasoning process that is an integral element of the Gricean picture seems questionable, at least partly. Of course, this is a criticism only if one takes the Gricean model to be an empirical theory. That may apply to some of the applications made of it in empirical linguistics, but it does not do justice to Grice's original intention, which was to make a philosophical point.

27.2 The author

H.P. Grice (1913 – 1988) was an English philosopher, born in Birmingham, who received his training at Oxford University. He taught at Oxford until 1969, when he moved to the US to take up a position at the University of California at Berkeley. He remained active at Berkeley throughout his years there until his death.

Grice started out in philosophy at more or less the same time and in the same intellectual environment as Strawson. Six years the latter's senior, he was his supervisor for a while, but very soon they became colleagues and they also co-authored an influential paper.[2] Like for Strawson, J.L. Austin was a major reference point for Grice in developing his own ideas. One of his early papers, on perception, he argues against Austin, and also elements in his work on meaning can be seen as implicit reactions to positions that Austin defended.

Grice did not publish very much, but has left a substantial oeuvre. He mainly worked on topics in philosophy of language, philosophy of mind and epistemology. The range of topics is quite diverse, — Grice wrote on perception, ethics, meaning, philosophical psychology, and philosophical methodology —, and people have struggled to find a common thread that ties them together.[3] Grice's work on meaning is undoubtedly the most influential. He has proposed and worked out in some detail a view on meaning that takes the intentions of the speaker as basic.[4] These ideas have been taken up mainly by philosophers and have not been very influential outside that circle.

But his ideas about conventional and conversational implicature, the role of the Cooperation Principle and the conversational maxims that can be derived from it, have been tremendously influential, not only in philosophy, but also in linguistics, in cognitive science, and in various other disciplines that study language and communication.

Grice's ideas on these issues have defined an entire sub-discipline: Gricean pragmatics was for a long time the 'go-to' theoretical framework for semanticists who were grasping the limitations of referential theories of meaning. And despite critical analyses of some of its assumptions, and the rise of alternative approaches, Gricean pragmatics remains the most widely used theoretical framework in linguistic pragmatics.

27.3 The text

The text, 'Logic and Conversation' (Grice, 1975), comes from the William James Lectures that Grice gave at Harvard in 1967. It starts with a short stage setting. First, Grice notes that many have argued that there are discrepancies between the meanings of natural language expressions and their formal logical counterparts. Then Grice pits the 'formalists', who hold that logic has the final say, against the 'informalists', who maintain the autonomy of natural language, also with respect to inference. Grice then states he wants to remain neutral on the general issues, but wants to show that there are in fact no discrepancies as summed by both formalists and informalists.

Then Grice introduces the fundamental distinction between what is said and what is implied, i.e., between 'implication' and 'implicature'. The former is related to conventional meaning. The latter comes in two varieties: conventional implicatures, which are not part of what is said but which do arise in virtue of conventional meaning. And conversational implicatures, which depend on general features of discourse.

Grice introduces the Cooperative Principle as the overarching principle: it states that one should makes one's contribution to a conversation as is required at a certain stage of the conversation by its accepted purpose. This gives rise to four categories of conversational maxims: Quantity, Quality, Relation, and Manner.

Quantity deals with informativeness; Quality with truthfulness; Relation with relevance; and Manner with form. Each gives rise to a number of maxims and sub-maxims that spell out what is required for a contribution to a conversation to be in accordance with the Cooperative Principle

Grice then continues with a discussion of the nature of these maxims, specifically of what is the source of their normativity. He acknowledges that in most situations people would act in accordance with the maxims because they are raised that way, but that does not explain their normative impact.

Rather the normativity, Grice suggests, needs to be located in the fact that discourse is a rational, goal-directed joint undertaking. This view underlies the effects that occur when a participant in a discourse does not fulfil a maxim.

Grice distinguishes four different cases of nonfulfillment: violating: e.g., lying, or withholding information; opting out: explicitly stating that one does not (cannot) fulfil one or more maxims; clashing: maxims making irreconcilable demands; flouting: blatantly not fulfilling a maxim. The case of flouting a maxim is an interesting one because it gives rise to conversational implicatures: flouting is the exploitation of one or more maxims to produce an implicature.

Thus a conversational implicature can be characterised as follows: A implicates q by saying p iff (i) A is presumed to obey the Cooperative Principle; and (ii) p by itself would constitute a flouting of a maxim, but acceptance of q resolves that, i.e., makes p in accordance with the maxim in question. Such conversational implicatures arise through a reasoning process of other participants in the discourse along these lines.

Grice then goes on to list a number of examples of conversational implicatures, grouping them in accordance with how they arise in relation to the maxims.

A final distinction that Grice introduces is that between particularised conversational and generalised conversational implicatures. The former arise on a particular occasion and depend on specific features of the context. The latter are (relatively) independent and arise under (almost) all circumstances.

Grice concludes with noticing three features of conversational implicatures: they are cancellable; non-detachable; not part of meaning; not part of what is said; and they can be of a disjunctive nature (since it may not be clear which maxim is involved).

27.4 Study and discussion questions

Study questions

- How does Grice the positions of the formalists and the informalists?
- Are indexicals (such as personal pronouns and verb tenses) part of what is said or part of what is implied?
- Give your own example of a conventional implicature.
- Try to construct your own examples of the various kinds of implicatures that Grice discusses on pp. 51–55.
- What is cancellability of an implicature? And detachability?

Discussion questions

- How does Grice's position relate to that of formalists and informalists?
- Is the distinction between particularised and general conversational implicatures an absolute one?
- Can all forms of non-cooperative discourse be explained in terms of the violation of maxims?

27.5 Further reading

Grice's work on implicatures has been very influential, both in philosophy of language as well as in natural language semantics and pragmatics. see Chapman (2013) for an overview. See also the work of Sperber and Wilson on relevance theory (Sperber & Wilson, 1995, 2002), which has developed Grice's ideas systematically and which has been influential also on work in psychology and discourse studies.

A

Set-theoretic Essentials

What follows lists a few core concepts of set theory that are used in this book.

A.1 Sets

A *set* is a collection of objects. The objects making up a set are called the *elements* of the set.

Here are some examples of sets:

- the set of Chinese provinces
- the set of natural numbers
- the set consisting of Peter, Paul, and Mary
- the set consisting of the number 12, the current president of the Royal Dutch Academy of Sciences, the *SS Titanic*, and the loaf of bread John bought on December 12, 2018
- ...

Some sets 'make sense', i.e., they consist of objects that share a significant property. Others don't: they are just arbitrary collections of objects that do not have anything in common.

Some sets are finite, others have an infinite number of elements.

The notation for sets uses curly brackets $\{,\}$. Thus : $\{d_1, \ldots, d_n\}$ is the set consisting of the elements $d_1, \ldots d_n$, and $\{x \mid \phi(x)\}$ is the set consisting of all x that satisfy the condition ϕ

This illustrates two main ways in which sets can be defined:

- *by enumeration*, i.e., by listing all of its elements; for example, the set $\{$Peter, Paul, Mary$\}$
- *by condition*: ie., by specification of a necessary and sufficient condition of set membership; for example, the set $\{n \in \mathbb{N} \mid n \text{ is odd}\}$

Typically, sets that are defined by a condition make sense, if the condition makes sense, of course.

$A, B, \ldots, A_1, A_2, \ldots$ are used as variables for sets; $x, y, \ldots, x_1, x_2, \ldots$ are used as variables for set elements.

Some additional notation:

- $x \in A$, $x \notin A$: x is an element of A, x is not an element of A

A special set is the empty set, i.e., the set without elements, for which $\emptyset$ is used.

A basic relation between sets is that of one set being part of another. This is called the 'subset'-relation, and it is defined as follows:

- $A \subseteq B$, A is a subset of B, iff for all x: if $x \in A$, then $x \in B$

And the 'proper subset' relation is defined as follows:

- $A \subset B$, A is a proper subset of B, iff for all x: if $x \in A$ then $x \in B$ and there is at least one x such that $x \in B$ and $x \notin A$

An important property of sets is expressed by the *Extensionality Principle*: a set is completely defined by its elements. Immediate consequences of the extensional nature of sets are:

- if $A \subseteq B$ and $B \subseteq A$, then $A = B$
- $\emptyset$ is a unique set
- $\emptyset \subseteq A$, for any set A.

A.2 Operations on sets

The following are standard operations on sets:

- Union: $A \cup B = \{x \mid x \in A \text{ or } x \in B\}$
- Intersection: $A \cap B = \{x \mid x \in A \text{ and } x \in B\}$
- Difference: $A - B = \{x \mid x \in A \text{ and } x \notin B\}$
- Powerset: $\mathcal{P}(A) = \{B \mid B \subseteq A\}$

Some simple facts:

- If $a \in A$ and $A \subseteq B$, then $a \in B$
- If $A \subseteq B$ and $B \subseteq C$, then $A \subseteq C$
- $a \in A$ iff $\{a\} \subseteq A$
- $A \cap B \subseteq A, \subseteq B$
- $A, B \subseteq A \cup B$
- $\emptyset, A \in \mathcal{P}(A)$

A.3 Ordered n-tuples

A two-element set $\{x, y\}$ is the same set as $\{y, x\}$: only the elements define the set, order plays no role.

An ordered pair $\langle a, b\rangle$ is a two-element construct in which order *does* matter: $\langle a, b\rangle \neq \langle b, a\rangle$ (unless $a = b$).

Definition 48 (Cartesian product)
$A \times B = \{\langle a, b \rangle \mid a \in A \text{ and } b \in B\}$

This can be generalised:

Definition 49 (n-fold Cartesian product)
$A_1 \times \cdots \times A_n = \{\langle a_1, \ldots, a_n \rangle \mid a_i \in A_i\}$

The n-fold Cartesian product of a set A is also written as A^n.

Note that the introduction of ordered n-tuples does not extend the set-theoretic universe. We can define n-tuples in terms of sets. For example, we can regard $\{a, \{a, b\}\}$ as the counterpart of $\langle a, b \rangle$, since $\{a, \{a, b\}\} \neq \{b, \{a, b\}\}$.

A.4 Relations, functions

Definition 50 (n-place relation)
An n-place relation R on a set A is a subset of A^n

Definition 51 (Function)
A function f from A to B is a subset F of $A \times B$ such that: if $\langle x, y \rangle \in F$ and $\langle x, z \rangle \in F$, then $y = z$

The generalisation to functions with more than one argument is straightforward:

Definition 52 (n-place function)
An n-place function from $A_1 \times \cdots \times A_n$ to B is a subset F of $A_1 \times \ldots A_n \times B$ such that: if $\langle x_1 \ldots x_n, y \rangle \in F$ and $\langle x_1 \ldots x_n, z \rangle \in F$, then $y = z$

Notes

Notes to chapter 1

1. Aristotle (384 – 322 BCE) was the first to study reasoning patterns of a certain kind systematically, by categorising them and providing means to distinguish valid from invalid patterns.

2. Mozi (470 – c. 391 BCE) founded the Mohist school, the works of which covered a wide range of areas, from mechanics to fortification, from ethics to optics, and which also included a systematic treatment of reasoning patterns.

3. Gottlob Frege (1848 – 1925) and Bertrand Russell (1872 – 1970) are generally considered as founders of modern logic. For more see chapter 2.

Notes to chapter 2

1. An explicit example is provided by Spinoza's *Ethics*, which bears the subtitle 'more geometrico demonstrata' ('demonstrated in the way of geometry'). Another example is Leibniz and his work on a 'characteristica universalis', a universal language for science.

2. Of course, Frege's work did not come out of the blue. As was already mentioned, Bolzano and Peirce were working on these problems at more or less the same time and came up with comparable results. And the earlier work of De Morgan and Boole was also important. The problem of relational judgments was, of course, well-known, and had occupied the minds of people such as Leibniz in the seventeenth century, and before him that of many of the Scholastic logicians. That they had not solved the problem may explain why Kant, in the preface to the the second edition of his *Critique of Pure Reason* could claim that 'logic since Aristotle has not been forced to take a step back, but also has not been able to take a step forward, and thus appears to be closed and completed.'

3. See e.g., Dummett (1973b, chapter 19) for an argument along these lines.

4. A similar misrepresentation has for a long time dominated the appreciation of Wittgenstein's work. He, too, was 'annexed' by the analytic tradition, and the role played by the continental tradition and his socio-cultural environment only gradually became clear.

5. See Sluga (1975, 1980).

6. See Mill's form of empiricism, in which even logical and mathematical laws are considered to be empirical generalisations, based on observable reality. Mill's ideas form an important impetus for Frege's radically different analysis of the concept of number in the *Grundlagen* (Frege, 1884). The radical scientific naturalistic empiricism in German philosophy was the result of a number of developments: the rise of the empirical sciences that produced results that appeared not to be in accordance with the idealism of Schelling, Fichte and Hegel, as it developed after Kant; the transition from

an agricultural to a pre-industrial society with the corresponding shift from speculative to practical thinking; the political criticism of traditional philosophy developed by Feuerbach, Marx and Engels.

7. Frege agrees with Kant's view of geometry as synthetic a priori.

8. It was continued by Russell, who formulated his theory of types to block the paradox. Based on that he continued the programme of logicism together with Whitehead, which resulted in their *Principia Mathematica*, which appeared in 1912 – 1913 (Russell & Whitehead, 1910, 1912, 1913). The demise of logicism came with Gödel's second incompleteness theorem (Gödel, 1931).

9. For more extensive discussion, see Stokhof (2007).

10. The subtitle raises an interesting question: 'As a field for scientific method in philosophy': so despite his misgivings about the results that philosophy has been able to come up with so far in history, for Russell there *is* a way in which philosophy can produce knowledge: by employing a scientific method. Is that the method of science? Then wouldn't philosophy be distinct only in topic, not in method? Or is it a method that is specific for philosophy, but one that can be regarded as scientific (unlike the methods of traditional philosophy)?

Notes to chapter 3

1. Also called 'atomic sentences', 'atomic propositions', 'elementary sentences', or 'elementary propositions'.

2. An alternative form for this type of definition would run as follows:
The formulas of L, given V_L, is the smallest set of expressions:

1. All proposition letters in V_L are formulas of L
2. If ϕ is a formula of L, then so is $\neg\phi$
3. If ϕ and ψ are formulas of L, then so are $(\phi \wedge \psi)$, $(\phi \vee \psi)$, $(\phi \rightarrow \psi)$, and $(\phi \leftrightarrow \psi)$

So the effect of clause (4) is now taken care of by stating that the set of formulas of L is the smallest set that satisfies clauses (1)–(3).

3. The reason is that where natural languages are used for communicative purposes, and thus can count on the context of use to solve ambiguities, sort out vagueness, and so on, this is different for formal languages. These do not serve a communicative purpose: they are not used, but applied. We will come back to the role of communicative use in chapter 26.

4. The qualification 'material' in 'material implication' is used to distinguish it from logical implication.

5. Another term often used is 'recursive'. A definition of objects that have some property P is recursive if it contains one or more clauses that define P-objects in terms of other, less complex P-objects. Such clauses are called 'recursive clauses'.

Notes to chapter 4

1. The terms, though not these exact definitions, go back to McTaggart's argumentation on the unreality of time; see McTaggart (1908).

2. See Kuhn & Portner (2002) for an overview. We will discuss some elements of tense logic in chapter 22.

NOTES TO CHAPTER 5

1. That does not mean that logic cannot be applied in the study of other types of sentences such as interrogatives and imperatives. See, e.g, Groenendijk & Stokhof (2011 (1997) for the first, and Portner (2016) for the second.

NOTES TO CHAPTER 6

1. He is also a well-known advocate of the 'open access' movement, which aims to make all results of publicly funded scientific research accessible to everyone, without charge or embargo.

NOTES TO CHAPTER 7

1. There are other considerations as well, but they concern not the expressive power of the language, but the definition of the concept of validity; see below, section 7.6 for more on this issue.

2. To increase readability we write $\phi \wedge \psi \wedge \chi$ instead of $\phi \wedge (\psi \wedge \chi$ (or $(\phi \wedge \psi) \wedge \chi$. This is justified by the associativity of $\wedge$.

3. Named after Henry Maurice Sheffer, who used it in 1913 to provide an axiomatisation of Boolean algebras. The current use if due to Jean Nicod.

NOTES TO CHAPTER 8

1. This view, a.k.a., 'Logic in Action', informs a wide variety of dynamic approaches to the concept of validity. See van Benthem et al. (2016) and https://logicinaction.org for more details.

2. For an accessible overview of Harman's ideas on a wide variety of philosophical questions, see the contributions on https://philosophy.princeton.edu/about/great-and-good/gilbert-harman.

3. Assuming for the moment that my beliefs are 'closed under logical consequence', i.e., that if some ϕ follows logically from my set of beliefs Γ, then ϕ is contained in Γ.

4. That Harman conceives of logic as classical logic is important: there are a number of logical approaches to belief revision, but none of them are classical. see Hansson (2022) for an overview.

5. The issue of the normativity of logic and the relation between logic and the psychology of reasoning, i.e., accounts of how people actually reason, will be taken up in more detail in chapter 20.

6. Note that there seems to be a threat of circularity here: in order to classify something as a mistake one already needs a normative criterion, so how can one base a normative theory on a description and analysis of mistakes?

7. Note that this assumes that triviality is a property of beliefs that is independent of whether one entertains that belief or not. This seems dubious. First, probably anyone recalls a certain number of 'trivia' that are 'useless', yet are (often explicitly held) beliefs. Otherwise, games such as Trivial Pursuit, or pub quizzes, would not exist. Second, triviality seems to be highly context- and individual-dependent: ask any parent and their children. Harman may have a point when it comes to logically trivial beliefs, but then again, logic was not supposed to have anything to do with it.

8. More on this in chapter 14, where we see how this situation is dealt with in a semantic theory of truth.

NOTES TO CHAPTER 9

1. The tableaux method was developed by Evert Beth, see Beth (1955); it is widely used, in particular in modal logic and automated proof systems; see D'Agostino et al. (1999) for an overview.

2. Note that since ϕ and ψ are meta-variables, this formulation of $I_\wedge$ is the same as:

$$\begin{array}{lll} 1. & & \\ \vdots & & \\ m_1. & \psi & \\ \vdots & & \\ m_2. & \phi & \\ \vdots & & \\ n. & \phi \wedge \psi & I_\wedge, m_1, m_2 \end{array}$$

or

$$\begin{array}{lll} 1. & & \\ \vdots & & \\ m_1. & \psi & \\ \vdots & & \\ m_2. & \phi & \\ \vdots & & \\ n. & \psi \wedge \phi & I_\wedge, m_1, m_2 \end{array}$$

3. As is also illustrated by the existence of other axiomatisations.

4. Such as Dag Prawitz, and Michael Dummett. See chapter 10 for more details.

NOTES TO CHAPTER 10

1. Wittgenstein's notation of his method is different from the truth-table notation that we are using nowadays, which goes back to independent work by Emil Post in the early 1920s. The basic ideas, by the way, can already be found in work of Charles Sanders Peirce from 1893, 1902 and 1909 (see Anellis (2012)). To what extent Wittgenstein, and Post were acquainted with each other's works is unclear.

2. On this point Gentzen was in line with Wittgenstein's famous dictum in *Tractatus Logico-Philosophicus* 4.0312, in which it is stated that 'logical constants do not represent'.

3. Other terms used for that relation are 'denotation' and 'signification'.

4. Augustine of Hippo (354 – 430) was a theologian and philosopher who converted to Christianity and become one of the most important thinkers in the Christian tradition. His *Confessions* is an autobiographical work that Wittgenstein greatly admired.

5. It should be noted that interesting attempts have been made to turn Wittgenstein's ideas into a more theoretical format, but that is not the same as ascribing a theory to him. A notable example is the work of Paul Horwich (Horwich, 1998, 2005). In a similar fashion, Brandom's inferential semantics (Brandom, 1994) should be seen as an approach inspired by Wittgenstein (and others), not as a reconstruction of his ideas.

6. The framework is referred to elsewhere in the paper as well in a way that assumes familiarity with it; it suffices to know that in a game-theoretic semantics each logical constant is associated with moves that the two players can make: the proponent who tries to show that a particular proposition is true, and the opponent who is trying to show that it is not. Each can do different things with, e.g., a conjunction: the proponent needs to show that both conjuncts are true, whereas the opponent aims to show that at least one of them is not. see for more details Krabbe (1985); Hintikka (2000).

NOTES TO CHAPTER 11

1. Meta-properties are properties of a logical system such as decidability, completeness, compactness. We will take a first look at this in chapter 21.

2. In the work of Frege, Peirce, Russell and a number of other authors; their systems diverge on some points (and not all of them are strictly first-order), but in spirit predicate logic was what these pioneers were concerned with.

3. See the discussion in chapter 1.

4. We cannot resist the temptation to refer to this passage in Lewis Carroll's *Alice in Wonderland* :

> "I see nobody on the road," said Alice.
> "I only wish *I* had such eyes," the king remarked in a fretful tone. "To be able to see Nobody! And at that distance too! Why, it's as much as I can do to see real people, by this light!"

5. For more on generics, see e.g., Carlson (2011).

NOTES TO CHAPTER 12

1. 'Vulcan' was the name given by Le Verrier in the 19th century to a planet that he postulated between Mercury and the sun in order to explain certain peculiarities in Mercury's orbit. There is no such object. And the observed peculiarities are adequately explained by relativity theory.

2. The argument is used by Plato in the *Timaeus*, hence it goes by the name 'Plato's Beard'.

3. This position was explicitly adopted and defended in the late nineteenth century by Alexius Meinong, an Austrian philosopher. His ideas were dismissed by Russell, and, without mentioning him by name, also by Quine ('Wyman' acts as a substitute for Meinong.) The logical theories that Russell and Quine used were extensional and did not leave room for possible entities. This changed with the development of suitable semantics for quantified modal logicin the 1960s. Quine objected to their use, mainly for the kind of reasons he also employs in this paper.

NOTES TO CHAPTER 13

1. Also called 'denotational semantics'.

2. Actually, in the standard way the semantics is specified the latter is obscured. Syntactically, the connectives are introduced syncategorematically, i.e., they are not expressions belonging to an independently specified category, but are introduced by syntactic rules. At the semantic level this is mirrored in the fact that connectives are interpreted, not as expressions by themselves, but through semantic rules that correspond with the

syntax. But that is a matter of presentation, as is shown by the discussion on functional completeness, where connectives are associated with semantic objects as their reference, viz., truth functions.

3. This is the principle of compositionality at work.

4. See chapter 14 for more on Tarski's analysis of the semantic conception of truth (Tarski, 1944), in which the notion of satisfaction also occurs prominently.

5. On pain of paradox, see appendix A.

6. When the context makes clear which model M is referred to, we may omit the subscript M.

7. Another term for an onto function is 'surjective function'.

8. A more general definition is possible, and will be introduced later, in chapter 15, but for now we can make do with this one.

9. From the point of view of natural language it is definitely not a realistic assumption to make, but that does not really constitute an argument: there is no reason why an instrument, in this case a logical language, should resemble what it is applied to, in this case a natural language.

10. Historically, the substitutional interpretation finds its roots in work of Peter Geach, Henry Leonard, and most prominently, Ruth Barcan Marcus, see Dunn & Belnap (1968). It has been discussed extensively in the literature, both from a philosophical as well as a logical perspective. Prominent early critics are Leslie Tharp and John Wallace, see Tharp (1971); Wallace (1971), and Peter van Inwagen, van Inwagen (1981). Saul Kripke has argued that their objections rest on a mistake, see Kripke (1976), but his analysis has been questioned Hugly & Sayward (2002).

Notes to chapter 14

1. See Russell (1918–19). A modern version can be found in Mulligan et al. (1985).. Truth maker semantics is also being applied in the semantics of natural language, e.g., in the analysis of counterfactuals. See Fine (2017) for details.

2. It also goes by the names of 'redundancy view', 'disquotational view', 'minimalist view'. As usual, there are subtle variations on the common theme. See Armour-Garb et al. (2023) for an overview..

3. For a detailed and comprehensive overview of various theories of truth, see Künne (2003).

4. It is worth emphasising that 'object language' and 'meta language' do not refer to different kinds of languages, but signal the ways in which a language is used. I.e., these qualifications indicate functional characteristics.

Notes to chapter 15

1. See Church (1936a,b). At more or less the same time Alan Turing proved a similar result, see Turing (1936). So the theorem is also known as the 'Church-TuringTheorem'.

Notes to chapter 16

1. Recall the following equivalences from the previous chapter:
   - $\forall x\phi \Leftrightarrow \forall y[y/x]\phi$, provided y free for x in ϕ
   - $\exists x\phi \Leftrightarrow \exists y[y/x]\phi$, provided y free for x in ϕ

One could arrange the semantics of the language of predicate logic in such a way that distinct variables do refer to different objects, as, for example, Wittgenstein does in the *Tractatus Logico-Philosophicus*, but that is really not very convenient.

2. Alternatively, instead of fixing the interpretation of $=$ through a restriction on the interpretation functions in suitable models, we could also take care of things in the truth definition, i.e., in the definition of $V_{M,g}(\phi)$, by adding a clause that defines the interpretation of atomic formulas of the form $s = t$ directly:

$$V_{M,g}(s = t) = 1 \text{ iff } V_{M,g}(s) = V_{M,g}(t)$$

Examples:

$$V_{M,g}(a = b) = 1 \text{ iff } V_{M,g}(a) = V_{M,g}(b) \text{ iff } I_M(a) = I_m(b)$$

$$V_{M,g}(a = x) = 1 \text{ iff } V_{M,g}(a) = V_{M,g}(x) \text{ iff } I_M(a) = g(x)$$

3. Note that we read 'P' here as a variable, and one that is implicitly quantified over universally. In first-order predicate logic we do not have variables that range over properties and we only have quantification over individuals, so we actually cannot express this precisely. For that we need to be able to also quantify over properties and relations. That is done in second-order logic. We add variables $X, Y, \ldots$ that range over properties and then we can express Leibniz's law as $\forall X \forall x \forall y(x = y \rightarrow (Xx \rightarrow Xy))$.

NOTES TO CHAPTER 17

1. This translation, though widely used, has not gone unchallenged, but that need not concern us here.

2. See further chapter 25.

3. The problem of non-referring names has already come up in our discussion of Quine's paper 'On What There Is'.

4. The two-fold distinction here is a simplification, in the literature many different forms of each of the two main trends can be found. However, for present purposes we can restrict ourselves to these two.

5. Do note that in higher-order logic quantified phrases can be treated as denoting expressions. So the problem is specific for the case of first-order logic.

6. For reasons of simplicity we stick to the case of 1-place predicates.

7. Recall Frege's considerations about the relationship between natural and formal languages in the preface of *Begriffsschrift*.

8. This is an unfortunate but common conception of what the basic structure of natural language is. It is based on a particular, relatively small set of languages that do indeed exhibit such a structure: Greek, Latin, English and sundry Indo-European languages. To take that set as representative for all the world's language is unjustified, but nevertheless, certainly among philosophers, quite common.

9. Meinong's ideas are presented in Quine's paper 'On What There Is' by the imaginary opponent 'Wyman'.

10. For those who are interested, recommended reading is Brogaard (2006) (a critical evaluation that rejects the argument as incoherent) and Rosenkrantz (2017) (a reconstruction that argues that within the context of an ideal language the argument makes sense).

NOTES TO CHAPTER 18

1. The term 'relation' is used because, due to its symmetry, an equivalence relation does not induce an order on the elements in a strict sense. An equivalence relation is thus more a 'grouping together' than an ordering of the elements of a set.

NOTES TO CHAPTER 19

1. We discussed the concept of a conservative extension earlier on, on page 32. The matter will also be taken up in the next chapter 20.

NOTES TO CHAPTER 20

1. In philosophy there have been a few dissidents as well, at an early stage. One of them is the Norwegian logician and philosopher Arne Naess, who already in the late fifties and early sixties advocated a thoroughly empirical take on logic and semantics.

2. We leave it to the reader to determine what Wason considered to be the right answer.

3. Other well-known experiments concern argument that involves the so-called 'strengthening of the antecedent', ie., $(\phi \rightarrow \psi) \rightarrow ((\phi \wedge \xi) \rightarrow \psi))$, which is classically valid, but is another inference pattern that many subjects do not 'get right'. Also relevant are studies that investigate the reasoning practices of people with different social and cultural backgrounds.

4. See Cosmides & Toolby (1992).

5. See Stenning & van Lambalgen (2008).

6. The situation in logic is thus not unlike that of modern mathematics, although there pluralism started earlier than in logic.

7. See Johnson-Laird (1983).

8. Compare the case of adding, e.g., conjunction $\wedge$ to a propositional language that contains negation $\neg$ and implication $\rightarrow$. That does not allow derivations that were not allowed before, so it is a conservative extension of the language.

9. The terms is used in a similar manner by John Rawls, as was noted in the discussion of Harman's principles of revision in chapter 8.

NOTES TO CHAPTER 21

1. What follows is concise, and at some points sketchy. Also, we will only deal with the relatively simple case of soundness and completeness of proposition logic and leave out the more complicated case of predicate logic.More information and further details can be obtained from any of the many introductions to mathematical logic, such as Enderton (2001), Mendelson (2015) or Westerståhl (2023).

NOTES TO CHAPTER 22

1. 'Two is company, three is a crowd.' Notice also that we speak of 'more values', not 'more truth values': in almost all cases the additional values are not considered to be truth values.

2. A similar story can be told about the uniqueness claim that is connected with descriptions.

3. It is also referred to as 'the paradox of the heap' ('Sorites' in classical Greek means 'heap'). This refers to the original formulation, which does not involve bald people but heaps of sand:

- A million grains of sand is a heap
- A heap from which one grain is removed is still a heap
- So, one grain of sand makes a heap

4. Note that the format of truth tables used here deviates from that used in the chapter on proposition logic. The current format is more economical when dealing with more than two values, and we assume that its use is straightforward.

5. Kleene, an American mathematician and logician, published his system in Kleene (1950). For an extensive analysis of this system , including its application in various fields, see Fitting (1991).

6. See Bochvar (1938 (1981); Kleene (1950).

7. See Bergmann (2008) for an overview.

8. See Malinowski (2009) for an overview.

Notes to chapter 23

1. Since the second and the third premise are structurally the same, we can focus on either one of them.

2. And, by parity of reasoning, the third one; see above.

3. These epistemological concerns play a key role in G.E.M. Anscombe's famous treatment of Aristotle's sea-battle argument in Anscombe (1956).

4. In the definition we also use the inverse $>$, 'later than'. No confusion should arise from this.

5. In order to keep things readable we do not adorn the nodes also with '$Pp, \ldots$', like we did above. We trust the above has made clear how to add that information.

6. See MacFarlane (2003) for a fairly recent overview.

7. Some details have been already given in the chapter on the syntax of predicate logical languages.

8. See also the Excursus in chapter 11.

9. And at this point we should note that Aristotle's work still continues to play an important role in attempts to develop a so-called 'natural logic', a logical system that stays as close as possible to the grammatical form of natural language sentences. This revival was instigated by the work of Fred Sommers in the 1980s, and is currently carried forward by, e.g., Neil Tennant, Larry Moss, Christopher Manning.

10. The original Greek title is *Peri Hermeneias*, but the work is best known under the title of the Latin translation.

11. Note that it is assumed that $T\neg p$ and $\neg Tp$ are equivalent.

Notes to chapter 24

1. We ignore the case of formulas with free variables, as this does not really impact the issue here.

2. As will become clear in what follows, these three kinds of considerations are not completely independent.

3. Early attempts to deal with the paradoxes of material implication gave rise to so-called 'relevance logics': see the references in chapter 6. In the semantics of natural

language, where conditionals are, of course, an important construction, there is a long tradition of analysing them using various kinds of intensional logics: see Lewis (1969); Veltman (1976); Kratzer (1979) for some influential early approaches.

4. If one wants to maintain extensionality such a change cannot be brought about without sacrificing completeness: Constable & Bickford (2014). In view of the non-validity of the principle of excluded middle, $\phi \vee \neg\phi$, giving up excluded middle would appear another option, but neither using a finite many-valued logic (see Gödel), nor an infinitely-valued logic (cf. Heyting) will do the trick.

5. See Kripke (1963). Kripke-semantics was not the first semantics for intuitionistic logic, that is the algebraic semantics that was developed by Brouwer's student Arend Heyting in 1930, see Heyting (1930).

6. Traditionally ascribed to Diodorus Cronus, a Greek philosopher of the late third, early second century BC.

7. The example is due to Barbara Partee.

8. The example comes from Quine, see Quine (1943).

9. Interestingly, what the number of planets is depends, not only on actual astronomical facts but also on what currently counts as the definition of 'planet': in 2006 the International Astronomic Union adopted a new definition that excludes Pluto, discovered as the ninth planet in 1930. So in fact now the number of planets is eight. But, as we know, for an argument to be valid, the actual truth or falsity of premises and conclusion is irrelevant.

10. A similar sentiment is expressed by Georg Steiner in his book on translation, *After Babel* (Steiner, 1975):

> Hypotheticals, 'imaginaries', conditionals, the syntax of counter-factuality and contingency may well be the generative centres of human speech.
>
> [*p. 219*]

11. Recall that we are for now only looking at things from the semantic perspective; the proof-theoretic approach will be briefly discussed in section 24.6.

12. Thus there are close connections between modal principles on the one hand and properties of relations on the other. This raises a number of questions. For example, not all properties of relations are definable in first order predicate logic, some can only be stated in higher-order logic: are there modal principles that correspond to such properties? And conversely, are all modal principles first-order expressible? The many, intricate connections between modal logics and predicate logics are the subject of what is called 'modal correspondence theory'. This was first explored in the 1970s by Sahlqvist and Van Benthem; see van Benthem (1984) for an overview. More generally, the theme of the expressive power of modal logics remains a widely researched topic.

13. See McNamara & Van De Putte (2021) for an overview.

14. See Hawke et al. (2020) for a recent overview.

15. See e.g., Payne (2015) for details.

16. The distinction between expressions of the form $\Box\forall x\phi$ and $\forall x\Box\phi$ (and $\Box\exists x\phi$ and $\exists x\Box\phi$) is traditionally described as a distinction between 'modality *de dicto*' and 'modality *de re*'. The idea behind this terminology is that the first kind of formula asserts the necessity (possibility) of the truth of a statement ('dictum') , whereas the second kind asserts the necessity (possibility) of objects ('res') having a certain property.

17. See Barcan Marcus (1946).
18. See Lewis (1973, p. 86).
19. We will encounter the question of realism again in the next chapter.

NOTES TO CHAPTER 25

1. See (Frege, 1892b, 1948).
2. Besides the already mentioned 'Über Sinn und Bedeutung' ('On Sense and Reference', (Frege, 1892b)) also 'Funktion und Begriff' ('Function and Concept', Frege (1891)), 'Über Begriff und Gegenstand' ('On Concept and Object', Frege (1892a)), 'Der Gedanke' ('The Thought', Frege (1918–1919a)), and 'Die Verneinung' ('Negation', Frege (1918–1919b)); English translations can be found in Frege (1980), Frege (1977) and Beaney (1997)
3. Other English terms are sometimes use to translate the German 'Bedeutung'. Thus we find, among others, 'meaning', 'nominatum', 'denotation'. The matter is subtle, but we stick here to what is the most commonly used terminology.
4. Which is why a referential semantics fits a realist view on mathematics, but not a constructivist one.
5. 'Über die wissenschaftlichen Berechtigung einen Begriffsschrifts', see Frege (1964, 1882).
6. Among others by Michael Dummett, who wrote very influential and insightful overviews of Frege's works, see Dummett (1973b, 1976, 1981, 1991a).
7. A prominent author who has defended this view is Hans Sluga, see Sluga (1975, 1982, 1980)
8. Relation semantics is also often referred to 'Kripke semantics', and relational models as 'Kripke models'. The use of the neutral term 'relational semantics' reflects the fact that other authors, among others, Stig Kanger and Jaakko Hintikka, developed similar ideas around the time Kripke formulated his.
9. The connection between the analyses of Marcus and those of Kripke has been subject of heated debate; see Smith (1995b,a); Burgess (1996) for positions and arguments.
10. The sense and reference of predicates is not discussed in 'On Sense and Reference' and we will therefore not go into Frege's views on that here; see the already mentioned Frege (1892a, 1891) for further details.
11. It should be noted that sense determining reference is a functional characteristic: Frege does not assume that in each situation sense determines an actual reference, there can be expressions with sense that lack reference. More on that below. For Frege's extensive analysis of the nature and status of mental associations, see Frege (1918–1919a).
12. What kind of realism of sense should be attributed to Frege is a matter of debate; see e.g., Burge (1992); Weiner (1995). For present purposes that need not concern us here.
13. In Frege (1918–1919a) another aspect of meaning that differs from sense is identified: the 'force' ('Kraft') with which an utterance is made. Thus 'Does water boil at 100 degrees Celsius?' and 'Water boils at 100 degrees Celsius' express the same thought, i.e., have the same sense, but differ in their communicative function.
14. Further qualifications of the positions in the sky and the times at which the object is visible need to be added of course.

15. Which is analogous to the extensionality principles we have encountered before, see section 24.1.

16. Note that this construes 'reference' in a purely factual manner. Of course, we can also ask questions about reference and truth within the context of fiction or myth. To be sure, those questions are answered using different criteria, but the fact remains that fictionality does not necessarily completely suspend notions of truth and reference. For more on this, see Woods & Alward (2004).

17. Which is why in the translation of a report of direct speech the reported speech is not translated.

18. Oddly, there is no explicit reference to Frege's analysis in 'On Sense and Reference'.

19. Quine made the point in a rhetorical manner by asking us how many possible fat men fit in the doorway of the room we are in; see Quine (1948).

20. This form of possible worlds realism is defended by David Lewis., see Lewis (1986).

NOTES TO CHAPTER 26

1. See Morris (1938). Similar distinctions are made by other semioticians, such as Peirce and de Saussure, but it is the formulation of Morris that is most commonly used nowadays.

2. This is the use that Richard Montague, one of the founders of formal semantics for natural language, makes of the term in his Montague (1970).

3. See the discussions in chapter 17 and chapter 25. The most extensive treatment of sense is given in Frege (1918–1919a).

4. I.e., on a realist conception of mathematics; intuitionists, of course, beg to differ.

5. And a very efficient one. Indexicality gives natural languages efficient tools, and Jon Barwise and John Perry once illustrated this with the following example:

- *A* to *B*: I'm right, you're wrong!
- *B* to *A*: (No,)I'm right, you're wrong!

Exactly the same words, completely opposite messages: it doesn't come more efficiently than that ...

6. This is of course why effective disagreement (see footnote 5) works.

7. See Kaplan (1989).

8. We use 'context' to cover various more concrete parameters, such as time and the location, speaker and addressee, ...

9. Which is due to Saul Kripke, who first drew attention to this kind of phenomenon in Kripke (1979).

10. It becomes even more complicated if, unbeknownst to *A*, Jones is also raking leaves, but somewhere else. Has *A* now all of a sudden said something that is true after all? And what if Jones is raking leaves, but Smith is not? What if it just appears that he is from a distance?

11. See Donnellan (1966).

12. Allegedly because *B* could no longer stand Smith's constant raking of leaves ...

13. See e.g., Travis (2006).

14. For an account of the so-called 'Travis cases' that uses semantics and logic to produce the results that Travis claims, see Dobler (2019).

Notes to chapter 27

1. We already encountered some discussion about the relationship between the material implication → and conditional sentences in English in the discussion of the papers of Suber and Sandford in chapter 6.

2. 'In Defense of a Dogma', that was directed against Quine's 'Two Dogmas of Empiricism' and in which Grice and Strawson argued that the analytic–synthetic distinction was a valuable one, despite Quine's qualms about it. Co-authoring, still quite rare in philosophy, was at the time quite exceptional.

3. For an interesting attempt, see Chapman (2005); see also Grandy & Warner (2017).

4. See Grice (1957, 1968).

Bibliography

Abbott, Barbara. 2008. Issues in the semantics and pragmatics of definite descriptions in English. *Reference: Interdisciplinary Perspectives*.

Allo, Patrick. 2016. Logic, reasoning and revision. *Theoria*, 82(1), 3–31.

Anderson, Alan Ross & Belnap, Nuel D. 1975. *Entailment: The Logic of Relevance and Necessity*. Princeton University Press, Princeton, NY.

Anellis, Irving H. 2012. Peirce's truth-functional analysis and the origin of truth tables. *History and Philosophy of Logic*, 33(1), 87–97.

Anscombe, G.E.M. 1956. Aristotle and the sea-battle. *Mind*, 65(257), 1–15.

Arlo-Costa, Horacio. 2019. The logic of conditionals. In: Zalta, Edward N., ed., *The Stanford Encyclopedia of Philosophy*. Metaphysics Research Lab, Stanford University, summer 2019 edn.

Armour-Garb, Bradley, Stoljar, Daniel, & Woodbridge, James. 2023. Deflationism About Truth. In: Zalta, Edward N. & Nodelman, Uri, eds., *The Stanford Encyclopedia of Philosophy*. Metaphysics Research Lab, Stanford University, Summer 2023 edn.

Bach, Kent. 1988. Review of Gilbert Harman: *Change in View.*. *Philosophy and Phenomenological Research*, 48(4), 761–764.

Barcan Marcus, Ruth. 1946. A functional calculus of first order based on strict implication. *Journal of Symbolic Logic*, 11, 1–16.

Beaney, Michael. 1996. *Frege. Making Sense*. Bloomsbury.

Beaney, Michael, ed. 1997. *The Frege Reader*. Blackwell.

Belnap, Nuel D. 1962. Tonk, plonk and plink. *Analysis*, 22(6), 130–134.

Belnap, Nuel D., Perloff, Michael, & Xu, Ming. 2001. *Facing the Future: Agents and Choices in Our Indeterministic World*. Oxford University Press, Oxford.

Belnap, Nuel D. & Steel, Thomas. 1976. *The Logic of Questions and Answers*. Yale University Press, New Haven.

van Benthem, Johan F.A.K. 1984. Correspondence theory. In: Gabbay, Dov & Guenthner, Franz, eds., *Handbook of Philosophical Logic. Volume II*. Reidel, Dordrecht.

van Benthem, Johan F.A.K., et al. 2016. *Logic in Action*. Universiteit van Amsterdam. Institute for Logic, Language and Computation, 2nd edn.

Bergmann, Merrie. 2008. *Introduction to Many-Valued and Fuzzy Logic: Semantics, Algebras, and Derivation Systems*. Cambridge University Press, Cambridge.

Besson, Corine. 2009. Understanding the logical constants and dispositions. *Baltic*

International Yearbook of Cognition, Logic and Communication:, 5.

—. 2012. Logical knowledge and ordinary reasoning. *Philosophical Studies*, 158(59–82).

Beth, Evert W. 1955. Semantic entailment and formal derivability. *Mededelingen van de Koninklijke Nederlandse Akademie van Wetenschappen, Afdeling Letterkunde*, 18(13), 309–342. Reprinted in Hintikka (1969).

Bimbó, Katalin. 2006. Relevance logics. In: Jacquette, Dale, ed., *Philosophy of Logic*, pp. 723–789. Elsevier, Amsterdam.

Blackburn, Patrick, de Rijke, Maarten, & Venema, Yde. 2001. *Modal Logic*. Cambridge University Press, Cambridge.

Bochvar, A.D. 1938 (1981). On a three-valued calculus and its application to analysis of paradoxes of classical extended functional calculus. *History and Philosophy of Logic*, 2, 87–112.

Brandom, Robert. 1994. *Making It Explicit*. Harvard University Press, Cambridge, Mass.

Brogaard, Berit. 2006. The 'Gray's Elegy' argument, and the prospects for the theory of denoting concepts. *Synthese*, 152(1), 47 – 79.

Browne, Stanley M. 1988. A contribution to the theory of reasoning. *Behaviorism*, 16(1), 93–96.

Burge, Tyler. 1992. Frege on knowing the third realm. *Mind*, 101, 633–650.

Burgess, John. 1996. Marcus, Kripke, and names. *Philosophical Studies*, 84(1), 1–47.

Carlson, Greg. 2011. Genericity. In: Maienborn, Claudia, Heusinger, Klaus von, & Portner, Paul, eds., *Semantics: An International Handbook*, vol. 2, chap. 4, pp. 1153–1185. De Gruyter, Berlin.

Chapman, Siobhan. 2005. *Paul Grice: Philosopher and Linguist*. Palgrave Macmillan.

—. 2013. Grice, conversational implicature and philosophy. In: A., Capone, F., Lo Piparo, & M., Carapezza, eds., *Perspectives on Pragmatics and Philosophy*. Springer, Cham, Switzerland.

Chellas, Brian. 1980. *Modal Logic: An Introduction*. Cambridge University Press, Cambridge.

Church, Alonzo. 1936a. A note on the Entscheidungsproblem. *Journal of Symbolic Logic*, 1(40–41).

—. 1936b. An unsolvable problem of elementary number theory. *American Journal of Mathematics*, 58, 345–363.

Cohnitz, Daniel & Estrada-González, Luis. 2019. *An Introduction to the Philosophy of Logic*. Cambridge University Press, Cambridge.

Constable, R. & Bickford, M. 2014. Intuitionistic completeness of first-order logic. *Annals of Pure and Applied Logic*, 165, 164–198.

Copeland, B. Jack. 2002. The genesis of possible worlds semantics. *Journal of Philosophical Logic*, 31, 99–137.

Cosmides, Leda & Toolby, John. 1992. Cognitive adaptations for social exchange. In: Barkow, J., Cosmides, L., & Tooby, J., eds., *The Adapted Mind*. Oxford University Press, Oxford.

D'Agostino, M., et al., eds. 1999. *Handbook of Tableau Methods*. Springer.

Davidson, Donald. 1967. Truth and meaning. *Synthese*, 17, 304–23. Reprinted in Davidson (2001).

—. 2001. *Inquiries into Truth and Interpretation*. Oxford University Press, Oxford, 2nd edn.

Dobler, Tamara. 2019. Occasion-sensitive semantics for objective predicates. *Linguistics and Philosophy*, 42(5), 451–474.

Donnellan, Keith. 1966. Reference and definite descriptions. *The Philosophical Review*, 75(3), 281–304.

Dummett, Michael. 1973a. *Frege. Philosophy of Language*. Duckworth, London.

—. 1973b. *Frege. Philosophy of Language*. Duckworth, London.

—. 1976. Frege as a realist. *Inquiry*, 19, 455–68. Reprinted in: *Frege and Other Philosophers*, Oxford University Press, Oxford, 1991, pp. 79–96.

—. 1981. *The Interpretation of Frege's Philosophy*. Duckworth, London.

—. 1985. *The Interpretation of Frege's Philosophy*. Duckworth, London.

—. 1991a. *Frege. Philosophy of Mathematics*. Duckworth, London.

—. 1991b. *The Logical Basis of Metaphysics*. Harvard University Press.

—. 1992. *Frege's Philosophy of Mathematics*. Duckworth, London.

Dunn, Michael J. & Belnap, Nuel D. 1968. The substitution interpretation of the quantifiers. *Noûs*, 2(2), 177–185.

Enderton, H.B. 2001. *A Mathematical Introduction to Logic*. Academic Press, New York, 2nd edn.

Engel, Pascal. 2006. Logic, reasoning and the logical constants. *Croatian Journal of Philosophy*, VI(16), 219–35.

Field, Hartry. 1972. Tarski's theory of truth. *Journal of Philosophy*, 59.

Fine, Kit. 2017. Truth-maker semantics. In: Hale, Bob & Wright, Crispin, eds., *A Companion to the Philosophy of Language*, pp. 556–577. Blackwell, Oxford, 2nd edn.

von Fintel, Kai. 2011. Conditionals. In: Heusinger, Klaus von, Maienborn, Claudia, & Portner, Paul, eds., *Semantics: An international handbook of meaning*, vol. 2, pp. 1515–1538. Mouton/de Gruyter, Berlin/Boston.

Fitting, Melvin. 1991. Kleene's logic, generalized. *Journal of Logic and Computation*.

Fitting, Melvin & Mendelsohn, Richard. 1998. *First-Order Modal Logic*. Springer.

Frege, Gottlob. 1879. *Begriffsschrift. Eine der arithmetischen nachgebildete Formelsprache des reinen Denkens*. Louis Nebert, Halle a.S. English translation in van Heijenoort 1970.

—. 1882. ́Uber die wissenschaftliche Berechtigung einer Begriffsschrift. *Zeitschrift f́ur Pilosophie und philosophische Kritik*, pp. 48–56. English translation in Frege (1964).

—. 1884. *Die Grundlagen der Arithmetik*. Verlag Wilhelm Koebner, Breslau. English translation by J.L. Austin, *The Foundations of Arithmetic*, Blackwell, 1950.

—. 1891. Funktion und begriff. *Jenaischen Gesellschaft f́ur Medizin und Natuurwisschenschaft*. English translation in Frege (1980).

—. 1892a. ́Uber Begriff und Gegenstand. *Vierteljahrschrift f́ur wissenschaftliche Philo-*

sophie, 16, 192–205. English translation in Geach and Black, 1980, pp 42–55.

—. 1892b. ʾUber Sinn und Bedeutung. *Zeitschrift fʾur Philosophie und philosophische Kritik*, 100, 25–50. English translation in Geach and Black, 1980, pp 56–78.

—. 1895. *Grundgesetze der Arithmetik. I.* Pohle, Jena. English translation (of §§1–) by M.Furth, *The Basic Laws of Arithmetic*, University of California Press, 1967.

—. 1918–1919a. Der Gedanke. *Beitrʾage zur Philosophie des deutschen Idealismus*, 1. Band, 58–77. English translation in Frege (1977).

—. 1918–1919b. Die Verneinung. *Beitrʾage zur Philosophie des deutschen Idealismus*, 1. Band, 143–57.

—. 1948. On sense and reference. *The Philosophical Review*, 57, 209–30.

—. 1964. On the scientific justification of a concept-script. *Mind*, 73, 155–60. Translated by J.M. Bartlett.

—. 1977. *Logical Investigations*. Blackwell, Oxford. Translated by P.T. Geach.

—. 1980. *Translations from the Philosophical Writings of Gottlob Frege*. Blackwell, Oxford. Translated by P.T. Geach and M. Black.

Garson, James. 2006. *Modal Logic for Philosophers*. Cambridge University Press, Cambridge, 2nd edn.

Gödel, Kurt. 1931. Über formal unentscheidbare sätze der principia mathematica und verwandter systeme, i. *Monatshefte für Mathematik und Physik*, 38(1), 173–198.

Grandy, Richard E. & Warner, Richard. 2017. Paul Grice. In: Zalta, Edward N., ed., *The Stanford Encyclopedia of Philosophy*. Metaphysics Research Lab, Stanford University, winter 2017 edn.

Grice, H.P. 1957. Meaning. *The Philosophical Review*, 66, 377–88.

—. 1968. Utterer's meaning, sentence meaning and word meaning. *Foundations of Language*, 4, 225–42.

—. 1975. Logic and conversation. In: Cole, Peter & Morgan, Jerry, eds., *Syntax and Semantics. Volume 3: Speech Acts*, pp. 41–58. Academic Press, New York.

Griffin, Nicholas, ed. 2003. *The Cambridge Companion to Bertrand Russell*. Cambridge University Press, Cambridge.

Groenendijk, Jeroen & Stokhof, Martin. 2011 (1997). Questions. In: van Benthem, Johan & ter Meulen, Alice, eds., *Handbook of Logic and Language*, pp. 1059–1131. Elsevier/MIT Press, Amsterdam/Cambridge Mass., 2nd edn.

Grover, Dorothy, Camp, Joseph, & Belnap, Nuel D. 1975. A prosentential theory of truth. *Philosophical Studies*, 27, 73–124.

Hansson, Sven Ove. 2022. Logic of belief revision. In: Zalta, Edward N., ed., *The Stanford Encyclopedia of Philosophy*. Metaphysics Research Lab, Stanford University, summer 2022 edn.

Harman, Gilbert. 1986a. *Change in View. Principles of Reasoning*. MIT Press, Cambridge, Mass.

—. 1986b. The meanings of logical constants. In: LePore, Ernest, ed., *Truth and Interpretation: Perspectives on the Philosophy of Donald Davidson*, pp. 125–134. Blackwell.

Hawke, Peter, Ögün, Aybüke, & Berto, Franz. 2020. The fundamental problem of logical omniscience. *Journal of Philosophical Logic*, 49, 727–766.

Heyting, A. 1930. Die formalen Regeln der intuitionistischen Logik. *Sitzungsberichte der Preussischen Akademie der Wissenschaften*, 42, 42–71, 158–169.

Hintikka, Jaakko, ed. 1969. *The Philosophy of Mathematics*. Oxford University Press.

Hintikka, Jaakko. 2000. Game-theoretical semantics as a challenge to proof theory. *Nordic Journal of Philosophical Logic*, 4(2), 127–141.

Hintikka, Jaakko & Sandu, Gabriel. 1995. The fallacies of the new theory of reference. *Synthese*, 104(2), 245–283.

Hofweber, Thomas. 2020. Logic and ontology. In: Zalta, Edward N., ed., *The Stanford Encyclopedia of Philosophy*. Metaphysics Research Lab, Stanford University, summer 2020 edn.

Horwich, Paul. 1998. *Meaning*. Oxford University Press, Oxford.

—. 2005. *Reflections on Meaning*. Oxford University Press, Oxford.

Hughes, G.E. & Cresswell, Max J. 1996. *A New Introduction to Modal Logic*. Routledge, London.

Hugly, Philip & Sayward, Charles. 2002. There is a problem with substitutional quantification. *Theoria*, 68(1).

van Inwagen, Peter. 1981. Why I don't understand substitutional quantification. *Philosophical Studies*, 39(3), 281–285.

Jago, M. 2013. Recent work in relevant logic. *Analysis*, 73(526–541).

Johnson-Laird, P.N. 1983. *Mental Models*. Cambridge University Press, Cambridge.

Kaplan, David. 1989. Demonstratives. In: Almog, Joe, Perry, John, & Wettstein, Howard K., eds., *Themes from Kaplan*, pp. 481–563. Oxford University Press, Oxford.

Kleene, S.C. 1950. *Introduction to Metamathematics*. Van Nostrand, New York.

Krabbe, Erik C. W. 1985. Formal systems of dialogue rules. *Synthese*, 63(295–328).

Kratzer, Angelika. 1979. Conditional necessity and possibility. In: Bäuerle, Rainer, Egli, Urs, & von Stechow, Arnim, eds., *Semantics from Different Points of View*, pp. 117–147. Springer.

Kripke, Saul A. 1963. Semantical considerations on modal and intuitionistic logic. *Acta Philosophica Fennica*, 16, 83–94.

—. 1971. Identity and necessity. In: Munitz, Milton K., ed., *Identity and Individuation*, pp. 135–164. New York University Press, New York. Reprinted in Schwartz, Stephen P., editor, *Naming, Necessity and Natural Kinds*, pp. 66–101. Cornell University Press, Ithaca/London, 1977.

—. 1975. Outline of a theory of truth. *The Journal of Philosophy*, 72, 690–716.

—. 1976. Is there a problem about substitutional quantification? In: Evans, Gareth & McDowell, John, eds., *Truth and Meaning: Essays in Semantics*, pp. 325–419. Clarendon, Oxford.

—. 1979. Speaker's reference and semantic reference. In: French, Peter A., Uehling jr., Theodore E., & Wettstein, Howard K., eds., *Contemporary Perspectives in the Philosophy of Language*, pp. 6–27. University of Minessota Press, Minneapolis.

—. 1980. *Naming and Necessity*. Blackwell, Oxford.

—. 1982. *Wittgenstein on Rules and Private Language*. Blackwell, Oxford.

Kuhn, Steven T. & Portner, Paul. 2002. Tense and time. In: Gabbay, Dov M. & Guenthner, Franz, eds., *Handbook of Philosophical Logic.*, vol. 7. Springer, Dordrecht.

Künne, Wolfgang. 2003. *Conceptions of Truth*. Clarendon Press, Oxford.

Lapointe, Sandra, ed. 2018. *Logic from Kant to Russell: Laying the Foundations for Analytic Philosophy*. Routledge, London/New York.

Lemmon, E.J. 1977. *An Introduction to Modal Logioc*. No. 11 in American Philosophical Quarterly Monograph Series. Blackwell, Oxford. In cooperation with Dana Scott. Edited by Krister Segerberg.

Lewis, David K. 1969. *Convention: A Philosophical Study*. Harvard University Press, Cambridge, Mass.

—. 1973. *Counterfactuals*. Blackwell.

—. 1986. *On the Plurality of Worlds*. Clarendon Press.

Łukasiewicz, Jan. 1920. O logice trójwartościowej. *Ruch filozoficzny*, 5, 170–171. English translation: On three-valued logic, in L. Borkowski (ed.), Selected works by Jan Łukasiewicz, North–Holland, Amsterdam, 1970, pp. 87–88.

MacFarlane, John. 2017. Logical constants. In: Zalta, Edward N., ed., *The Stanford Encyclopedia of Philosophy*. Metaphysics Research Lab, Stanford University, winter 2017 edn.

MacFarlane, John Gordon. 2003. Future contingents and relative truth. *The Philosophical Quarterly*, 53(212), 321–36.

Malinowski, Grzegorz. 2009. Many-valued logic and its philosophy. In: Gabbay, Dov & Woods, John, eds., *Handbook of the History of Logic Volume 8. The Many Valued and Nonmonotonic Turn in Logic*. Elsevier.

McNamara, Paul & Van De Putte, Frederik. 2021. Deontic Logic. In: Zalta, Edward N., ed., *The Stanford Encyclopedia of Philosophy*. Metaphysics Research Lab, Stanford University, Spring 2021 edn.

McTaggart, J. M. E. 1908. The unreality of time. *Mind*, 17(68), 457–474.

Mendelson, Elliott. 2015. *Introduction to Mathematical Logic*. CRC Press, Boca Raton, sixth edn.

Montague, Richard. 1970. Pragmatics and intensional logic. *Synthese*, 22(1-2), 68–94.

Morris, Charles. 1938. *Foundations of the Theory of Signs*. No. 2 in International Encyclopedia of Unified Sciences. The University of Chicago Press.

Mulligan, Kevin, Simons, Peter, & Smith, Barry. 1985. Truth-makers. *Philosophy and Phenomenological Research*, 44(3), 287–321.

Noonan, Harold. 2013. *Routledge Philosophy Guidebook to Kripke and Naming and Necessity*. Routledge, Abingdon.

Øhrstrøm, Peter & Hasle, Per. 2020. Future contingents. In: Zalta, Edward N., ed., *The Stanford Encyclopedia of Philosophy*. Metaphysics Research Lab, Stanford University, summer 2020 edn.

Pacuit, Eric. 2017. *Neighbourhood Semantics for Modal Logic*. Springer, New York.

Payne, Jonathan. 2015. Natural deduction for modal logic with a backtracking operator. *Journal of Philosophical Logic*, 44(3), 237–258.

Pears, David F. 1967. *Bertrand Russell and the British Tradition in Philosophy*. Collins, London.

Peregrin, Jaroslav. 2012. Inferentialism and the normativity of meaning. *Philosophia*, 40(1), 75–97.

Portner, Paul. 2016. Imperatives. In: Aloni, Maria & Dekker, Paul, eds., *The Cambridge Handbook of Formal Semantics*, Cambridge Handbooks in Language and Linguistics, pp. 593–626. Cambridge University Press.

Priest, Graham. 2008. *An Introduction to Non-Classical Logic: From If to Is*. Cambridge University Press, Cambridge.

Prior, Arthur N. 1957. *Time and Modality*. Oxford University Press, Oxford.

—. 1960. The runabout inference ticket. *Analysis*, 21(2), 38–39.

—. 1967. *Past, Present, and Future*. Clarendon Press, Oxford.

Putnam, Hilary. 1975. The meaning of 'meaning'. In: *Mind, Language, and Reality*, pp. 215–71. Cambridge University Press, Cambridge.

Queiroz, Ruy de. 2008. Reduction rules, meaning-as-use, and proof-theoretic semantics. *Studia Logica*, 90(211–247).

Quine, Willard Van Orman. 1943. Notes on existence and necessity. *Journal of Philosophy*, 40(5), 113–137.

—. 1948. On what there is. *The Review of Metaphyics*, 2, 21–38. Reprinted in Quine (1953).

—. 1953. *From a Logical Point of View*. Harper & Row, New York.

—. 1960. *Word and Object*. MIT Press, Cambridge, Mass.

—. 1974. *The Roots of Reference*. Open Court, LaSalle, Illinois.

—. 1992. *Pursuit of Truth*. Harvard University Press, Cambridge, Mass., 2nd edn.

Ricketts, Thomas & Potter, Michael, eds. 2010. *The Cambridge Companion to Frege*. Cambridge University Press, Cambridge.

Romanos, George D. 1983. *Quine and Analytic Philosophy*. MIT Press, Cambridge, Mass.

Rosenkrantz, Max. 2017. A reconstruction of Russell's Grey's Elegy argument. *Journal of the History of Analytical Philosophy*.

Russell, Bertrand. 1903. *The Principles of Mathematics*. Unwin, London.

—. 1905. On denoting. *Mind*, 14, 479–93. Reprinted in Russell, 1956, pp 39–56.

—. 1912. *The Problems of Philosophy*. Williams and Norgate, London.

—. 1914. *Our Knowledge of the External World*. Open Court, Chicago.

—. 1918–19. The philosophy of logical atomism. *The Monist*, 28–9, 495–527, 32–63, 190–222, 345–80. Reprinted in *Logic and Knowledge*, 1956, pp 175–282.

—. 1945. *A History of Western Philosophy*. Allen and Unwin.

—. 1956. *Logic and Knowledge: Essays 1901–1950*. Allen and Unwin, London. Edited by R. C. Marsh.

Russell, Bertrand & Whitehead, Alfred North. 1910, 1912, 1913. *Principia Mathematica*. Cambridge University Press, Cambridge. 2nd revised edition 1925–1927.

Sanford, David. 1989. *If P then Q. Conditionals and the Foundations of Reasoning*. Routledge.

Schroeder-Heister, Peter. 2018. Proof-theoretic semantics. In: Zalta, Edward N., ed., *The Stanford Encyclopedia of Philosophy*. Metaphysics Research Lab, Stanford University, spring 2018 edn.

Shain, Ralph. 2011. A defence of Aristotle's 'sea-battle' argument. *Pli*, 22, 124–137.

Shapiro, Stuart. 2013. Tarski's theorem and the extensionality of truth. *Erkenntnis*, 78(5), 1197–1204.

Sluga, Hans. 1975. Frege and the rise of analytical philosophy. *Inquiry*, 18, 471–87.

—. 1980. *Gottlob Frege*. The Arguments of the Philosophers. Routledge & Kegan Paul, London.

—. 1982. Frege as a rationalist. In: Schirn, Matthias, ed., *Studien zu Frege I. Logik und Philosophie der Mathematik*, pp. 27–48. Fromman-Holzboog, Stuttgart.

Smith, Quintin. 1995a. Marcus and the new theory of reference: A reply to Scott Soames. *Synthese*, 104(2), 217–244.

—. 1995b. Marcus, Kripke, and the origin of the new theory of reference. *Synthese*, 104(2), 179–189.

Soames, Scott. 2014. *The Analytic Tradition in Philosophy. Volume 1: The Founding Giants*. Princeton University Press, Princeton, NY.

Sperber, Dan & Wilson, Deirdre. 1995. *Relevance: Communication and Cognition*. Blackwell, Oxford, 2nd edn.

—. 2002. Pragmatics, modularity and mind-reading. *Mind and Language*, 17(1–2), 3–23.

Steinberger, Florian. 2017. The normative status of logic. In: Zalta, Edward N., ed., *The Stanford Encyclopedia of Philosophy*. Metaphysics Research Lab, Stanford University, spring 2017 edn.

Steiner, George. 1975. *After Babel. Aspects of Language and Translation*. Oxford University Press, Oxford.

Stenning, Keith & van Lambalgen, Michiel. 2008. *Human Reasoning and Cognitive Science*. MIT Press, Cambridge, Mass.

Stevenson, J.T. 1961. Roundabout the runabout inference ticket. *Analysis*, 21(6), 124–128.

Stokhof, Martin. 2007. Hand or hammer? On formal and natural languages in semantics. *Journal of Indian Philosophy*, 35(5–6), 597–626.

Strawson, Peter F. 1950. On refering. *Mind*, 59(235), 320–44.

—. 1959. *Individuals*. Methuen, London.

—. 1962. Freedom and resentment. *Proceedings of the British Academy*, 48, 1–25.

—. 1966. *The Bounds of Sense: An Essay on Kant's 'Critique of Pure Reason'*. Methuen.

Tarski, Alfred J. 1935. Der Wahrheitsbegriff in den formalisierten Sprachen. *Studia Logica*, 1, 152–277.

—. 1944. The semantic conception of truth and the foundations of semantics. *Philosophy and Phenomenological Research*, 4, 341–75.

Tharp, Leslie H. 1971. Truth, quantification, and abstract objects. *Noûs*, 5(4), 363–372.

Travis, Charles. 2006. Insensitive semantics. *Mind and Language*, 21(1), 39–49.

Turing, Alan M. 1936. On computable numbers, with an application to the Entscheidungsproblem. *Proceedings of the London Mathematical Society*, 42(230–265). A correction, 1937, 43 (544–546).

Veltman, Frank. 1976. Prejudices, presuppositions and the theory of conditionals. In: Groenendijk, Jeroen & Stokhof, Martin, eds., *Amsterdam Papers in Formal Grammar*, vol. 1, pp. 248–281. Centrale Interfaculteit, University of Amsterdam, Amsterdam.

Wallace, John. 1971. Convention T and substitutional quantification. *Noûs*, 5(2), 199–211.

Weiner, Joan. 1995. Realism *bei* Frege: Reply to Burge. *Synthese*, 102(3), 363–382.

Westerståhl, Dag. 2023. *Foundations of Logic: Completeness, Incompleteness, Computability*. CSLI.

Williamson, Timothy. 2013. *Modal Logic as Metaphysics*. Oxford University Press, Oxford.

Wittgenstein, Ludwig. 1960. *Tractatus Logico-Philosophicus*. Suhrkamp, Frankfurt a/M.

—. 2009. *Philosophical Investigations*. Wiley-Blackwell, Oxford. Translated by G. E. M. Anscombe, P. M. S. Hacker and J. Schulte. Revised fourth edition by P. M. S. Hacker and J. Schulte.

Woods, John & Alward, Peter. 2004. The logic of fiction. In: M., Gabbay Dov & Franz, Guenthner, eds., *Handbook of Philosophical Logic. Volume XI*. Kluwer, Dordrecht, 2nd edn.

Index